LAW OF EVIDENCE IN NIGERIA
Practice and Procedure

SECOND EDITION

LAW OF EVIDENCE IN NIGERIA
Practice and Procedure

SECOND EDITION

Professor Simon Uchenna Ortuanya, *SJD, FCIArb*

malthouse

Malthouse Press Limited

Lagos, Benin, Ibadan, Jos, Port-Harcourt, Zaria

First Published 2021
Second Edition 2025
ISBN (paperback): 978-978-61135-0-0
ISBN (e-book): 978-978-61135-1-7

Malthouse Press Limited
No. 7 Adele Road, Off Warehouse Road,
Apapa, Lagos Mainland, Nigeria
E-mail: malthouselagos@gmail.com
Facebook:@malthouselagos
Twitter:@malthouselagos
Istagram:@malthouselagos
Tel: 0802 600 3203

International Outlet
African Books Collective, Oxford, UK
Email: orders@africanbookscollective.com
Website: http://www.africanbookscollective.com

DEDICATION

To Aruotoma and Enyoha, my parents both of blessed memory.
You taught me the core values of truth, hard work, integrity and justice.

ACKNOWLEDGEMENTS

I am overwhelmed by the love and providence of my Heavenly Father. Indeed, it is not of him who wills nor of him who runs, but of God who shows mercy. Thank you, God.

I am eternally grateful to His Excellency, Rt. Hon. Dr. Ifeanyi Ugwuanyi, Governor of Enugu State of Nigeria, for providing the impetus that has become more of a catalyst for this work.

I am humbled by the staggering personalities whom God has brought into this project for guidance and assistance. I would like to begin by thanking my dear friends and colleagues of the Faculty of Law, University of Nigeria, Enugu Campus, where I taught Law of Evidence and Procedure for almost a decade, for their encouragement and invaluable advice. Same gratitude goes also to my colleagues at the Faculty of Law, Enugu State University of Science and Technology. I especially would want to thank Dr. Uju Obuka, who read and made insightful contributions to this book.

Another, whose impact extends far beyond his contribution is Late Prof. George Sopuruchukwu Amadi, a humanist, poet, writer and former Dean, Faculty of Law of the University of Nigeria, Enugu Campus. You are no longer here with us, but your indelible mark remains.

Acknowledging also my bosom friend of blessed memory, Hon. Chijioke Lawrence Ugwueze, “Aguiyi”, your lessons on courage in the face of adversity has paid off. You will never be forgotten.

I thank my staff for their unflinching support, especially Barr. Ijeoma Oluchi Mbah Esq, a phenomenal woman of substance and intellect. Thank you for your dutifulness and support.

To Emmanuel Martins Nyia Esq, Onuora Monday Okeke Esq, Kenechukwu Aneke Esq, Callistus Ugwuafia Esq and Mrs. Ebere Nome, I thank you all.

To you, Ngozi Ezigbo, thank you very much.

To my Siblings, Duke, Dr. Emeka and Barr. Ijeoma and their families, many thanks.

To the Ortuanya Pack, my phenomenal children – Obumneme, Kachi, Afamefuna, Nkemcherem and Akalaka, thank you for never giving me any cause to worry.

To all my friends and family, who took part in the shaping and support of this book, your help is inexpressibly appreciated. I pray the Lord will repay you all in kind.

PREFACE TO THE SECOND EDITION

The First edition of the book, *Law of Evidence in Nigeria: Practice and Procedure* has been a veritable tool in the hands of every lawyer both the Bar and the Bench alike. Law students in various universities across Nigeria have also found the first edition of this book very valuable. This can be gleaned from the high demands of copies of the work with goodwill messages as to the detailed, comprehensive and analytical presentation of evidential issues.

Having taught Law of Evidence in two public Nigerian Universities with plethora of paper presentations and publications on the subject matter for many years, an intrinsic nature of our law is its dynamism. Thus, Law in its dynamic nature is ever changing. It changes with the changing circumstances of the society in which we live in. The Law governing the reception of evidence in our courts is not left out in this wave of change. As new technologies emerge to assist man in his daily transactions, this created a yawning gap deserving of a legislative action to bring the Evidence Act 2011 up to speed with the current technological changes and advancements. The second edition of this book thus, stands as a bridge to close the yawning gap brought about by these technological advancements and innovations

The first edition of this book was published in 2021 premised primarily on the Evidence Act of 2011. Just barely two years after its publication, precisely on 12 June 2023, President Bola Ahmed Tinubu gave a nod to a call for advancement and change by signing the (Evidence Amendment) Act 2023 into Law. Though the amendment did not repeal in its entirety, the Evidence Act of 2011 (Principal Act). However, it introduced a number of new sections by repealing some sections in the Principal Act of 2011 as well as amending some of the old sections.

The Second edition of this book is thus significant in many ways. It critically x-rayed the eleven sections as contained in the new Evidence (Amendment) Act 2023 which comprises both amended sections of the Act and the new sections as introduced by the new Act. Firstly, amidst other things; it raised a discourse on the newly introduced admissibility of Statements in Electronic Records. Admittedly, it is now clear that records or data generated, image or sound stored, received or sent in an electronic form or microfilm are now admissible.

The topic on Confession discussed under chapter six was further broadened in this second edition to reflect the publication of regulations using Electronic Gazette as it relates to the exercise of powers conferred on the Federal Minister of Justice to make uniform regulation for receiving statements from suspects by law enforcement agencies. This is made possible through the instrumentality of new section 255 of Evidence (Amendment) Act 2023.

Chapter 22 that treats Affidavit Evidence, further examined the newly introduced section on Electronic Oath Taking (Affidavit) and the attendant conditions which are the prerequisites for its admissibility in our courts.

Chapter 23 on Admissibility of Computer and Electronic Evidence accommodated the introduction of new section 84A-84D and further analyzed its provision on Information in Electronic Form, Admissibility of Records in a Computer, Authentication of Electronic Record and Proof of Digital Signature. A copy of the Evidence (Amendment Act) 2023 has also been annexed to this second edition as an appendix for ease of reference of the innovative changes as introduced by the new Act.

It is hoped, therefore, that the book will continue to appeal to lovers of legal knowledge and continue to serve as a compass and a guide in reception of evidence in our courts.

Prof. Simon Uchenna Ortuanya, SJD, FCIArb.
Dean, Faculty of Law
Enugu State University (ESUT)
2025.

FOREWORD

The Evidence Act, 2011, repealed the old Evidence Act. In doing so, the new Act introduced some changes in the Law of Evidence. Ever since then, there has an urgent need for scholastic guidance in the proper approach to the interpretation of the provisions embodying those changes. This is, particularly, so as the courts have been issuing contradictory interpretations of these provisions.

Professor Simon Ortuanya, formerly, Associate Dean, Faculty of Law, University of Nigeria, Enugu Campus; Professor of Law, Faculty of Law, Enugu State University of Science and Technology, [ESUT], Enugu, has, percipiently, undertaken the challenge of offering the much-anticipated guidance to fill the yawning gap in the Literature.

In his new book, *Law of Evidence in Nigeria: Practice and Procedure,* the veteran author and urbane man of letters, Professor Simon Ortuanya, masterfully, plumbs the intention of the draft's persons of the Act. The result is the over Four-Hundred-and-Thirty-Six-page treatise of redoubtable erudition.

Structured on twenty-three, incisively articulated, Chapters, Chapter One deals with Conceptual Issues. This is followed by Chapter Two on Relevancy and Admissibility. Chapter Three takes the reader through the intriguing legislative landscape of Intention, Similar Facts and Defence of Accident. In Chapter Four, the author, painstakingly, explores the cogency of Improperly or Illegally-Obtained Evidence in criminal proceedings. The exquisite discourse in Chapter Five – Admissions - effortlessly, flows into the larger body of the forensic question of Confessions. The question of confessions so engages the scrupulous attention of the author that he, later in the book, emphasizes the need to incorporate the issue of electronic recorded video evidence of the confessional statement of the defendant in the Evidence Act. This, in his submission, must be so for this practice is already codified in the Administration of Criminal Justice Act.

Chapters Seven and Eight deal with Hearsay Evidence and Opinion Evidence, respectively. Character Evidence is dealt with in Chapter Nine whilst Chapter Ten examines the subject of Presumptions. The subjects of

Judicial Notice and Estoppel are dealt with in Chapters Eleven and Twelve, respectively. Chapter Thirteen discusses the subject of Proof of Custom. On its part, Chapter Fourteen examines the difficult question of Burden of Proof and Standard of Proof with the finery of a toothcomb. Taking of Oral Evidence and Examination of Witnesses feature in Chapter Fifteen.

Admissibility of Statements made in Special Circumstances is taken up in Chapter Sixteen. Corroboration; Official and Privileged Communications are dealt with in Chapters Seventeen and Eighteen, respectively. The last four Chapters, [Chapters Nineteen; Twenty; Twenty-One; Twenty-Two and Twenty-Three], treat, most methodically, the subjects of Competence and Compellability; Documentary Evidence; Primary and Secondary Documentary Evidence; Affidavit Evidence; Admissibility of Computer and Electronic Evidence, respectively.

The succinct titles of the different chapters are quite captivating just as the logical presentations of ideas are very illuminating. The book bears the imprints of the erudite author's versatility in the Law of Evidence – a course he has taught, admirably, in two public universities for some years now.

Judges and Justices; Senior Advocates of Nigeria; Law Professors and sundry litigation lawyers must be, truly, enamoured of the enormous efforts which Professor Simon Ortuanya invested into this precious book. Upon my intimate perusal of this excellent book, I am under obligation to commend it to all Justices of our appellate courts; Judges of disparate categories; Law Teachers and their Students, and to one and all! It is unputdownable!

Chima Centus Nweze, Ph. D.; JSC; Life Bencher; FCIArb
Justices' Chambers
Supreme Court, Abuja, Nigeria

CASES

STATUTES

Lagos State

FOREIGN

India

UK

INTERNATIONAL

CONTENTS

CHAPTERS

1 CONCEPTUAL ISSUES

2 RELEVANCE AND ADMISSIBILITY

6 CONFESSION

7 HEARSAY EVIDENCE

8 OPINION EVIDENCE

9 CHARACTER EVIDENCE

10 PRESUMPTIONS

11 JUDICIAL NOTICE

12 ESTOPPEL

13 PROOF OF CUSTOM

14 BURDEN OF PROOF AND STANDARD OF PROOF

15 TAKING OF ORAL EVIDENCE AND EXAMINATION OF WITNESSES

16 ADMISSIBILITY OF STATEMENT MADE IN SPECIAL CIRCUMSTANCE

17 CORROBORATION

18 OFFICIAL AND PRIVILEGED COMMUNICATION

19 COMPETENCE AND COMPELLABILITY

20 DOCUMENTARY EVIDENCE

21 PRIMARY AND SECONDARY DOCUMENTARY EVIDENCE

22 AFFIDAVIT EVIDENCE

23 ADMISSIBILITY OF COMPUTER AND ELECTRONIC EVIDENCE

Chapter 1

CONCEPTUAL ISSUES

1. Preliminary Considerations

There is no gainsaying that in the determination of every dispute before a judicial or quasi-judicial body, the rules of evidence remain indispensable. Thus, where a party to a particular dispute asserts a fact upon which he bases his claim and the other party opposes the existence of that fact, an umpire would be obliged to make a finding as to the existence or otherwise of that fact since the proper determination of that dispute depends on whether the fact exist or not.

To discover the truth about that fact, processes must be undergone. The question then becomes, what are the processes that should be undergone in order to discover the truth of the fact? This is the question that has, perhaps, given rise to the formulation of the rules of evidence.

Primarily, the rules of evidence have been formulated to determine four principal problems to wit:

1. what facts may be proved?
2. what facts ought to be excluded from the umpire's cognizance?
3. for the fact that ought to be proved, on whom rests the burden of proving them.
4. how should the facts be proved? Put in another way, what modes of proof are acceptable?

The above listed issues are what the law of evidence concerns itself with.

2. Meaning of the Law of Evidence

Without much ado, the law of evidence is the branch of law which governs the giving and reception of evidence in proceeding. In a nut shell, the court in *Mr. Felix Olusegun Orogun & Anor* v. *Fidelity Bank PLC*[1] summarized the entire purport of the Law of Evidence per IKYEGH JCA. His Lordship stated thus:

---

[1](2018) LPELR-46601(CA) P. 46, para. B.

I believe the essence of the law of Evidence is discovery of the truth.

It is, indeed, as the title implies "the law of Evidence". Thus, to understand its true meaning, it is imperative to understand the meaning of evidence. In the recent case of *Muogbo* v. *Equinox Microfinance Bank Ltd*,[2] the Court of Appeal defined Evidence as the means whereby a court is informed as to the issue of facts as ascertained by the pleading, that is, the testimony, oral, documentary or real, which may be legally received in order to prove or disprove some facts in dispute.

According to *Black's Law Dictionary*,[3] "evidence" is "...something (including testimony, documents and tangible objects that tends to prove or disprove the existence of alleged facts." It has also been defined as "Any matter of fact which is furnished to a legal tribunal, otherwise than by reasoning or a reference to what is noticed without proof, as the basis of inference in ascertaining some other matter of fac*t*.'[4] Kumai Bayang Aka'ahs JSC in *Arum* v. *Nwobodo*[5] attempted to define the subject matter in the following terms:

> In its broad sense, Evidence encompasses and includes the means employed for the purpose of proving a disputed fact.

Extrapolating from the above definitions is the view that the term evidence means no more than the means by which facts in issue are established before a judicial tribunal. According to Michael Hirst,[6] he posited thus:

> The law of evidence encompasses rather broader functions: it includes rules regulating the means and by which facts may be proved to the satisfaction of the Court; it allocates burden of proof as between the parties, and it prescribes the standard of proof which the court must require before it can make a finding on a given issue. The law of evidence also includes within its broader compass, rules prescribing the relative functions of judge and jury in respect of the receipt and evaluation of evidence.

[2](2019) LPELR-47161(CA) P. 24, para. E.

[3] Brian A. Garner, *Black's Law Dictionary (9th* edn. West Publishing Company, 2004), p. 635.

[4] B.T Thayer 'Presumptions and the Law of Evidence' (1989) 3 Harv. LR. 141 at 142.

[5] (2013) 10 NWLR (Pt. 1362) P.374.

[6] Michael Hirst, *Andrews & Hirst on Criminal Evidence* 4th Edition, (UK: Lexis Nexis 2001) P. 1.

Though as sound as the position of the learned author is, S.T. Hon in his book[7] approved in part Michael Hirst's definition of evidence, but went further to make it more elaborate to remark that it ought to be extended to cover such areas like presumptions and judicial notice,[8] which though do not arise necessarily out of 'proof', but are necessary aspects of the law of evidence, incorporated in almost all principal statutes of Evidence Act 2011.

On the other hand, the law of evidence, broader as it is, concerns the laws, rules, practice and procedure that regulate the means or methods of proving facts or adducing evidence before a court of law.[9] Such evidence could be oral testimony of a person who actually perceived the facts or documentary evidence which deals with production of documents to prove facts which are in dispute or real evidence which is a production of material objects other than document. We have copiously mentioned the word "fact" as the fulcrum of the law of evidence. The question then is, what is a fact? Section 258 of the Evidence Act describes a fact as including:

A. anything, state of things or relation of things, capable of being perceived by the senses; and
B. any mental condition of which a person is conscious;

In essence, a fact is anything which is subject to perception and (or) consciousness.

3. Sources of the Nigeria Law of Evidence

a. The Evidence Act

This is the primary source of the evidence rules we have today. Currently, what operates in Nigeria is the Evidence Act of 2011 which came into effect on June 3, 2011 and which has repealed the previous Act.[10]

b. Other Sources of Nigerian Law of Evidence

In enacting laws, the legislature may make provisions relating to evidence. For instance, section 221 of the Criminal Code[11] which creates the offence of defilement of girls under sixteen requires that a person charged with the offence cannot be convicted "upon the uncorroborated evidence of one witness. This is a provision relating to evidence and there is no gainsaying that it has the force of law notwithstanding that it is contained in the

---

[7] S.T. Hon, *S.T. Hon's Law of Evidence in Nigeria,* Vol. I, 2nd Edn. (Port Harcourt: Pearl Publishers, 2013) pg. 3
[8] Presumption and Judicial Notice are deeply treated under chapter 10 and 11 of this book respectively.
[9] S.T. Hon, *op. cit.*, Pg.2
[10] Evidence Act 2004. It has been repealed by Section 257 of the Evidence Act 2011.
[11] Cap C38, LFN 2004.

Criminal Code and not the Evidence Act. In this regard, section 3 of the Evidence Act provides that:

> Nothing in this Act shall prejudice the admissibility of any evidence that is made admissible by any other legislation validly in force in Nigeria.

It is, however, submitted that the width of the provision herein quoted above is alarming and has sweeping legal effects. It has the capability of raising several legal issues. Firstly, it has the capacity of importing English rules of evidence. It can be recalled that the Common Law of England, doctrines of Equity and Statutes of General Application in England on January 1, 1900 have all been received into Nigeria.[12] What it means is that Common Law rules of evidence are validly received by the Interpretation Act which is "legislation validly in force" in Nigeria within the meaning of section 3 of the Evidence Act quoted herein above. However, it ought to be quickly noted that on any issue of admissibility of Evidence, recourse must first be made to the Act. It is only where the latter is silent on that issue that the received English law, only insofar as it deals with the admissibility of the evidence in question, will become admissible.[13] Another matter arising from section 3 of the Evidence Act is a constitutional one. What is the meaning of the phrase "any other legislation validly in force in Nigeria" used in that section? Does it accommodate legislation passed by state House of Assembly? It can be recalled that "evidence" is a subject matter under the Exclusive Legislative competence of the National Assembly.[14] It follows therefore that any state which makes an "Evidence Law" has acted *ultra vires* and such legislation will, by virtue of section 1(3) of the Constitution, be null and void. It is, therefore, submitted that the interpretation of the phrase "any other legislation" used in section 3 of the Evidence Act must be confined to Acts of National Assembly. However, would it be equally correct to argue that state laws which are enacted for other matters within the state legislative competence cannot embody evidential rules? Put in another way, what is the fate of an evidential rule contained in a state law covering a subject matter within the state's legislative competence? Is such evidential rule null and void even though it may have been tacitly made by the state legislature because it was incidental to the principal matter dealt with? It is submitted that such evidential rules should have the force of law in so far as

[12] See section 32(1) of the Interpretation Act.

[13] See *R* v. *Itule* (1961) All NLR 462.

[14] See item 23, part 1 of the second Schedule to the 1999 Constitution of the Federal Republic of Nigeria (as amended).

the laws embodying them are not primarily made for evidence. The court should look at the pith and substance of the law (particularly the preamble, to know what the law is set to achieve). If the evidential rule is only incidental to the principal provisions of the law, then it should be as forceful as any pure evidential rule.

c. Judicial Decisions

It is now a cliché to lawyers, judges and even law students that by the doctrine of *stare decisis*, courts of law have over the years, rigidly adhered to previous decisions. By the doctrine of binding precedents, a lower court is bound to follow the decision of a superior or higher court in appropriate cases. Therefore, all decisions of superior courts (especially the Supreme Court) in respect of admissibility of evidence or mode of proving facts, are to be followed by lower courts in deserving situations as those decisions form part of the Nigeria *corpus juris* on Evidence.[15]

4. Applicability of the Evidence Act

The Evidence Act does not apply in all courts in Nigeria. It is provided in section 256(1) of the Act that the Act shall apply to "all judicial proceedings in or before any court established in the Federation of Nigeria." A "court" is defined as including all judges and magistrates excepting arbitrators, but includes persons legally authorized to take evidence.[16] The Act "shall not apply to:

(a) proceedings before an arbitrator;
(b) a field general court martial;
(c) judicial proceedings in any civil cause or matter in or before any Sharia Court of Appeal, Customary Court of Appeal, Area or Customary Courts.[17]

However, the Act applies to Sharia Courts of Appeal, Customary Courts of Appeal, Area Courts and Customary Courts if the power to enforce the Act is conferred upon those courts by an order published in the Gazette and authorized by the Constitution. In any judicial proceeding in any criminal matter before an Area Court, the latter shall be guided by the Evidence Act.[18]

---

[15] See *Nwabueze* v. *The People of Lagos* (2018) LPELR-44113 (SC) pp. 26-27, paras. E-A. where Muhammad, JSC held that: "It is therefore settled that a court lower in the judicial ladder is bound by its own or the *ratio decidendi* of a higher court in an earlier case, if the issues of fact and the legislation the State Court considers subsequently are same or similar."

[16] Section 258(1) of the Evidence Act 2011.

[17] *Tongding* v. *Kakshak* (2018) LPELR-46169(CA) P. 11, paras. D-G.

[18] See section 256 (2) of the Evidence Act 2011.

Also, in all judicial proceedings in criminal cause or matter, an Area Court shall be bound by section 134 to 140 of the Act, dealing with standards and burdens of proof.[19]

In *Kusumu* v. *Udom,*[20] it was held that there is nothing in the Evidence Act which makes it applicable in Area Courts. Similarly, in *Osu* v. *Ogiri,*[21] the Supreme Court held that Customary Courts are not bound by the provisions of the Evidence Act. The apex court further warned that courts hearing appeals from Customary or Area Courts or District Courts should be wary to apply the strict technicalities of procedure of the Evidence Act in reviewing appeal. It has been further stated by the apex Court that even the regular Courts like the High Court, Court of Appeal and even the apex Court itself, to which the Evidence Act ordinarily applies, cannot apply it when hearing civil appeals from those courts expressly exempted from the applicability of the Evidence Act.[22]

The reason for non-application of the Act to those courts is glaring. Those courts are usually constituted by person who is knowledgeable in customary matters but not legal matters. Most of them are not even learned in legal rules and principles let alone the technicalities associated with the law of evidence.

5. Human Rights and the Law of Evidence

Human Rights are those rights which inhere in a person by reason of being human. In democratic societies, those rights are recognized and entrenched in a written Constitution.[23] Thus, the constitutional provisions embodying the recognition of human rights and which carry a reasonable extent of relationship with the law of evidence are too numerous to mention. For example, section 36(1) of the Constitution, mandates that in all circumstances where his rights are to be determined by any court or tribunal, a person shall be entitled to "fair hearing". The only way a person can be heard, practically, is that such person should be allowed to call all pieces of relevant and admissible evidence which he has to rely on for his case and to have opportunity to contradict any piece of evidence relied upon against him. This is an indispensable particle of the fair hearing principle

[19] See section 256 (3) of the Evidence Act 2011.

[20] (1990) 1 NWLR (Pt. 127) 426.

[21] (1988) 1 NWLR (Pt. 69) 221.

[22] *Tongding* v. *Kakshak, supra.*

[23] See Chapter IV of The Constitution of the Federal Republic of Nigeria, 1999 (as amended); See also The Chapter III of the Indian Constitution.

and all that it entails.[24] In *Sule & Ors* v. *Orisajimi;*[25] Bayang Aka'ahs, JSC observed as follows:

> It is a fundamental principle of fair hearing enshrined in Section 36 (1) of the Nigerian Constitution that no one should be condemned unheard.

However, a sort of controversy and abuse surrounding this immortal principle of fair hearing was aptly captured in the recent decision of the Supreme Court in *Governor of Imo State & Ors* v. *E. F. Network (Nig) Ltd* & *Anor.*[26] per C.C. Nweze JSC thus:

> The complaint on the breach of the appellants' right to fair hearing reminds me of the eloquent formulation in *Adebayo* v. *AG, Ogun State* (2008) LPELR-80 (SC) 23-24. For its bearing on the fortune of the appellant's case, I crave Your Lordships' indulgence to quote this Court's view *in extenso*: I have seen in recent times that parties who have bad cases embrace and make use of the constitutional provision of fair hearing to bamboozle the adverse party and the Court, with a view to moving the Court away from the live issues in the litigation. They make so much weather and sing the familiar song that the constitutional provision is violated or contravened. They do not stop there. They rake the defence in most inappropriate cases because they have nothing to canvass in their favour in the case. The fair hearing provision in the Constitution is the machinery or locomotive of justice; not a spare part to propel or invigorate the case of the user. It is not a casual principle of law available to a party to be picked up at will in a case and force the Court to apply it to his advantage. On the contrary, it is a formidable and fundamental constitutional provision available to a party who is really denied fair hearing because he was not heard or that he was not properly heard in the case.

Albeit, this may not be a human right text, however the dictum of the Law Lord above provokes an irresistible need to reproduce same for better appreciation of this subtopic. Also, the presumption of innocence in the constitution implies that the onus of proving a person's guilt is on the person who asserts it and not the contrary.[27] This is in consonance with the

---

[24] See *Garba* v. *UNIMAID* (1986) 1 NWLR (Pt 18) 550.
[25] (2019) LPELR-47039(SC) P. 25, paras. A-B.
[26] (2019)LPELR- (2019) LPELR-46938(SC) Pp. 29-30, Paras, D-C.
[27]See section 135 (1) Evidence Act 2011; See also *State* v. *Shonto* (2019) LPELR-47431(SC).

accusatorial system of criminal justice administration which Nigeria has adopted.[28]

Ultimately, it is submitted that all the principles of fair hearing as contained in section 36(1) to (2) of the constitution have some bearing on the law of Evidence.

5. Direct and Circumstantial Evidence

Direct evidence otherwise known as original evidence is a testimony concerning a fact actually perceived by a witness with one or more of his senses. For example, if the fact in dispute is whether Mr. Franklin had been driving on the wrong side of the road, Mr. Emmanuel gives evidence of having seen Franklin drive his car at the time in question, on the wrong side of the road, Emmanuel's testimony is direct evidence. In this regard, section 126 of the Act provides that oral evidence must be direct in all cases. Therefore, if the oral testimony relates to a fact that can be seen, it should come from a witness who saw the fact. If it relates to a fact that can be heard, it should come from a witness that heard it. If the fact can be perceived by any sense or in any manner, it should be testimony of a witness who says he perceived the fact in such sense or manner.[29] Evidence must be direct at all times except where it relates to the contents relating to Part III of the Evidence Act. The court is duty bound to accept evidence that is direct. The court can expunge evidence that is not direct from its records where it was admitted.

On the other hand, circumstantial evidence as the name implies, is evidence not based on personal knowledge but on surrounding circumstances. Where direct testimony of an incident is not available, the law allows the courts to infer from the proven facts, the existence of such other facts that may be logically inferred.[30] His Lordship, John Inyang Okoro JSC, while delivering the leading judgment in the recent case of *State* v. *Sunday,*[31] summarised the description of circumstantial evidence in the following appetising prose:

> Under our criminal jurisprudence, circumstantial evidence is defined as evidence of surrounding circumstances which by undersigned coincidence is capable of proving a proposition with mathematical exactitude, and that where direct evidence is unavailable, circumstantial evidence which is

---

[28] See *Uso* v. *C.O.P.* (1972) JELR 33877 (SC)

[29] See generally, *Akinlu* v. *The State* (2015) LPELR 25986 (SC).

[30] See L. Atsegbua, *Law of Evidence* (Benin City: Justice Jeco Printing & Publishing, 2012) pg. 10.

[31] (2019) LPELR-46943 (SC) Pp. 24-25, paras. D-A.

> cogent, compelling and pointing irresistibly and unequivocally to the guilt of the accused is admissible to sustain a conviction. Circumstantial evidence consists of various pieces of evidence which in themselves alone cannot ground conviction, but when put together can constitute a good solid case for the prosecution...

The law is trite that for a person to be convicted on circumstantial evidence, such evidence must be sufficient to establish the guilt of the accused beyond reasonable doubt.[32] The evidence must be cogent and compelling, pointing to the guilt of the accused person with the accuracy of mathematics. While concurring with the leading judgment of Mary Ukaego Peter-Odili JSC in *Ogogovie* v. *The State,*[33] John Inyang Okoro JSC also summarized this position in the following terms:

> May I state here that our laws on circumstantial evidence are well settled...the circumstances relied upon should point unequivocally, positively, unmistakably and irresistibly to the fact that the offence was committed and that the accused committed the offence.

In *Basil Akpa* v. *The State,*[34] the deceased travelled to visit the accused so as to collect the money which he (the accused) owed him (the deceased). He never returned from his journey. Upon investigation, although the body of the deceased was not found, drops of human blood were found in the house of the accused. The drops of blood connected themselves by dots which led to a pit toilet behind the accused's house. Upon digging the toilet, human legs and hands were found. There was also a mattress in the accused's house which was soaked in blood. There was yet evidence showing that the deceased was seen around the accused's house. Notwithstanding the absence of direct evidence as to the killing, the court convicted the accused on the strength of the pieces of circumstantial evidence against him. His appeal to the Supreme Court failed.

7. Real Evidence and Best Evidence

Real Evidence is neither oral testimony nor documentary evidence. It is evidence of objects used in bringing about the fact in issue and which is tendered for the court's inspection. The definition of Real Evidence in

---

[32] See also *Ikomi* v. *State* (1986) 3 NWLR (Pt. 28) 414; *Atano* v. *A.G., Bendel State* (1988) N.W.L.R (Pt. 75) 201.

[33] (2016) LPELR 40501 (S.C).

[34] (2008) 14 N.W.L.R (Pt. 1106) 72.

section 258(1) of the Act is nebulous. The section defines it as "anything other than testimony, admissible hearsay or a document, the contents of which, are offered as evidence at a trial, which is examined by the court as a means of proof of such fact." Be that as it may, real evidence includes objects such as knife, machet, gun, gallon, mattress, etc. In a murder trial, the machet with which the alleged killing was done could be tendered in evidence. Such machet is real evidence. Although documents are not real evidence, where a document is tendered as an object and its contents are not in dispute, such document is real evidence and not documentary. For example, if Okeke is being tried for stealing Clement's West African Examination Certificate (WAEC) and during trial the prosecution tenders the stolen property (the certificate), the latter is real and not documentary evidence in such situation as the contents of the certificate is not the fact in issue but whether there was a stealing or theft.

By section 127 of the Evidence Act, a court of law is empowered to inspect any object, whether moveable or immoveable, the inspection of which, is material to the determination of the fact in dispute.[35] Parties before the court give evidence and tender document(s). There are certain instances where the real evidence to be produced in court is not movable, the court will adjourn to visit or inspect the real evidence. For instance, land, houses, ship and the likes cannot be moved to the courtroom in order for the judge and the parties to inspect same. In that case, a visit to the *locus* becomes necessary. A visit to the *locus* to inspect the real evidence is only necessary where there is conflict in the evidence presented by the parties.[36] It is otiose to inspect real evidence where the existence of a fact is not in dispute before the court. The court has held that this form of evidence is more 'reliable than the vagaries of "I believe" of oral testimony.'[37]

On the other hand, "Best Evidence", as the name implies, is the best evidence which a party to a proceeding can rely upon in support of his case. In criminal trials, evidence of an eyewitness is the best evidence as it is direct and provides an "on the spot" narration of the commission of the crime.[38] The law of evidence requires that a party to a proceeding should call that

---

[35] In *Brigs* v. *Brigs* (1992) 3 N.W.L.R (Pt. 228) 128 at 140 G, (2003) 2 NLLC P. 652 at 674K, it was held that it is only when there is conflict in evidence of the parties that a visit to the locus is necessitated. The court cannot substitute its opinion on the visit to the locus to the concrete evidence and facts placed before the court.

[36] *Brigs* v. *Brigs* (*supra*).

[37] See *Brigs* v. *Brigs* (2003) NLLC (*supra*), page. 674.

[38] *Kola Akanji* v. *The State* (2020) LPELR-49531 (CA) P. 40, paras. F.

evidence which will prove his case. This is regarded as the "best evidence rule".[39] In debt recovery cases and civil proceedings generally, evidence of the lender is regarded as the best evidence.[40] In pre-election matters, the best evidence of the records of the primary election conducted by a political party is a record of the result of the election coming from the custody of the political party and confirmed by it as its document.[41]It is therefore trite that, when a document is duly pleaded and admitted in evidence, that document becomes the best evidence of its contents and therefore speaks for itself, and the court cannot disregard it.[42]

In *Purification Technique (Nig) Ltd. & Ors* v. *Jubril* & Ors,[43] Ngwuta, JSC articulated the best evidence rule, thus:

> Under the best evidence rule, best or primary evidence is that particular means of proof which is indicated by the nature of the fact under investigation as the most satisfactory; it is the best evidence the nature of the case admits...

Going by the above principle herein quoted, the best evidence to prove the commission of a crime is the evidence of an eyewitness who saw the commission of the offence.[44] Also, in the absence of duress or undue influence, the voluntary confession of an accused person could be the best evidence against him.[45] In the same vein, the best evidence to prove the contents of a document is the production of the document itself.[46] The best evidence to establish the juristic personality of a company is the company's certificate of incorporation.[47] And in the assessment of damages payable in respect of total destruction of a chattel, the evidence of an expert is the best evidence.[48]

---

[39] See *PDP & Anor* v. *INEC & Ors* (2008) 8597 (C.A).
[40] See *Okpokam* v. *Treasure Gallery LTD & Anor* (2017) LPELR-42809(CA).
[41] See *Chidoka* v. *Ugokwe & Ors* (2019) LPELR-46705(CA) 50, para. E.
[42] *DG, Bureau of Lands, Kwara State & Anor* v. *Alabi & Anor* (2018) LPELR-44487(CA).
[43] (2012) LPELR 9727 (SC).
[44] See *Obot* v. *State* (2018) LPELR-45185(CA) P. 10, para B; *Agu* v. *State* (2017) LPELR-41664 (SC) P.28, para B.
[45] See *Iliya* v. *State* (2019) LPELR-47728(CA) Pp.24 -25, paras. F-A; *Kayoele* v. *The State* (2016) LPELR 40028 (S.C); *Salahudeen* v. *The State* (2013) LPELR 21851 (C.A); *Musa* v. *The State* (2013) LPELR 19932 (SC).
[46] See *Agbareh & Anor* v. *Mimra & 2 Ors* (2008) vol. 2 M.J.S.C. 134.
[47] *Motorcycle Transport Union of Nigeria & Ors* v. *Delta State Motorcyclists Association & Ors* (2010) LPELR 4503 (C.A.)
[48] *Oando Nig. Plc* v. *Adijere West Africa Ltd.* (2013) LPELR 20591 (SC).

8. Proved facts, Disproved facts and facts not proven

When is a fact said to be proved?

A fact is deemed to be proved when the court, after considering the matter before it, either believes it to exist or considers its existence so probable that a prudent man ought, in the circumstances of a particular case, to act upon the supposition that the fact truly exists.[49] On the other hand, a fact is disproved when the court, after considering the matters before it, believes that it does not exist or considers its non-existence so probable that a prudent man ought, in the circumstances of a particular case, to act upon the supposition that it does not exist.[50] A fact is not proved if it is neither proved nor disproved.

[49] See section 121(a) of the Evidence Act 2011.
[50] See section 121 (b) Evidence Act, 2011.

Chapter 2

RELEVANCE AND ADMISSIBILITY

1. Preliminary considerations

In the preceding chapter, we mentioned that the law of evidence is mainly concerned with the establishment or proof of facts or their disproof. The question then is, what are the facts relevant to be proved? In any dispute before the court, it is incontestable that it is not all the facts leading to the dispute that is necessary. For example, if the dispute before the court is whether A was murdered by B, the testimony of C who says that he saw A and B entering the room immediately before the killing occurred, is obviously relevant. In such a case, the testimony of D who says she was passing with her tray of groundnuts to Artisan market but knows nothing more about the killing, will not be relevant because it has no bearing on the dispute before the court. Therefore, it is not every fact that is relevant to be proved. In this chapter therefore, we will be dealing with those facts that are relevant. Whether a fact is relevant or not is to a very huge extent, a question of law because the court is not given a blank cheque to determine what facts are relevant. The Evidence Act has devoted a portion of itself to lay down the relevant facts in any case.

Before we go further, it is worthy to also mention quickly that the phrase "relevance and admissibility" is as old as the law of evidence itself. Just as we have used examples to explain above, a fact is relevant if it is material to the dispute in court.[1] It follows that a piece of evidence is relevant if it is material in a trial before the court. In *Okonji* v. *Njokanma,*[2] the Supreme Court held that a relevant piece of evidence is that which is intended to prove or disprove any question of fact in the issue inter parties.

Admissibility on the other hand means the capability of a piece of evidence to be admitted. Admissibility poses no problem at all as the law is settled, that relevance is the bedrock or touchstone of admissibility.

---

[1] *Ajose-Adeogun & Anor* v. *Olojede & Ors* (2018) LPELR-43683 (CA).

[2] (1999) 12 SCNJ 259.

Therefore, once a fact is relevant, it automatically becomes, as a general rule, admissible,[3] hence, admissibility is as submissive to relevance as a wife, to her husband. However, it should be quickly noted that a relevant fact may be excluded by the court if it is in all material respect, too remote for the determination of the dispute in court.[4] It should be noted that a document that is admitted for one purpose may be rejected for another purpose. For instance, a document rejected for failure to comply with registration legislation when the purpose is to show that title to land was conveyed may be admissible for the purpose of showing that consideration was paid in respect of the piece of land.

Also in the case of documents, the journey of admissibility does not end at relevance as the document must be such that is prescribed by the Act. For example, where a certified copy is statutorily required, the document must be appropriately certified before it can be admitted notwithstanding that its contents may have some nexus with the fact in issue.[5]

2. Facts in issue and facts relevant to the facts in issue

By section 258(1) of the Evidence Act, a fact in issue includes "any fact from which either by itself or in connection with other facts, the existence or non-existence, nature or extent of any right, liability asserted or denied in any suit or proceeding necessarily follows." To cut the long story short, a fact in issue is a fact in dispute. If Mr. A asserts that he owns a piece of land and B disagrees, saying that he (B) owns the land, then we can say that both parties (A and B) have joined issues on the ownership of the land. Thus, the fact in issue is the ownership of the land and therefore, in determining the ownership, only facts tending to establish the ownership of the parties would be necessary. This is why section1 of the Act provides that evidence shall be given of facts in issue or relevant facts but of no others.

In civil litigation where pleadings are used, parties are expected to deny vividly, any asserted fact which they do not agree with. This is so because any fact not denied is deemed admitted; our law reports are in abundance of this principle.[6] It is only when a fact is denied that it becomes a fact in issue. The

---

[3] *Ifaramoye* v. *State* (2017) LPELR -42031 (SC)

[4] See Section 1(a) of the Evidence Act 2011; see also *Obiagwu & Ors* v. *Okoroafor* (2019) LPELR-46689 (CA) and *Starline (Nig) Ltd & Anor* v. *Onyeagocha & Anor* (2018) LPELR-44268 (CA) Pp.19-20, paras. F-A.

[5] *Taiwo* v. *FRN* (2019) LPELR-47635 (CA) P. 14 paras. A-E. See also the notes on Documentary Evidence.

[6] See section 123 of the Evidence Act. See also *Ogunleye* v. *Oni* (1990) 2 NWLR (Pt 735) 745.

court has no business with admitted facts or facts not in contest. The courts only determine facts in dispute. So if a fact is admitted, it is not in dispute.[7]

3. Facts forming part of the same transaction

Section 4 of the Evidence Act provides:

> Facts which, though not in issue, are so connected with a fact in issue as to form part of same transaction, are relevant, whether they occurred at the same time and place or at different times and places.

It is important in explaining the above provision to introduce the doctrine of *Res gestae*. Section 4 of the Act appears to be an importation of that common law doctrine. The expression "*res gestae*" is a Latin expression meaning "things done" or "things transacted."[8] In the law of evidence, it is an expression used in reference to fact or facts closely related, connected or surrounding the fact or facts in issue so as to form the same transaction with the fact in issue.[9] In *Ajose-Adeogun & Anor* v. *Olojede & Ors,*[10] the Appellants had claimed declaratory and injunctive reliefs against the Respondents. Their claims were predicated on the traditional evidence that their forebearer; one Chief Sasore-Abapo was the first settler on the land they claimed. By the unchallenged evidence of 4th-6th Respondents, Langbasa, Ijoyi-Nla and Ijoyi-Kekere and Abegede Villages were founded by their ancestor who owned them. The Appellants did not dispute that the land they claimed is not situate at Ijoyi-Nla or/and Ijoyi-Kekere, even though they did not call their own Ijoyi, either Nla or Kekere. In the above circumstances, the trial Court held that Exhibit "L" which dealt with the history of the villages including Langbasa, Ijoyi-Nla and Ijoyi-kekere was relevant to the issues canvassed by the parties in the case before it as the Exhibit 'L' went directly to the issues raised in the case of the 4th - 6th Respondents and so relevant for determination of the case even if the Appellants did not join issues with the 4th - 6th Respondents, on Langbasa. As rightly stated by the trial Court, facts which, though not in issue, are so connected with a fact in issue as to form part of a transaction, are relevant,

---

[7] See *Olufosoye* v. *Olorunfemi* (1989) 1 NWLR (Pt. 95) 26.

[8] L. Atsegbua, *op. cit.,* pg. 54.

[9] *Adesuba & Anor* v. *The State* (2012) LPELR 9722 (S.C).

[10] (2018) LPELR-43683(CA) Pp. 38-39, paras. G-A.

whether they occurred at the same time and place, or otherwise. Such facts are admissible in evidence in proof or disproof of facts in issue in judicial proceedings.

A fact found by court as forming part of *res gestae* becomes a relevant fact to assist in establishing the fact in issue before the court. For example if the fact in issue is whether Franklin killed the deceased, the fact that Franklin was armed with a machet on that day and the fact that the deceased had two days before he was killed, received a life-threatening text message from Franklin, are all part of the *res gestae* and are all relevant to establish the fact in issue which is whether it is Franklin that killed the deceased.

To form part of *res gestae* at common law, a fact must satisfy the following requirements:

(a) it must explain the fact in issue;

(b) it must be contemporaneous with the fact in issue.

Let us explain them seriatim.

(a) It must explain the fact in issue: For a fact to be deemed as following part of *res gestae*, the common law insists that it must explain the fact in issue. In *R* v. *Bliss*,[11] the court was confronted with the question whether a road was a public or private road. There was an adjacent land to the road in question. The owner of that land during his lifetime planted a tree there and in the course of doing so, he made a declaration that he was planting the tree "to mark the boundary of the road and his land." During the hearing of this case, evidence of this statement was sought to be tendered. The court rejected it as being irrelevant and not forming part of the *res gestae* as the fact in issue before the court was not about boundary but whether the road was public or private.

(b) It must be contemporaneous with the fact in issue.

The common law insists that a fact cannot form part of *res gestae* unless it is contemporaneous or spontaneous with the fact in issue. The rationale behind this common law rule is that if the fact is contemporaneous, then it is purely part of the fact in issue but if it happens before or after the happening of the fact in issue, there is possibility of it being a connection. Thus, in the celebrated case of *R* v. *Bedingfield*,[12] the accused was charged with murder of a woman he was living with. The woman's throat was cut. The defence

[11] (1837) 7 Ad & El 550.

[12] (1879) 14 Cox CC.341.

was that she committed suicide. The prosecution wanted to give evidence of a statement made by the deceased with her cutthroat when she staggered out of the room and shouted "oh aunt, see what Harry has done to me". She died shortly afterwards before getting any assistance. Cockburn CJ (as he then was) rejected the statement because it was made after the event and after the fact in issue (the act of killing) was completed. According to his Lordship, if she had said anything at the time of cutting the throat, that would have been admissible but since the statement in question was made after the act, it was not contemporaneous with the fact in issue and could not form part of its *res gestae.*

We have earlier remarked that section 4 of the Act is a codification of the doctrine of *res gestae*. However, it is very imperative to note that, that section has modified the doctrine to wit: it has dispensed with the requirement of contemporaneity which the common law paid serious respect to. The last phrase of section 4 provides that once a fact is connected with the fact in issue, it remains relevant for the proof of the fact in issue whether that fact "occurred at the same time and place or at different times and places" with the fact in issue. The implication of this is that if *Bedding field* should be decided in Nigeria today, that statement made by the deceased would have been admissible as forming part of *res gestae*. In *Okoro* v. *The State,*[13] the deceased was the bell ringer of his church at Imo State. One morning, the deceased went to ring the bell for morning prayers. Shortly afterwards, he was heard shouting "Anthony Okoro has shot me." His wife recognized the voice of her husband and ran to the *locus criminis* only to find her husband in a pool of blood. The deceased was taken to the hospital where he also narrated the whole incident to his wife before giving up the ghost. It was held that the shout at the *locus criminis* together with the story at the hospital where he also narrated the whole incident to his wife before giving up the ghost, all formed part of *res gestae* and admissible under section 7 of the Evidence Act, Cap E14, LFN 2004 (now section 4 of the Evidence Act 2011). It can be recalled that but for the provision of the Act, the story told by the deceased to his wife at the hospital could not have been treated as *res gestae* because it was not contemporaneous with the shooting. It is submitted that our statutory provision on *res gestae* is better than the common law position which is capable of occasioning miscarriage of justice as we obviously saw in the *Bedding field's* case.

---

[13] (1988) NWLR (Pt. 74) 255.

4. Facts which are the occasion, causes or effects of the fact in issue

Section 5 of the Act states thus:

> Fact which are the occasion, cause or effect, immediate or otherwise, of relevant facts, or facts in issue, or which constitute the state of things under which they happened, or which afforded an opportunity for their occurrence or transaction are relevant.

Under section 5 of the Act, facts which in fact caused the happening of the fact in issue or which created an enabling environment for the fact in issue to exist, are relevant to prove the fact in issue. For example, if A enters B's land and destroys his crops and one week later, B retaliates by also entering A's land to destroy A's crops, in an action for damages for trespass by A against B, what A did to B's crops will be relevant because it was what he did that caused the fact of B's trespass. Again, in allegation of murder, the fact that the limbs and legs of the deceased were discovered in the pit toilet of the Accused is relevant. Also in suit for negligence, the fact that the Defendant was drunk or had worn out tires at the time the vehicle had accident and killed a person is relevant to show reckless driving.

5. Facts Showing motive, preparation and prevision or subsequent conduct

Section 6(1) of the Evidence Act states: *'Any fact is relevant which shows or constitute a motive or preparation for any fact in issue or relevant fact.'* This section deals with facts which are the motive behind the occurrence of the fact in issue. It can be recalled that motive is not a relevant point to consider for the purpose of criminal responsibility,[14] but as can be gleaned from section 6 of the Evidence Act, it is a relevant fact. In this case, envy, avarice, ostentatious living, hatred, etc., are relevant to prove criminal liability.[15] Thus, in *Nweke* v. *The State,*[16] the fact in issue was whether it was the appellant that murdered his deceased wife. To establish this, the prosecution

---

[14] See Criminal Code, Cap C38 LFN 2004, S. 24.

[15] The Federal High Court, on Wednesday, 19th day of July, 2017 ordered a temporary seizure of property at Banana Island, Lagos reportedly bought for 37.5 million dollars belonging to Diezani Allison-Madueke. According to the Federal Government the property was bought during her service as a Minister. Counsel to the EFCC told the court that EFCC "reasonably suspected that the property was acquired with proceeds of alleged unlawful activities of Diezani."

[16] (2011) FWLR (Pt 40) 1595.

led evidence to show that the accused nursed grudges for his wife because he alleged that she got pregnant for another man while under his roof. It was held that this fact was relevant as it formed the motive for the killing.

Section 6(2) of the Act states that:

> The conduct, whether previous or subsequent to any proceeding-
>
> (a) of any party to any proceedings, or an agent to such party, its reference to such suit or proceeding or in reference to any fact in issue in it or a fact relevant to it; and
>
> (b) of any person an offence against whom is the subject of any proceedings, is relevant in such proceedings if such conduct influences or is influenced by any fact in issue or relevant fact.

This sub-section is wider that section 6(1) of the Act. Under this sub-section, a conduct of any party or his agents must relate to a (1) previous proceedings or (2) subsequent proceedings. The conduct of a party or his agent in relation to that proceeding, when a fact in issue is to be determined is relevant. The fact that a party is a greedy and a habitual liar and it is disclosed in a previous proceeding, is relevant to show in subsequent proceedings when the fact in issue is to show that the same party is a greedy and a habitual liar.

Section 6(3) of the Evidence Act states that the "conduct" does not include "*statements, unless those statements accompany and explain acts other that the statements, but this provision shall not affect the relevance of statements under any other section.*" A statement that is not accompanied by positive acts will not give rise to criminal liability. A mere threat to bodily harm will not be admitted to prove murder when it is not accompanied by positive acts.

6. Facts necessary to explain or introduce relevant facts

Section 7 of the Evidence Act states that:

> Facts-
>
> (a) necessary to explain or introduce a fact in issue or relevant fact;or
>
> (b) which support or rebut an inference suggested by a fact in issue or relevant fact; or
>
> (c) which establish the identity of anything or person whose identity is relevant; or

> (d) which fix the time or place at which any fact in issue or relevant fact happened; or (e) which show the relation of parties by whom any such fact was transacted, are relevant in so far as they are necessary for that purpose.

Firstly, section 7(a) of the Act supports the laying of foundation for the admissibility of lost documents before the photocopy could be admitted by the court. The relevant fact is the photocopy of the document to be tendered before the court. Facts which explain or introduce how the original document was lost is relevant for the admissibility of the photocopy of the document.

Secondly, section 7(b) of the Act is a little wider than section 7(a) of the Act, in that, fact which "rebuts an inference suggested by a fact in issue or relevant fact" is relevant. For instance, Mr. Okon was alleged to have stolen a goat belonging to Mr. Odoh in Umahia. The fact that Mr. Onehi saw Mr. Okon on the faithful day in Obalende in Lagos buying wares is relevant. The fact in issue was the fact that, Mr. Okon stole a goat belonging to Mr. Odoh. The fact which rebuts that inference suggested was the fact that Mr. Onehi saw Mr. Okon on the fateful day in Obalende in Lagos. The evidence of Mr. Onehi that he saw Mr. Okon in Lagos will be relevant in rebutting the inference suggested that Mr. Okon was the one that stole the goat.

Section 7(c) tends to establish the identity of something or someone whose identity is in question. It is the foundation for the practice of identification parade. Let us make some observations in respect thereof. Evidence of identification generally, is evidence tending to show that the person charged with an offence is the person who was seen committing the offence.

In the most recent decision of the apex court in *Ugwu* v. *The State*,[17] His Lordship Amina Adamu Augie, J.S.C posited thus:

> What then is an identification parade? It is an identification procedure of the police, in which a criminal suspect and other physically similar persons are shown to the victim or witness to determine whether the suspect can be identified as the perpetrator or one of the perpetrators of the crime. It is otherwise called and referred to as line up.

The purpose of identification evidence or parade is to ensure that the person charged is indeed the criminal so as to avoid a miscarriage of

[17](2020) LPELR-49375(SC) Pp. 25-26, para, E-A.

justice.[18] Therefore, the procedure is used to unmask the identity of the offender where his identify is not clear. It follows therefore that where the identity of the offender is clear as where the victim knew the offender before the commission of the offence or an eye witness cogently identifies the offender, identification parade is unnecessary.[19] Identification parade is also unnecessary where the Accused is positively fixed at the scene of the crime. For instance, where Mr. Edoh was caught "red handed" in the course of committing the crime and brought to the police station, identification parade will be obviated. As a matter of procedure, the police are required to display the accused person with a good number of other suspects of same physical characteristics and ask the witness to identify the accused without any assistance. In *Bazin* v. *The State*,[20] the Appellant who was sentenced to death by the High Court appealed against his conviction. In the Court of Appeal, it was shown that it was the police who pointed out the appellant for the witness as the "armed robber." The Court of Appeal however dismissed the appeal. On further appeal to the Supreme Court, Oputa, JSC (of the blessed memory) reacted to the identification parade in these terms:

> The identification of a suspected person must be carefully conducted and it is very wrong to point out the suspected person and say: is that the man? The usual and proper way is to place the suspected person with sufficient number of others and ask the witness to identify or pick the accused without any assistance.

7. Things said or done by conspirators in reference to common intention

Section 8 provides that where the issue before the court is whether there is a conspiracy, any statement made by a co-conspirator regarding the conspiracy is relevant to prove that the maker of the statement or anyone whom it affects, is a party to the conspiracy. But the statement shall not suffice to prove the doing of any act in furtherance of the conspiracy. The rationale behind this provision is obvious. Albeit conspiracy is a crime complete upon the unlawful agreement, it can hardly be established where

---

[18] See *Egbuji* v. *The State* (2014) LPELR 24092 (C.A); *Timothy* v. *People of Lagos State* (2015) LEPELR 24812 (C.A).

[19] See also *Egufor* v. *The State* (2013) LPELR 20688 (C.A); *Ikemson & Anor* v. *The State* (1989) 3 NWLR (pt. 110).

[20] (1985) 2 NWLR (Pt 8) 465.

there are no further acts from which reference can be drawn. In *Omotola & Ors* v. *The State,*[21] Oguntade, JSC held thus:

> In order to get conviction on a count of conspiracy, the prosecution must establish the element of agreement to do something which is unlawful or to do something which is lawful by unlawful means. Conspiracy is an offence which is difficult to prove because it is hatched in secrecy. Circumstantial evidence is often used to point to the fact that the confederates had agreed on the plan to commit crime. There must be an overt act from which to infer the conspiracy.

One notable fact is that, the offence of conspiracy involves more than one person. A man cannot conspire by himself alone.

8. When facts not otherwise relevant become relevant

Section 9 enacts that facts which are not relevant become relevant where they are inconsistent with the fact in issue or where by themselves or in connection with other facts, they render the existence of the fact in issue probable or improbable. For example, that Johnbosco was away in Lagos celebrating Valentine's Day with his girlfriend may not be a relevant fact. But this fact could be relevant if Johnbosco is charged with the murder of Omego who was killed in Enugu on 14th February. It is not logical to hold Johnbosco who was in Lagos on Valentine's Day responsible for Omego's death which occurred in Enugu unless there is further evidence to link both facts. This is so because the law does not believe that any human being is omnipresent or ubiquitous. Thus, section 9 of the Evidence Act is the pillar upon which the defence of *Alibi* stands and we wish to make some observations in respect thereof. In the most recent decision of the Supreme Court in *Chijioke Ugwu* v. *The State,*[22] it was held that "*Alibi*" is a defence raised when a person charged with an offence says that he was not at the scene of the crime at the time the alleged offence was committed.

According to my Lord, Awotoye J.C.A. in *Yauri* v. *The State,*[23] the term "*alibi'* means "elsewhere." In the legal parlance, *alibi* is used to refer to a defence set up by an accused person wherein he asserts or seeks to establish that he was absent from the *locus criminis* at the time of the commission of the offence and cannot be logically held for the actual commission of the

---

[21](2011) Vol. 9 LRCNCC P. 73 at p. 103 KP.
[22](2020) LPELR-49375(SC) P. 22, para. E.
[23] (2016) LPELR-40118 (C.A).

offence.[24] For the defence of *alibi* to stand, it must satisfy the following conditions:

(a) it must be raised at the earliest opportunity to warrant an investigation into it and not be raised at trial;[25]

(b) the accused must raise it with sufficient facts to enable an investigation because a defence of alibi without sufficient facts to enable investigation is tantamount to sending the police on a wild-goose chase. Such defence of *alibi* is porous and cannot avail the accused.[26]

For example, if Frank is charged with an offence, and he wishes to raise alibi, it is not sufficient for him to say: "I was not even in Enugu." He must say where he was and in whose company he was, what he went there to do, and all other facts that are necessary so that the police can confine their investigation within those facts. Saying "I was not even in Enugu" without more means that Frank is sending the police to all parts of the world to discover where he was at that time. This is undesirable and unacceptable.

(iii) Finally, the defence of *alibi* will fail if there is a cogent and compelling evidence of an eyewitness fixing the accused at the *locus criminis*.[27]

9. Certain facts are relevant in proceedings for damages

Where the court is expected to award damages, any fact that will enable the court to arrive at the quantum of damages to be awarded in that circumstance is relevant under section 10 of the Act. This section plays out more obviously in a claim for special damages.

10. Facts showing existence of state of mind or of body or bodily feeling

Section 11 provides that a person's state of mind such as goodwill, negligence, rashness, etc. is relevant where such state of mind is in question. For example, if Kosi has failed to provide necessaries for her little house-help, Blessing, and the latter dies as a result of that, in a charge of murder against Kosi for omission to provide necessaries[28] and Kosi tells the court that she has been nice to Blessing, evidence of Kosi's hatred towards Blessing

---

[24] See *Idemudia* v. *The State* (2015) LPELR 24835 (S.C).

[25] See *Adebayo* v. *The State* (2014). LPELR 22988 (S.C).

[26]See *Halilu* v. *The State* (2016) LPELR 4026 (C.A).

[27] See *Ayan* v. *The State* (2013) LPELR 20932 (S.C).

[28] It is an offence for any person not to provide necessaries for young persons under their care and the consequences of the failure to provide such necessaries is to be borne by the one on whom the law imposes the duty. See Criminal Code Cap C38, LFN 2004, SS 300-302; See also *R* v. *MacDonald* (1904) St. R. Qd. 151.

may be given as her state of mind towards Blessing where her state of mind is in issue.

11. Facts showing the existence of a course of business

When there is a question before the court as to whether a fact existed, any ordinary course of business under which the fact will exist is relevant. This is the provision of section 13 of the Act. If for example, the issue before the court is whether Mr. Tamuno is a graduate of a tertiary institution, evidence of the fact that Tamuno has just finished his National Youth Service is relevant because going for Youth Service is an ordinary course of business for those who have graduated from Nigeria tertiary Schools and this fact could serve as a relevant fact to prove the existence of the fact in issue which is whether Tamuno has graduated.

Chapter 3

EVIDENCE OF INTENTION, SIMILAR FACTS AND DEFENCE OF ACCIDENT

1. The General Rule

It is pertinent to reiterate that the law frowns at the desperation of a prosecutor who tries to secure the conviction of an accused person by all means. Sometimes, in an attempt to 'nail' the accused person, a prosecutor goes into a voyage of discovery to dig out past criminal records of the accused. As a general rule, any evidence adduced with the primary or lone purpose of bringing to bare, the past similar misconduct or offence of an accused person and thus, proving his disposition or propensity to conduct himself in a particular manner so as to prove the present charge(s) against him is inadmissible.

This general rule on exclusion of evidence of similar facts and its recognized exception has received judicial blessings and attention in the celebrated case of *Makin* v. *Attorney General for New South Wales*[1] whereby Lord Herschel posited in his erudition thus:

> It is undoubtedly not competent for the prosecution to adduce evidence tending to show that the accused has been guilty of criminal acts other than those covered by the indictment, for the purpose of leading to the conclusion that the accused is a person likely from his criminal conduct or character to have committed the offence for which he is being tried. On the other hand, the mere fact that the evidence adduced tends to show the commission of other crimes, does not render it inadmissible if it be relevant to an issue before the jury and it may be so relevant if it bears upon the question whether the acts alleged to constitute the crime charged in the indictment were designed or accidental, or to rebut a defence which would otherwise be open to the accused.

The Law Lord gave an expository insight into the principle of similar fact evidence and its correlation with the defence of accident and Intention as will be treated under the exceptions where similar fact evidence can be

---

[1] (1894) AC 57 at 67.

admitted having in mind the principle of relevance of evidence. Suffice it to say that there is a very close inter-connection between the exclusion of similar fact evidence and the presumption of innocence encapsulated under section 36(5) of the 1999 Constitution (as amended).This is essentially glare, since the prohibition of similar fact aims to ensure that the accused is not pre-judged by evidence of his past behaviour or disposition.

The remark of Oguntade, JCA (as he then was) in *Emeka* v. *State*,[2] while delivering the lead judgment of the Court of Appeal, is so germane to be overlooked. His Lordship, while illuminating on this principle and clothing himself with the impeccable garment of neutrality in the dispensation of justice remarked thus:

> I need to observe that the evidence before the lower court amply revealed that the 2nd and 3rd appellants were desperados who wanted to make money by any means. In their approach, they were ruthless. The evidence suggested they were bad boys...They might have lied before the lower court on some matters. But all these would not make them guilty of the offences as laid.

Nwadialo as submitted in his book[3] and rightly too, posited that although the rule as formulated by Lord Herschell in *Makin* v. *Attorney General for New South Wales*[4] applied to criminal cases, nothing stops it from being applied in civil proceedings as well. In the light of this, the apex court in *Akaninwo* v. *Nsirim*,[5] while relying on its earlier decision of *Yusuf* v. *Adegoke*,[6] captured the reason for the exclusion of this rule when it held that the reasons for rejecting such piece of evidence as in exhibits "A" and "B" are not far-fetched; similar facts, though often cogent, moral and weighty, i.e., logically relevant, are rejected as legal evidence on the grounds of policy and fairness; since they tend to waste time, embarrass the enquiry with collateral issues, prejudice the parties with the court and even encourage attacks without notice. This principle is well enshrined in the Latin maxim: *"Res inter alio sacta alter inocere non debet"* which when translated means; a man ought not to be prejudiced by what has taken place between others.[7]

---

[2] (1998) 7 NWLR (Pt. 559) 556 at 586.

[3] Fidelis Nwadialo, 'Similar Facts Evidence,' in Afe Babalola (ed.), *Law and Practice of Evidence in Nigeria*, (Ibadan: Intec Printers 2001) page 102.

[4] *Supra.*

[5] (2008) LPELR-321(SC) Pp.39-40, Paras. D-A.

[6] (2007) II NWLR (Pt. 1045) 332.

[7] See also *DPP* v. *Kilbourne* (1973) AC 729 at 758, per Lord Simon.

The underlying rationale for the rule excluding similar fact evidence is that, to allow it in every instance is to risk the conviction of an accused, not on the weight or probative nature of the evidence relating to the facts but because of past behaviours or disposition towards crime which invariably will raise its ugly head in the course of the judge's legal reasoning in judicial process. Such evidence without doubt has a prejudicial effect against the accused. At the root of the exclusionary rule is the risk of prejudice to the accused; the concern is that the trial would be unduly influenced by the fact that the accused has been guilty of similar crimes in the past and thereby succumb to the deductive reasoning that the accused has greater propensity to commit the present offence.

However, at times, similar facts can be so probative of guilt that to ignore it via the imposition of a blanket rule would hamper the search for truth. The basic dilemma confronting the reception of similar fact evidence is that while it constitutes extremely probative evidence, it is also thought to be capable of engendering substantial unfavourable sentiment against the accused. Regrettably, the prejudicial effect of similar fact evidence is simply not eliminated by not admitting it. In fact, once it has been presented to the judge, it is admitted into the mind of the judge. The prejudicial effect remains, even if the evidence is not admitted physically; this is the extent of havoc such similar fact evidence can wreck in the case of an accused.

There are, however, exceptions to the general rule, which shall be considered in the subsequent sub topics.

2. Exceptions to the rule against admission of similar facts

It is settled law that although, a particular court proceeding and judgment thereon may be inadmissible in the course of trial of an action on the ground that, as between the parties to the action in which it is proffered in evidence, it ought to be excluded on the well-known maxim of law of Evidence known as *res inter alio sacta alter inocere non debet.* However, there are numerous provisions of the Evidence Act under which an evidence of similar fact can be admissible. Suffice it to say that most of these exceptions are well captured under Part II of the Act that provides for Relevancy[8] which has been treated in details under the preceding chapter. It should be emphasized at this point that relevance is the bedrock or touchstone of admissibility and a fact is relevant if it is material to the dispute in court.[9] Once a piece of

[8] Specifically, see sections 4, 5, 6(2)-(4), 7, 9(b), 12 and 66 of the Act.
[9] *Ajose-Adeogun & Anor* v. *Olojede & Ors* (*supra*).

evidence is relevant to the fact in issue, it becomes admissible even when it tends to show evidence of similar fact. This summarises every other exceptions to be captured in this chapter.

3.Evidence of intention

As seen from the dictum of Lord Herschell in *Makin's case supra,* evidence of intention constitutes an exception to the rule against admissibility of similar fact evidence and thus becomes relevant to an issue before the court and may be so relevant if it bears upon the question whether the acts alleged to constitute the crime charged were designed or intended. Thus, it mostly becomes of particular importance and significance when the main issue is the state of mind of the accused. Where it is established that an accused committed the *actus reus* of the crime charged, evidence of a similar fact may often be of sufficient relevance to be admissible to show that he possessed the appropriate *mens rea* (guilty intention).

As an exception to the general rule of exclusion of evidence of similar fact, the law is that a person is presumed to intend the natural consequence of his actions.[10] This can be seen in section 316(2) of the Criminal Code, which provides that:

> Where a person who does grievous harm to another is liable to a charge of murder. If the victim dies, then his death is construed as the natural or probable result or consequence of such grievous act.

Intention has been defined in *Oseni* v. *State*[11] as the willingness to bring about something planned or foreseen; the state of being set to do something. It is the purpose or design with which an act is done.[12] In otherwords, it is the foreknowledge of the act, coupled with the desire of it, such fore-knowledge and desire being the cause of the act, in as much as they fulfil themselves through operation of the will. This is to say that an act is intentional if, and in so far as, it exists in an idea before it exists in fact, the idea realizing itself in the fact because of the desire by which it is accompanied. Before an act is committed, the court takes cognizance of the intention of the accused before the commission of the offence and if the intention is not secured, then it would be difficult to hold such party liable for the offence unless the prosecution lays down evidence to sustain his speculation that it was the accused and no one else that committed the

[10]See *Ukpong* v. *State* (2019) LPELR-46427(SC) P. 24, paras. F-G.
[11](2017) LPELR-42770(CA) P. 40, paras. B-C.
[12] Relying on the *Blacks Law Dictionary* (8th Edn) by Bryan A. Garner at p.826.

alleged offence. The court in *Oseni's* case while quoting Niki Tobi JCA (As he then was) in *Iden* v. *State*[13] poignantly submitted in an appetizing prose that:

> An intention is a design or fixation of the mind on a particular line of act or conduct. And until intention is overtly applied or executed in a particular way or direction, it is lost to any human being other than the Almighty God. Therefore the intention which the law punishes in respect of attempted murder is that which the accused overtly expresses by any action or inaction. It is therefore clear to me that intention is the state of the mind of the actor at the time he committed or performed the act. However, as the saying goes, not even the devil knows the intention of man. Only God who created us has that absolute prerogative. That being so, the only way the intention of a man can be presumed to be known is through the overt acts done by him in the execution of that presumed intention.[14]

In line with the above judicial approach to the concept of intention, once an accused has caused a grievous bodily harm to the person of another, the law imputes an intention to cause such other person, the harm done as a man intends the natural consequences of his action. The accused is thus, presumed to have intended to kill that person and he would be guilty of murder irrespective of his intentions.[15] The consequence of an act may be said to be probable, if a reasonable man would consider its occurrence to be the natural and normal effect of the act. This automatically negates the general rule that evidence of similar fact is inadmissible. For instance, in an offence of murder, intention, which is not tangible, can be inferred from the instrument used to commit the crime, the force used and the part of the body on which the injury was inflicted. Also, the force with which the accused applied the instrument on the deceased is also to be taken into consideration. In *Afolabiv*. *State*,[16] the court imputed an intention to cause bodily grievous harm to the person of the deceased when the appellant stated emphatically in Exhibit D that he aimed his gun at the chest of the deceased at close range and shot him.

In *Akerele* v. *The King*,[17] the appellant, a medical doctor was convicted of manslaughter of a child, on the ground that he had knowingly

---

[13] (1994) 8 NWLR (pt.365) (1994) LPELR 14608 (CA).
[14] See *James Afolabi* v. *The State* (2016) LPELR 40300 (SC).
[15] *Omotosho* v. *State* (2018) LPELR-44169 (CA) P. 12, para G.
[16] (2016) LPELR-40300 (SC).
[17] 1940 8 WACA 5, (1943) 1 All ER 367.

administered over-dose or poisoned injection on the child. The defence contended vehemently that the drugs administered on the child was not over-dose, and that the child had died because of his peculiar health conditions. To rebut this defence, however the prosecution tendered similar evidence concerning the symptoms, ill health and death of other children attended to by the appellant, using the same drugs. It was held by the Privy Council that this similar negative evidence adduced by the prosecution was properly received in evidence as a man intends the natural consequences of his action.[18] However, the court is to ascertain whether the accused nurtured such intention. If he did so, the court can *suo moto* presume the intention that the accused committed the offence. In another case of *R* v. *Nungu,*[19] it was held that a person is guilty of murder if he intends to do the person killed some grievous harm.On this premise, the accused person may not have formed the requisite intention that his act may occasion death but since death has occurred, it is presumed that he formed the intention unless a rebuttal is made.

In *Ishola* v. *The State,*[20] the appellant was charged for murder and the prosecution adduced evidence of the appellants previous similar conducts towards the deceased, such as previous assaults, previous stabbing of the deceased and destruction by the appellant of economic trees belonging to the witnesses and the deceased. The Supreme Court in rejecting the argument that evidence of such previous acts of the appellant was prejudicial to him, and ought not to have been admitted held that such evidence of previous similar facts was admissible both under Section 9 of the Evidence Act[21] and under the general rule enunciated in *Makin's* case.

Other exceptions asides relevance and intention include but not limited to when a previous bad character or similar facts evidence amounts to a crime or a civil wrong or to no wrong at all, in so far as the prosecution proposes to use such similar fact to negative any possible defence the accused might be raising especially where the accused person raises a defence of his good character. In this regard, there is no closed list of the sort of cases where such evidence is admissible. It is, however, well established that it may be admitted to rebut a defence of legitimate association for honest purposes,

---

[18]See also *Arije* v. *FRN* (2014) LPELR-24097 (CA) relying on *Akerele* v. *The King, Ishola* v. *The State and Makin's case.*

[19](1953) 14 WACA 379.

[20] (1978) 2 LRN 111.

[21] See s 6 of the Evidence Act, 2011. Though it has been slightly amended but the decision still stands in the face of the extant law.

as well as to rebut evidence of good character. Where the evidence is admissible on the first mentioned basis, it may be admitted as part of the case for the prosecution. When the trial judge in the exercise of his discretion admits similar fact evidence, an appellate court should not interfere with that discretion unless the learned trial judge has erred in principle.[22]

The Court of Appeal in a more recent case of *Starline (Nig) Ltd & Anor* v. *Onyeagocha & Anor*[23] while summarising the exceptions to similar fact with relevance to the copious provisions of section 3, 4, 5, 6(1)-(4), 7(a)-(e) and 9(a) and (b), the court was of the opinion that it is only commonsensical that where there is insufficient evidence to prove the particular issue or situation in question that there might be need to resort to adducing evidence in respect of similar facts.

It is unavoidably crucial to reproduce the fact of *Makin's case* for its pivotal place in the discussion of similar fact evidence. In that case, the accused, a husband and wife, were charged with the murder of a baby. Its body was found buried in their garden, and they were proved to have agreed to adopt it in return for payment of a small sum by its parents. The defence of the accused were that the child had died through natural causes and that their sole crime was to have buried it irregularly. The prosecution's case was that the child had been killed by the Makins pursuant to a scheme by which they took charge of infant in return of payments to be used for the infants care; then kill the infants and retain the sum paid. In support of this case, the prosecution led evidence that the bodies of twelve other infants had been discovered in the grounds of premises occupied at various times by the Makins, and that several of these infants had been placed in the care of the Makins in return of a payment of a small sum. The accused were convicted and appealed unsuccessfully to the Privy Council. The Privy Council held that the evidence had been properly admitted to establish that the baby's death was not of natural causes, but of the conduct of the Makins as the death of the child was actually intended.

4. Similar facts and the defence of accident

Unless otherwise expressly declared, the motive by which a person is induced to do oromit to do an act, or to form an intention is immaterial so far as regards criminal responsibility. Albeit, presence of motive usually

[22] See *R.* v. *Doughty* (1965) 1 WLR 331, 49 Cr. App. R. 110. See also Makin's case.

[23] (2018) LPELR-44268 (CA) P.22, paras. E-F.

strengthens the case of the prosecution depending on the circumstances of each case.[24] In relation to the admissibility of similar fact evidence, we shall make reference to section 24 of the Criminal Code on intention and motive.

Section 24 of the Criminal code provides for intention and motive. It provides thus:

> Subject to the express provisions of this code relating to negligent acts and omissions, a person is not criminally responsible for an act or omission which occurs independently of the exercise of his own will or for an event which occurs by accident. Unless the intention to cause a particular result is expressly declared to be an element of the offence constituted, in whole or part, by an act or omission, the result intended to be caused by an act or omission is immaterial.

An event is said to be accidental when the act by which it was caused was not done with the intention of causing it and when its occurrence as a consequence of such act is not probable that a person of ordinary prudence ought under the circumstances in which it was done to take reasonable precaution against it.[25] In *Makin's case,* the court was of the opinion that the baby's death couldn't have been by accident or by natural cause in view of the similar fact evidence led by the prosecution that bodies of twelve other infants had been discovered in the grounds of premises occupied at various times by the Makins; of course, this cannot be by accident.

It will be so much of a coincidence or accident for an accused person to commit series of related offences consecutively and when such is raised in his present trial, the court will be rendered helpless and thus forced to overlook the criminal tendency of the accused person on the ground that the law forbids him from admitting similar fact evidence. It should be stressed at this juncture that once such piece of evidence is relevant to the fact in issue, it becomes admissible in line with statutory exceptions to this rule. Finally, one point that should be borne in mind in the course of these intellectual analysis is that, relevancy is a key word and an integral determinant for the admissibility of any piece of evidence.

---

[24] *Onwuzulike* v. *State* (2017) LPELR-41889 (CA) P. 150, para. F relying on *Ishola* v. *The State* (1978) 2 LRN 111 at page 122 to page 123.

[25] *Musa* v. *State* (2016) LPELR-40798 (CA) P. 16, paras.A-B.

Chapter 4

IMPROPERLY OR ILLEGALLY OBTAINED EVIDENCE

1. The general rule

It is an antiquated principle of law premised on a hidden but resourceful truth that once any piece of evidence is relevant, it becomes admissible; the way and manner it was obtained notwithstanding.[1] This general rule gained statutory recognition under our body of laws '*corpus juris*' specifically section 14(a) and (b) of the Evidence Act 2011 which provides that evidence obtained improperly or in contravention of the law or in consequence of an impropriety or of a contravention of a law, shall be admissible unless the court is of the opinion that the desirability of admitting the evidence is outweighed by the undesirability of admitting evidence that has been obtained in the manner in which the evidence was obtained. This goes to underscore the time-hallowed principle that admissibility of evidence is primarily governed by relevance and not the circumstances under which it was obtained or proper custody.[2]

In so many cases, the law enforcement agencies employ detection by deception so as to fish and flush out criminals who wear the garb of innocence. This is a very topical issue in the determination and the admissibility of illegally obtained evidence under our law.

The highly celebrated case of *Igbinovia* v. *State*[3] is very germane to be reproduced herein for proper understanding of this subject matter. The facts of the case are that the appellant and the deceased are of Benin origin, friends and resident in Benin City. The appellant by occupation was a soldier and the deceased a taxi driver. On the 7th day of April, 1975 at between 7.00 p.m. and 8.00p.m., the appellant called at the house of the deceased (Sunday Egharevba, described in the evidence of P.W 1 as Sunday Igbinosun) at

[1]Section 14 of the Evidence Act, 2011. See also *the locus classicus* cases of *Karuma* v. *Queen* (1955) AC 197 at 203; *Igbinovia* v. *The State* (1981) 12 NSCC 63 at 68–69 and the recent decision in *Ayodeji* v. *FRN* (2018) LPELR-45839(CA).

[2] See *Omatseye* v. *FRN* (2017) LPELR-42719(CA).

[3](1981) LPELR-1446(SC).

Oziegbe Street, Benin City and invited him to come with him to buy petrol (which was scarce at that time). The deceased (a taxi driver) needed petrol to operate or run his taxi. The deceased accepted the invitation, followed the appellant and both drove off in the taxi, the appellant leaving a copy of his photograph with P.W.1 (widow of deceased) who was doubtful of the success of the mission to assure her that her husband would succeed and she should not be afraid.

At about 8.00p.m., P.W. 2, a sister of the deceased stopped the taxi at Uselu Motor Park as she saw the deceased drive past. She observed that besides her brother there were 4 passengers including the appellant in the car. The appellant alone sat in front with the deceased while the other three passengers whom she could not recognise sat at the back. The deceased then told her that the appellant invited him to follow him to purchase some quantity of petrol. The deceased did not return either alone or with the car that day. Neither did the appellant who invited him and took him away to buy the petrol call to report to P.W.1 having expected the return of her husband in vain. P.W.1, on the following day informed members of the family of the deceased of the failure of her husband to return since the appellant took him out to an 'unknown destination' the previous day. The police were contacted immediately by them. A search for the deceased by both the police and the family of the deceased started. The appellant was arrested (11 days) later along with other accused persons who were acquitted and discharged at the lower court except the accused person who was convicted.

Then on the 20th day of April, 1975, the decomposed body of the deceased was recovered by the police in a bush behind the Bendel Television House after an intensive search for the deceased. The body was found covered with blanket and some other clothes. It was shown from the fact that during the incarceration of the Appellant , the P.W.5, a police officer was planted in the same cell with the appellant wherein the appellant confessed that he took part in the killing of Sunday Igbinosun.

Being dissatisfied with the judgment, the appellant appealed to the Federal Court of Appeal and the appeal was dismissed for lack of merit. Further dissatisfied, he appealed to the Supreme Court. The Supreme Court while dismissing the appeal and affirming the decision of the High Court and Federal Appeal Court held that there is no doctrine of entrapment in Nigerian law and evidence obtained by means of agent's provocateurs is admissible.The appellant regarded P.W 5 as a trusted partner in crime and at the time of the confession, the P.W.5 was no more than a possible witness for the prosecution.

It should be noted that the ascribable weight to be attached to an evidence obtained in contravention of the law is for the court to determine by taking into cognizance, the provisions of sections 14(b) and 15(a)-(g) of the Evidence Act. This will be discussed extensively in subsequent sub-topic.

2. Admissibility of illegally obtained evidence

The law is clear on this point that the way and manner an evidence is obtained is not material to the admissibility of such evidence provided it is relevant.[4] However, it goes to the weight the court will attach to it. It should be noted that this is not a 'catch phrase.' The Evidence Act explicitly made provisions for what the court will put into cognizance while determining whether or not to admit an improperly obtained evidence under section 14 of the Act. This is provided under section 15 of the Act. It states thus:

> for the purpose of section 14, the matters that the court shall take into account include-
>
> (a) the probative value of the evidence;
>
> (b) the importance of the evidence in the proceeding;
>
> (c) the nature of the relevant offence, cause of action or defence and the nature of the subject-matter of the proceeding;
>
> (d) the gravity of the impropriety or contravention;
>
> (e) whether the impropriety or contravention was deliberate or reckless;
>
> (f) whether any other proceeding (whether or not in court) has been or is likely to be taken in relation to the impropriety or contravention;
>
> (g) the difficulty, if any, of obtaining the evidence without impropriety or contravention of law.

The provisions of section 14 of the Act on admissibility of illegally obtained evidence cannot be divorced from the provisions of section 15 of the Act. As a matter of fact, section 14 needs the helping hands of the provisions of section 15 to sail through. The admissibility of an illegally obtained evidence is a question of judicial discretion which the court must exercise judicially and judiciously having in mind, the factors encapsulated

---

[4] See *Ifaramoye* v. *State* (2017) LPELR-42031(SC).

under section 15 of the Act which the court is mandated and obligated to consider while exercising its discretion.[5]

In addition to the matters the court will take into account under section 15 of the Act, the court while analysing the probative value to be attached to a form of an illegally obtained evidence called "Police detection by deception," in *Igbinovia's case* gave a judicial insight and states that if the confession proceeds from remorse and a desire to make reparation for the crime, it is admissible. If it flows from hope or fear, exerted by a person in authority, it is inadmissible. The court went further to define who is "a person in authority". Though, we may not dwell much on this but suffice it to say that a person in authority means anyone who has authority or control over the accused or over the proceedings or the prosecution against him.

In *R.* v. *Murphy*,[6] Lord MacDermott, LCJ at page147 while considering and approving police procedure of detection, cautioned that it should be seldom used. The court stated thus:

> Detection by inspection is a form of police procedure to be directed and used sparingly and with circumspection but as a method, it is as old as a constable in plain clothes and, regrettable though the fact may be, the day has not yet come when it would be safe to say that law and order could always be enforced and the public safety protected without occasional resort to it.

Detection of crime is the primary assignment of the law enforcement agencies and offenders or miscreants that pollute the air of good governance, public security and public safety cannot be allowed to continue circumventing the full weight of the law by the manner in which evidence against them was obtained. Their activities are shrouded in secrecy and masked with the garb or toga of innocence.

In *Ayodeji* v. *FRN*,[7] the Appellant and another person Mohammed Dogonyaro Audu (a.k.a Abdullahi Dogonyaro Muhammed) as 1st Defendant were arraigned before the High Court of Federal Capital Territory on a ten-count charge of conspiracy and fraudulent acquisition of property

---

[5] Note the use of the word "shall" in section 15 of the Act. Note also the use of the word "include" to enumerate what the court must consider in admitting an evidence obtained in contravention of the law. This means that the factors listed under section 15 of the Act is not exhaustive in itself as the trial court is at liberty to take into account any other considerations that will further the interest of justice, demands of fair hearing, due process and rule of law.

[6](1965) N.I.138

[7] *Supra.*

contrary to sections 26 and 12 of the ICPC Act, 2000. The Defendant pleaded not guilty to the counts on 23rd February, 2017. Three witnesses testified for the prosecution. At the end of the trial and adoption of addresses of learned counsel to the accused persons, the Appellant was found guilty on counts 1, 3, 4, 5 and 9 of the charge. He was sentenced to seven years imprisonment on Counts 1, 3, 4, 5 and 9 and the term was to run concurrently. Dissatisfied with the decision, the Appellant appealed to the Court of Appeal and subsequently to the Supreme Court On the whole, the Supreme Court found no merit in the appeal and accordingly dismissed same.

The contention of the Appellant's counsel is that the evidence of PW2 who is an investigating officer in the matter was hearsay evidence. What the PW3 (IPO) did was to give evidence on what he actually saw or had witnessed, or discovered in the course of his work as an investigator. The court held that the law is now trite that whatever comes to the knowledge or attention of an IPO or Investigating Police Officer in the course of investigation particularly facts discovered which can incriminate or exculpate an accused or defendant is not hearsay evidence.[8] Such evidence are clearly admissible notwithstanding that such evidence was found or discovered in the course of investigation.

The Court went further at page 45 to hold thus:

> It is an acceptable and settled principle of law in this country that it does not matter how or by what method evidence (oral or documentary) capable of sustaining the prosecution's case against an accused/Defendant was/is obtained. Relevancy is the underlying requirement coupled with the fact that such evidence is not rendered inadmissible by any other enactment aside from the provisions of Evidence Act.

The legal emphasis here is that it is the relevancy of a piece of evidence that is the major determinant of whether that piece of evidence is admissible or not. The way and manner through which it is obtained is immaterial and inconsequential provided that the court has considered the matters listed in section 15 of the Act and any other ancillary matters that will foster the interest of justice.

---

[8] See also *Ibrahim Kamila* v. *The State* (2018) 8 NWLR (PT 1621) 252 AT 271 D - E per Sanusi, JSC and *Lekan Olaoye* v. *The State* (2018) LPELR -43601 (SC) P. 23, paras. D-E.

3. Wrongly admission and rejection of evidence

The law is trite that the court is not infallible as the Justices of the court are human and may by inadvertence or oversight, wrongfully admit an evidence which ordinarily should be inadmissible. This often times, gives rise to a party agitating by way of appeal which the appellate court is bound by law to overrule such a decision based on a wrongfully admitted evidence.

Section 251 of the Act should be borne in mind on the attitude of the court on the nature of wrongfully admitted evidence. Section 251 of the Evidence Act provides thus:

> (1) The wrongful admission of evidence shall not of itself be a ground for the reversal of any decision in any case where it shall appear to the court on appeal that the evidence so admitted cannot reasonably be held to have affected the decision and that such decision would have been the same if such evidence had not been admitted.
>
> (2) The wrongful exclusion of the evidence shall not of itself be a ground for the reversal of any decision in any case if it appears to the court on appeal that had the evidence excluded been admitted, it may reasonably be held that the decision would have been the same.

The import of section 251 of the Act is to the effect that although a wrongfully admitted evidence can be a ground for appeal,[9] however, it is not every shadow of wrongfully admitted evidence that is sufficient to cause a reversal of a decision on appeal. Such wrongfully admitted evidence must be such as to have affected the decision. The apex court in *Ugo-Ngadi* v. *FRN*[10] held thus:

> A wrongful admission of evidence or a wrongful consideration of an issue which is alien to the case under consideration cannot be a ground for reversal of a decision where it appears on appeal that such evidence or wrongful consideration of such issue cannot reasonably be held to have affected the decision and that the decision would have been the same if such evidence had not been admitted and the consideration of the issue complained of had not been made.

---

[9] See *Badung* v. *COP Plateau State Command* (2019) LPELR-47033(CA).

[10] (2018) LPELR-43903(SC) Pp. 20-21, paras. E-A; See also the following: *Itu* v. *State* (2016) LPELR 26063 (SC); *Ezeoke* v. *Nwagbo* (1988) 1 NWLR (Pt.72) 616, *Umeojiako* v. *Ezenamuo* (1990) 1 NWLR (Pt.126) 253 and *Ayeni* v. *Sowemimo* (1982) 5 SC 60.

In determining whether to set aside a decision predicated on a wrongfully admitted evidence, the court while applying the provisions of section 251(2) of the Act in *Ayabam* v. *C.O.P. Benue State*[11] held thus:

> The appellant has the onus of showing that, if the public documents had been expunged by the learned trial Judge or this court, the decision would not have been the same. See Section 251(1) of the Evidence Act, 2011. The appellant has to further show that had the learned trial Judge not wrongfully excluded all the exhibits the appellant is complaining of, but had admitted them in the Court below or on the orders of this Court, it may reasonably be held that the decision would have not favoured the appellant.[12]

when a party desires to exclude a piece of evidence which he conceives to be inadmissible from being admitted in evidence, the said party is duty bound to object to the piece of evidence in question at the point it is being tendered.[13] However, even when parties do not raise an objection or make it a ground of appeal, the court can raise it *suo motu* and call the parties to address it on the issue.[14] A ruling wrongly rejecting or admitting a piece of evidence in the course of trial is an integral part of the trial which can be appealed against as an error in the final decision of the trial Court,[15] and leave is not required for filing an appeal which is hinged on a complaint of wrongful admission or rejection of a particular exhibit, as it is evidently a ground of law alone.[16] The law sees the question of wrongful admission with a stern look that even the parties cannot by consent, confer on an inadmissible evidence, the toga of admissibility.[17]

It should be noted also that evidence which is legally admissible under the Evidence Act cannot be rendered inadmissible by a state law.[18] This is because evidence is under item 23 in the Exclusive Legislative List, Second

---

[11](2019) LPELR-47283 (CA) P. 5-6, paras. F-B; see also *Dalyop* v. *C.O.P, Plateau State Command* (2019) LPELR 47031 (CA) and *Edong* v. *State* (2014) LPELR-23989 (CA).

[12]See also *Bonum (Nig) Ltd* v. *Ibe & Anor* (2019) LPELR-46442 (CA); *Nomany* v. *FRN* (2018) LPELR-44546 (CA.).

[13]See *Okoye* v. *Okonkwo & Ors* (2017) LPELR-42855(CA) P.24, paras. D-E.

[14] See the recent decision in *Weekly Insight and Communication Network Ltd & Anor* v. *Peter & Ors* (2019) LPELR-46847(CA) P.18, Paras.A-C; See also *Rosehill Ltd* v. *GTB Plc* (2016) LPELR-41665 (CA) P. 24, paras. B-C; *Abdullahi* v. *State* (2016) LPELR-43753 (CA) Pp.13-14. Paras. F-A and *Ekpo* v. *Ukaonu & Ors* (2013) LPELR-22535(CA) P. 37, paras. B-D; see also *ACN* v. *Lamido & Ors* (2011) LPELR-9174 (CA) and *AG Kwara State & Anor* v. *Alao & Anor* (2000) LPELR-10457 (CA).

[15] See *Ogbebor* v. *Onojakpor & Ors* (2019) LPELR-47176 (CA).

[16] See *Ogoejofo* v. *Ogoejofo & Ors* (2018) LPELR-43950 (CA).

[17] *Weekly Insight and Communication Network Ltd & Anor* v. *Peter & Ors.* (*supra*).

[18]See *Taiwo* v. *Ogunwale* (2019) LPELR-47058(CA).

Schedule to the Constitution of the Federal Republic of Nigeria 1999 (as amended) and not within the legislative competence of states to legislate on.

Generally, section 215(2) of the Act hinges on the effect on appeal of wrongful exclusion of evidence. Having captured the provision of section 215(2) of the Act in the preceding paragraphs, it suffices to say that in considering this provision, the appellate court determines each case with their peculiar circumstances so as to do what the justice of the case demands.[19]

4. Discretionary powers of the court to admit evidence

The usual catch phrase is that admissibility of evidence is governed by relevancy.[20] The court have always held that relevancy is the precursor or touchstone of admissibility. However, the Act to some extent vested on the court, the discretionary powers to admit evidence based on relevancy and other ancillary considerations expressly stated under section 211 of the Evidence Act.

Section 211(1) of the Act provides that when either party proposes to give evidence of any fact, the court may ask the party proposing to give the evidence in what manner the alleged fact, if proved, would be relevant; the court shall admit the evidence if it thinks that the fact, if proved, would be relevant and not otherwise.

The expression '*the court shall admit the evidence if it thinks*' used in the provision above confers some degree of judicial discretion on the court while applying judicial reasoning in legal process as to do what the justice of the case demands.

In the recent case of *Baba* v. *Iyeghe*[21] the Court of Appeal while citing the Supreme Court in *Zakirai* v. *Muhammad*[22] held that judicial discretion is described as a sacred power that inheres to a judge, and which should be employed judicially and judiciously. In the judicious and judicial exercise of discretion, a Court must be guided by the spirit and principle of law. The exercise has to be judicious in the sense that it must be based on sound decision marked by discretion, wisdom and good sense.

---

[19] Finally, under section 251(3) of the Evidence Act, it is provided that the term "decision" as used in section 251 of the Act "includes a judgment, order finding or verdict."

[20] *Royork (Nig) Ltd* v. *A.G. & CJ, Sokoto State & Anor* (2017) LPELR-42506 (CA), P. 23,para.B.

[21] (2019) LPELR-46933 (CA) P. 8, paras. C-F.

[22] (2017) 17 NWLR (Pt. 1594) 181 at 192.

For a party to succeed in showing that a trial judge exercised his discretion wrongly, he has the onus to justify the fact that the discretion was exercised in an arbitrary manner or without due regard to all the relevant considerations or that the trial judge engaged in the consideration of unnecessary factors or relied upon wrong principles. In other words, to have the order made in exercise of Courts discretion reversed, the appellant must show that the trial Court exercised its discretion wrongly or did not give due weight to relevant considerations, which resulted to injustice done to such party.

Section 211(2) of the Act, also provides that if the fact proposed to be proved is one of which evidence is admissible only upon proof of some other fact, such last mentioned fact must be proved before evidence is given of the fact first mentioned, unless the party undertakes to give proof of such fact, and the court is satisfied with such undertaking.

Finally, if the relevancy of one alleged fact depends upon another alleged fact being first proved, the court may in its discretion, either permit evidence of the first fact to be given before the second fact is proved, or require evidence to be given of the second fact before evidence is given of the first fact.[23]

5. Custody and weight of Evidence

The issue of proper custody of documents has been settled long ago in *Obianwuna Ogbunyiya & Ors* v. *Obi Okudo & Ors.*[24] The court later in *Uwagboe & Anor* v. *Eriyo & Anor*[25] while expounding on what it means for a document to emanate from proper custody submitted thus:

> What after all, is meant by expression proper custody of a document? It means no more than its deposit with a person and in a place where, if authentic, it might naturally and reasonably be expected to be found, and proof of production from proper custody is required not as a ground for reading the document...but to afford the Judge reasonable assurance of it as being what it purports to be.

It is the law that admissibility should be based on relevance and not proper custody. Once a matter, be it a document or oral evidence is relevant, it is admissible. Proper custody only raises the issue of presumption, or to

---

[23] Section 211(3) of the Evidence Act, 2011.

[24](1979) All NLR (Reprint Edition) Page 105 at 112 Per Idigbe JSC. See also Phipson on *Evidence* 12th Edition (UK: Sweet & Maxwell Ltd 1976) Page 731.

[25] (2017) LPELR-42512(CA) P. 12, paras. A-E. The court relied on the Supreme Court decision of *Obianwuna Ogbunyiya & Ors* v. *Obi Okudo & Ors. supra.*

put it more clearly, the weight to be attached to the evidence, whether documentary or otherwise. For evidence, documentary or otherwise to be admissible, it is sufficient that proper ground of its relevance is laid.[26] Section 156 of the Act defined proper custody thus:

> Documents are said to be in proper custody within the meaning of section 148 to 155 of this Act if they are in the place in which, and under the care of the person with whom, they would naturally be, but no custody is improper if it is proved to have had a legitimate origin, or if the circumstances of the particular case are such as to render such an origin probable.

The proviso "no custody is improper if it is proved to have had a legitimate origin, or if the circumstances of the particular case are such as to render such an origin probable" underscores the position of relevancy in documents emanating from custody of a person whose duty it is to keep same or otherwise provided it is within the bounds of law. In *Lawal* v. *Hon. Commissioner for Lands, Housing & Survey Oyo State*[27] the Appellant filed a motion for an order of mandamus compelling the respondent, the Honourable Commissioner for Lands, Housing and Survey Oyo State, to forthwith issue him a Certificate of Statutory Right of Occupancy in respect of Plot 4, Block III at the Oyo State New Government Reservation Area, Samoda, Bodija, Ibadan since he had paid all the prescribed fees following the allocation of the plot to him.

The court granted the order of mandamus on 28/1/2008. The respondent however filed a motion on notice on 15/2/2008 which sought an order of stay of execution of the ruling granting the order of mandamus.The same was struck out on 18/3/2008. Before then, on 21/2/2008, the respondent filed a motion on notice to set aside the ruling of 28/1/2008 on the ground that he was not aware of the hearing date and as such was denied fair hearing. After a detailed consideration of the said motion, the learned trial Judge on 2/5/2008 set aside his earlier ruling. He then considered the motion on notice for an order of mandamus on the merits. On 30/6/2008, he delivered his ruling. He ruled that the application for the order of mandamus lacked merit and therefore dismissed it. The appellant being dissatisfied with that ruling, appealed to the Court of Appeal. In conclusion, the appellate judge

[26] See *Torti* v. *Ukpabi & Ors* (1984) LPELR-3259 (SC) P. 19, paras. D-E.
[27] (2013) LPELR-21114(CA) P. 19, paras. A-B.

> However, an admission, in order to bind the party admitting, must be clear, unequivocal and total. Admission is not a game of chance. It is not a subject of speculation or conjecture. On the contrary, it is a total and comprehensive statement orally made or in writing suggesting a clear and unequivocal inference as to any fact in issue or relevant fact unfavourable to the conclusion contended by the person by whom or in whose behalf the statement is made.

Thus, to ascertain this sacred condition for bindingness of admission on the maker, the court is saddled with the great task of determining the collateral circumstances under which an admission was given so as to decide what weight to attach to it. Thus, the law is that in order to determine whether a party either, expressly or by necessary implication, has made an admission or admitted a relevant fact(s) in his pleadings, all the averments in the pleadings must be looked at and considered holistically in the circumstances of the case and not in isolation.[6]

Extrapolating from the totality of the aforementioned statutory and judicial exposition, it is evident that two vital points are deducible from the meaning of admission as a general principle. These are the question as to whether the statement or document is an admission and the circumstance under which the statement or document was made.

2. Formal and informal admissions

For clarity and to avoid weaving the cloth of the evidential topic of admission with the thread of confusion, admissions are either classified into formal and informal admission.

Formal admissions

This is otherwise referred to as judicial admissions. It refers to admission made by a party to civil proceedings so as to relieve the other party of the necessity of proving the matters admitted.[7] As a general rule, this suffices to mean that formal admissions are conclusive and dispense with any need for further proof.[8] It is now a settled position of law with statutory backing and

---

[6] See *Mobil Producing (NIG) Unltd* v. *Ayeni & Ors* (2019) LPELR-47481 (CA).

[7] *Tejuoso* v. *Asset Mgt. Corporation of Nigeria & Ors* (2015) LPELR-24677 (CA) P. 23, Para. A.

[8] See *Aondo* v. *Benue Links (Nig) Ltd* (2019) LPELR-46876(CA) P59, para. C; *Oki & Anor* v. *First Bank* (2019) LPELR-47542 (CA); *A.G. Imo State & Anor* v. *Imo Rubber Estates Ltd & Ors* (2019) LPELR-47579 (CA), P.31, paras E and *Ignobis Hotel Ltd* v. *Bentec Elect Ltd* (2015)1 NWLR (pt. 411 – 630).

a legion of decided authorities that what is admitted needs no further proof as proof is about disputed facts and not otherwise.[9]

This evidential principle has received statutory expression under section 123 of the Evidence Act. The said section provides thus:

> No fact needs to be proved in any civil proceeding which the parties to the proceedings or their agents agree to admit at the hearing or which, before the hearing, they agree to admit by any writing under their hands, or which by any rule of pleading in force at the time they are deemed to have been admitted by their pleadings: provided that the court may in its discretion, require the facts admitted to be proved otherwise than by such admissions.

This was the gravamen of the decision in *NURTW & Ors* v. *First Continental Insurance Co. Ltd.*[10] However, an admission does not *ipso facto* amount to conclusive proof of the matter admitted as the trial court is duty bound to take into account the collateral circumstances under which it was made and thereby determine the weight to attach thereto.[11]Unless explanations are given which satisfy the court that admissions should not be regarded, due weight should be given to them as such.[12]

As stated earlier, admission by a party does not *per se* amount to conclusive proof of the matter admitted, rather, it only strengthens the weight of probative value the court attaches to the evidence adduced by the other party.[13] Thus, section 27 of the Evidence Act provides that though admissions are not conclusive proof of the matters admitted but they may operate as estoppel under certain circumstances under sections 145 to 174. Formal admissions are usually contained in pleadings by way of express admissions made by parties in their pleadings and such are usually taken as established without further proof.[14] It may also take the form of clear admissions filed or made by a party to a civil proceeding or by his counsel in the service of the trial of a civil suit. The court however, even in the case of a formal admission in a civil proceeding has discretion to require the admitted fact to be proved by some other evidence other than by the admission itself.

---

[9] *Barau & Ors* v. *Consolidated Tin Mines Ltd & Ors.* (2019) LPELR-46806 (CA) Pp.31-32, paras. F-A; See also *Aliyu* v. *Bulaki* (2019) LPELR-46513 (CA) P.40, para. E.

[10] (2019) LPELR-48005 (CA).

[11] *Tejuoso* v. *Asset Mgt. Corporation of Nigeria & Ors.* (*supra*) at P. 22, paras. E-F.

[12] Per Niki Tobi JSC (of the Blessed Memory) in *Odi & Ors* v. *Iyala & Ors* (2004) LPELR-2213 (SC).

[13] *Kay Dee Venture Ltd* v. *The Honourable Minister of FCT & Ors* (2010) 2 SCNJ 276 at 301.

[14] See *Tejuoso* v. *Asset Mgt. Corporation of Nigeria & Ors.* (*supra*) at P. 23, paras. B-C.

For any averment contained in any paragraph of a statement of claim to amount to an admission of some paragraphs on the statement of defence, it must be raised by any of the parties. By so doing, it averts the mind of the other party to address it as failure to do so by a party or usurpation of such task by the court is a flagrant disregard of evidential proof and have all the possibilities of occasioning a miscarriage of justice as was held by the Supreme Court in *Shashi* v. *Smith.*[15]

Extrapolating from the fore-going or fleet of relevant statutory and judicial authorities, formal admission only applies to civil cases as the prosecutor in criminal case cannot be relieved of the onus of proving the fact which constitutes the offence by admission. However, under the short summary trial procedure in the magistrate court, the Criminal Procedure Act and Criminal Procedure Code respectively provide that if the accused admits the content of the First Information Report (FIR) or charge, the court may convict thereon without formal proof of the facts constituting the offences charged.

Informal admission

Conversely, informal admission has its terminus from section 20 of the Evidence Act 2011. Thus, it suffices to mean that it takes the form of a statement, oral or documentary, made by a person which suggests an inference as regards to a fact in issue or relevant fact. Informal admissions, on the other hand, do not necessarily or strictly speaking bind their maker and may therefore be explained or contradicted. The weight of an informal admission depends on the circumstances under which it was made and these circumstances may always be proved to impeach or enhance its credibility. Thus, an informal admission, unless it amounts to an estoppel, may be established by the party against whom it is tendered to be incorrect, untrue or to have been made under a mistake of law or fact or some compelling or vitiating circumstances. Accordingly, the value of an informal admission depends on the particular circumstances under which it was made and it is for the trial court to determine the issue and to give due weight to the alleged admission and the explanatory circumstances thereof.[16]

Generally speaking, admission is binding only if it is clear, unequivocal and not based on misapprehension of facts. The Supreme Court re-echoed

---

[15] (2009) 12 SCNJ 200 at 221 per Muntaka-Coomasie JSC.

[16] See *Tejuoso* v. *Asset Mgt. Corporation of Nigeria & Ors* (*supra*).

the principle in *Mba* v. *Mba*[17] that it is well settled that any admitted facts, or fact not disputed or not specifically denied, need no further proof and will be deemed established.

Admission can also be by conduct. Thus, it is well settled law that if a clear and direct accusation is made against a person, in his presence, in circumstances which should warrant instant denial, refutation or protestation against the grievous allegation, neither of which the person makes, evidence of such could be given against him as evidence of admission by conduct.[18] In loan transaction with bank, the law is settled and clear that where a bank makes demands for settlement of debt by letters and the amount of debt is contained in the letter and the debtor does not query the figure written in the letter as the overall debt due but rather writes letters in response explaining the reasons for non-payment of the debt, or refuses to respond at all, the debtor will be deemed to have impliedly admitted the quoted figure as the amount of debt due.[19] This muteness of the debtor as a 'sacrificial lamb' amounts to admission by conduct.

Another genre of admission is admission against interest. It is to the effect that where the evidence proffered at a party's instance, favours the opponent's case, it is seen as tantamount to a solemn admission of the opponent's case.[20] However, in *Orakwe* v. *Orakwue & Ors,*[21] it was held that for an admission against interest to be relied on and accepted by the court as proof of the matter or a fact in issue, it must be weighed along with the entire evidence on record in order to determine its correctness and proper probative value. An admission based on mistaken belief of the facts and true position of the law is not an admission against interest. It is against all sense of justice to rely on admission against interest when the truth of the admission is not borne out by other material pieces of evidence on record and/or does not reflect the position of the law.

To surmise it, despite the glaring provision of section 123 of the Evidence Act to the effect that an admitted fact needs no further proof, there is a provision embedded in the same section 123 of the Act vesting on the court enormous discretion to require facts admitted to be proved other than by the admission *simpliciter*. Thus, it is expedient and pertinent for the court to

---

[17](2018) LPELR-44295 (SC) P. 25, para. D.

[18] N.O Obiaraeri, *op. cit.,* at P. 57.

[19]*Registered Trustees Anacowa Motorcycle Owners & Riders Association & Ors* v. *Nut Endwell Micro Finance Bank Ltd* (2018) LPELR-46749 (CA) 22-23 F-B.

[20]*Doherty & Anor* v. *Sunmonu & Ors* (2018) LPELR-46725 (CA) P. 21, paras B-C.

[21](2018) LPELR-44763 (CA) P.29, paras. A-C.

take into cognizance, the circumstances under which the admission was made as to determine the weight to attach to it.

3. Persons who can make admission

The persons who can make admissions are enumerated but not limited to the persons provided for in sections 21-23 of the Evidence Act 2011. These include: the party to the proceedings himself or his duly authorized agent, a person suing or being sued in a representative capacity, a person whose position must be proved as against party to a suit as a witness cannot admit facts outside his knowledge. Let us discuss them seriatim.

A. Admission may be made by the party to the proceeding or his agent

Under section 21(1) of the Evidence Act, it is provided with high precision that statements made by a party to the proceeding or by an agent to any such party, whom the court regards in the circumstances of the case, as expressly or impliedly authorized by him to make them are regarded as admissions. Here, the law takes into cognizance of the antiquated rule of law, if not a long aged principle of law premised on a hidden but resourceful rule of agency relation that an agent can only bind the principal where the court having considered all the collateral circumstances of the case and, it is announced that the agent acted within the scope of his authority which can either be implied or express.[22] Thus, what this means is that an admission by an agent can be against the principal only if it is shown by cogent and credible evidence that the agency is still subsisting.[23]

To cap it, an oral admission by a counsel or other lawful agent of a party to a civil suit is admissible in evidence against the interest of such party. It has been held that a party is bound by the acts of his or her counsel, including any admissions made by that counsel.[24] Thus, it is trite that a counsel while functioning as such has the implied authority to make admission of facts thereby dispensing with proof of the particular fact and the admission may be binding if not retracted by the client before judgment.[25]

---

[22] *Adeosun* v. *Afolabi* (2018) LPELR-46115(CA) P. 32, para. B.
[23] *Chukwu & Anor* v. *Chukwu & Ors.* (2018) LPELR-45482 (CA).
[24] *Okusanya & Ors* v. *Adetona & Ors.* (2018) LPELR-44876 (CA) p.32, Para. C.
[25] Ibid.

B. Admission may be made by privies or suitors in a representative capacity

Section 21(2) of the Evidence Act 2011 provides *ipssima verba* that statements made by privies to suits, suing or sued in a representative character are not admissions unless they were made while the party making them held that character. What this means is that assuming but not conceding that the statement was made when he does not possess that character, the fact that he once occupied that position cannot suffice as admission. Example of the persons that can make admission under this section is where A sues or defends an action on behalf of his family in a representative capacity, statement made by A in that capacity is admission.

C. Admission may be made by party interested in the subject matter or by person from whom interest is derived

Section 21(3) of the Act reads thus:

> Statements made by persons:
>
> (a) who have any proprietary or pecuniary interest in the subject matter of the proceedings and who made the statements in their character of person so interested, or
>
> (b) From whom the parties to the suit have derived their interest in the subject matter of the suit, are admissions, if they are made during the continuance of the interest on the person making the statements.

Thus, where A has some proprietary and pecuniary interest in a property, statement made by A in respect of the property which is the subject matter of a suit is admission.

In *Ajeigbe* v. *Odedina,*[26] the plaintiffs brought an action against the defendants claiming possession of a parcel of land. He relied on a judgment in Suit No. 1/33A/64. He averred that the said Buraimoh Ojo Dalegan sold the land in dispute to each of the respondents during the pendency of the suit. The respondents contended that they were not aware of the dispute in Suit No 1/33A/64. The learned trial judge held that the respondents were not

---

[26] (1985) 1 NWLR (PT. 72) 548 SC

bound by the judgment since they bought and developed the land before the inception of the case.

The appellant appealed to the Court of Appeal which dismissed the Appeal. He further appealed to the Supreme Court which construed section 20(3)(a) and (b) of the Evidence Act (now Section 21(3)(a) and (b) of the Evidence Act 2011) which is relevant to the case. The court held that statement made by a witness in a previous proceedings who are witness in a latter one, can only be used to discredit or contradict such witnesses. Section 20(3)(a) and (b) of the Evidence Act[27] should not be construed as to bind a whole family with statements or documents tendered by an individual in a suit which he was sued as an individual and not as a representative of the family.

D. Admission may be made by persons expressly referred to by party to a suit

Statements made by persons to whom a party to the suit has expressly referred for information in reference to a matter in dispute are admissions.[28] Where X for instance brings an actions against Y in the High Court claiming ownership of a piece of land. X writes a letter to Z seeking for information concerning ownership of the land. The statement made by Z is an admission.[29] The case of *Elewuju* v. *Onisaodu*[30] is very germane in this regard. The facts of the case disclosed that a dispute arose between the families of the appellants and the respondents as to the ownership of a piece of land. Consequently, the appellants instituted an action at the High Court against the respondent claiming a declaration that they are entitled to certificate of customary right of occupancy in respect of the piece of land and also injunction restraining the respondents from further acts of trespass on the land. Both parties called witnesses to testify in support of their case. However, one of the witnesses (DW2) called by the respondent, testified during cross examination that the land in dispute belonged to the appellant's family. The trial court however did not accord or attach any weight to the testimony of the witness.

On appeal, the court of Appeal posited in its wisdom and held that by virtue of section 22 of the old Evidence Act (now section 23 of the Evidence Act 2011), statements made by persons to whom a party to the suit has

---

[27] Now Section 21(3) (a) and (b) of the Evidence Act, 2011.
[28] Section 23 of the Evidence Act 2011.
[29] Nwadialo, *Modern Nigerian Law of Evidence*, 2nd edn (Lagos: University of Lagos Press 1999) p 273.
[30] (2003)3 NWLR (Part 647) p. 95.

expressly referred for information in reference to a matter in dispute are admissions. The court, having the totality of the fact and the misplaced probative value which ordinarily would have been accorded to the testimony of DW2, categorically and without mincing words, held that the admission by DW2 that the land in dispute belongs to the appellants' ancestor is against the interest of the respondents who called him as a witness ostensibly to establish the fact that the land in dispute belongs to them (respondents).

It must be noted also that under section 24 of the Act, admission are relevant and may be proved as against the person who makes them or his representative in interest and not against a third party. However, exceptions apply in the following cases:

I. an admission may be proved by or on behalf of the person making it when it is of such a nature that if the person making it cannot be called as a witness, it would be relevant as between third parties under section 39 to 45 of the Act;

II. an admission may be proved by or on behalf of the person making it. When it consists of a statement of the existence of any state of mind or body, relevant or in issue, made at or about the time when such state of mind or body existed, and is accompanied by conduct rendering its falsehood improbable;

III. an admission may be proved by or on behalf of the person making it, if it is relevant otherwise than as an admission.

Pursuant to section 25 of the Act, oral admissions as to the contents of a document are not relevant, and thus inadmissible and until the party proposing to prove them shows that he is entitled to give secondary evidence of the contents of such document under part V or unless the genuineness of a document produced is in question. For clarity and precision, part V (sections 83 to 120) relate copiously to admissibility of documentary evidence.

E. Admission may be made by persons whose position must be proved as against party to the suit

Under section 22 of the Act, statements made by persons whose position or liability is necessary to prove as against any party to the suit, are admissions if such statements would be relevant as against such persons in relation to such position or liability in a suit brought by or against them and, if they are made whilst the person making them occupies such position or is subject to such liability. A practical example is where A guarantees a loan given by B to

C in an action to recover the loan brought by B against A, statements made by C are admissions against A.

From our foregoing discussion on persons who can make admissions, one word has permeated the whole subheadings on who may make admission. It is the word “statement”. Thus, it will be deprivation of academic flavour and precision, if it goes without prescient definition pursuant to section 258(1) of the Evidence Act. “Statement” therefore, includes any representation of fact whether made in words or otherwise.

Chapter 6

CONFESSION

1. Definition and Nature of Confession

The meaning of confession has attracted so many scholarly work as many authors have defined it in different ways. Before taking a voyage into the definition proffered by some -authors, it is of paramount importance to bring to light, section 28 of the Evidence Act 2011 which defined confession thus:

> A confession is an admission made at any time by a person charged with the commission of a crime stating or suggesting the inference that he committed the crime.

This definition gained judicial recognition in the recent case of *Michael Ori* v. *The State.*[1] It is correct to say that this definition gave credence to the effect that confession is a specie of admission as it is an admission of guilt. According to Professor Yemi Osinbajo,[2] he defined confession as an incriminating admission. He further opined that a confession need not be direct acknowledgement of guilt. Thus an admission from which guilt could be inferred will be sufficient. Imhanobe[3] on his own part defined confession as an admission of guilt by a person charged with an offence. According to this erudite writer, it is not a defence; it only strengthens the case of the prosecution and in proper case, reduces the challenges of establishing the guilt of the accused.

In the same vein, the statutory definition of confession under section 28 of Evidence Act has received judicial blessings and recognition in the recent case of *Akibu* v. *State.*[4] The court submitted in its wisdom that confession in criminal procedure, like admission in civil procedure, is the strongest

---

[1](2020) LPELR-49554(CA) 24 B-C.

[2] Yemi Osinbajo, *Cases and Materials in Nigeria Law of Evidence* (Nigeria: Macmillan Nig Ltd, 1992) p. 116

[3] Sylvester O. Imhanobe, *Law of Evidence* (Nigeria: Imhanobe Law Books, 19…)

[4] (2019) LPELR-47630 (SC). See also *Ikemson* v. *The State* (1989) 3 NWLR (pt. 110) @ 455; *FRN* v. *Iweka* (2013) 3 NWLR 9Pt 1341) 285 SC; *Obi* v. *State* (2013) 5 NWLR (Pt.1346) 68 CA.

evidence of guilt on the part of an accused person.[5] It went further in the same case to posit that it is stronger than evidence of an eyewitness because the evidence comes out from the "horse's mouth" who is the accused person. There is no better evidence and there is no need for further proof since what is admitted needs no further proof.[6] As a matter of fact, in the recent decision of the apex court in *The State* v. *Ali Ahmed*,[7] His Lordship Ariwoola JSC posited thus:

> It is trite law that confessional statement, so long as it is free and voluntary and it is direct, positive and properly proved, is in itself enough to sustain conviction.

In other words, it is a settled law that confession alone is sufficient to support conviction without corroboration, so long as the court is satisfied of the truth of the confession. However, the weight to be attached by courts to such confession is a question of fact deducible from the nature of the confession; that is, whether it is voluntarily made or not as both attract different approaches by court. The nature as to whether a statement is confessional is a question of fact.[8]

A confession is relevant when it proves the fact that constitutes one of or all the elements of the crime to be proved and or identifies the person who committed the offence. If the confession is relevant and is free and voluntary, it is admissible in evidence and when once admitted, the weight to be attached depends on its probative value and pure truth content.

Thus, once there exists a confessional statement which is direct, cogent and unequivocal to the fact that the accused committed the offence complained of, the prosecution need not prove further elements of the offence charged.[9] It is important to stress succinctly at this juncture that before a confessional statement is admissible in evidence, it must be voluntary.[10]

In other words, a free and voluntary confession of guilt that is direct and positive and if duly made and satisfactorily proved, is sufficient without any

---

[5] See also *Ogedengbe* v. *State* (2014) 12 NWLR pt. 207 and *Akpa* v. *State* (2008) 14 NWLR (pt. 1106) p. 74.

[6] *Barau & Ors* v. *Consolidated Tin Mines Ltd & Ors.* (2019) LPELR-46806 (CA); See also *Ignobis Hotel Ltd* v. *Bentec Elect Ltd* (2015) 1 NWLR (Pt. 411 – 630) CA.

[7] (2020) LPELR-49497(SC) P. 16, para. E.

[8] *Ogedengbe* v. *State supra*

[9] Per Niki Tobi JSC. (*supra*) *Mustapha Mohammed* v. *State.* Suit No. 184/2006 of 26th April 2007.

[10] Rhodes Vivour JSC in *Shurumor* v. *State* (2010) 44 NSCOR 177.

corroborative evidence so long as the court is satisfied as to the truth of the confession. It is only then, can it be said that the confession is voluntary. Where an accused person contends that he did not make the statement voluntarily, that is to say, that the statement emanated from some threat or fear of the unexpected proceeding from a person in authority, usually a police officer, justice demands that the court would direct a trial-within-trial. The purpose is to test the truth of what the accused person is saying. A confession found by the court to have been obtained by threat, inducement, etc., would be rejected. On the other hand, if after trial-within-trial, it is found that the confession was made voluntarily, it would be admitted in evidence and considered with other evidence led in the trial.[11] The courts also have added the elements of positivism and directness for a confession to ground conviction. In *Akpa* v. *State*,[12] the confession of the appellant to the killing of the deceased was positive and direct. The court in the recent case of *Afolabi* v. *State*[13] while citing Akpa's case with approval adopted the dictum of Niki-Tobi, JSC (As he then was) thus:

> In law, where an accused person confesses to a crime, in the absence of an eye witness of killing, he can be convicted on his confession alone once the confession is positive, direct and properly proved.[14]

This opportunity of the trial court to observe the demeanour of the witness during their testimonies cannot be interfered by the appeal court when it is shown that such finding is not perverse. The court in *Ogedengbe* v. *The State*[15] held that the voluntary confessional statement of an accused person provides the best evidence to herald his conviction. It should also be noted that the retraction of a confessional statement during a trial does not automatically vitiate its admission as a voluntary statement. Thus, where an accused person denies making a confessional statement, the trial court is expected to admit the statement in evidence as an exhibit and in its judgment, decide whether or not such retraction or denial avails the accused person. It stresses to mean that a confession does not become inadmissible merely because an accused person denies having made it. Rather the court

---

[11] *FRN* v. *Borisade* (2015) 5 NWLR (Pt. 1447).

[12] (2008) 14 NWLR (Pt. 1106) Page 72 at 92.

[13] (2019) LPELR-47731(CA) p. 35 paras. C-D.

[14] See also the most recent case of *Ori* v. *State* (2020) LPELR-49554(CA).

[15] *Ogedengbe* v. *State*, *supra*.

should look for independent evidence outside what is contained in the retracted statement to establish or prove the offence.[16]

According to a legal giant and a political doyen, Professor Yemi Osinbajo, in his book,[17] confessions are broadly of two types: judicial (formal) confessions and extra judicial confessions. The former refers to confessions made in court where the accused formally pleads guilty while the latter concerns admissions made by the accused outside a formal trial after an offence has been committed. It is this type of confession with which the rules on admissibility of evidence are mainly concerned.

2. Confession obtained by oppression

It is a notorious principle of law beyond equivocation that any confessional statement obtained by use of oppression is inadmissible. A court is legally bound to scrutinize an alleged confessional statement of a defendant or an accused person presented by the prosecution with the eye--s of an eagle in determining the truth.[18] A confessional statement of an accused person must not be allowed to sail through as if it were a magic wand that the prosecution will invoke and flash to secure an automatic or irreversible conviction of an accused person.

Section 29(5) of the Evidence Act 2011 defined "Oppression" to include:

> Torture, inhuman or degrading treatment, and the use of threat of violence, whether or not amounting to torture.

The broad definition of the word "oppression" under our Evidence Act to include torture, inhuman or degrading treatment is a laudable movement on the legal trend as it can conveniently overlap or dovetail into the already developed human rights jurisprudence on the provision of section 34(a) of the 1999 Constitution (as amended) recognizing the right to dignity of human person.

In the light of this topic, the definition of the word "torture" has gained judicial interpretation in the supreme court decision of *Uzoukwu & Ors* v. *Igwe Ezeonu II*[19] to include "mental harassment" as well as physical

---

[16] *Sunday Abiodun* v. *The State* (2012) 15 NWLR (Pt. 1111) p. 594.

[17] Yemi Osinbajo, *Cases and Materials in Nigeria Law of Evidence* (Nigeria: Macmillan Nig Ltd, 1992) p. 06

[18] N.O Obiaraeri, *op. cit.*, p. 69.

[19] (1994) 10 SCNJ at p 20, See also *Ogugu & Ors* v. *State* (1994) 9 (Pt. 366) 1 SC.

brutalization" while "inhuman treatment" characterizes "any act without feeling for the suffering of the other."

In the more recent decision in *Igweokolo* v. *Akpoyibo & Ors,*[20] the court of Appeal defined torture in the following words:

> The online electronic dictionary, Dictionary.com defines the noun torture, inter alia, as the act of inflicting excruciating pains, as punishment or revenge, as a means of getting a confession to information or for sheer cruelty. The English Dictionary Wiktionary org. defines the verb torture as to intentionally inflict severe pain or suffering. The Blacks Law Dictionary, 8th Edition, defines torture as the infliction of intense pain to the body or mind to punish, to extract a confession or information, or obtain sadistic pleasure.

A degrading treatment connotes "the element of lowering the societal status, value or position of a person in the eye of a right thinking members of the society. The immortal dictum of Baron Parke in the old English case of *R* v. *Baldry*[21] is germane to reproduce here.

The legal colossus posited thus:

> In order to render a confession admissible in evidence, it must be perfectly voluntary; and there is no doubt that any inducement in the nature of a promise or of a threat held out by a person in authority vitiates a confession. It has further being submitted that it is a fundamental principle of law that no answer to a question and no statement is admissible unless it is shown by the prosecution not to have been obtained in an oppressive manner and to have been voluntary in the sense that it has not been obtained by threats or inducement.

It is very pertinent to note that juristic ink has flown in an attempt to give an etymological meaning of what inducement connotes. The court has posited in a plethora or avalanche of cases[22] that influence of a chief or juju will not amount to an inducement so as to import the toga of involuntariness of confessional statement. The court further held that to find otherwise, would be getting previously near to the fallacious theory that a genuine belief in witchcraft might be a defence to a charge of murder, in so far as it might reduce the charge to manslaughter or even an acquittal by

[20] (2017) LPELR-41882(CA) Pp. 19-20 paras. G-C.

[21] (1852) 2 Den 430 at p 44.

[22] *Udoaka Eka* v. *Ebong* (1947) WACA 139.

reason of self defence. Another point worthy of note which is a sharp contrast and a paradigm shift from the repealed Act was abrogation of the sentence under section 28 of the old Evidence Act which provides that the threat must proceed from a person in authority.

It is submitted that it remains mandatory and obligatory that our courts should reject as admissible and irrelevant, any confession that is involuntary. The test of voluntariness being:

(a) whether there was oppression of the maker of the statement; or

(b) whether there was anything said or done at the time of making the statement that will likely --make it unreliable.

If the court is able to resolve the two question or issues in affirmative, then it is crystal clear that the statement is involuntary and thus inadmissible. However, where the court answers the question in the negative, then, the statement is voluntary thus, relevant and admissible. This view as submitted by authors and from the import of the totality of section 29 of the Act, is adopted with approval because the law provides, that the court "shall not" allow involuntary confession to be given in evidence under section 29(2) of the Evidence Act 2011. Thus, it is mandatory, obligatory, incumbent and not within the discretionary powers of the court to treat confessional statement obtained by oppression as inadmissible and irrelevant. Thus, the judicial interpretation given to the word "shall" in a long line of cases[23] as used in the wording of the section under discourse.

The meaning of oppression as a word has not only gained statutory blessing under our municipal law in section 34(a) of the 1999 Constitution which is a fountain head from which every other laws within the municipal confines of Nigeria derive their validity and life, it has transcended this municipal boundaries to gain a prime place of importance under international conventions, protocols and charter.

Some of these international charters are Article 5 of the Universal Declaration of Human Right 1948 and Article 5 of the African Charter on Human and People Right 1981 to say but a few.

3. Voluntariness and Burden of Proof of Confession

The burden of proving the voluntariness of a confessional statement lies on the prosecution and this must be proved beyond reasonable doubt and not on the shadow of doubt. Thus, the burden of proving that confession was

---

[23] *Yakubu* v. *Ibrahim & Ors* (2016) LPELR-41496 (CA). See also *Agbiti* v. *Nigerian Navy* (2011) 2 SCNJ at 25 and the *locus classicus* of *Ifezue* v. *Mbadugha* (1984) 15 SCNJ 427.

not obtained in contravention of section 29(2)(a)&(b) is on the prosecution.[24] It is a cardinal constitutional provision under section 36(5) of the 1999 Constitution (as amended) that a person accused of an offence is presumed innocent until the contrary is proved. To proceed otherwise is an infraction, and antithetical to the letters, spirit and the provision of the constitution.

Myriad of cases abound to substantiate this constitutional provision. Thus, in *Sunday Ani & Anor* v. *The State,*[25] the Supreme Court in its wisdom adopted the dictum in *Kinnami* v. *Bauchi Native Authority*[26] with approval to hold that it is not the duty of the accused to prove his innocence; it is the duty of the prosecution to establish his guilt.

In the more recent case of *Hamzat* v. *State,*[27] Barka JCA while citing Ogunbiyi JSC in the case of *C.O.P.* v. *Amuta,*[28] posited in his erudition thus:

> The constitutional provision on the presumption of innocence of an accused person is sacrosanct and settled. The burden is always on the prosecutions to prove the guilt of the accused and not his business to prove his innocence. He can decide to keep mute from the beginning of the trial right through to the end. This has been the position of the law ever since, and through the ages...

The burden or onus of proof of the commission of a crime is always on the prosecution. This burden of proof or *onus probandi* is static; it does not shift to the accused. However, it is only after full trial and the accused person is convicted of the offence charged that the presumption of innocence in favour of the accused fizzles out and atrophies. In *Emeka Eze* v. *The State,*[29] it was emphasized that it is a time hallowed principle of law that the guilt of an accused person can be proved by:

(a) his confessional statement;
(b) circumstantial evidence; or
(c) evidence of eye witnesses of the crime.[30]

---

[24] Section 29(3) of the Act; See also *Yinusa* v. *State* (2018) LPELR -43942 (CA); *Mohammed* v. *State* (2018) LPELR-43872; *Olabode* v. *State* (2009) 11 NWLR p. 261.
[25] (2009) 6 SCNJ 98 at 108.
[26] (1957) 1 NRNLR p 42 per Baraiman, SPJ (as he then was).
[27] (2019) LPELR-47406 (CA).
[28] (2017) All FWLR (Pt. 879) 760 at 783.
[29] (2001) 14 NWLR (pt. 734) 666 see also *Igabele* v. *State* (2006) 6 NWLR (Pt. 975) 100.
[30] See also *Hamzat* v. *State* (*supra*).

Therefore, the prosecution can secure the conviction of an accused person based on his confessional statement which the court has adjudged to be free and voluntary.

Section 29 of the Evidence Act, requires that in any proceeding where the prosecution proposes to give in evidence, a confessional statement made by a defendant, the court may on its own motion require the prosecution, as a condition for allowing it to do so, to prove that the confession was not obtained contrary to the provisions of section 29(2) (a)(b) of the Act. This is a movement in the right trend, novel and significantly progressive. Here, the court may *suo motu* without the prompting of the prosecution or defence and as a condition precedent, require that the prosecution should discharge the burden placed on it. Thus, where from the proof of evidence filed, the prosecution intends to rely on a confessional statement to secure the conviction of the accused, and the court is free to call upon it to discharge the burden beyond reasonable doubt. Where the court decides not to adopt this procedure, it may not however affect the outcome of the proceedings if it did not occasion any miscarriage of justice as the requirement is not obligatory or mandatory as the law provides that the court "may" and not that it "shall".[31]

In the recent case of *State* v. *Ahmed*,[32] it was graphically explained that proof beyond reasonable doubt is not proof beyond all iota of doubt or proof to the hilt.[33] What it portends is that once all the essential ingredients of the offence charged have been satisfactorily proved by the prosecution, the charge is proved beyond reasonable doubt. Earlier in the old English *locus classicus* of *Miller* v. *Minister of Pensions*,[34] the Law Lord, Lord Denning, J. (as he then was) in his usual and characteristic candour had adumbrated thus:

> Proof beyond reasonable doubt does not mean proof beyond the shadow of doubt. The law would fail to protect the community if it admitted fanciful possibilities to deflect the course of justice. If the evidence is so strong as to leave only a remote possibility in the favour of the prosecution which can be dismissed with the sentence of "of course it is possible but not in the least probable", the case is proved beyond reasonable doubt, but nothing short of that will suffice.

---

[31] See Section 29(3) of Evidence Act.

[32] (2020) LPELR-49497 (SC) P.18, paras, E-F.

[33] See also *Ukpongv*. *State* (2019) LPELR -46427(SC) P. 20 Para. B; *Ayinde* v. *State* (2019) LPELR -47835 (SC) P.16 para. 16.

[34] (1947) 2 ALLER 372 cited in *Jua* v. *The State* (2010) 2 SCNJ 224.

This established principle was relied on in *Sunday Ani & Anor* v. *The State*[35] by Tobi JSC (as he then was) when he expounded on the expression "beyond reasonable doubt" in evidence to mean:

> Fully satisfied, entirely convinced...Reasonable doubt which will justify acquittal is doubt based on reason and arising from evidence or lack of evidence, and it is doubt. Reasonable doubt is such a doubt as would cause a prudent man to hesitate before acting in matters of importance to him.

Thus, in the final analysis, it is trite law and an antiquated settled principle of law like the rock of Gibraltar that the *onus probandi* or burden of proving the voluntariness of a confessional statement rests squarely on the prosecution.

4. Confession and Co-accused

It is a cardinal evidential provision under Section 29(4) of the Act that, where more persons than one are charged jointly with an offence and a confession made by one of such persons in the presence of one or more of the other persons so charged, is given in evidence, the court shall not take such statement into consideration as against any of such other person in whose presence it was made unless he adopted the said statement by words or conduct.[36] The import of this principle of law was poignantly elucidated in the Supreme Court decision of *Salawu* v. *State,*[37] where the court in its wisdom posited that the Act provides that each accused persons can be damnified on the basis of his own confessional statement and not the basis of what other accused persons had confessed to. However, where a charge is woven round conspiracy, the evidence given by one of the accused persons should be examined to see if there is a linkage between the evidence and the admission of his co-accused person. In the instant case (Salawu's case) the charge against the appellant was woven round conspiracy and the statements made by the 1st accused person gave an insight as to the role played by every accused person including the appellant. The statements of the 1st accused person revealed the common intention by the accused persons to avenge the

[35] *Supra*, p. 180.
[36] See the following: *Udoh & Anor* v. *State* (2019) LPELR-47934 (CA); *Akokhia* v. *State* (2018) LPELR-44163 (CA) and *Suraju* v. *State* (2018) LPELR-43658 (CA).
[37] (2015) 2 NWLR (Part 1444) P. 595.

death of one Kasali Shittu which they successfully executed by killing the deceased.

The same principle of law has also gained judicial blessing and attention in *Akokhia* v. *State*.[38] The old case of *Evbuomwan* v. *Commissioner of Police*[39] had this to say on this point:

> It is settled law by statute and judicial decisions that the confessional statement of a co-accused is no evidence against an accused person who has not adopted the statement.

In *Ajaegbo* v. *State*,[40] one Innocent Ekeanyanwu made a statement while in detention. However, before the commencement of the trial, he died in detention. He confessed to killing the deceased person and further mentioned the appellant as one of the persons who aided him in the actual act of the killing. The entries in the said statement were neither made in the appellant's presence nor did he adopt them. Regrettably, the trial court accepted them as the whole truth as regards what happened on the day in question. Unfortunately, the lower court perpetuated the same error. The apex court while allowing the appeal held thus:

> This cannot be so. A free and voluntary confession of guilt by an accused person, whether under examination before a Magistrate or otherwise, if it is direct and positive and is duly made and satisfactorily proved, is sufficient to warrant convictions without any corroborative evidence so long as the court is satisfied of the truth of the confession...However, a man's confession is only evidence against him and not against his accomplices...In effect, the confessional statement of an accused person is not binding on a co-accused person, except the statement was adopted by the co-accused person. This must be so for where an accused person makes a confessional statement to the Police as to his participation or culpability in the crime charged, he is not confessing for his co-accused person. Thus, his confession is only evidence against him and not against the co-accused person.

Consequently, the Supreme Court earlier in *Ozaki* v. *State*[41] per Obaseki JSC held, *inter alia*, that:

---

[38](2018) LPELR-44163 (CA) P.24, para. A.

[39] (1961) WNLR 257.

[40](2018) LPELR-44531 (SC) P.40, Paras. A-F.

[41] (1990) 1 NWLR (Pt.124) P.92; See also *Bassey* v. *State* (1993) 7 NWLR (pt. 306) 409 CA. See also *Titilayo* v. *State* (1998) 2. NWLR (pt. 537) 235 CA and *Dele* v. *State* (2011) 1 NWLR (Pt. 1229) 508.

(a) a confessional statement of an accused person once expunged from the record of the court, no longer constitutes evidence for the purpose of the judgment of the court;
(b) a confessional statement of a co-accused is no evidence against an accused person unless the latter has adopted the statement either by words or conduct.

In the instant case, as the 1st appellant did not adopt or confirm the statement of the 2nd appellant in court but instead denied it; it is no evidence against the 1st appellant upon which he can be convicted.

The learned and erudite justice in an appetizing prose thus posited:

> It is an error in law to convict an accused on the statement of another accused to the police. It is a travesty of justice and a gross violation of all known rules of evidence. Section 27 of the Evidence Act (now section 29 of the Act), forbids the use of such statement even when it is confessional. It is my opinion that an incriminating statement made even in the hearing of an accused defence, even in the occasion which could reasonably be expected to call for some explanation from him is not evidence against him on his trial of the facts therein stated save in so far as he has accepted the statement and where the statement is used to found or secure a conviction, the conviction must on appeal, be quashed.

5. Confession under Secrecy, Deception or otherwise

It is the law that confession otherwise relevant does not become irrelevant merely because, it was made under a promise of secrecy, or in consequence of a deception practiced on the defendant for the purpose of obtaining it, or when he was drunk or because it was made in answer to questions which he need not have answered, whatever may have been the form of these questions, or because he was not warned that he was not bound to make such statement and that evidence of it might be given.[42]

The notorious case of *James Igbinovia* v. *The State*[43] is best illustrative of this principle. The Supreme Court held in that case that the confession made by the appellant in consequence of a deception on him by the police was admissible as a confession. In this case, the police investigating a case of murder disguised some policemen to be locked up in a cell where the suspects were also locked up. One of the policemen boasted to the suspect that he was a notorious criminal and murderer. As a result of this, one of

[42] See section 31 of the Evidence Act 2011.
[43] (1981) 2 SC 5.

the suspects confessed that he took part in the killing of the deceased and mentioned the date and time. The confession was held admissible. The court in that case further amplified the position of the law vis-à-vis the meaning of influence from person in authority as it affects the admissibility of a confessional statement thus:

> If the confession proceeds from remorse and a desire to make reparation for the crime, it is admissible. If it flows from hope or fear excited by a person in authority, it is inadmissible. If it flows from a sense of sadistic pride not induced by a promise or threat, it is admissible.

It is humbly submitted that this position of law in the aforementioned case, with all intents and purposes is right and justifiable as the law enforcement agencies should be able to beat the criminals in their own game by adopting means towards deciphering and unveiling the veritable ingredients of the offence charged in so far as it is within the bounds of the law.

6. Trial-within-trial and denial of authorship of Confessional Statement

The Supreme Court has re-echoed the position of the law in *Mathew* v. *State*[44] to the effect that the test of admissibility of a confessional statement is its voluntariness. In a more recent decision of the Supreme Court in *Ofordike* v. *State,*[45] the court, on the test of admissibility of confessional statement held thus:

> It is a positive rule of our accusatorial jurisprudence that no statement of an accused person is admissible against him unless it is shown by the prosecution to have been made voluntarily. This principle is as old as the Laws received from England. In England, the principle is as old as Hale.

However, once the issue of involuntariness is raised, it must be resolved or settled one way or the other before its admission or otherwise. According to Obiaraeri, in his book,[46] when admissibility of a statement is challenged on the ground that it was not made voluntarily, the following procedural safeguards which have crystallized over the years should be noted:

---

[44](2018) LPELR-45519 (CA).

[45](2019) LPELR-46411 (SC) P. 39, Paras. E- F.

[46] N.O Obiaraeri, *op. cit.,* p. 75 also prescribed under sec 29(3) of Evidence Act 2011.

i. the issue as to proper time to raise an objection as to the voluntariness of a confessional statement is at the point when it is to be tendered in evidence so that the voluntariness or otherwise would be determined before it is admitted in evidence. Hence, the objection must be raised timeously at the trial and not as an afterthought or face saving gambit, ploy or stratagem;
ii. it is also incumbent on the judge to call upon the prosecution to establish that it was voluntarily made by conducting a trial-within-trial and that the procedural step of trial-within-trial must be taken at the point when the objection is raised.

Trial-within-Trial defined

Trial-within-trial or *voire dire* or mini trial as the name implies is a mini trial conducted by the court before ruling on the substantive case so as to arm itself with the procedural mechanism for sifting the chaff of involuntariness from the wheat of confessional statement of an accused person where the accused objects to his confessional statement as voluntarily obtained.

According to the court in *Abubakar* v. *State*,[47] the court while taking refuge in the reasoning of Nweze JSC in *FRN* v. *Borisade*,[48] held thus

> The *raison d'etre* of the evolution of the mini trial or *voire dire* procedure is to arm the trial Court with a procedural mechanism for sifting the chaff of involuntary and hence inadmissible evidence from the wheat of admissible evidence whose cogency and probative value are indubitable.

In the most recent case of *The State* v. *Soyinka*,[49] the Court of Appeal reiterated the essence of trial-within-trial in the following words:

> The main purpose of a trial within the main trial is to test whether the Confessional Statement to be tendered by the Prosecution was made voluntarily by the accused person or whether he was forced or induced to make it. Once a trial within trial is ordered by the trial Judge, the main trial is suspended until the conclusion of the trial within trial.

---

[47](2019) LPELR-47393 (CA) P. 20, paras. A-B.
[48] (2015) 5 NWLR (pt. 1447).
[49](2020) LPELR-49493 (CA) P. 7 paras. A-B

Thus, the gravamen or crux of trial-within-trial as enunciated in the case above is to determine whether the accused person made the disputed statement voluntarily.[50]

It should be noted that failure of the trial court to conduct this mini trial where the voluntariness of a confessional statement is in issue, becomes fatal to the whole gamut of the case, the quantum of dexterity invested in such case notwithstanding. Thus, it stands the perilous chance of disposing into the trash can, the judgment of the trial court decided upon such procedural mishap through the appellate court. Thus, the court has in its erudition restated in *Koku* v. *State*[51] that a counsel representing an accused person owes a duty to raise an objection to the admissibility of an extra judicial statement at the point of tendering same and not at the address stage. Failure to do so at that point is conclusive evidence that it was made voluntarily. A counsel who failed to object to the admissibility of a confessional statement at the point of tendering cannot be heard to later challenge its voluntariness. This is to buttress the position of the law in a litany of cases to the effect that where an accused person wishes to attack the voluntariness of a confessional statement, he must raise an objection to the admission of that statement at the point where it is sought to be tendered.[52] The Court of Appeal in *Adio* v. *State*[53] aptly captured it when it held thus:

> The settled position of the law is that the appropriate time to challenge the admissibility of a statement projected as confessional statement of an accused on ground of involuntariness, inadmissibility or any other vices or inadequacy that may be afflicting such statement is at the time and point when the prosecutor seeks to tender the statement or document in evidence and not at Appellate Court.

The court while relying on *Joseph Ubi* v. *The State*[54] went further to posit that the objection to a confession is required to be raised at the tendering of the confessional statement. This is ordinarily so during presenting of the prosecution's case at the main trial. Thus, it was on record that the learned respondent's counsel did not raise any objection at the point of tendering the statement. It was after the confessional statement had been

---

[50] See also *Ogudo* v. *State* (2011) 18 NWLR (pt. 1178) 1; *Ibeme* v. *State* (2013) 10 NWLR (pt. 1362) 333.

[51] (2019) LPELR-48121 (CA) Pp. 29-30, Paras. F-B.

[52] See *Tope* v. *State* (2019) LPELR-47837 (SC) P. 19, paras. C-D and *Adunbi* v. *State* (2018) LPELR-45005 (CA) P.16, paras. B.

[53] (2018) LPELR-45720 (CA) P.21.

[54] (2012) 16 NWLR (PART 1327) 522 at 545, para. E.

admitted that the respondent retracted the statement in the course of giving evidence in his defence. This, the court ruled and rightly too, as an afterthought, for if she was uncomfortable with the statement, the point of tendering and admissibility should have been when to object. It was late in time to have retracted at the stage she did. The confessional statement not having been objected to, was admissible as evidence, and the learned trial court was not in error in ascribing probative value to it. Thus, it is inappropriate to raise it at the stage after the confessional statement has gone in.[55] Furthermore, the Supreme Court per Rhodes-Vivour, JSC in *Eke* v. *State*[56] held that failure of the trial court to conduct trial-within-trial where necessary was fatal to the case. In this case, at the point of tendering the confessional statement, the accused claimed that he was beaten up and forced to write the statement. The trial court ought to have ordered a trial-within-trial to find out if the accused person's contention that he did not write the statement voluntarily was true. The Court posited thus:

> Failure to conduct a trial-within-trial was wrong. The Court of Appeal fell painfully into the same error when it said on page 91 of the record that the learned trial judge was right to admit the document as exhibit 5 without having to conduct a trial-within-trial.

The trial-within-trial procedure as aforesaid is designed to determine if the confession was voluntary as failure, refusal or neglect to carry out the mandatory trial-within-trial is fatal to the trial. It is immaterial how trivial and seemingly inconsequential, the issue of involuntariness may appear, the court is bound to determine and subject such confessional statement to the crucible of trial-within-trial. In *Julius Berger & Anor* v. *Toki Rainbow Community Bank Ltd,*[57] the Supreme Court per Eko JSC held that the law has for long been settled in criminal cases that it is the duty of the trial court to consider a defence no matter how weak or feeble it may appear.

This is to say that it is settled beyond any argument that a court, including the appellate Court, has a sacred duty to consider all the defences raised by an accused person, which is in evidence before it, no matter how weak or unreasonable it may be. The adjudication process in this our adversarial system of administration of justice demands that every defence

---

[55] *Elewanna* v. *State* (2019) LPELR-47605 (CA) P.47, para. F.
[56] (2011) 3 NWLR (Pt.1235) P. 589 at 609.
[57] (2019) LPELR-46408 (SC) P.47, paras. B-C.

available to the accused on the evidence and facts before the court must be considered by the court. To refrain from a consideration of the defence because it is considered weak, far-fetched, foolish, conflicting, unfounded and false is to err seriously in the discharge of one's duty as a judge. Where there is no evidence to warrant consideration of the defence, the trial judge has no duty to consider the defence. It is not the duty of the judge to scout round for defences where there are none and where the evidence does not suggest one.[58]

This suffices to mean that failure to consider and examine a defence by the trial judge does not only raise reasonable doubt in the case of the prosecution but also amount to failure to perform a vital duty imposed on that judge and as such will amount to a miscarriage of justice which must result in the decision appealed against to be set aside and the conviction quashed.[59] In a long line and avalanche of cases, it has been showed and ascertained that failure to conduct trial-within-trial where the voluntariness of a confessional statement is questionable is fatal to the case.[60]

It should be noted however, that if the omission, refusal, neglect and failure to conduct a trial within trial does not lead to miscarriage of justice or the other evidence led and accepted are so over whelming and conviction can easily be sustained without the confessional statement, the appellate court can overlook it. Thus, the Supreme Court had earlier in *Eke* v. *State*[61] per Fabiyi JSC, posited, *inter alia,*

> It is clear to me that the trial judge at the tribunal goofed in failing to carry out the mandatory trial-within-trial to determine the voluntariness of the statement credited to the appellant. To my mind, Exhibit 5 was admitted to no avail. However, the conviction of the appellant was not based solely on exhibit 5, the saving grace was that without Exhibit 5, the evidence adduced by PWI and PW2, the victims of the offence of armed robbery assisted by PW3 and PW4, who got the appellant arrested sufficiently put the appellant in a tight corner where he failed to extricate himself.

It suffices to say that the wrongful admission of evidence shall not of itself be a ground for the reversal of any decision in any case where it appears to

---

[58] *Afolabi* v. *FRN* (2019) LPELR-47731 (CA) 24-25, paras. D-C. Per Aliyu JCA. See also *Abubakar* v. *State* (2019) LPELR-47046 (CA).

[59] See *Williams* v. *State* (1992) 8 NWLR (pt. 261) 515.

[60] See *Giki* v. *State* (2018) LPELR-43604 (SC); *Ogu* v. *COP* (2017) LPELR-43832 (SC) P.39, paras. B-C. and *Abacha* v. *State* (2018) LPELR-46358 (CA).

[61] (2011) LPELR-1133 (SC), pp. 11-12, Paras, F-A.

the court that the evidence so admitted cannot reasonably be held to have affected the decision and that such decision would have been the same if such evidence had not been admitted.[62]

Another procedural safeguard is that at the trial within trial, the accused person must give evidence before witnesses called by him to give evidence.[63] In the same wavelength, at the end of the trial-within-trial, if the court is satisfied that the confessional statement was not voluntary, the said statement would not be admissible in evidence as an exhibit and the trial judge should rule accordingly; this is the requirement arising from the provision of section 29(2) of the Evidence Act.

A confessional statement found not to have been voluntary is worthless and inadmissible. However, when there was no objection challenging the admissibility of a statement made by an accused person to the police on the ground that it was not made voluntarily, there is no basis to embark on a trial within trial as was held in *Adio* v. *State.*[64]

To surmise it, the court in *Mathew* v. *State*[65] laid a procedural approach to be followed in assessing the quality of a confessional statement and to determine the question whether or not it is retracted. These are:

1. is there anything outside the confession which shows that it may be true?;
2. is it corroborated no matter how slight?;
3. are the facts made in it true as far as they can be tested?;
4. was the prisoner or accused one who had the opportunity of committing the offence?;
5. is the confession possible?; and
6. is it consistent with other facts which have been ascertained and proved in the matter?

Denial of Authorship of a Confessional Statement

Denial of authorship of confessional statement is an outright and complete denial by an accused person that he did not make the confessional statement. Thus, denial of authorship should be distinguished from "denial of voluntariness" as both are diametrically at variance or opposed to each other and radically different.[66] To say the least, these are like two parallel lines that

---

[62]Section 251(1) of the Evidence Act; See also *Fulani M* v. *State* (2018) LPELR-45195(SC) pp. 22-23, paras. E-A.

[63]*Eke* v. *State* (*supra*) per Rhodes-Vivour JSC.

[64] *Supra.*

[65](2018) LPELR-45519(CA) P.18, paras. B-C.

[66] See the recent decision of the Supreme Court in *Afordike* v. *State* (*supra*).

cannot meet or two rivers that have no confluence as both have received different judicial approaches. Thus, if an accused person alleges that he made a confession under an oppressive circumstance, he acknowledges that he authored the statement contained in the document but asserts that he is unwilling to be bound by its contents by virtue of the oppressive circumstance under which he made it. This lends itself to the conduct of trial-within-trial already discussed in the preceding paragraph of this topic. It is a different kettle of fish where a confessional statement is challenged on the sole ground that the accused person did not make the statement at all. In this latter case, the statement should be admitted since its admissibility is not affected; thus, trial-within-trial here is unnecessary, unwarranted and inappropriate.

Where there is outright denial of authorship, that is to say it is canvassed by the defence that the "accused person did not make the statement," it is settled law that the question whether the statement was made voluntarily or otherwise does not arise for consideration. The trial court is expected to admit the statement in evidence as an exhibit and in its judgment, decide whether or not such denial avails the accused person. It is an established principle of law that a confession does not become inadmissible merely because an accused person denies having made it.

In the recent case of *Aliyu* v. *State*,[67] the Supreme Court per Sidi Dauda Bage JSC, reiterated the position of law as regards denial of authorship of confessional statement. In the words of his Lordship,

> A confessional statement does not become inadmissible even if the accused person denied having made it. This has been the settled position in our jurisprudence of criminal justice.

This is because, such a denial is an issue of fact to be decided in the judgment as the issue does not affect admissibility of the statement as the statement must be considered alongside the entire evidence and the circumstances of the case for evidential value to be attached to it as decided in myriad of cases like *Amos* v. *State*,[68] *Egwuche* v. *State*,[69] *Ibrahim* v. *State*[70] and *James* v. *State*[71] to mention but a few.

---

[67](2019) LPELR-47421(SC) P. 11 Paras. B-C
[68] (2018) LPELR -44694 (SC).
[69](2018) LPELR-43975 (CA).
[70] (2018) LPELR-44256 (CA).
[71] (2017) LPELR-42721 (CA).

7. Evidence of Confessions in other proceedings admissible

Evidence in other proceedings amounting to confession may or may not be admissible and relevant depending on the circumstance under which the defendant is confronted with the previous confession. Under section 32 of the Act, evidence in other proceedings amounting to confession is admissible and relevant to secure the conviction of an accused person even if the said confession may have been given on oath. It does not affect the admissibility even if the present proceeding may be related to the previous proceeding where the confession was made, or that the witness refused to answer the question put to him.

However, the previous confession is irrelevant and rendered inadmissible if the maker was improperly compelled to admit the making of the previous confession.[72]

There is no gainsaying the fact that the prosecution will be required to prove beyond reasonable doubt, that the confession adopting the previous confession was voluntarily made by the accused person and not otherwise.

8. The Inconsistency Rule and the Judges' Rule

The Inconsistency rule is concerned with the weight and probative value of admitted evidence. This is predicated on the fact that it does not begin to operate until the inconsistency arises on the evidence at the trial. For the purposes of the "inconsistency rule", the provision of section 232 of the Evidence Act is important and germane. Under the aforementioned section, a witness may be cross examined as to previous statements made by him in writing or reduced into writing and relative to matters in question in the suit or proceeding in which he is cross-examined without such writing being shown to him or being proved but if it is intended to contradict such witness by the writing, his attention must, before such writing can be proved, or such contradictory proof given, be called to those parts of the writing which are to be used for the purpose of contradicting him, provided always that it shall be competent for the court at any time during the trial to require the production of the writing for its inspection and the court may thereupon make use of it for the purposes of the trial, as it deems fit.

Where extrajudicial statement is inconsistent with oral testimony in court, it attracts very careful legal considerations and may attract severe consequences, thus the inconsistency.

---

[72] See Section 32 of Evidence Act.

In *Orisa* v. *State*,[73] the Supreme Court categorically stated without mincing words and with a high degree of statistical certainty that the law is settled that where a witness made an extrajudicial statement which is inconsistent with his sworn testimony on oath in court and he gives no reasonable explanation for the inconsistencies, the only option available to the Court is to regard his evidence unreliable. The inconsistency rule is that such a testimony at the trial is treated as unreliable while the earlier statement is not regarded as evidence on which the court can act. In this case, the Supreme Court treated the testimony of the appellant as unreliable.

In *Uzoma* v. *State*,[74] the Court of Appeal held that the law is long settled that the Inconsistency Rule does not apply to an accused person. Cases where an accused person's confessional or extra judicial statements run contrary to his testimony in court are not covered by the inconsistency rule. The Court is at liberty to convict on the retracted confessional statement of an accused person provided the testimony and confession of the accused person and all other evidence are properly evaluated. Once an accused person's confessional statement is voluntary and true but inconsistent with his evidence in Court, a Court may convict.

According to Amina Audi Wambai J.C.A in *Ahmed* v. *State*,[75]

> The law has been well laid down on the treatment of oral testimony of an accused person which is different or inconsistent with his extra judicial statement to the police. The inconsistency rule which applies to a witness who has previously given an extra judicial statement inconsistent with his evidence in Court does not apply to an accused person whose extra judicial statement is inconsistent with his oral evidence in Court. The inconsistency rule is that where a witness makes an extra-judicial statement which is inconsistent with his testimony at the trial, such testimony is to be treated as unreliable while the statement is not regarded as evidence on which the Court can act...
>
> Where the inconsistency is between a voluntary confessional statement of the accused and his oral evidence in court, the law is that the oral evidence should be treated as unreliable and liable to be rejected while the contents of the confessional statement be upheld unless a satisfactory explanation of the inconsistency is proffered. The appellant herein offered

---

[73](2018) LPELR-43896 (SC) P. 24, paras. A-B. See also *Egboghonome* v. *The State* (1998) SCNJ (pt. 1) 1, *Bature* v. *State* (1994) 1 NWLR (Pt. 320) 267, *NEMI & Ors.* v. *State* (1997) 10 SCNJ 1.

[74](2018) LPELR-44765 (CA) P. 25, paras. D-F.

[75](2018) LPELR-46606 (CA).

> no explanation for the obvious inconsistency, why he was resiling from his voluntary statement which is obviously inconsistent with his oral evidence in Court.

It is submitted that the inconsistency rule has not been an inflexible rule of law or practice. In order to ensure that its operation did not eventuate to injustice, the courts had developed a safeguard. Thus, in addition to considering the totality of the evidence, the witness is given an opportunity to explain the inconsistency in his previous unsworn statement and his evidence in court, or the inconsistency rule, indeed be minor or unsubstantial, in which case, the inconsistency may fail to discredit the entire testimony. Thus, it is only where the witness is unable to explain the inconsistency satisfactorily that the rule is applied.[76] It follows therefore that an accused person should be wary in setting up inconsistent testimony with his earlier statement to the police or any other investigating authority and should stand prepared at all material times to explain the disparity or nuances if any, to the satisfaction of the court and without any prompting.

The Judges' Rules

The Judges' Rules were first formulated in 1912 by judges in England. It was later revised in 1964. These rules are administrative directives and do not have the force of law.[77] These rules were devised to govern questioning by the police. These rules have received judicial application in *Abubakar* v. *State*[78] as a veritable tool for effective and efficient administration of justice. The Court of Appeal held that Judges Rules are rules made by English Judges to guide English Police Officers and though not rules of law but rules of administrative practice made for the more efficient and effective administration of justice. However, it should not by any stretch of imagination be used to defeat justice. The Courts must take care not to deprive themselves by new artificial rules of practice of the best chances of learning the truth. It went further to state that the sole purpose of the Judges Rules is to ensure that confessions are voluntary.[79]

---

[76] See *Ahmed* v. *State* (*supra*). It has been established that Inconsistency Rule does not apply to previous confession of an accused person and his evidence in court. See the following *Roland* v. *FRN* (2018) LPELR-43686 (CA) and *Smart* v. *State* (2016) LPELR-40827 (SC).

[77] *R* v. *Voism* (1918) 1 KB 531.

[78] (2017) LPELR-43197 (CA) 21 -22 F-B.

[79] See the following *Smart* v. *State* (2016) 9 NWLR (Pt. 1518) 447 and *Hassan* v. *State* (2017) 5 NWLR (Pt. 1557)

It appears apparently that Rules 2 and 3 of the judges' rule are most widely used by police officers in Nigeria. Rule 2 requires that as soon as a police officer has evidence which would afford reasonable grounds for suspecting that a person has committed an offence, he shall caution that person or cause him to be cautioned before putting to him any questions, or further questions relating to that offence. The caution will be pertinent to be reproduced here *ipssima verba*:

> You are not obliged to say anything unless you wish to do so, but what you say may be put into writing and given in evidence.

Rule 3 stipulates that where a person is charged with or informed that he may be prosecuted for an offence, he shall be cautioned in the following terms.

> Do you wish to say anything? You are not obliged to say anything unless you wish to do so, but whatever you say will be taken down in writing and may be given in evidence.

In Nigeria, the rules have been held to be applicable even though failure to apply or strictly follow the rules as prescribed will not necessarily render the statements inadmissible in evidence.[80]

In a more recent decision of the court in *Sagbanimu* v. *FRN*,[81] the court while addressing whether the failure to comply with Judges' Rules will vitiate a confessional statement or document, engaged in an elaborate explanation, origin and the jurisprudence of this principle thus:

> One of the primary functions of the police is to investigate all crimes which are brought to their notice and wherever possible to bring the perpetrators before the Courts, together with all the relevant evidence. Controversies associated with methods used by law enforcement agents in the interrogation of suspected persons and the value of evidence obtained thereby has always been a source of judicial and societal concern. In an attempt to achieve a balance between the need to ensure that law enforcement agents are enabled to investigate crimes thoroughly and the need to ensure the protection of the innocent as well as the rights of the suspect, Judges in England developed what was known as Judges Rules, meant to guide the police on how far they should go when

---

[80] Aguda, *op. cit.*, p 55 to 64.

[81] (2018) LPELR-43924 (CA) Pp. 7-10, Paras. G-B. See also *Nnajiofor* v. *FRN* (2018) LPELR-43925 (CA).

> interrogating or taking statements from suspects or prisoners. These Rules were not rules of law but more in the nature of rules of caution. They, in effect provided a code of behaviour for the guidance of the police in investigation. *The purpose of the Rules was to ensure, as far as possible, that all statements admitted in evidence, more so if confessional in nature, were obtained freely and voluntarily. Nevertheless, failure to observe the Rule would not, ipso facto, render the statement inadmissible, as long as the statement in issue was made freely and voluntarily.* The fact that the police have adhered to these Rules in their investigation of a crime would guide the Judge in determining the weight to be attached to any confessional statement made by the accused. On the application of the Judges' Rules in Nigeria, the Supreme Court, per Oputa, JSC in *Ojegele* v. *The State* (1988) NWLR (Pt. 71) 414, (1988) LPELR-2370 (SC), at pages 15 - 16 of the E-Report elucidated: "The Judges, Rules are rules made by English Judges for the guidance of English police officers. -Nobody, however, disputes the wisdom behind those Rules. But having said that, it is necessary to add that the rules are not rules of law but merely rules of administrative practice. They are rules made for the more efficient and effective administration of justice and therefore should never be used to defeat justice. Even in England, the Court of Appeal felt bound to observe that "the Court must take care not to deprive themselves by new artificial rules of practice of the best chances of learning the truth" *R.* v. *Richardson* (1971) 2 QR 484 at p. 490: (1971) 2 All ER 777. Here in Nigeria there is a consensus of judicial opinion that the practice set out in the Judges Rules "accords with prudence and that where it is practicable, especially in serious cases of felony, where the only material evidence against an accused person is his confession contained in his Statement made to a junior police officer that practice should be followed...

Thus, legal reform should be an ongoing activity. The importance of these commendable practices to our justice delivery cannot be over-emphasized. Thus, the Nigerian case of *R* v. *Ugwuogo & Anor*[82] is very illustrative of the application of judges' rule in Nigeria. The court said:

> The so-called 'judges rule' which lay down *inter alia* that persons in custody should not be questioned without the usual caution being first administered, are rules form of caution laid down by the judges in England as the procedure to be followed in that highly civilized country.

[82] (1943) 9 WACA 74 at p. 74.

> They should be followed *mutatis mutandis*, so far as it is possible and practicable in this country.

In the same vein, in *Edeme Ugarma* v. *R*,[83] the police took a photograph of the accused after the commission of a murder. The photograph showed the accused, one of his co-accused and an accomplice all standing in a group and pointing towards a spot which they identified as the place the murder was committed. The court held that, before a person under arrest is invited to pose for a photograph which may strengthen the case against him, it should be in accordance with the spirit of the rules for him to be cautioned again and told that he is not obliged to pose for any photograph.

However, there is need for these commendable practice to be given force of law in a discernible local statute or regulation and thus making them binding and obligatory on law enforcement agencies. There is no doubt that the judges' rule has played a significant role in protecting the rights of accused persons in England and Nigeria. It is in attempt to fully provide for such laws that the omnibus clauses provided in section 255 of the Evidence Act 2011 is germane. Coincidentally, it is provided in section 255 of the Act that "the minister of justice may from time to time make regulations generally prescribing further conditions with respect to admissibility of any class of evidence that may be relevant under this Act." This is a novel provision; ostensibly this will, if fully cultivated, fast track the administration of justice process as well as enhance the functionality of our evidentiary rules. The Attorney-General and Minister of Justice is therefore enjoined to latch on the powers conferred on him by the provision of this section and make binding uniform regulations on procedure for recording the statement of suspects by law enforcement agencies.

Thus uniform set of rules streamlining the minimum requirements or mandatory safeguards for obtaining evidence of a suspect during interrogation will definitely not be out of place now. Evidence being a matter within the exclusive legislative list,[84] the Federal Minister of Justice is required to use his wide powers under section 255 of the Evidence Act, 2011 to make uniform regulation for receiving statements from suspects by law enforcement agencies and other bodies vested with criminal jurisdiction in Nigeria.

---

[83] (1959) 4 FSC 218.

[84] See Item 23, part 1 in the 2nd schedule of the 1999 Constitution (as amended).

Chapter 7

HEARSAY EVIDENCE

1. Definition of Hearsay

The doctrine of hearsay is of immense popularity in the law courts. This popularity is born from its repeated usage by the courts to render a piece of evidence inadmissible. Hence, it has become of the utmost importance in the Nigerian law of evidence. The Evidence Act 2011 defines hearsay in section 37 as follows:

> Hearsay means a statement-
>
> (a) oral or written made otherwise than by a witness in a proceeding; or
>
> (b) contained or recorded in a book, document or any record -whatever, proof of which is not admissible under any provision of this Act, which is tendered in evidence for the purpose of proving the truth of the matter stated in it.[1]

The court in the recent case of *Harka Air Ltd & Anor* v. *Sterling Bank*[2] posited that *hearsay evidence is evidence which does not derive its value solely from the credit given to the witness himself but which rests also, in part, on the veracity and competence of some other person. In an earlier case of Opionachie* v. *Fayemi,*[3] the court while relying on *FRN* v. *Mohammed Usman & Anor*[4] posited that hearsay evidence is secondary evidence of an oral statement best described as 'second-hand' evidence.

In the same trend, the Supreme Court in *Bamidele Simeon* v. *The State,*[5] posited in its erudition that a piece of evidence is hearsay if it is evidence of the contents of a statement made by a witness who himself is not called to testify. It presupposes that if any fact is to be proved against anyone, it ought

---

[1] See *Abass* v. *FRN & Ors.* (2018) LPELR-43695 (CA) P. 17, paras. D-F.
[2](2019) LPELR-47638 (CA) P.28, para. A.
[3](2018) LPELR-44134 (CA).
[4](2012) 3 SC (PT 1) 128.
[5](2018) LPELR-44388 (SC) P. 25, Para. G per Kekere-Ekun JSC.

to be proved in his presence by the testimony of a witness sworn to speak the truth and testifying to facts within his personal knowledge, subject to recognised exceptions.

2. The General Rule

The general rule is that hearsay evidence is not admissible in evidence.[6] It is only admissible where the Evidence Act states it is or where any other Act provides for same. It follows therefore that by virtue of section 126 of the Evidence Act, 2011, oral evidence must be direct. This is to say: if the evidence is a fact which could be seen, heard, perceived or refers to an opinion or to the grounds on which that opinion is held; it must be evidence of a witness who saw the fact, heard the fact, perceived the fact or holds the opinion on those grounds, respectively. Oral evidence which is not at-tune with section 126 of the Evidence Act, is adjudged hearsay evidence and inadmissible in law.

The reason for the hearsay rule is to ensure that a person is not accused or found guilty for an offence he did not commit. By this rule, courts are under duty not to admit and or convict an accused person based on the testimony of a witness who did not see, hear or perceive the facts given in his testimony at a trial; this rule is sacrosanct except for where a statute provides an exception. Accordingly, where a trial court convicts an accused upon hearsay evidence, an appellate court will quash the conviction, if there is no other legal evidence upon which the conviction hinges.[7]

From the provision of section 37 of the Act, there are two forms of hearsay evidence recognized by the Act. The first is a statement, whether oral or written, made otherwise than by a witness in a proceeding for the purpose of proving the truth of the matter therein. The phrase "otherwise than by a witness in a proceeding" refers to a person who is himself called as a witness. In *Aina* v. *State*[8] the Court of Appeal, expounding on the doctrine of hearsay, stated thus:

> Undoubtedly, by the provisions of Section 37 and 38 of the Evidence Act, 2011, evidence; oral or documentary, given or made by a person who is not called as a witness in the proceedings of a court of law, is hearsay and inadmissible in evidence, if its purpose is to prove the truth of what is

---

[6] See section 38 of the Evidence Act. See also *Abubakar* v. *State* (2019) LPELR-47046 (CA) P. 28, paras. D-E. See also *Osinowo* v. *Nigerian Navy* (2019) LPELR-46429 (CA).
[7] *Abdullahi* v. *State* (2016) LPELR-43753 (CA).
[8] (2018) LPELR-45566 (CA) P. 9, paras. C-D, P 11, paras. A-C.

> contained therein...The underlying principle of the position of the law on hearsay evidence is that it is evidence which does not derive its value solely from the credibility of the witness himself, but also rests in part, on the veracity, credibility and competence of some other person who does not appear in the proceeding before the court as a witness. Thus, it is a tale, retold and retorted that is unreliable for the purpose of proving the truth of the content.

Also, as stated in section 37, it must be for the purpose of proving the truth of the matter therein.[9] This rule as to a statement being hearsay and inadmissible only applies when it is given for "the purpose of proving the truth of the matter therein.[10] This rule traces its roots to the Common Law rule in *Subramanian* v. *Public Prosecution.*[11] In that case, Subramanian had been captured by Chinese terrorists and forced into training in a large camp. When later captured by the Malayan force, he was charged with being in possession of ammunition without lawful authority, contrary to Emergency Regulations in force at the material time. Both in his extra judicial statement to the police and his evidence in court, he insisted that though he was in possession of ammunition, he had them because he was acting under duress as a result of threats by the Chinese terrorist. He described how he was forced to accompany the terrorists, one of whom walked in front and two behind, who told him he was being taken to their leader. At this stage, the trial judge interrupted him saying that his conversion with bandits was not admissible unless they were called; otherwise, it amounted to hearsay. On appeal to the Privy Council, it stated:

> Evidence of a statement made to a witness by a person who is not himself called as a witness may or may not be hearsay. It is hearsay and inadmissible when the object of the evidence is to establish the truth of what is contained in the statement. It is not hearsay and is admissible when it is proposed to establish by evidence, not the truth of the statement, but the fact that it was made.

Thus, the conviction was quashed because the excluded evidence was not hearsay as it was tendered to prove the fact that threats were made and not

---

[9] Ibid.
[10] *Sunday* v. *State* (2018) LPELR-46131 (CA) Pp. 20-21, paras. F-A.
[11] (1956) 1 WLR 965.

to prove the truth of what the terrorist said. In *Osho* v. *The State,*[12] the Court of Appeal, having quoted the dictum in the Subramanian case, stated that hearsay evidence imports the purpose of which it is intended to be given and not the quality of the evidence itself.

The second form of hearsay in section 37 is a statement contained or recorded in a book, document or any record whatsoever, proof of which is not admissible under any provision of the Act which is tendered in evidence for the purpose of proving the truth of the matter stated in it. This is obviously a wide provision and brings within its ambit, every statement contained in a document as aforestated, which is inadmissible in evidence.

The rational for the exclusion of hearsay evidence is stated in *Chief Otu Gregory Apph & Ors* v. *Mr. Mathias Oturie.*[13] In that case, the Court of Appeal stated thus:

> The rationale for excluding hearsay evidence is the great difficulty of assessing what if any, weight that can properly be given to a statement by a person whom the jury have not seen or heard, and which has not been subject to any test of reliability by cross-examination.

Hearsay evidence cannot be a basis of any evidence before the court and the court will not rely on same to give his judgment.[14]

There is an abundance of case law in respect of hearsay evidence. In *Zubairu* v. *The State,*[15] the deceased had broken the widescreen of the 4th accused's car. When this was discovered, the 4th accused, according to the daughter of PW 1, sent his sons, the 1st and 3rd accused person to get the deceased, after which he was beaten thoroughly before being taken to the police station. The deceased died shortly after at the hospital. PW1, who gave evidence as to what happened at the 4th accused's house stated that her daughter, who was the source of her information, had seen it. The Supreme Court held that this was obviously hearsay as its object was to establish the truth of what happened in the house of the 4th accused person. In *Uwa* v. *The State,*[16] the appellant was charged with the offence of armed robbery and a confessional statement was tendered in evidence. However, the appellant, while giving evidence denied any involvement in the crime. There

---

[12] (2012) 8 NWLR (pt. 1302) 234 C.A.
[13](2019) LPELR-46301 (CA) P. 22, paras. B-C.
[14]*Bashiru Popoola* v. *The State* (2018) LPELR-43853 (SC).
[15] (2015) 16 NWLR (Pt. 1486) 504.
[16](2015) 4 NWLR (Pt. 1450) 438 C.A.

was no independent statement corroborating the confessional statement, which the appellant stated he did not make, apart from the oral evidence of PWI who was not at the scene of the crime. The Court of Appeal held that as the evidence of PWI was not based on his personal knowledge, it amounted to hearsay.

In view of the doctrine of hearsay, the court of Appeal in *Ayo* v. *The State*[17] stated that where the only eyewitness to a crime is the accused person, whatever any other witness would testify to as to the unlawful act is hearsay. Hence, in that case, it was held that since the witnesses for the prosecution merely relied on what the accused person, the sole witness of the incident said, the prosecution's evidence amounted to hearsay. Similarly, the Supreme Court held in *Ikara* v. *the State,*[18] that since the prosecution's witnesses were not at the scene of the armed robbery which the accused was alleged to have committed, their testimonies amounted to hearsay.

Unless an interpreter who wrote down the statement of the accused is called as a witness, it would amount to hearsay.[19] An investigating police officer's evidence as to the investigation he carried does not amount to hearsay as it is based on his personal knowledge,[20] but where such investigating police officer is not called as a witness and his reports are tendered by another police officer, it is indisputably hearsay evidence.[21]A deposition laced with hearsay has no probative value[22] as to do otherwise is like asking the court to sieve the oral evidence (in the form of written statement on oath) of witnesses to determine which part of it is hearsay or not[23]

If hearsay evidence is admitted, even if this is done unknowingly, the trial court is duty-bound not to act on it and if it does, such judgment can be overturned on the ground that it was reached on the basis of inadequate evidence. Such evidence has no evidential value.[24] Thus, in *Hakair Ltd & Anor* v. *Sterling Bank,*[25] the court of Appeal while relying on the Supreme

---

[17] (2015) 16 NWLR (Pt.1486) P. 53.
[18] (2014) 1 NWLR (Pt. 1389) 639 S.C.
[19] *Bashiru Popoola* v. *The State* (*supra*).
[20] See *Yahaya Yusuf Ayodeji* v. *Federal Republic of Nigeria* (2018) LPELR -45839 (CA) P44. Paras. D-G. See also *Sunday* v. *State* (2018) LPELR-46131 (CA).
[21] *Okpa* v. *The State* (2014) 13 NWLR (pt 1424) 225 C.A
[22] *Kakih* v. *PDP* (2014) 15 NWLR (pt 1430) 374 S.C
[23] Ibid., at pages 418-419.
[24] *Shide* v. *State* (2018) LPELR-45038 (CA).
[25](2019) LPELR-47638 (CA) P. para. 29 A.

Court decision of *Olalekan* v. *The State*[26] stated the law with judicial sagacity when it held that *neither the court nor the consent of the parties is capable of making such evidence admissible in law.*

3. Exceptions to the Rule against Hearsay Evidence

Although hearsay evidence is generally inadmissible, the provisions of section 38 of the Act make it clear that the law regarding hearsay is not cast in iron. There are exceptions to the rule. The main exceptions to the hearsay rule are contained in Part IV of the Evidence Act, 2011. These exceptions to hearsay are examined copiously with a direct reference to the provisions of the Evidence Act. They include the following:

i. Statement made by persons who cannot be called as witnesses

The Evidence Act contains 11 exceptions to the hearsay rule, from section 40-50. However, these exceptions can only avail a party if any of the conditions in section 39 is fulfilled. Section 39 of the Act provides thus:

> Statements, whether written or oral of facts in issue or relevant facts made by a person;
>
> (a) Who is dead;
>
> (b) Who cannot be found;
>
> (c) Who has become incapable of giving evidence; or
>
> (d) Whose attendance cannot be procured without an amount of delay or expense which under the circumstances of the case appears to the court unreasonable, are admissible under section 40-50.

The court, reinforcing this provision, stated in *Orjiakor & Anor* v. *Mbachu & Anor*[27] that by the aforementioned provision of the Evidence Act, statements made by any of the categories of persons mentioned may be admitted in evidence where the maker of the statement is not called as a witness by reason of death or incapability stated in the provisions. In the instant case, one fact that is not in dispute is that Agabus Mbachu is dead and it was practically impossible for him to be called as a witness. The evidence of what he said is permissible under Section 39(a) of the Evidence Act 2011.

---

[26](2001) LPELR -2561 (SC), Per Karibi-Whyte.

[27](2019) LPELR-47713 (CA) Pp.62-63, Paras. E-A.

In the recent decision of the Supreme Court in *Adeusi Adesina* v. *The People of Lagos State,*[28] the medical report of a medical doctor whose attendance could not be procured was tendered by an IPO and was held admissible as an exception to hearsay under section 39 and 41 of the Act.

These statutory exceptions will now be discussed.

A. Statements relating to cause of death or Dying Declarations

The Evidence Act states that "a statement made by a person as to the cause of his death, or as to any of the circumstances of the events which resulted in his death in cases in which the cause of that person's death comes into question is admissible where the person who made it believed himself to be in danger of approaching death although he may have entertained at the time of making it hope of recovery."[29]

This statement in legal parlance is referred to as a "Dying Declaration." The Act further states that such a statement shall be admissible whatever may be the nature of the proceeding in which the cause of death comes into question.[30] From the above, the conditions for a successful plea of "dying declaration" are:

(a) the statement must relate to the cause of his death or to any of the circumstances of the events which resulted in this death;

(b) he must have believed himself to be in danger of approaching death. It is immaterial he might have had some hope of recovery. This has abolished the common law rule that provided that the victim must be in "a settled hopeless expectation of death" to come within a dying declaration;

(c) It must have been made in a proceeding, whether civil or criminal.

A dying declaration may seem similar to "*res gestae*" as provided under section 4 of the Evidence Act but it differs from "*res gestae*" as the above elements need not be fulfilled when a statement is sought to be admitted as "*res gestae*". The hallmark of *"res gestae*" is a connection so strong with the facts in issue to form part of the same transaction. It is therefore not limited to occasions where a deceased makes a dying declaration.

---

[28](2019) LPELR-46403 (SC) Pp. 20-21, para. F. per Peter-Odili, JSC.

[29] Section 40 (1) of the Evidence Act.

[30] Section 40 (2) of Evidence Act.

The subject of dying declarations was examined in *Ezeugo* v. *The State*.[31] In that case, the appellant, the General Overseer of a church, was alleged to have set fire on the deceased and five other witnesses for the prosecution. According to all the other witnesses and PW4, the appellant, after beating the deceased and his other victims severely, asked PW4 to pour petrol on them. Upon which he lit a matchstick and set fire on them. Before the deceased's death, she had made a statement at the hospital that she had suffered injuries and burns from a generator fire accident at the appellant's residence. She also told PW4 and the IPO that she had suffered her injuries from a fire accident. However, the other victims of the fire incidence and PW5 testified that the appellant had told the deceased and them to say that at the hospital and to the police. The appellant contended that the statement, both oral and written, of the deceased constituted a dying declaration in proof of his innocence. However, the trial court held that the statement did not constitute a dying declaration as the deceased was not in expectation of death at the time she made the statement. Consequently, the appellant was convicted. Dissatisfied with this decision, the appellant appealed to the Court of Appeal. The Court of Appeal, dismissing his appeal, held as follows:

> For a statement to qualify as a dying declaration under section 33(1) (a) of the Evidence Act (now section 40(1)), the person making the statement must believe himself to be in danger of approaching death. The belief in the danger of approaching death is subjective, not objective. The person making the declaration must believe himself to be in danger of approaching death, as nobody would wish to die with a lie on his lips. The danger of approaching death cannot be inferred from surrounding circumstance or opinion of third parties. In this case, the statement made by the deceased were not made with the belief that she was in danger of approaching death. In the circumstance, the statement were not dying declarations. Furthermore, the appellant's argument that the deceased's belief in the danger of approaching death could be garnered and inferred from the surrounding circumstances of the case or from the evidence of PW6 and PW8 was not correct.

Though the Court in the above case was completely right when it stated that "the belief in the danger of approaching death is subjective, not objective, and there was no convincing evidence as to the deceased's belief at the time of making the statements, it is submitted, with respect, that the

[31] (2013) 9 NWLR (Pt. 1360) 508 CA.

Court of Appeal was wrong in stating that "the danger of approaching death cannot be inferred from surrounding circumstances." This statement is far-reaching and will only make the task of proving a dying declaration herculean. One need not "unfold the innermost recesses" of the heart of the deceased to know a deceased's belief at the material time. Evidence of such belief can only be gotten from an examination of all the surrounding facts and circumstances of the case.

In *Hassan Wakili* v. *The State,*[32] the Court of Appeal while relying on *Olabode* v. *State*[33] where the PW1 and PW2 gave evidence of what they heard directly from the mouth of the deceased both at the scene of the-crime and at the hospital held that the pieces of evidence by witnesses which represent what they saw and heard from the deceased do not constitute hearsay. Their evidence was not hearsay evidence at all.

B. Statements made in the course of business

A Statement is admissible when made by a person in the ordinary course of business, and in particular, when it consists of any entry or memorandum made by him in books, electronic device kept in the ordinary course of business, or in the discharge of a professional duty, or an acknowledgement written or signed by him of the receipt of money, goods, securities or property of any kind, or of a document used in commerce written or signed by him or of the date of a letter or other document usually dated, written or signed by him.[34] However, the maker of the statement must have made it contemporaneously with the transaction recorded or so soon thereafter that the court considers it likely that the transaction was still fresh in his memory.[35] A recourse to appraisal of judicial decisions will be of utmost relevance in the comprehension of this exception to the rule against hearsay.

In *Brila Energy Ltd* v. *FRN*[36] the evidence before the court adduced through PW9 (though not the maker of the document) was that the Lloyds' List Intelligence Report, admitted in evidence as Exhibits P23-P25 was to the effect that Exhibits P23-25 consisted of a business record about the movement of ships worldwide kept by Lloyds and made available to business organizations or individuals who subscribed to it by payment of prescribed fees. PW9 was not the maker but to the extent that the Report consisted of a

---

[32](2016) LPELR-40237 (CA).

[33](2009) 11 NWLR (Pt.1152) 270.

[34] Section 41 of the Evidence Act. See also *Adeusi Adesina* v. *The People of Lagos State (supra).*

[35]Ibid.

[36](2018) LPELR-43926 (CA) P. 151, Paras E-F.

business record regularly maintained in the ordinary course of business, the Court of Appeal while relying on sections 41 and 51 of the Act held that they could be tendered through PW9, who though not the maker, had subscribed to website, and thus, did not therefore constitute hearsay evidence. The Court of Appeal while rejecting such statement made in the course of movement of ships worldwide as hearsay, further gave a stamp of approval to this genre of exception to state that one of the exceptions to hearsay rule is in respect of records made or kept in the course of regularly conducted activity of a business, organization, occupation or calling, whether or not for profit. However, in *Simth* v. *Blakey,*[37] it was held that a letter written by the deceased branch manager to the plaintiffs informing them that the defendant had sent three cases of shoes to the branch office was inadmissible evidence as it was not the deceased branch manager's duty to do a particular act and record it.

C. Statement against interest of maker with special knowledge

A statement is admissible where the maker had peculiar means of knowing the matter stated and such statement is against his pecuniary or proprietary interest; and (i) he had no interest to misrepresent the matter or (ii) the statement, if true, would expose him to either criminal or civil liability.[38] One vital element of this exception to hearsay is that the statement must be against the pecuniary or proprietary interest of the maker. An example of this is a statement in which a deceased person shows that the quantum of his interest in property is less than it appeared. In *Sly* v. *Sly,*[39] a deceased occupier of land who was thought to hold an absolute interest in land declared that he only held a life interest under a will with two named persons as executors. The declaration was held to be against the deceased declarant's interest and thus, admissible to prove the existence of the Will and also the Executors. This case can be contrasted with the *Sussex Peerage Case*[40] where a deceased clergyman made a declaration exposing himself to the risk of criminal prosecution for irregular celebration of marriage. It was held that the statement did not come within the exception for the interest of the clergyman affected.

---

[37] (1867) L.R. 2 QB 326.
[38] Section 42 of the Evidence Act.
[39] (1877) 2 PB 91 cited in F Nwadialo, *op. cit.,* pg 242.
[40] (1844) 11 Cl and F85 at 110-115.

D. Statements of opinions as to public right or custom and matters of general interest

When a statement gives the opinion of a person as to the existence of any public right or custom or matter of general interest, the existence of which, if it existed, the maker would have been likely to be aware, such statement is admissible as long as it was made before any controversy as to such right, custom or matter, had arisen.[41] The rationale behind this exception is that it may be extremely difficult to prove a long existing public right or custom by direct evidence.

E. Statement relating to the existence of a relationship

A statement which relates to the existence of relationship by blood, marriage or adoption between person as to whose relationship by blood, marriage or adoption the person making the statement had special means of knowledge, is admissible provided that:

(i) it is deemed to be relevant only in a case in which the pedigree to which it relates is in issue, and not to a case in which it is only relevant to the issue;[42] and

(ii) it must be made by a declarant shown to be related by blood to the person to whom it relates,[43] or by the husband or wife of such a person. However, a declaration by a deceased parent, that he or she did not marry the other parent until after the birth of the child is relevant to the question of the paternity of such child upon any question arising as to the right of the child to inherit real or personal property under any legislation;[44] and in proceeding for the declaration made by a person who, if an order were granted, would stand towards the petitioner in any of the relationship mentioned in (ii) above is deemed relevant to the question of the identity of the parents of the petitioner; and the statement must be made before the question in relation to which it is to be proved had arisen, but it does not cease to be admissible because it was made for the purpose of preventing the dispute from arising.[45] If any of the three conditions above is not fulfilled, the statement will be inadmissible. Therefore in *Johnson* v. *Lawson*,[46] evidence of declaration by a deceased

---

[41] Section 43(1) and (2) of the Evidence Act.
[42] Section 44(2) (a) of the Evidence Act.
[43] Section 44(2) (b) of the Evidence Act.
[44] Section 44(2) (b) (i) of the Evidence Act.
[45] Section 44 (2) (c) of the Evidence Act.
[46] 2 Bing 86 (9 E.C.L.R).

housekeeper who had known the family for over twenty years was rejected because he was an outsider and not one related by blood to the person to whom declarations relates to or the husband or wife of such a person.

F. Declarations by testators

The declarations of a deceased testator as to his testamentary intentions and as to the content of his Will are admissible when;

(a) His Will has been lost, and when there is a question as to what were its contents; or

(b) the question as to whether an existing Will is genuine or was improperly obtained or the questions as to whether any or which of the more existing documents than one constitute his Will.[47] Also, it is immaterial whether the declarations were made before or after the making or loss of the Will.[48]

G. Admissibility of certain evidence for proving, in subsequent proceeding, the truth of facts Stated in it

Section 46 of the Evidence Act makes evidence given in previous proceedings admissible in a subsequent proceeding for proving the truth of the facts stated in it. It provides that evidence given by a witness in a judicial proceeding, or before any person authorized by law to take it, is admissible for the purpose of proving in a subsequent judicial proceeding or in a later stage of the same proceeding the truth of the facts which it states, when the witness cannot be called for any of the reasons specified in section 39, or is kept out of the way by the adverse party. Provided that-

a. the proceeding was between the same parties or their representative in interest;
b. the adverse party in the first proceeding had the right and opportunity to cross-examine; and
c. the question in issue were substantially the same in the first as in the second proceeding.[49]

For the purpose of section 46, a criminal trial or inquiry shall be deemed to be a proceeding between the prosecutor and the defendant.[50] This provision is of the utmost importance for without it, there would be undue

[47] Section 45(1)(a)(b) and (c) of the Evidence Act.
[48] Section 45 (2) of the Act.
[49] Section 46 (1) of the Act.
[50] Section 46 (2) of the Act.

delay and even a denial of justice when for instance, due to one reason or the other, parties are unable to proceed with trial after evidence has been given and have to start de novo before a new judge. However, the conditions stipulated in section 39 must exist before section 46 is applicable, otherwise, the trial will be nullified on appeal. In *Danish Car Carries* v. *F. S. and Co. (Nig) Ltd,*[51] the respondent's claim against the appellants, at the trial court was for the sum of DM18,28.00 deutschmark or its naira equivalent at the prevailing exchange rate at the date of judgment and ₦2,231,126.00 with 21 per cent interest from November 2001 till judgment and settlement thereof. After filing and exchange of pleadings, the matter proceeded to trial before Hon. Justice Olomojobi. The respondents called one witness in the person of the 2nd respondent and tendered twenty-two exhibits to prove their claim. The appellants similarly called one witness in their defence without tendering any exhibit. Both parties concluded their evidence and closed their case before Hon. Justice Olomojobi, who ordered both parties to file and exchange written address and fixed 21st June 2007 for adoption of the written addresses. The respondents, however, could not file their written addresses until the trial judge retired from service. The case was then reassigned to another judge. On the 21st of April 2008, the respondents' counsel told the trial court that they had already concluded evidence and that they had done the trial and had filed written addresses and were yet to adopt same before the previous judge retired. The trial judge ordered and directed the parties to file and serve written address within ten weeks and adjourned the case for adoption of written addresses. Subsequently, both parties filed and exchanged written addresses and adopted same on the adjourned date. The trial judge reserved judgment which he delivered on the 28th July 2008. The appellant being dissatisfied with the judgment of the trial court filed an appeal before the Court of Appeal. He contended that the court was wrong when having taken over a part-heard suit declined to commence the trial *de novo*. The Court of Appeal, unanimously allowing the appeal, stated as follows:

> The learned judge who never was a trial judge in this case was in serious blunder by merely writing and delivering judgment in respect of a case heard by another judge. A trial judge must hear evidence in court, assess the witnesses who testified before him, form impression about them and evaluate their evidence in the light of such impression. Failure to take

---

[51] (2012) 2 NWLR (pt 1284) 237 C.A.

> evidence afresh had effectively reduced the foundation upon which the judgment was based to hypothesis. The trial conducted by the previous judge cease to be relevant in the proceeding except in such circumstances as provided under section 34 of the Evidence Act Cap. E14, L.F.N, 2004 (now section 46 of the present Act)...The lower court was in grievous error by adopting such peculiar and lazy procedure in trial conducted by another judge to prepare and deliver judgment.[52]

Also, the conditions stipulated in section 46 of the Act must be fulfilled. Thus, the Court held in *Lateja* v. *Fabayo*,[53] that as the respondent in that case was not a party to the suit tendered as an exhibit, the provision of section 46 could not be brought into operation. However, though evidence given in a previous proceeding is not admissible in a subsequent proceeding to prove the truth of the facts alleged in such evidence, it can be used for cross-examination with the aim of discrediting a witness called to testify in the subsequent proceeding or later case.[54]

H. Statement made under any criminal procedure legislation

A statement in accordance with section 290 and 291 or section 319 of the Criminal Procedure Act, may afterwards be used in evidence on the trial of any person accused of an offence to which the same relates, if the person who made the statement cannot be called for any of the reasons specified in section 39, and if reasonable notice of the intention to take such statement was served upon the person against whom it is to be read in evidence and he had, or might have had, if he had chosen to be present, full opportunity of cross-examining the person making the statement.[55]

I. Any statement made by a defendant at a preliminary investigation or at a coroner's inquest may be given in evidence.[56]

Statutorily, the Evidence Act under section 48 provides that statement of defendant at preliminary investigation or coroner's inquest may be given in evidence and thus, is admissible as an exception to the hearsay rule.

[52] At pp. 250-251.
[53] (2012) NWLR (Pt. 1304) 159 C.A.
[54] *Aremu* v. *Chukwu* (2012)1 NWLR (Pt. 1288) P 587.
[55] Section 47 of the Evidence Act.
[56] Section 48 of the Evidence Act.

J. Admission of written statement of investigating police officer in certain cases

Where in the course of any criminal trial, the court is satisfied that for any sufficient reason, the attendance of the investigating police officer cannot be procured, the written and signed statement of such officer may be admitted in evidence by the court if-

(a) the defence does not object to the statement being admitted; and
(b) the court consents to the admission of the statement.[57]

The conditions for this exception to arise may be stated as follows:

(1) there must be evidence that the attendance of the investigating police officer cannot be procured due to a sufficient reason in the opinion of the court;
(2) the statement of such investigating police officer is written and signed by him;
(3) the defence does not object to the statement being admitted;
(4) the court consents to the admission of the statement.

In *Yahaya Yusuf Ayodeji* v. *Federal Republic of Nigeria*[58] this issue came up for determination. In that case, the Appellant and another person Mohammed Dogonyaro Audu (*aka*) Abdullahi Dogonyaro Muhammed) as 1st defendant were arraigned before the High Court of Federal Capital Territory on a ten count charge of conspiracy and fraudulent acquisition of property contrary to sections 26 and 12 of the ICPC Act, 2000. The defendant pleaded not guilty to the counts on 23rd February, 2017. Three witnesses testified for the prosecution. At the end of the trial and adoption of addresses of learned counsel to the accused persons, the appellant was found guilty on counts 1, 3, 4, 5 and 9 of the Charge. He was sentenced to seven years imprisonment on counts 1, 3, 4, 5 and 9 and the term was to run concurrently. At the trial court, the learned senior counsel also took serious exception to the recognition accorded evidence of PW2 who is an investigating officer in the matter contending that the evidence given was hearsay evidence. Dissatisfied with the decision of the trial court admitting the evidence of the IPO, the Appellant appealed to the Court of Appeal. In a well-considered judgment of the Court of Appeal, while relying on *Lekan*

[57] Section 49(a) and (b) of the Evidence Act.
[58] (2018) LPELR-45839 (CA) P.44, paras. D-G.

Olaoye v. *The State,*[59] *Ibrahim Kamila* v. *The State*[60] and *Ijeoma Anyasodor* v. *The State,*[61] it held thus:

> The law is now trite that whatever comes to the knowledge or attention of an IPO or Investigating Police Officer in the course of investigation particularly facts discovered which can incriminate or exculpate an accused or defendant is not hearsay evidence. Such evidence are clearly admissible notwithstanding that such evidence was found or discovered in the course of investigation. Once it is relevant to the facts in issue in the criminal trial or even to a fact relevant to the fact in issue. IPO's evidence constitutes one of the vital and important exceptions to hearsay evidence.[62]

Thus, an IPO only narrates to the court, the outcome of his investigation or enquiries or what he recovered or discovered in the course of his duty. This is because he must have discovered or recovered some pieces of evidence vital to the commission of the crime which trial courts normally consider in arriving at a just decision one way or the other.[63]

K. Absence of public officers

In the case of a person employed in the public service of the Federation or of a state who is required to give evidence for any purpose connected with a judicial proceeding, it shall be sufficient to account for his non-attendance at the hearing of the said judicial proceedings, if there is produced to the court, either a Federal or State Gazette or a telegram, an e-mail or letter purporting to emanate from the head of his department, sufficiently explaining to the satisfaction of the court his apparent default.[64]

L. Family or communal traditional history in land cases

Section 66 of the Evidence Act provides that when title or interest in family or communal land is in issue, oral evidence of family or communal tradition concerning such title or interest, is admissible. This becomes an exception to the rule excluding hearsay evidence only when the source of the oral evidence is dead.[65] If such person is still alive, it will certainly constitute

---

[59](2018) LPELR 43601 SC 1 AT 23 - 24 per Sanusi, JSC.

[60](2018) 8 NWLR (PT 1621) 252 at 271, paras. D-E.

[61](2018) 8 NWLR (PART - 1620) 107 AT 125, para. D.

[62] See also *Rowaye* v. *FRN & Ors* (2018) LPELR-45650(CA) Pp. 66-68, paras. C-B.

[63] See also *Umar* v. *State* (2018) LPELR-44430 (CA) and *Musa* v. *State* (2018) LPELR-46037 (CA) Pp. 16-18, paras. F-C.

[64] Section 50 of the Evidence Act.

[65]*Muhammad & Ors* v. *Gani* (2019) LPELR-47190 (CA) Pp. 21-23, paras. E-C.

hearsay evidence and be inadmissible. In *Barau & Ors* v. *Consolidated Tin Mines Ltd & Ors,*[66] the Court of Appeal held thus:

> I wish to only add, in further answer to learned silks contention about hearsay evidence that, hearsay evidence is actually admissible in proof of traditional history of land ownership, exception having been made for its admission by Section 66 of the Evidence Act. In fact, it has been said too by high authority that the rationale behind this statutory exception is the universal condition of illiteracy of years past, and that the provision applies not only to claims in land cases but to all claims (including chieftaincy claims founded on traditional history) which owe their origin to antiquity and could only be proved by oral evidence.[67]

In *Bala Barau Bako & Anor* v. *Haruna Audu & Anor,*[68] a matter arose out of a land dispute and the respondents, as plaintiffs, commenced the action in the High Court against the appellants, as defendants, claiming ownership of a parcel of land lying and situate in Bagel Village in Dass Local Government Area of Bauchi State. Among other things, the respondents claim for a declaration that the sale of the land by the first appellant to the second appellant was null and void, damages for trespass and injunction to restrain further trespass. The appellants counterclaimed for a declaration of ownership of the land in dispute, a declaration that the sale transaction between them was valid and for an injunction. The case of the respondents on the pleadings before the High Court was that the land in dispute was founded and first cultivated by their grandfather, late Galadima Kundel, and that the parcel of land is bounded on the north to the west by the farmland of Umaru Sambo Bagel, on the east by the farmland of Hashimu Wambai Bagel and on the south by the land which was loaned to the father of the second Appellant, Ba'ade, for use and return and which land the second appellant retained possession of after the death of his father. It was their case that their late grandfather was succeeded on the land by late Audu Galadima Kundel and that late Audu Galadima Kundel begat three children, Haruna Audu (the first Respondent), Maidawa Audu and Hassan Audu and that the three children succeeded their father on the land in dispute and that both Maidawa Audu and Hassan Audu have since died and that the second respondent is the son of Maidawa Audu.

---

[66](2019) LPELR-46806 (CA), pp. 35-36, Paras. E-B.
[67] The court also relied on *Popoola* v. *Adeyemo* (1992) 3 NSCC 46 at 59 60.
[68](2018) LPELR-44394 (CA) Pp. 40-42, para. C.

It was the case of the respondents that the father of the first appellant migrated from Dajin village to Bagel Village and he was accommodated by Hashimu Wambai Bagel and he subsequently approached the first Respondent and his brothers to request for land to farm and which would be returned on demand. It was their case that they granted the request of the first Appellant's father and granted him the land in dispute on loan and to be returned whenever demanded and that they informed their boundary men of the transaction. It was their case that on the death of his father, the first appellant took over the land and that they took the first Appellant before the Village Head of Bagel to demand for the return of their land, but that the first Appellant pleaded that he should be allowed to use the land to farm for some time to enable him feed his family. It was their case that they granted the request of the first Appellant to use the land temporarily and that they were surprised when they learnt that the first Appellant sold the land in dispute to the second Appellant and that the sale was without their knowledge or consent.

The Appellants denied the entire case of the Respondents and it was their case that the land in dispute was bounded on the north by a bush, on the south by the second Appellant, on the west by untarred road leading to Pegin Doka and on the east by Hassan Tata and that it was the first appellant that first cultivated the land as virgin land during the reign of one Mallam Saidu, the father of the present village Head of Bagel, and that he had been on the land for over fifty-two years without challenge from anybody, including the respondents. It was their case that it was only around three years ago that he was called before the village Head by the respondents in respect of the land in dispute and the matter was resolved in his favour and that it was correct that he sold part of the land in dispute to the second appellant and that he had the right to sell the land as it belonged to him. Counsel to the appellants contended that the evidence given by all the plaintiff witnesses amounted to hearsay because they all stated that the facts they rendered in their respective testimonies were as told them by their respective fathers. At the conclusion of trial, High Court entered judgment granting the claims of the respondents and dismissing the counterclaim of the appellants. Dissatisfied with the decision, the Appellant appealed to the Court of Appeal.

While refusing this argument and dismissing the appeal, the Court of Appeal held thus:

> As stated earlier, the case of the respondents was predicated on evidence of traditional history. Traditional history, by concept, deals with an event which is beyond human memory, or is ancient through recollecting beyond record, or is what happened at a time out of mind and therefore qualified to be immemorial...The unique feature of traditional history is that it is evidence of historical fact transmitted from generation to generation in respect of family communal land or chieftaincy. It is given by witnesses who, by their close association, interaction or special relationship with the land-owning family are knowledgeable enough to give cogent and relevant traditional evidence in respect of ownership of the land...

The court went further at page 41, to state that the law thus recognizes and accepts that evidence of traditional history is no more than hearsay evidence because it deals with events which occurred long ago and the history of which has been handed down from father to son or from generation to generation. It is evidence as to rights alleged to have existed beyond the time of living memory. Hence, although evidence of traditional history is hearsay, Section 66 of the Evidence Act 2011 accords it some potency, some respectability and probative force, and it is thus admissible in proof of title to land.[69]

M. Depositions in Affidavit

Section 107 of the Evidence Act provides that a court may in any civil proceeding make an order at any stage of such proceeding, directing that specified facts may be proved at the trial with or without the attendance of the deponent for cross-examination provided that where a party desires the attendance of such deponent for cross-examination, the court shall require his attendance for that purpose where this would not result in unjustifiable delay or expense. Furthermore, when a person deposes to his belief in any matter of fact, and his belief is derived from any source other than his own personal knowledge, he shall set forth explicitly the facts and circumstances forming the ground of his belief,[70] but the name of his informant shall be stated and reasonable particulars shall be given with respect to the informant and the times, place and circumstance of the information.[71]

---

[69] See also *Ogbaji* v. *Utahile & Ors* (2019) LPELR-47186(CA).
[70] See also section 115 (3) of the Evidence Act.
[71] Section 115 (4) of the Evidence Act.

Indeed, affidavit deposed to by people based on information received from someone else is commonplace in proceedings. In *Apph & Ors* v. *Oturie*,[72] the court had opined that hearsay in an affidavit is admissible, provided the source and grounds of information or belief are disclosed therein.

N. Evidence Admitted on the Principle of Corporate Personality

A company or a corporate entity, being an artificial person, cannot give evidence on its own. This must be done through its servants and agents, even if they were not a party to the transaction of which evidence is given. The position was aptly stated by the Supreme Court in *Ishola* v. *Societe Generale Bank*:[73]

> It cannot be over-emphasized that a company being a legal person or a juristic person can only act through its agents or servants and any agent or servant of the company can therefore give evidence to establish any transaction entered into by the company. Where the officer giving the evidence is not one who actually took part in the transaction on behalf of the company, such evidence is nonetheless admissible and will not be discountenanced or rejected as hearsay evidence. The fact that such official did not personally participate in the transaction on which he has given evidence, may in appropriate cases, however, affect the weight to be attached to such evidence.

In *Okolo* v. *FRN*,[74] the Court of Appeal while admitting the evidence of a servant or agent of a company on transaction or activity of the company which he never took part in held that the evidence of Pw2 and Pw3 (servants or agents of the company) are certainly not hearsay and admissible evidence as they were both the human agencies through which the corporate persons of Access Bank Plc and the Aminu Kano Teaching Hospital Kano acted. The court went further to pose some rhetorical questions when it stated "How could the juristic *personam* which are legal figments clothed with legal personality sue and be sued? How can they ventilate their claims or defend them in the case of suits or in any dealing? It has to be through the instrumentality of the human with flesh, blood, hands, legs and eyes and brains. That is why the alter ego of a corporate entity can be discerned.

---

[72](2019) LPELR-46301 (CA) P. 25, paras.D-E.
[73] (1997) 2 SCNJ 1 cited in S. Imhanobe, *op. cit.*, pg 107.
[74](2018) LPELR-45431(CA) Pp. 25-26, paras. G-C.

Also in *Impact Solutions Ltd & Anor* v. *International Breweries PLC,*[75] the Court of Appeal had this to say:

> ..It cannot be over emphasized that a company being a legal person or a juristic person can only act through its agents or servants and any agent or servant of a company can therefore give evidence to establish any transaction entered into by that company. Where the official giving the evidence is not the one, who actually took part in the transaction on, behalf of the company, such evidence is nonetheless relevant and admissible and will not be discountenanced or rejected as hearsay evidence. The fact that such official did not personally participate in the transaction on which he has given evidence may in appropriate cases, however, affect the weight to be attached to such evidence.

O. Admissibility of Documentary Evidence as to facts in issue

Section 83 of the Evidence Act which governs admissibility of documentary evidence incorporates the hearsay rule in sub-section (1) but provides that "the condition that the maker of the statement shall be called as a witness need not be satisfied if the maker is dead, or unfit by reasons of his bodily or mental condition to attend as a witness, or if he is outside Nigeria and it is not reasonably practicable to secure his attendance, or if all reasonable efforts to find him have been made without success." If any of those conditions exists, the document will be admitted in evidence.[76]

[75](2018) LPELR-45441 (CA).

[76]*NIMASA* v. *Hensmor (Nig) Ltd* (20115) 5 NELR. See generally section 83 of the Act.

Chapter 8

OPINION EVIDENCE

1. The General rule

It is the duty of the court to draw inferences and conclusions from proved facts. This was the kennel of the decision in *Nyavo* v. *Zading*.[1] Thus, the court is entitled to draw inferences from the evidence before it.[2] In other words, conclusions and proved facts lie in the domain of the court and not the lawyers or their litigants. Therefore, as a general rule, a witness will be disallowed from giving his opinion as to the existence or non-existence of the fact in issue or of any relevant fact.[3] Opinion evidence is made totally inadmissible by section 67 of the Act and the parties cannot by consent override the clear provision of the law.[4]

2. Exception to the General Rule

However, it is provided in section 67 of the Act that in circumstances envisaged in section 68 to 76 of the Act, opinion evidence could be relevant and admissible. The exceptions created by these sections cover the opinions of expert and non-experts. Opinion of experts will be relevant and admissible when the court is to form its own opinion with respect to foreign law, native law and custom, science or art, handwriting or finger impressions.[5] Conversely, Opinion of non-experts will be relevant and admissible when the court is to form an opinion with respect to general custom or right, certain usages and tenets, existence of the relationship of one person to another.

3. Opinion of Experts

An expert is a person specially skilled in the field in which he is giving evidence.[6] Although expertise, for evidential purposes, cannot be

---

[1] (2018) LPELR-44086 (CA) P. 19, paras. F.

[2] See *MTN* v. *Corporate Communication Investment Ltd* (2019) LPELR-47042 (SC) P. 24, para. D per Kekere-Ekun JSC

[3] See section 67 of the Evidence Act 2011.

[4] *G & T Investment Ltd* v. *Witt & Bush Ltd* (2011) 8 NWLR (Pt. 1250) 500.

[5] See section 68 (1) of the Evidence Act.

[6]See section 68(2) of the Evidence Act. *Lawal & Anor* v. *Umaru* (2018) LPELR-46695 (CA) P5. paras. F-G; *UBA Plc* v. *Patkan Ventures Ltd* (2017) LPELR-42392 (CA) P.13, paras F.G.; *Seismograph Services*

equiparated with scholastic knowledge or professorial attainment, an expert is, all the same, a person who is specially skilled in the field he is giving evidence.[7] In *Adebayo* v. *Nigerian Navy*,[8] an expert witness is one who has made the subject upon which he speaks a matter of particular study, practice or observation and he must have a particular and special knowledge of the subject. The Supreme Court in its judicial exercise[9] gave an interpretation of this provision when it held that a person is an expert when there is evidence that:

A. he has special knowledge, training or experience in the matter in question; or
B. he has made a special study of the subject or acquired a special experience on the subject matter.

Thus, these two conditions must operate disjunctively to establish who an expert is. The court held in *SPDC* v. *Gbeneyei & Ors*[10] that *expert opinion is only necessary where an expert can furnish the court with scientific or other information of a technical nature that is likely to be outside the experience and knowledge of the Judge.* Thus, where there is an expect evidence which is unchallenged and uncontradicted, the court is entitled to accept and act on it.[11] Conversely, where there are conflicting expert opinions, the court is free to evaluate and pick out of the opinions before it[12] as the court is not bound to accept such an opinion if it conflicts or is inconsistent with common sense of logic.[13] It thus suffices to say that expert opinion should not derail from the ordinary logic and clear thought of nature; it must not be a distortion of facts of general knowledge. Thus, in *Aladu* v. *The State*,[14] the court rejected the opinion of a medical doctor that a round wound of S inch in diameter was caused by sharp edge instrument or knife because round wounds are consistent with gunshots. Where more than one expert testifies and there is conflict in their testimonies, the court may reject or accept one

---

Nig. Ltd. v. *Akpororo* (1974) 6 SC 119, See also, *Azu* v. *The State* (1993) 6 NWLR (Pt. 229) 303 and *Shell Petroleum Co. Ltd* v. *Otoko* (1990) 6 NWLR (Pt. 159) 693.

[7] *Emmanuel* v. *Umana & Ors.* (2016) LPELR-40037 (SC) (2016) LPELR-40037(SC) P. 64, paras. B-C.

[8] (2018) LPELR-45957(CA) while relying on *Omisore & Anor* v. *Aregbesola & Ors.* (2015) LPELR-24803 SC

[9] Ibid.

[10] (2019) LPELR-47819(CA) P. 29, paras. E-F.

[11] See *Access Bank* v. *K.C. Intl Ltd* (2018) LPELR-43668 (CA) P.68, paras. E-F.

[12] *SPDC* v. *Gbeneyei & Ors* (*supra*).

[13] See *Okoh* v. *The State* (1971) NMLR 140.

[14] (1998) 8 NWLR (Pt. 563) 618.

or more of the testimonies and the court is not bound to give reasons for its decision in respect thereof.[15]

In *Ameh & Anor* v. *Suleiman & Ors,*[16] the court held that for the evidence of an expert to be given weight, it should be given by an independent party and not a party to the suit.

It has been held that where a party is seeking to persuade the court to accept the opinion of an expert expressed in textbooks which expect cannot be called as witness, such party cannot do so by merely tendering the textbook.[17] The party must put such an opinion to any other expert in the same field who is a witness in the case for confirmation after which it properly becomes part of the evidence in the case and will be considered as such by the court.[18]

By section 68(1) of the Act, evidence of an expert is relevant to enable the court form its own opinion on any point of science or art. It is noteworthy that such expert must be specially skilled in the area of science or art he is called upon to give evidence and must confine his evidence to that area of specialty otherwise his evidence will be irrelevant.[19] The term science and art are used in their widest sense and would include any point which is covered by any branch of the study of science or art. For example, in a murder trial, the determination of the cause of the death of the deceased person will come under this heading as well as the range or distance from which the shot was launched where the deceased was killed by a gunshot. A medical doctor will be considered as an expert for these purposes.[20] Finally, the term "science and art" will also include valuation of property in an action where the value of the property is relevant as in an action claiming *mesne* profit. The landlord will have to prove current rental value of the property if he claims a sum that is more than the rent and would therefore require expert evidence, of say, an estate valuer, to prove his claim.

In *Access Bank* v. *K.C. Intl Ltd,*[21] the expert opinion of a chartered accountant and member of the Institute of Chartered Accountant was held admissible as an expert evidence. The court went further to hold that the expert witness can sign such Report even though it does not necessarily

---

[15]See *S.P.D.C.* v. *Ferah* (1995) 3 NWLR 148; *Ozigbo* v. *C.O.P.* (1976) 2 SC 67.
[16](2018) LPELR-46543 (CA) P. 19, para. C.
[17] See *Concha* v. *Murieta* (1889) CHD. 543.
[18]*Corier* v. *Simpson* (1931) 5C& P 73.
[19] See *Tittibale* v. *Sokoto N.A.incomplete citation.*
[20] See *Ogunze* v. *The State* (1998) 5 NWLR (Pt.551) 521.
[21] *Supra.*

emanate from him. Hence, the law is that a credible member of a firm can sign the report or decision of the firm which they produced. Whether it is a firm of chartered accountants or law firm. However, where such expert cannot take questions on it, the court attaches little or no evidential value to such testimony as the expert who prepared such record was not called as a witness in the case.[22] It should be noted that where an adverse party cross examines an expert to test his credibility at the trial court, he will be estopped from challenging the competence of the expert on appeal. In *Union Bank* v. *Onwukwe*,[23] the court had this to say:

> Appellant had argued, strenuously, that the CW1 (Mr. Michael Chibuike Agulahi) an Accountant, who tendered the Audit Report (Exhibit A), prepared by him and his Accounting firm, was not an expert witness, not being a Chartered Accountant, himself...Of course, the Report was admitted without any objection, and when the witness was cross-examined, on the report and generally on the testimony he gave, there was no challenge as to his competence as an expert in accounting and auditing. Having presented himself as an Accountant and a member of the Chartered Institute of Cost and Management, and working with Uguma Amako & Co., Chartered Accountant, which produced the Exhibit A (Audit Report), it was for the Appellant, while at the Lower Court, to rebut the claims of the witness and/or ask questions to puncture his credentials and claims of expertise and/or credibility, by challenging the admissibility of the audit report by his company. Appellant never did that, instead cross examined the CW1, extensively, on the substance of his audit report and evidence, only to wake up, on appeal, to contest the competence/expertise of the witness!
>
> The evidence also shows that Appellant had given the CW1 (an Accountant) and his Accounting firm all the support and co-operation, needed to accomplish the services to the Respondent, by supplying the firm the necessary information, as requested by the Respondent, in the auditing of the Respondents account.. It is therefore, too late in the day for Appellant to turn round (on appeal) and try to discredit the CW1, trying to impeach his credibility, as expert witness for the purpose of this case, after believing in him and working with him to produce the report.

---

[22]See *Union Bank* v. *Onwukwe* (2017) LPELR-43279 (CA) P.27, para. C. The court relied on *Okereke* v. *Umahi* (2016) 11 NWLR (Pt.1524) 438 at 472.

[23] *Supra* at P. 29, para. B & G. P, 30, paras. A-G and P. 32, paras. C-D.

It is the expectation of section 68(1) of the Act that where a court of law wants to form an opinion on any point of foreign law, expert evidence is required. Such expert must be a person who by virtue of their profession, are acquainted with such foreign law. The witness therefore need not to have practiced or be qualified to practice law in the foreign country; it is sufficient if he knows the position of that foreign law, by virtue of the position or profession. Thus, in *Ajani* v. *Comptroller of Customs*[24] a bank manager of a bank in Nigeria authorized to deal in foreign currency was allowed to give evidence that *Franc* notes were legal tender in French West Africa. In the same wavelength, in *Sharing Cross Educational Service Ltd* v. *Umaru Adamu Enterprises Ltd & Ors,*[25] while relying on the erudition of the privy Council in *Ajani* v. *Comptroller of Customs,*[26] the Court of Appeal held that a person who is an expert in the area of foreign currency by virtue of his long experience in the banking sector and by his position as the branch manager of a bank and who was authorized to deal in foreign currency can elucidate as an expert on the law and practice regarding the question as to which currency was legal tender in French West Africa even though he was not a lawyer. Thus, *the practical knowledge of a person who is not a lawyer may be sufficient in certain cases to qualify him as a competent expert on a question of foreign law.*

It is noteworthy that an expert witness on foreign law is allowed to produce to the court, any book which he declares to be a work of authority on that foreign law in question and the court will be free, after necessary explanations from the expert, to construe for itself.[27] Where the court is to form its opinion on any point of native law or custom, section 68(1) says that the opinion of any person skilled in that native law is relevant.

Thus, in proving a custom or native law, expert opinion is required. Experts in this circumstance are traditional rulers, chiefs or other persons having special knowledge of such native law and custom.[28] The mere fact that a person is a President of a Customary Court does not necessarily make him an expert in customary laws.[29] It is also noteworthy that in proving customary law, any book or manuscript recognized by natives as legal

---

[24](1952) 14 WACA 34.
[25](2015) LPELR-24661(CA) P.36, paras. D-F.
[26](1954) 14 WACA 37.
[27] See section 69 of the Evidence Act.
[28] See section 70 of the Evidence Act.
[29] See *Edokpolor* v. *Idehen* (1961) WNLR 11.

authority representing their custom is relevant.[30] Such book or manuscript must, however, be tendered in evidence at the trial.[31]

Under section 68(1), expert opinion may be utilized to prove handwriting. The expert must be specially skilled in the identification of handwritings. In this regard, a police officer specially trained in handwriting and finger prints will be regarded as a handwriting expert as well as a solicitor who has acquired knowledge of handwriting as an amateur could also be treated as an expert in hand writing.[32] The facts still remain that it is for the trial court to reach a final decision on the admissibility of the expert opinion of a person trained in handwriting through adduction of evidence.[33]

4. Non–Expert Opinion

Opinion of non-experts could be relied upon to prove handwriting, the existence of general custom or right, usages and tenets and existence of a relationship.[34] In the case of handwriting, it is provided in section 72(1) of the Act that when the court is to form an opinion as to the person by whom a document was written or signed, the opinion of any person acquainted with the handwriting of the person by whom it is supposed to be written or signed, is relevant and admissible. A person is deemed to be acquainted with the handwriting of another person if:

(i) he has seen that other person write; or

(ii) he has received documents purporting to be written by that other person in answer to documents written by himself or under his authority and addressed to that other person; or

(iii) in the ordinary course of business, documents purporting to be written by that other person are habitually submitted to him.[35]

It should also be noted that even the court is empowered by the law to compare signatures without recourse to experts in handwriting.[36] In *Orjiakor* v. *State*,[37] the court held that the Evidence Act 2011 provides that

---

[30] Section 70 of the Evidence Act; *Adedibu* v. *Adewoyin* (1951) 13 WACA 198.

[31] See *Idundun* v. *Okumagba* (1976) 9 & 10 SC. 227.

[32] See *R* v. *Sliverlock* (1894) 2 Q. B 766.

[33] See *Sterling Bank Plc* v. *Suleiman & Ors* (2016) LPELR-41261 (CA) P. 16, para. C.

[34] See sections 72-75 of the Evidence Act, 2011.

[35] Section 72 (2) of the Evidence Act 2011.

[36] See section 101 (2) of the Evidence Act 2011.

[37] (2017) LPELR-42739 (CA) P.19. However, the power to compare and draw conclusions on finger impressions given to the court by the Evidence Act 2011 as it existed in past legislation has been argued not to be a progress in the right direction. This is because even finger print experts in the past have been found to make grievous mistakes which have led to gross miscarriage of justice and sadly, innocent people wrongly sent to the gallows. Thus, it is submitted that the correct methodology in such instance is to use

there is no limitation to the power of a court to examine document and form its opinion on hand writing, signature or finger impression. The Act provides that the court can form its own opinion as to handwriting or finger impression by comparing a genuine/specimen with a disputed one. By section 73(1) of the Act, the opinion of non-expert could prove the existence of any general custom or right. The witness here should be someone who is likely to know the existence of such general custom or right. It can be recalled that we earlier relied on a judicial authority to argue that the mere fact that a person is a President of a Customary Court does not make him an expert in customary law, it is submitted that the evidence of such person may be admissible under section 73(1) as opinion of non-expert. "The expression "general custom or right" includes customs or right common to any considerable class of persons.[38]

When the court is to form an opinion on the existence of any usage or tenet of any body of individuals or family or the constitution and government of any religious group or charitable organization or the meaning of words or terms used in a particular district or by a particular class of persons, the opinion of anyone having special means of knowledge of such usage or tenet, constitution and government or meaning of words, is admissible under section 74 of the Evidence Act. For example, a young man from Orlu in Imo State who has served in a local bar for five years in Eket, should be capable of testifying that the term "404" is used to refer to dog meat at Eket. It is submitted that his testimony is covered by section 74 (particularly paragraph (c) because by serving in a local bar for five years at Eket, he should be deemed to have special means of knowing the name given to dog meat by the habitants of that place or locality. Finally, by section 75 of the Act, opinion of a non-expert may aid the court when the latter wants to form opinion as to the relationship of one person to another, provided that such opinion shall not suffice as evidence for the proof of a valid marriage in proceedings for dissolution of marriage or action for damages for adultery or in a criminal trial for bigamy. It is also noteworthy that whenever the opinion of any person who is alive is admissible, the grounds upon which he holds the opinion becomes admissible.[39]

---

artificial intelligence to discover similarities in handwriting, voice and thumb print. One may ask why the section calling for dependence on human intelligence found its way back into the statute books in this age despite the provisions of Section 68 which deals with the admissibility of Expert opinion. It is hoped that this could be resolved in the future.

[38] See section 73(2) of the Act.

[39] See section 76 of the Act.

Chapter 9

CHARACTER EVIDENCE

1. Meaning of Character

Character Evidence or evidence of character belongs to that category of evidence which is generally inadmissible and thus excluded by the court even though it may be relevant. Character is defined by the Evidence Act as "reputation as distinguished from dispositions." It goes further to state that except as mentioned in sections 78 to 87 of the Act, "evidence may be given only of general reputation, and not of particular acts by which reputation or disposition is shown."[130] The restriction of the meaning of "character" as used in the Act to "general reputation" was derived from *R* v. *Rowton.*[131] In that case, Cockburn CJ explained character evidence to be "evidence of his general character founded on his general reputation in the neighbourhood in which he lives." He distinguished this from evidence of witness' opinion of the party's character which he described as "disposition".

Thus, "character" as used in the Evidence Act means the reputation of an individual in the neighbourhood or community in which he lives. Such reputation may raise a presumption in a judge's mind that an accused is incapable of committing an offence, or if the accused's character or reputation is bad, it raises a presumption that the accused is likely to have committed the offence. It is this bias in a judge's mind caused by evidence of character that justifies its general exclusion by the Evidence Act. This has a nexus with the rational for the exclusion of similar fact evidence under our law save and except some recognized exceptions.

2. General Principle of Evidence of Character

Character Evidence should not be confused with the character of a witness who is being cross-examined. For while a party's character is generally inadmissible in evidence, a witness' character is always relevant to his credit.[1] They are diametrically opposed to each other. The implication of this is that

---

[130] Section 77 of the Evidence Act.
[131] (1865) Le & Ca. 530.
[1] F. Nwadialo, *op. cit.*, pg 179.

"character evidence" as used in sections 77 to 82 of the Evidence Act refers only to the evidence of character of a party, not a witness. Hence, section 233 of the Evidence Act states that the credit of a witness may be, impeached by the evidence of a person who testify that they, from their knowledge of the witness, believe him to be unworthy of credit, and by proof that the witness has been bribed, or has accepted the offer of a bribe, or has received any other corrupt inducement to give his evidence. The credibility of a witness could be impeached during the trial if his extra-judicial statement contradicts his evidence during the trial. The Court is duty bound to reject the evidence as unreliable once the extra-judicial evidence of an accused contradicts his evidence at the trial. The dictum of Ogbuagu, JSC in *Agbo* v. *State*[2] is very instructive here. His Lordship stated thus:

> It is settled that the character of the witness for habitual veracity, is an essential ingredient in his credibility. For it is said, that for a man who is capable of uttering deliberate falsehood (as in this case leading to this appeal), in most cases, is capable of doing so under solemn oath. If therefore, it appears that he has formally said or written the contrary of that which he has sworn, his evidence should not have much weight with a jury (I add a court without a jury) and if he has formally sworn the contrary, the fact is conclusive against his credibility.

The import of section 223 of the Act is to cross-examine and ask any questions which tends to test the accuracy, veracity or credibility of the accused; discover who the accused is and what is his position in life and shake his credit, by injuring his character.

The admissibility or otherwise of evidence of character is governed by different rules, depending on the nature of the proceeding.

3. Character Evidence in Civil Cases

Section 78 of the Evidence Act contains the general rule as to character evidence in civil cases. It states as follows:

> In civil cases evidence of the fact that the character of any person concerned is such as to render probable or improbable any conduct imputed to him is inadmissible except in so far as such character appears from facts otherwise relevant.

[2](2006) Vol. 135 LRCN P. 808 at p. 840PZ. See also *Dogo* v. *State* (2001) 1 SNJ 315 at 336.

From the above, evidence of character, whether good or bad, is generally inadmissible in law. However, the general rule is subject to the following exceptions.

a. Where such character appears from facts otherwise relevant

This exception is contained in the closing part of section 78 as seen above. The phrase "facts otherwise relevant" refers to relevant facts in the proceeding apart from the character of the party itself. This is usually the case when the character of a party is in issue. An instance of this is in an action for defamation where the defendant, while raising the defence of justification, gives evidence of the bad character of the plaintiff which was the subject matter of the libellous article or slander. In *Din* v. *African Newspaper Ltd,*[3] the plaintiff sued for libel. The court held that evidence of his previous conviction was admissible because the parties had, in their pleadings, joined issue on the good character of the plaintiff. However, if unlike this case, a defendant does not by his defence assert the truth of the statement complained of, the defendant is not entitled on the trial to give evidence in chief with a view to mitigation of damages, as to the circumstances under which the libel or slander was published, or as to the character of the plaintiff, without the leave of the judge, unless seven (7) days at least before the trial, he furnishes particulars to the plaintiff of the matters as to which he intends to give evidence.[4] In *Iloabachie* v. *Iloabachie,*[5] the appellant brought an action against the respondent for libel claiming the sum of ₦5,000.00 as special and general damages and for an injunction restraining the respondent from further production of the defamatory words. At the trial, the respondent set up, *inter alia*, the defence of justification, which was not pleaded. At the end of the trial, the trial court held that the defence of justification was established. The appellant, dissatisfied with the judgment, appealed to the Court of Appeal where he argued that the respondent could not raise the defence of justification, having not pleaded it. The Court of Appeal after construing the provision of section 71 of the Evidence Act 2004, now section 80 of the present Act, held that section 71 only applied to evidence elicited during examination in chief. Thus, the respondent acted within the provision, as the dent made on the

---

[3] (1990) 3 NWLR (Pt. 139) 392 S.C.
[4] Section 80 of the Evidence Act.
[5] (2000) 5 NWLR (Pt. 656) 178. CA.

appellant was not from the testimonies of the respondent but from the evidence given by the appellant himself extracted under cross-examination from the documents tendered by the respondents with a view to mitigate damages.

The exception of "character appearing from facts otherwise relevant" has also become an express route to the admissibility of previous convictions in subsequent civil proceeding. In *Onyewole* v. *Kelani*,[6] the court held that evidence of conviction for an offence is not admissible in a subsequent civil trial. However, in view of the exception in section 78 of the Evidence Act and the express provision of section 63 of the Act,[7] the decision in *Onyewole* v. *Kelani* no longer represents the law. The admission of conviction for an offence in a subsequent civil matter was beautifully explained by Hon.[8] The learned writer states as follows:

> In civil suits, relevancy is determined by the nature of pleadings, hence if an accident, for instance occurs and Mr. A was convicted, say for recklessness, and this fact is pleaded by B in a subsequent civil suit for damages resulting from the accident, nothing stops B in that civil suit from tendering in evidence the record of conviction of A in the previous criminal trial, because such (record of) conviction would "appear from" (or be linked with) "facts otherwise relevant", which are the accident and other collateral matters like negligence, etc.

Another instance where the character of a party may be a fact in issue is an action for breach of promise to marry. Therefore, a defendant may raise a plaintiff's bad character as a defence for the breach of promise to marry.

In the same vein, in an action for libel where the plaintiff sues for damages, claiming to be of good reputation or character, and the defendant raises the defence of justification and pleads previous conviction (in effect puncturing the plaintiff's claim of good character), evidence of such previous conviction will be admissible in proof of such defence of justification.[9] Evidence of such bad character of the plaintiff may also be admissible in an action for defamation of character, to mitigate the quantum of damages.[10]

---

[6] (1948) 12 WACA 327.

[7] This section makes the evidence of conviction for an offence admissible in civil proceedings if relevant to any issue in such civil proceeding.

[8] S.T Hon, *op. cit.*, pg 1315.

[9] *Din* v. *African Newspapers Ltd.* (1990) 3 NWLR (Pt. 139) 392 SC.

[10] *Associated Newspapers Ltd.* v. *Dingle* (1961) AC 371.

b. Mitigation of damages

Notwithstanding section 78 of the Act, in civil cases, the fact that the character of any person is such as to affect the amount of damages which he ought to receive may be given in evidence.[11] Evidence of bad character of the plaintiff may also be admissible to mitigate damages in a divorce proceedings where adultery is relied on.[12]

Finally, evidence of bad character of the plaintiff may be admissible to mitigate damages in an action for breach of promise to marry.[13]

Evidence of Character in Criminal Proceedings

For ease of comprehension and proper appreciation of evidence of character in criminal proceedings, we shall streamline our discussion into two categories to wit: Evidence of good character and evidence of bad character making recourse to exceptions under each stated category.

a. Evidence of Good Character: In Criminal proceedings, evidence of the fact that a defendant is of good character is admissible.[14] This rule accords with common sense. Evidence of good character benefits a defendant in two ways. Before a defendant is convicted for an offence, evidence of his good character will certainly render his evidence more credible and may influence the judge when giving judgment, especially when there's no substantial incriminating evidence against the defendant. It must be quickly noted, however, that only in the most exceptional cases should a judge be swayed mainly by the good character of a defendant for it does not in the slightest, prove innocence though it can play a role during allocutus as an extenuating factor. In *Haruna* v. *Police,*[15] the defendant was charged with abetting armed robbery of a bank. The oral testimony of the bank manager to the effect that the defendant was financially sound and never got into trouble was held admissible.

In addition, evidence of character may be important after the conviction of a defendant. This becomes the case when the court takes into consideration the defendant's clean records etc. in mitigation of the sentence of the defendant. Thus, such good character helps to reduce the defendant's sentence which might otherwise have been heavy and thus serve as an extenuating circumstances in punishment and sentencing.

---

[11] Section 79 of the Evidence Act

[12] *Butterworth* v. *Butterworth* (1836) P. 126 @ 145

[13] See *Jefferson* v. *Paskell* (1916) 1 KB 57.

[14] See section 81 of the Evidence Act.

[15] (1967) NMLR 145.

b. **Evidence of Bad Character:** The general rule is that evidence of an accused's bad character is not admissible. This is in line with the statutory provision under Section 82(1) of the Evidence Act which states that "Except as provided in this section, evidence of the fact that a defendant is of bad character is inadmissible in criminal proceeding." It went further to provide that the fact that a defendant is of bad character is admissible in the following circumstances: This underscores the circumstances under which evidence of bad character can be admissible. They are:

i. When the bad character of the defendant is a fact in issue[16]

The evidence that an accused has a bad character is admissible if that fact is in issue.[17] The fact is said to be in issue when it is an ingredient of the offence or offences which the defendant is charged with.

Such evidence of bad character is usually evidence of previous conviction.[18] Some examples of such offences are the offence of being a rogue and vagabond under section 250(1) of the Criminal Code. Similarly, in order to prove guilty knowledge in a charge of receiving stolen property under section 427 of the Criminal Code, the fact that within the five years preceding the date of that charge, the accused was convicted of any offence involving fraud or dishonesty may be proved.[19] If the character of the defendant is not in issue, evidence of bad character remains inadmissible. In *Odogwu* v. *The State,*[20] the appellant was charged with murder of the deceased. During the trial, one of the prosecution's witnesses stated:

> from my observation of the accused, she has a good temperament but she is slippery. The accused does immoral things and immediately you accuse her she will be crying. The accused's moral life is questionable. On several occasions, the accused travelled outside the state with other men and the accused herself rang the deceased from Lagos to Owerri announcing her whereabout (sic).

The Court of Appeal, while demolishing this evidence stated:

> Above all, the evidence tainting the appellant with immorality and showing her generally as bad character (sic) was received in violation of

[16] Section 82 (2) (a) of the Evidence Act.

[17] See section 82(2) (a) of the Evidence Act. See also *Okeke* v. *State* (2016) LPELR-40024 (CA) Pp. 21-22, paras. B-A.

[18] *Din* v. *African Newspapers of (Nig) Ltd* (1990) LPELR-947(SC) P.18, para. A.

[19] Section 36(1)(b) of the Evidence Act.

[20] (2013) 14 NWLR (Pt. 1373) 74 SC.

> section 82 of the Evidence Act...The character of the appellant was not in issue. What was in issue was whether or not she killed the deceased. She had not testified at the time the witnesses gave evidence and so she could not have made her character an issue in the trial, nor did she do so in her statement other than a denial of the charge.

What the court is enjoined to consider, in overall, is the probative value of the accused before the court vis-à-vis the evidence that is presented before the court in arriving at a just determination of the case, and to do otherwise is to put on the scale, the prejudicial value of the accused in the determination of the case. This, the law abhors and frowns at.

ii. When the defendant has given evidence of his good character[21]

Another exception to the inadmissibility of bad character of a defendant is captured under section 82(2)(b) of the Evidence Act. Thus where the defendant has given evidence of his good character, the prosecution, naturally, has to rebut this evidence; otherwise, the defendant may not be convicted. Where the accused person creates a false impression or pads his character where he ought not to have, the prosecution could lead evidence to show the contrary. We may seek reliance on the persuasive Canadian case of *Less* v. *R*[22] In this case, the defendant had given evidence of a clean record and evidence from a psychiatrist that he was of no danger to the community. In reply, the prosecution called evidence to show that he was planning another robbery, having spent all the money he made from the first robbery. The Supreme Court of Canada held that the evidence of bad character called by the prosecution was admissible. Conversely, where the defendant has not put evidence of his good character in line, evidence of his bad character remains inadmissible. Coming back home, in *Musa* v. *State,*[23] the allusion by the prosecution and the learned trial judge to the bad character of the Appellant, based on Exhibit "A" was punctured and faulted by the appellate Court as being in bad taste. The court went further to hold that evidence of bad character of the appellant was irrelevant to the consideration of his conviction and sentence since he did not give evidence of good character. The evidence of the appellant's bad character was not in issue before the

---

[21] Section 82 (2) (b) of the Evidence Act.

[22] (1979) 10 C.R (3d) 5-17. The position of the common law is that evidence of rebuttal must be proportionate to the same limits as that to which is in answer.

[23] (2012) LPELR-20428 (CA).

lower court and the allusion to it as quoted by the learned trial judge is wrong. Regrettably, this influenced the opinion of the lower court in passing sentence but was upturned on appeal.

iii Evidence of bad character in the circumstances mentioned in paragraph (g) of the proviso to section 180

Section 82(3) of the Evidence Act states that, "a defendant may be asked questions to show that he is of bad character" in the circumstances mentioned in paragraph (c) [24] of the proviso to section 180.

Section 180 (g) provides as follows:

> A person charged and called as a witness in pursuance of this section shall not be asked, and if asked, shall not be required to answer, any question tending to show he has committed or been convicted of or been charged with any offence other than that with which he is then charged; or is of bad character unless-
>
> (i) The proof that he has committed or been convicted of such other offence is admissible evidence to show that he is guilty of the offence with which he is then charged, or
>
> (ii) He has personally or by his legal practitioner asked questions of the witnesses for the prosecution with a view to establish his own good character or has given evidence of his good character or the nature or conduct of the defence is such as to involve imputations on the prosecutor or the witness for the prosecution, or he has given evidence against any other person charged with the same offence.

Permit me to say that section 180(g) is identical with section 1 of the Criminal Evidence Act 1898 of England. Hence, decisions of the English courts will be largely relied upon in interpreting the above provisions. The expression "tending to show" was expounded upon in the English case of *Jones* v. *DPP.*[25] In that case, an accused disclosed in his examination-in-chief that he had previously been in trouble with the police in connection with an earlier conviction for another offence and the prosecution cross-examined him on the similarity between the explanations he gave about his movements on the occasions of that offence and the one under trial. The

---

[24] This is obviously a typographical error as it should read section 180(g).

[25] (1962) AC 647.

court held that "tending to show" as used in the Criminal Evidence Act 1898[26] meant tending to reveal or disclose for the first time rather than tending to prove. Therefore, it was held that the cross-examination was proper as the fact of the earlier conviction was revealed by the accused himself.

The exceptions to the rule provided in section 180 (g) (i), (ii), (iii), are examined below for proper appreciation of the subject matter.

i. Section 180 (g) (i): Where previous conviction or commission of the offence is relevant to prove guilt of accused

When proof that the defendant had committed or been convicted of an offence is relevant to prove guilt of the defendant for the offence charged, the defendant may be asked questions to show that he has been convicted of or been charged with that offence. This may arise when evidence of similar facts is admissible under section 12 of the Evidence Act. However, the questions asked by the prosecution must relate to whether he has committed or been convicted of an offence and not whether he has been charged and acquitted of it.[27]

ii. Section 180(g) (ii)

If the defendant has put his character in issue, either personally or by his legal practitioner, by asking questions with a view to establishing his good character or gives evidence of his good character, the prosecution may ask him questions which shows he has previously committed or been convicted of or been charged with an offence other than that with which he is presently charged with. Similarly, if the defendant puts prosecution witnesses' character in issue by making imputations on the prosecutor or their witnesses, the prosecution may also ask questions as to whether he had committed or been convicted or been charged of an offence other than that with which he is presently charged. However, the defendant does not give evidence of his good character when such good character is elicited from him during cross-examination by the prosecution[28] or when evidence of good character is inadvertently given.[29] A good instance of where a

[26]Identical with section 180(g) of the Evidence Act 2011.
[27]*R* v. *Cokar* (1960) 2 QB 207.
[28]*R* v. *Beecham* (1921) 2 KB 464.
[29]*R* v. *Redd* (1923) KB 104.

defendant put his character in issue is captured in *R* v. *Samuel*.[30] In that case, the defendant was charged with stealing a camera found in his possession some weeks after. The defendant gave evidence at the trial that on two earlier occasions, he had found items belonging to other person and returned them to their owners. Consequently, the prosecution had to rebut his claim of honesty by cross-examining him as to his previous conviction. In respect of the second arm of section 180 (g) (ii), a defendant may make imputations against the persecutor or witnesses for the prosecution in many ways such as alleging that a witness for the prosecution was the actual person who committed the offence,[31] or alleging that the prosecution had bribed the defendant to confess to the crime,[32] or that the prosecutor is drunk.[33] However, the court noted in *R* v. *Rouse*[34] that a mere denial of the allegation of the prosecution, even if done in very strong terms, cannot amount to imputations on the accused. Also, in *R* v. *Cook*,[35] it was held that a judge should warn the defence of the consequences of giving evidence or acting in such a way as would put his character or the prosecution's witnesses' character in issue, though a failure to do this will usually not lead to the conviction of the defendant being quashed.

iii. Section 180 (g) (iii)

Evidence by an accused against a co-accused opens the floodgates to examination of the accused as to previous conviction of an offence or commission of an offence or as to whether he has been previously charged with an offence other than that with which he is presently charged with. In *Anyanwu* v. *The Queen*,[36] the Federal Supreme Court held that where an accused giving evidence had made himself liable to cross examination as to his character or convictions by giving evidence against another person charged with the same offence, the judge has no overriding discretion to allow or disallow such cross-examination as it might be put as a matter of right. This is opposed to the first two exceptions where the trial judge "must weigh the prejudicial effect of the questions against the damage done by the attack on the prosecution's witnesses and must generally exercise his discretion so as to secure a trial that is fair both to the prosecution and the

---

[30] (1956) 40 CAR 8.
[31] *R* v. *Hudson* (1912) 21 KB.
[32] *R* v. *Wright* (1910) 5 Cr App R 131.
[33] Holmes (1899) 43 SJ 219.
[34] (1904) 1KB 184 at 187.
[35] (1959) 2 QB 340.
[36] (1963) 1 All NIR 273.

defence[37] and may, therefore, disallow questions barred by section 180(g) even if they come within its exceptions.[38] Though a co-accused is entitled to examine an accused as to previous convictions or charge by virtue of section 180(g) (iii), he cannot establish an accused's previous conviction of or commission of a different offence through an independent witness even if the accused had given evidence against him.[39]

---

[37] *R* v. *Burke* (1985) 82 Cr App R 156.
[38] *R* v. *Watts* (1983) 77 Cr App R 126.
[39] *R* v. *Butterwasser* (1948) 1KB 4.

Chapter 10

PRESUMPTIONS

Introduction

The term presumption can be construed as an inference as to the existence of one fact from the existence of some other facts, founded on a previous experience of their connection. For someone to presume, there must be a connection between the known and the inferred facts as to such a nature that the existence of one thing, which is established, admitted or assumed or an existence or an inference as to the existence of the other. Presumptions may be certain or not certain and is capable of being rebutted by contrary proof. As a general rule, presumption amounts to a proof of fact when it is the usual, but not invariably consequential. Presumptions are weak, it carries no weight, and it could be legal or artificial depending on the basis of such presumption.

In ordinary sense, presumption is derived wholly by means of a common experience of mankind or from the courses of nature and the ordinary habits of society. Presumption in its legal parlance can be referred to as an inference, to infer on the existence or non-existence of a fact which can be seen as a fact in issue. The evidence Act used the word presumption in various sections, but did not define it. However, a presumption is a conclusion that may not be drawn from a given set of circumstances unless and until the contrary has been proved. In other words, the court is at discretion to come to a conclusion.[1] The court in *Karimu* v. *State*,[2] elucidated that the term presumption is better described than defined. On a bid to give an exhaustive meaning of the word, "to presume" means to infer though there is a possibility of rebuttal.

Classifications of presumption

1. Presumption of Law

Presumption of law is classified into irrebuttable presumptions of law and rebuttable presumptions of law. Presumption of law is a preliminary rule of

---

[1] Tony Ukam, *Evidence Compendium*, (Cross River State: Orak Wise Publication 2012) P. 239.

[2] (2005) ACLR 438 at 443.

law which may appear in the face of rebuttal evidence. However, in the absence of no evidence to the contrary, the presumption stands.[3]

Presumptions of law are in reality, rules of law and part of the law itself, and a court may draw the inference whenever the requisite facts are developed in the pleadings.[4] Presumptions are unstintingly founded on reasons of public policy, social convenience and safety which are warranted by the legal experience of courts in the administration of Justice. At times, presumptions are to be conceived as conclusive rules of law, otherwise known as, irrebuttable presumptions of law. Other presumptions of law may be regarded as prima facie evidence and may be rebutted. Lawrence Atsegbua,[5] in his erudition, posited that presumptions of law can be either absolute or conclusive, notwithstanding that certain presumptions of law are rebuttable. Section 145(1)(2) and (3) of the Evidence Act provides for rules as to presumptions by the court.

Section 145(1) provides thus:

> Whenever it is provided by this Act that the court may presume a fact, it may either regard such fact as proved unless and until it is disproved, or may call for proof of it.
>
> (2) Whenever it is directed by this Act that the court shall presume a fact, it shall regard such fact as proved unless and until it is disproved.
>
> (3) When one fact is declared by this Act to be conclusive proof of another, the court shall, on proof of the one fact, regard the other as proved and shall not allow evidence to be given for the purpose of disproving it.

The above provision is geared towards laying a foundation as to the presumptive measures and mechanism on the part of the court to obviate certain facts either as conclusive or resplendently ruminated.

2. Irrebuttable presumption of law

An irrebuttable presumption of law can be seen as the process whereby the court draws a conclusion from proved facts, especially on the proof of certain facts where evidence in rebuttal is not allowed. Section 30 of the

---

[3] S. A. Awomolo: "Presumptions" in Afe Babalola ed., *Law and Practice of Evidence in Nigeria* (Ibadan: SIBON Books 2001) at P. 361.

[4] Ibid.

[5] Lawrence Atsegbua, *Law of Evidence* (Benin: Justice Jeco printing and Publishing Global, 2012) p?

Criminal Code provides that a child below the age of seven years is presumed to be incapable of committing an offence. The same view is expressed by section 50 of the Penal Code.[6] These are instances of irrebuttable presumption of law.

It is an irrebuttable presumption of law that a male child under the age of 12 year is presumed incapable of having carnal knowledge of a woman or a girl.[7] It is trite law that every judgment delivered by a court of competent jurisdiction is a conclusive proof of the matter decided therein, except where the court in question lacks the locus in quo or the veritable jurisdiction to entertain such matter. Where the latter is the case, it can be said that such judgment is null and void.[8]

Irrebuttable presumption of law is expressed in the Latin maxim "*eaque alia estiuris*". Section 145(3) of the Evidence Act deals predominantly with irrebuttable presumptions of law. Presumptions of law are usually in favour of the defendant or the accused person. They are conclusive and final. It must be stressed that presumptions of law are prescribed by law. Consequently, the procedure for the application and implementation of presumptions of law are fixed and uniform and therefore alters the burden of proof in an issue.[9]

3. Rebuttable presumptions of law

A rebuttable presumption is the conclusion which must be drawn unless and until rebutted by evidence to the contrary. Examples of such presumptions are: presumption of innocence, presumption of marriage, presumption of legitimacy and presumption of sanity plus a lot more of presumptions.

In *Isma'il* v. *State*,[10] the Supreme Court made an expository remark on the subject matter thus:

> In the Halsbury's Law of England Fourth Edition Re-Issue Volume 11(2), paragraph 1108 9 page 883, which deals with rebuttable presumptions of law, the authors encapsulated the presumption thus: "A rebuttable presumption of law is one which leads to a decision on a particular issue in favour of the party who establishes it or relies upon it, unless it is rebutted. Rebuttable presumptions of law may be created by statute, or may exist as common law, and may cast either a legal or an evidential

---

[6] Penal Code, Section 50.
[7] Section 50 of the Criminal Code 1990.
[8] Section 54 (1) of the Evidence Act 2011.
[9] Lawrence Atsegbua, *op. cit.*, at pg 245.
[10] (2011) LPELR-9352 (SC) P. 39 paras C-F.

> burden on the party seeking to rebut the presumption, except that it is a rule of the common law that (save in the case of a defence of insanity) the accused cannot be required to discharge the legal burden of proof.

Rebuttable presumption of law is statutorily recognised under section 145 (2) of the Act. The inoculate effect of rebuttable presumptions of law is to shift the burden of proof until it is disproved by contrary evidence. When the law presumes a fact, such fact could be rebutted if there is a contrary evidence or testimony presented to the court. It is within the discretion of the court in view of the evidence adduced, to decide either way as to when a presumption has been rebutted.

Under the presumptions of law which are considered rebuttable, we shall examine several areas and fields of law to ascertain whether or not they could be termed irrebuttable or rebuttable.

4. Presumption of Innocence

It is a cardinal constitutional requirement that every person charged with a criminal offence shall be presumed innocent until proven guilty.[11] This is common presumption of law. Where an accused person has been charged with a criminal offence, to this extent, it is presumed that he is innocent until evidence has been led to show that he is guilty of the offence charged. Under the Nigeria criminal jurisprudence, an accused person has a fundamental right as to the presumption of his innocence under the constitution. However, the burden or the onus is on the prosecution to prove the guilt of an accused beyond reasonable doubt and any slightest doubt raised by the accused shall lead the court to resolve the doubt in favour of the accused which may lead to his discharge and acquittal. While the prosecution must prove the guilt of an accused person, there is no corresponding burden laid on the accused person to prove his innocence. An accused person is presumed to be innocent until his guilt of the offence is established. The above view was captured by the court in *Nweneke* v. *State.*[12] The court reiterated the position of this constitutional safeguard with respect to the presumption of innocence as contained in section 36(5) of the Constitution in *Ekele* v. *FRN.*[13] In the words of the learned justice of the Court of Appeal, IGE JCA,

[11] Section 36 (5) 1999 Constitution of the Federal Republic of Nigeria as Amended.
[12](2019) LPELR-47018 (CA) P.21, para. F.
[13](2018) LPELR-45831 (CA) Pp. 11-12, Paras. G-B.

> The presumption of innocence is the legal principle in criminal cases that one is considered innocent until proven guilty. This basically means that until a judicial pronouncement on the guilt or otherwise of the accused person is made, he/she is to be treated the same as a regular person, any suggestion to the opposite would be a breach of the fundamental human rights of the individual. Section 36(5) of the Constitution of the Federal Republic of Nigeria 1999 as amended guarantees this right.

The court in *Auta* v. *The State*[14] posited that the Constitution of the Federal Republic of Nigeria, 1999 (as amended), by virtue of the provision made thereto under section 36(5) provides that any person who is charged with a criminal offence is presumed to be innocent until he is proved guilty by due process of the rule of law. This trite principle of law has universal applicability, at least in those jurisdictions, where the principles of Common law are in place. Thus, the principle or doctrine of presumption of innocence has all through, guided the courts of the land in all criminal prosecutions. The court went further to state that the general aim of this principle of presumption of innocence is to protect the accused person against any judicial decision or other statement by state officials relating to an assessment of the guilt of any person without him having previously been proved guilty according to law.

On this note, it is submitted that where the law presumes the innocence of an accused, such presumption is rebuttable upon the presentation of adequate, substantive and credible evidence. The above view was captured by the court in *Amadi* v. *State.*[15] Presumption of innocence can only be rebutted by proof beyond reasonable doubt.[16]

5. Presumption of Legitimacy[17]

The law has always acknowledged the right of a woman to say who the father of her child is, and of course, where a child is born within wedlock, the presumption is conclusive, that the child is the seed or product of the marriage.[18] Thus, presumption of legitimacy is provided for under section 165 of the Act and section 115 of the Matrimonial Causes Act. There is a

---

[14](2018) LPELR-44490 (CA) Pp. 16-17, paras. E-C.

[15] (2018) LPELR-46077 (CA). See also *Ekele* v. *FRN* (2018) LPELR-45831 (CA).

[16] Ibid.

[17] *Idahosa* v. *Idahosa & Ors* (2010) LPELR-9072 (CA) Pp. 39-40, paras. C-A.

[18] See *Tony Anozia* v. *Mrs. Patricia Okwunwa Nnani & Anor* (2015) LPELR-24277 (CA) P. 18, paras. C-D. See also *Anozie* v. *Uwakwe & Anor* (2016) LPELR-40554 (CA) and *Duru* v. *Duru* (2016) LPELR-40444(CA) P. 37, paras. E-F.

presumption that a child conceived and born during the continuance of a valid marriage between a man and a women or within 280 days after the dissolution of the marriage, if the mother remains unmarried, is the legitimate child of the man. This view applies to both statutory and customary marriages. It is a cardinal requirement that before such presumption is invoked, sexual intercourse must have taken place between the spouses.[19]

The Supreme Court judicially activated the above in *Elumeze* v. *Elumeze*[20] by stating that any child born by the wife of a valid marriage is the legitimate child of the husband or if he was born within 280 days after the dissolution of the marriage. Unless it can be proved that the husband and wife had no access to each other or no sexual Intercourse took place between the spouses.

In *Egwunwoke* v. *Egwunwoke,*[21] the petitioner filed an application for dissolution of marriage. While the petition was still pending, the respondent filed an application against the petitioner for payment of maintenance with respect to the child alleged to be the child of the marriage. It was held that until the contrary is proved, where a child is born in wedlock, intercourse is presumed to have taken place between the husband and wife resulting in the birth of the child. Since it was not disputed that the child was born during the subsistence of the marriage, there is presumption that the child is the legitimate child of the marriage.

Where a marriage occurs between a husband and a wife and such conjugal matrimony lasted, there is a presumption that a child conceived or born during its continuance is legitimate unless it can be shown that the husband and wife had no access to each other and that the circumstances of the access, if any, was to render it highly improbable that sexual intercourse took place between them.[22]

Consequently, where a man and a woman in law are proved to have lived together as husband and wife, it is presumed by law unless the contrary is proved, that they are living together in consequence of a valid marriage and not in a state of concubinage.[23] Imagine a situation where a Yoruba man is married to "Miss A", under the marriage Act and during the subsistence of

---

[19] Lawrence Atsegbua, *op. cit.*, at Pg. 248.
[20] (1969). All NLR 311 at 317.
[21](1966) 2 All NLR1.
[22]*Ogbole* v. *Onah* (1990) 1 NWLR 357.
[23] Ibid.

that marriage, he had a child "P" by another woman, who also had a second child for him. Six weeks after the death of the wife, he acknowledges the two children as his children. After the birth of the second child, he got married again to yet another woman "Miss B" under the marriage Act. The Court will infer that "P" is not a legitimate child under the recognized system of law. There is a presumption of legitimacy in favour of second child under customary law.[24]

Presumption is rebuttable by the presentation of evidence showing that it is repugnant to natural justice equity and good conscience.[25] In *Anozia* v. *Nnani*,[26] the court held that a presumption can be rebutted by evidence showing that it would be repugnant to natural justice equity and good conscience and also contrary to public policy.

6. Presumption of sanity

Ordinarily, in law, everyone is presumed to be sane and of sound mind and accountable for his actions, unless the contrary is proved. But where there is defect or incapacity of the understanding, as there can be no consent of the will, the act is not punishable as a crime.[27]

It is a general principle of law that everyone is presumed to be of sound mind until the contrary is proved.[28] This presumption also includes that an accused person is fit to stand trial until the contrary is proved.[29] The onus to rebut such presumption encapsulated by law is on the defence to prove and establish insanity on the balance of probability especially where the defence of insanity is raised *in limine* (at the very beginning) of the trial.[30]

When a person is presented to the court to give testimony or evidence about a given fact, the court looks at the following: what is the mental capacity of the witness at the time he was brought to testify? Does he possess the mental moment vis-à-vis the *corpus mentis* to give evidence in court. The above must be established before rendering admissible any evidence or statement made by such person.[31] The Court of Appeal in *Oseni* v. *State*[32] held that:

---

[24] *Olubunmi Cole* v. *P.A. Akinyele & Anor* (1960) 5 F.S.C. 84.
[25] *Mariyana* v. *Sadiku Ejo* (1961) NRNLR. 81.
[26] (2015)8 NWLR Pt. 1461 p. 244.
[27] See *Adamu* v. *State* (2014) LPELR-22696(SC) P. 25, paras. B-C. per Ariwoola JSC. See also *State* v. *John* (2013) LPELR-20590 (SC) P. 18, paras. C-D per Rhodes Vivour JSC.
[28] Section 27 (1) of the Criminal Code 1990.
[29] *Queen* v. *Ogor* (1961) All NLR 70 at 75.
[30] Criminal Code Act Section 28(1).
[31] *Oladele* v. *State* (1993) 1 S.C.N.J. 60.
[32] (2017) LPELR-42770 (CA) P. 42, Paras, A-E.

Generally, however, the law presumes that every person, unless the contrary is proved, is sane and accountable for his actions. However, circumstances may arise when that presumption of sanity may be negatived or rebutted. One of such circumstances may arise where the actor or assailant is found to be afflicted by insanity or insane delusion. In the case of *Ani* v. *State* (2002) 10 NWLR (pt.776) p.644, Katsina-Alu, JSC (as he then was) said:

"Every person is, unless the contrary is proved, presumed by law to be sane, and to be accountable for his actions. But it (sic, if) there is an incapacity, or defect of understanding, as there can be no consent of the will, the act is not punishable as a crime. Whether the accused person was sane in the legal sense at the time when the act was committed is a question of fact to be decided by the trial Judge and not by medical men however eminent, and is dependent upon the previous and contemporaneous acts of the accused."

7. Presumption of Death

This presumption arises where a person has not been heard of for seven years, there is a presumption that he is dead; but as to what time between the period that he died is not a matter of presumption, but of evidence and the onus of proving that the death took place at any particular time within seven years lies upon the person who claims a right to the establishment of which that fact is essential.[33] There is no presumption in law in favour of the continuance of life though an inference of fact may be drawn that a person alive and healthy on a particular day was alive a short time afterwards.[34]

It is noteworthy that for this presumption to be invoked, two conditions must be met:

(A) the person must have been absent for seven years or more;

(B) those who would naturally heard of him have not heard of him.

The latter condition includes husband or wife, parents or children or guardians.

By virtue of Section 164 of the Act, there are certain circumstances in which a person is presumed dead or presumed to have died. Thus, the court in *Olude* v. *State*[35] illuminated on the law when it held that a person shown not to have been heard of for seven years by those, if any, who if he had been alive would naturally have heard of him, is presumed to be dead unless the

---

[33] See *Chinedu Ekuma* v. *The State* (2018) LPELR-44633 (CA) P. 14, paras D-E. See also *Kehinde Olude* v. *The State* (2018) LPELR-44070 (SC) P. 34, paras. B-C per Kekere-Ekun JSC.

[34] *Re- Phene's Trust* (1870) L.R 5 Chap 139.

[35] (2018) LPELR-44070 (SC) P. 34, paras. B-C.

circumstances of the case are such as to assume his death. However, there is no presumption as to the time when he died and the burden of proving his death at any particular time is upon the person who asserts it.[36] What amounts to hearing of someone include hearing from him and also hearing about him from someone who knows him. There is no presumption as to the age at which a person died.[37]

Section 164(2) of the Act provides for where two or more person dies simultaneously, say in an accident, it is presumed that the eldest of the persons died first for the purpose of determining title to property.

8. Presumption of Regularity

This presumption was coined from a Latin expression, *Omnia praesumuntur rite esse acta"* meaning: "All acts are presumed to have been done rightly and regularly." This presumption is commonly applied to official acts and documents. Thus, the court in *7up Bottling Co.* v. *Ugwu & Ors*[38] held that the law by section 168(1) of the Evidence Act, 2011 presumes the regularity of an official act until the contrary is proved by preponderance of evidence. There are indeed plethora of sections in the Evidence Act dealing with certain acts and documents. Section 146 of the Act provides that the court shall presume every document purporting to be a certificate, certified copy or other document, which is by law declared to be admissible as evidence of any particular fact and which purports to be duly certified by any officer in Nigeria who is duly authorized in that behalf to be genuine, provided that such document is substantially in the form and purport to be executed in the manner directed by law. Extrapolating from the above-mentioned section, there is as a general rule, a presumption as to the genuineness of certified copies of a document.

Also, section 147 deals with presumption as to documents produced as record of evidence. Section 148 also deals with presumption as to gazettes, newspapers, Act of the National Assembly, and other documents.[39] The court exercises the discretion of presuming whether a document or copies of documents are genuine depending on the manner in which such document is tendered. There is a presumption, though rebuttable, of regularity in the

---

[36] Section 164 (1) of the Evidence Act 2011.

[37] *Prudential Assurance Co* v. *Edmonds* (1877) 2 AC 487.

[38] (2017) LPELR-42685 (CA) P. 14, paras. C-D. See also *Adigun* v. *Ibadan North Local Govt.* (2016) LPELR-41385 (CA).

[39] See *Chiaghana & Anor* v. *Govt of Anambra State & Ors.* (2016) LPELR-42096 (CA) Pp. 31-35, paras. F-C.

registration of the document. However, the burden of adducing evidence in rebuttal is on the party challenging the document.[40] The court in *Anyanwu* v. *Nwachukwu & Ors*[41] while validating a document in line with section 155 of the Act held thus:

> I am also not oblivious of the fact that Exhibits B and C are registered instruments relating to title and that those documents are/were in fact over 20 (Twenty) years old being made in 1971 and 1978 respectively and ordinarily by the provisions of Section 123 Evidence Act, Laws of the Federation 2004 (now Section 155 Evidence Act, 2011): "Where any document purporting or proved to be twenty years old or more is produced from any custody which the court in the particular case considers proper, the court may presume that the signature and every other part of such document which purports to be in the handwriting of any particular person is in that persons handwriting, and, in the case of a document executed or attested, that it was duly executed and attested by the persons by whom it purports to be executed and attested" [42]

Other sections like section 149, 150, 151, 152, 153 down to section 163 are streamlined on document the court would presume upon the presentation of such document. It is worthy to note that the court is at discretion to presume certain facts and ascertain whether certain document could be admissible based on the court's intuitive presumption. The Supreme Court in *Michael Dan Udo* v. *Chief Christopher Eshiet*[43] per *Niki Tobi J.S.C.* postulated thus:

> It is the law that determines whether the court is entitled to presume the regularity of documents made until the contrary is proved by way of rebuttal.

The court has the capacity to presume the regularity of judgments or rulings until it is set aside on appeal.[44] The above judicial decision was extracted and adhered to by the court placing reliance on the relevant sections of the Evidence Act. Section 168 of the Act deals with the

---

[40] See *Ayodele Ilori & Ors* v. *Alhaja Risikat Ishola & Anor* (2018) LPELR-44063 (SC).
[41] (2017) LPELR-42849 (CA).
[42] See also *Jagaba & Ors* v. *Umar* (2016) LPELR-40466 (CA) P. 42, paras. B-F.
[43] (2004) 8 NWLR, pt. 363, 483 at 500.
[44] *Albion Construction Company Ltd* v. *R.A.O Investment & Properties Ltd.* (1992) NWLR (Pt.219) p. 583 at p 595.

presumption of due execution of document which entitles a person to be the beneficial owner of property. In a recent decision of the Supreme Court in *Architect Hudu Ibrahim Mamonu & Anor* v. *Joseph D. Mato Dikat & Ors.*[45] Eko JSC posited thus:

> Equity follows the law. It takes as done that which ought to be done. Section 168(1) of the Evidence Act, 2011 provides that when an official act, as done by the presiding officer in the instant case, is shown to have been done in a manner substantially regular, it is presumed that formal requisites for its validity were complied with.

The court had applied the above section in an earlier case of *Aja* v. *Odin*[46] In this case, it was held that by virtue of section 64(3) of the Electoral Act, 2006, the presiding officer shall give to the polling agents and the police officer where available, a copy each of the completed forms after it has been duly signed. Such forms enjoy the presumption of regularity under the Act being an official act.

Also in *House of Reps* v. *S.P.D.C.N*,[47] the court held that section 146(1) of the Act which provides for the presumption as to genuineness of copies of document is admissible under the law, where the law will presume that a certified copy of such document is genuine and that it has been regularly certified as a copy of the original by the officer charged with the responsibility of doing so. Presumption of the regularity of a document is to be determined by the court and whether the parties had complied with the procedural requirements for the tendering of the documents in court as evidence in support is a question of fact.

9. Presumption of fact

Presumption of fact is the logic inference of the existence of one fact from the proved existence of other facts. In most cases, it exists as a form of inference from circumstantial evidence. By virtue of section 145(1) of the Evidence Act, whenever it is provided that the court may presume a fact, the court may either regard such fact as proved unless and until it is disproved or it may call for proof of it. Section 167 of the Evidence Act stipulates that the court may presume the existence of any fact which it deems likely to have

---

[45] (2019) LPELR-46560 (SC) P. 61, paras. C-E per Eko JSC.
[46] (2011) 5 NWLR pt. 1241, p. 509 at 516.
[47] (2012) 11 NMLR pt. 1205 p 213 and 220- 227.

happened, regard being had to the common course of natural events, human conduct and public and private business in their relationship to the facts of a particular case.[48] Section 167 of the Act provides for presumption of certain facts which are of frequent occurrence. The above section sets out various circumstances upon which the court can presume a fact and these circumstances would be examined in sequence.

In *Umar* v. *Bailey & Ors*,[49] the court held that in the Law of Wills, there is a common law presumption that a testator would ordinarily have regards to his estate particularly his family and dependants. Thus, where a testator by his Will denies or deprives legacies or bequest to such natural objects e.g. wife, sons, daughter, it ordinarily raises doubts and imposes a heavy onus on the proponents of that Will. In the case at hand, the testator Dr. A. Bailey adequately provided for his sons in his Will made on 11/3/98 which the testator further confirmed by two subsequent codicils of 21/5/2003 and 5/8/2004. For the testator to turn around and make Exhibit 'E' on 21/3/2005 thereby depriving his sons of the estate regardless of the dispositions by Will, raises the eyebrows and calls in operation section 167 of the Evidence Act.

10. Presumption of possession and guilty knowledge

As a deduction from the previous subtopic, section 167 provides that the court may presume the existence of any fact which it deems likely to have happened, regard shall be had to the common course of natural events, human conduct and public and private business, in their relationship to the facts of the particular case,[50] and in particular, the court may presume that: "(a) A man who is in possession of stolen goods soon after the theft is either the thief or has received the goods knowing them to be stolen, unless he accounts for his possession."[51] This evidential provision received judicial blessing and attention in *Ojubayo* v. *State*[52] where the court held thus:

> Appellant was found in possession of the handsets soon after the theft. He is deemed to be the thief or has received the goods knowing them to be stolen unless he can account for his possession by virtue of Section 167 Subsection (a) of the Evidence Act 2011

---

[48] *Bonum (NIG) Ltd* v. *Ibe & Anor* (2019) LPELR-46442 (CA) P. 33, paras. C-E. See also *Hwande* v. *Biem & Ors* (2019) LPELR-46868 (CA).
[49] (2018) LPELR-44285 (CA) Pp. 53-54, paras. C-A.
[50] Ibid. See also *Udoh* v. *State* (2017) LPELR-43733 (CA).
[51] See also *Ojubayo* v. *State* (2017) LPELR-43269 (CA) P. 19, paras. A-F.
[52] *Supra* at P. 19, paras. C-D.

A person who is in possession of a recently stolen property can only be presumed to be either a thief or a receiver but cannot be both. He cannot be a thief and at the same time a receiver to himself of the stolen property.

11. Presumption of Continuance

Section 167(b) provides that a thing or state of things which has been showed to be in existence within a period shorter than that within which such things or state of things usually cease to exist, is still in existence. In the above section, there is a presumption in favour of the continuance of human life. A person alive and healthy is generally presumed to be alive a short while after. The presumption is useful in establishing the fact that a person who occupies an office, prior to a given date, is in the absence of contrary evidence, sufficient to raise the presumption that he is still occupying the office.

In *Sani* v. *C.O.P.*[53] the court held that there is an irrebuttable presumption that he (the Accused) was the person driving the car at the time of the accident unless he can prove the contrary.

12. Presumption of course of business

Section 167(c) of the Act provides that the court may presume that the common course of business has been followed in particular manner. If a particular procedure is always adopted in a transaction, it may be presumed that the same procedure was adopted in a given instance of such transaction. The court in *Dr. Mohammed Ashard* v. *Commissioner of Police*[54] posited that it is presumed that a statement made by a witness to the police and reduced into writing was duly set forth in the case diary.

13. Presumption of Withholding Evidence

By virtue of section 167(d) of the Act, the court may presume that evidence which could be and is not produced would, if produced, be unfavourable to the person who withholds it. Before the presumption can operate, the court must be satisfied that:

(a) the evidence not called exists;
(b) it could be produced;
(c) it has not been produced;
(d) it has been withheld by the person who could produce it.

---

[53](1980) 1 NWLR (289).
[54](1963) NNLR 80.

In *Danbaba* v. *State,*[55] the prosecution withheld the evidence of one Kware Hospital to produce the report of the hospital affirming the mental state of the Appellant. The court while applying section 169(d) of the Evidence Act, held that the evidence withheld, thus raises the presumption that the defence failed to produce evidence, which could be produced, because its production would be unfavourable to their plea of insanity.

In the bid to amplify this rule, the court in *Yusuf* v. *State*[56] held that the rule in section 167(d) applies where a party fails to adduce evidence by withholding evidence which could have been but was not produced. The court while elaborating on the principle of withholding evidence stated that it must be pointed out that there is a distinction between failure to call a witness and failure to call or adduce evidence. The section deals with failure to call evidence and not failure to call a particular witness. The section applies to the prosecution in a criminal case only when it withholds evidence and not when it fails to call a particular witness. Therefore, the rule applies where a party fails to adduce evidence by withholding evidence which could have been but was not produced. While it is the law that the prosecution is not bound to call a particular witness where his case can otherwise be proved, its failure to adduce evidence at its disposal which it is supposed to adduce amounts to withholding of evidence.[57]

The court in *Solar Construction Services Ltd* v. *Hon. Minister of Federal Capital Territory & Ors*[58] posited that:

> The court may presume that evidence which could be and is not produced would, if produced, be unfavourable to the person who withheld it. What this means is that, where a document is in the custody of a party, that party owes it a duty to produce such a document before the court. Where such a party fails to do so, it raises the presumption under section 167(d) of the Evidence Act that if produced, it would be unfavourable to him.

14. Presumption of document creating obligation

Section 167(e) provides that where a document creating an obligation is in the hands of the obligor, the obligation has been discharged.[59] For instance, where an I.O.U note that ought to be with the creditor is found with the

---

[55](2018) LPELR-43841 (SC), p. 44, para. E.
[56](2018) LPELR-46718 (CA), pp. 28, paras. A-B.
[57]Ibid.
[58](2018) LPELR-46648 (CA), pp. 27-28, Paras. F-A.
[59] Section 167(e) of the Evidence Act 2011.

debtor, it will be constructed that the obligation has been discharged. However this presumption is rebuttable by evidence. For example, where the obligor/debtor stole the note or document or got it by false pretence or fraud, the creditor will be allowed to show evidence to prove this.[60]

Though there is a presumption under the provision of section 167(e) of the Act, creating an obligation, such obligation is seen as discharged, but a rebuttal could be made upon the presentation of a substantial evidence to discountenance with presumption encapsulated under the Act. In *FRN* v. *Usman & Anor,*[61] the court while applying the provision of section 167(e) of the Act held that a receipt generally is that document or a piece of paper which signifies that goods or services have been paid for. It is thus, an evidence of payment. It went further to state that the presumption of payment by 2nd respondent to the company through PW2 arose in favour of the respondents. The court agreed with the appellant's counsel that a receipt raises a presumption of payment which is rebuttable. This is on account of Section 167(e) of the Evidence Act, 2011 which provides that when a document creating an obligation is in the hands of the obligor, the obligation has been discharged. Though, being a rebuttable presumption, the burden fell on the prosecution to lead evidence in rebuttal of the presumption which the law requires to be strong, distinct, satisfactory and conclusive.[62]

Presumption of facts under common Law

Presumption of facts under common law would be examined under the following categories of presumptions and they are:

15. Presumption of intention

Under common law, there is an unstinting presumption of law that a person intends the natural consequence of his actions. This can be seen in section 316(2) of the Criminal Code, which provides that:

> Where a person who does grievous harm to another is liable to a charge of murder if the victim dies, then his death is construed as the natural or probable result or consequence of such grievous act.

The phrase, "intention" simply means a resolve, design or the determination of the mind. Before an act is committed, the court takes

---

[60] *Okele* v. *Nnolim* (2015) 5 NWLR Pt. 1453 Pg 444.

[61] (2018) LPELR-43894 (CA), pp. 12-14, paras. D-A. See also *Macaulay* v. *Seriki* (1925) 6 NLR 92.

[62] See *Idahosa* v. *Idahosa* (*supra*).

cognizance of the intention of the accused before the commission of the offence and if the intention is not secured, then it would be difficult to hold such party liable for the offence unless the prosecution lays down evidence to sustain his speculation that it was the accused and no one else that committed the alleged offence. This buttresses the dictum that even the devil knoweth not the heart of men. It is only hidden in the mind of an accused what his intentions are except through manifestation of an overt act. The court is to ascertain whether the accused nurtured such intention and if he did, the court can *suo moto* presume the intention that the accused committed the offence through merging his intention *(mens rea)* with the *actus reus.*

The court held in *R* v. *Nungu*[63] that a person is guilty of murder if he intends to do the person killed some grievous harm. On this premise, the accused person may not have formed the requisite intention that his act may occasion death but since death has occurred, it is presumed.

16. Presumption of Marriage

The validity of a marriage may be inferred by way of presumption. Two undisputable facts may be associated with this presumption. First, where it is proved that a man and a woman went through a regular ceremony of marriage either under the marriage Act or under the customary laws and values, a rebuttable presumption of the validity of the marriage is raised.

In *Obidiegwu* v. *Obidiegwu,* [64] relying on the Marriage (Validation) Act Cap 219 LFN 1990, under which marriages contracted in the Marriage Registries in "the Republic of Biafra" were validated by law, the marriage certificate issued by the Marriage Registry Owerri, Biafra was validated by law and held to be valid as statutory marriages celebrated in Nigeria. The court went further to state the conditions for validation of such marriages under the Marriage (Validation) Act to wit:

(a) it must be celebrated in duly designated marriage districts;
(b) it must be celebrated before duly appointed registrars of marriages; and
(c) it must be celebrated in duly appointed marriage offices.

In *Piers* v. *Piers,*[65] a marriage was solemnised by a regularly ordained clergyman of the Church of England, in a private house as if by special licence; there was in fact no such licence, nor any entry of its having been

[63] *Supra.*
[64] (2019) LPELR-47236(CA) P. 9, paras. C-E.
[65] (1849) 2HLC 331 relied on in *Obidiegwu* v. *Obidiegwu* (*supra*).

granted, nor could any registration of the marriage itself be found. The Bishop of the Diocese, thirty years after the solemnization of the marriage, testified that, in his belief, he had not granted the licence but that it might have been granted by his predecessor who died about one and a half years before the marriage. The court held that the grant of a special licence as well as the validity of the marriage must be presumed.

Secondly, where it is proved that a man and a woman cohabited and were treated as married by those who knew them, there is a presumption that they were living together in consequence of a valid marriage and not as concubines, unless there is proof to the contrary. It is notable to state that where a marriage is celebrated outside the place or authorized place permitted by law, such marriage may be declared null and void under section 32 of the Marriage Act. Though the court can presume a marriage but non-compliance with the statutory requirement for a valid marriage under the Marriage Act and Matrimonial Causes Act will render such marriage invalid and of no legal recognition.[66]

17. Presumption under *res ipsa loquitur*

Under this principle, where a thing is shown to be under the management or control of the defendant or his agent, and an accident occurs which in the ordinary cause of things does not happen if those who exercise management and control uses proper care, it affords reasonable evidence in the absence of reasonable explanation by the defendant that the accident arose from want of care.[67] The court in *Otti* v. *Excel-c Medical Centre Ltd & Anor*[68] stated that the doctrine of *res ipsa loquitur* means that the thing speaks for itself. It is an evidential rule, the implication of which is to shift the burden of proof to the defendant where it is shown that the event complained of was more likely than not to have been caused by negligence in the absence of an explanation. The doctrine shifts the burden to the defendant to explain what happened to negative the application of the doctrine. A claimant who relies on *res ipsa loquitur* only needs to prove the resultant accident and injury and then ask the court to infer or draw a presumption from that case of negligence on the part of the defendant.

---

[66]Lawrence Atsegbua, *op. cit.*, pg. 258.
[67]Ibid., pg. 259.
[68](2019) LPELR-47699 (CA) P.53, paras. D-E.

Chapter 11

JUDICIAL NOTICE

1. General Principles

By way of definition, judicial notice also known as judicial cognizance is the means by which the court takes as proven, certain facts without hearing evidence. There are matters which the court and the parties must have observed as proven without the necessity of leading evidence before the court. In *Commissioner of Police Adamawa State* v. *Maiyini Century Company Ltd & Anor,*[1] *Omoleye*, J.C.A explained thus:

> Judicial Notice is defined as, "the act by which a court, in conducting a trial, or framing its decision, will, of its own motion or on request of a party, and without the production of evidence, recognize the existence and truth of certain facts or law, having a bearing on the controversy at bar, which from their nature are not properly the subject of testimony, or which are universally regarded as established by common notoriety."

The point that has really been made above is that there are acts which silence the need for proof and thus dispense with the actual production of such document as the court takes judicial cognizance of them. As a matter of fact, the onus shifts to the other party to disprove such fact. The effect of taking judicial notice was aptly captured by the judgment of his Lordship, in *Prince Olumuyiwa Adekunle Ladejobi & Ors* v. *Otunba Ainofi Afolorunsho Oguntayo & Ors* [2] where his Lordship stated that, where a court takes judicial notice of a fact, it is no longer necessary to prove same save the other party intends to call evidence in disprove of same.[3]

---

[1](2017) LPELR-43025 (CA) P. 19, paras D-F. The court relied on the definition proffered in Black's Law Dictionary, 7th edn, p. 848.

[2](2015) LPELR-41701 (CA) P.96, para. D. See also *Joseph* v. *The State* (2011) LPELR 1630 (SC) per Olabode Rhodes-Vivour JSC.

[3] Ibid. The court can *exproprio motu* take judicial notice of a fact where it is prescribed by the operation of law. On the other hand, parties can invite the court to take judicial notice of a particular fact such as a particular custom. See *Okpowagha and Anor* v. *Ewhedoma* (1970) All N.L.R P. 208.

Extrapolating from the above is the fact that judicial notice is not conclusive; facts within the court's notice can still be disproved by cogent evidence and when this is done, the fact erodes the notice of the court. The court can take judicial notice of facts in two ways. Firstly it can do so *ex propriomotu,* that is, on its own accords.[4] Secondly, it can do so by being invited to take judicial notice. It is important to note that where a court is invited to take judicial notice, it may refuse to do so unless and until the party giving the invitation produces any such book or document as the court may consider necessary to enable it take judicial notice.[5]

2. Judicial Notice Under Section 122 (2) Of The Act

Section 122 of the Evidence Act has catalogued several matters of which the court should take notice of. It has been argued,[6] and rightly too in our view, that the court is under a mandatory obligation to take judicial notice of the facts in section 122 of the Act, as the operative words in section 122(2) of the Act say that "the court *shall* take judicial notice" of those matters listed thereunder.[7] Some of the matters in that section include: all laws passed by the legislature in Nigeria and the subsidiary legislation pursuant thereto, the course of proceedings of the legislature, the assumption of office of the President, a state Governor or the Chairman of the Local Government Council and their seals, all seals of courts in Nigeria, the division of time, the national flag, public holidays and festivals, all the states within the common wealth, etc.

This section gained judicial attention and approval in the case of *Uli Microfinance Bank (Nig) Ltd* v. *Okwuchukwu,*[8] where the court while applying section 122(2) of the Act on matters the court must take judicial notice of held thus:

> It is not necessary according to the Supreme Court to plead the Constitution, Acts of the National Assembly, Laws of State Houses of Assembly, Rules of Practice and Procedure of Courts of Justice nor call on

[4] See *Victino Fixed Odds Ltd* v. *Ojo* (2010) 8 NWLR (Pt. 1197) 486 at 505, per Adekeye JSC.

[5] See section 122(4) Evidence Act 2011; see also *S.P.O.C.* v. *Dino* (*supra*).

[6] N.O. Obiaraeri, *op. cit.,* at 170.

[7] It can be recalled that where the word "shall" appears in a statute, it operates to impose an obligation. See *Chevron (Nig.) Ltd* v. *Lowaz & Ors.* (2017) LPELR-42813 (CA) and *Ifezue* v. *Mbadugha* (1984) 1 SCNL 158.

[8] (2018) LPELR-44956 (CA) P. 50, para. A-C. See also *Independent National Electoral Commission & Anor* v. *Muri Edet Etim Asuquo & Ors* (2018) LPELR-43885 (SC).See also *Olagoke & Ors* v. *Governor of Osun State & Ors* (2017) LPELR-43301 (CA) P. 20, paras. C-D.

> the parties or learned counsel to address the court as the parties and the judges are presumed to be aware of their provisions and are bound to take judicial notice of them in the determination of the civil rights and obligations of litigants in the course of dispensing justice and putting an end to disputes.[9]

On this score, the law gives the court the unbridled licence to apply any relevant legislation to any proceedings. Indeed, the law is in the breast of a *judex* and he is entitled *ex debito justitiae* (in the interest of justice) to apply it in deserving circumstances.[10]

In *Joseph* v. *The State,*[11] one of the issues before the Supreme Court was whether the trial court and Court of Appeal were right in holding that by virtue of the Legal Notice No. 60 of 1977, the trial court was right in taking judicial notice of the Igbogial/Ibara-Orile/Sokoto express way as a Federal Highway under section 74 of the Evidence Act 2004 (now section 122(2) of the Evidence Act 2011). The Supreme Court held that both courts were correct. According to the apex court, the legal Notice designating that road as Federal Highway was a subsidiary legislation of which the court must take judicial notice of.

3. Judicial Notice under Section 16 And 17 of the Act

Section 16 of Evidence Act provides that a custom may be adopted as part of the law governing a particular set of circumstances if it can be shown to exist by evidence or by judicial notice. It is further provided in section 18(1) that where a custom cannot be established as one judicially noticed, it shall be proved as a fact. A combined reading of these two provisions reveal that judicial notice is one of the means by which a custom can be established as being in existence.

Pursuant to the old order under section 14 of the repealed Evidence Act 2004, a custom can only qualify for judicial notice if it has been acted upon severally by courts of co-ordinate jurisdiction in the same area to such extent that such custom gains notoriety. In *Romaine* v. *Romaine,*[12] it was held that a custom is a matter of evidence unless it qualifies for judicial notice and it

---

[9] See also *Sanni & Ors* v. *C.O.P.* (2018) LPELR-45049 (CA) P. 15, paras. A-F.

[10] See *Akanbi & Ors.* v. *A.G. Federation & Ors.* (2017) LPELR-43121(CA) Pp. 36-37, paras. C per Ogbuinya, JCA

[11] (2011) LPELR-1630 (SC) P.8, paras. B-C.

[12] (1992) 4 NWLR (Pt.238) 650. See also *Motoh* v. *Motoh* (2011) 16 NWLR (Pt. 1274) 474 at 522 decided on the premise of the old Evidence Act.

can qualify for judicial notice if and only if it has been so often proved, pronounced upon and acted upon by a court of superior or coordinate jurisdiction in the same area to such an extent that it can be said to have acquired notoriety. It is very imperative to point out that this decision and its likes were decided in accordance with the 2004 Act and are no longer good law to the extent that they decided that custom must gain notoriety before being judicially noticed. It is submitted and rightly too, that this is no longer the position of the law in view of the extant law. Thus, in view of section 17 of the new Evidence Act, once a custom has been adjudicated upon once by a superior court of record, the court shall take judicial notice. This is the position of the law in *Okusanya & Ors* v. *Adetona & Ors.*[13]

This provision is a paradigm shift from section 14(2) of Evidence Act 2004 which provided that: "A custom may be judicially noticed if it had been acted upon by a court of superior or co-ordinate jurisdiction in the same area to an extent which justifies the court asked to apply it in assuming that the persons or class of persons concerned in that area looked upon the same as binding in relation to circumstances similar to those under consideration."

Obviously, the novelty in section 17 of the Evidence Act 2011 is that it has jettisoned the following requirements in section 14(2) of the Old Act:

i. the requirements that the court ask to take judicial notice of a custom must be in the same area or fall within same jurisdiction as the court before which the said custom had been acted upon;
ii. frequency of poof or requirement of notoriety;
iii. the assumption by the court that the persons or class of persons concerned in the area look upon the custom as binding in relation to circumstances similar to those under consideration.

Consequently, it appears that under the new regime, all that a litigant who wishes that a court should take judicial notice of a custom need to do is to draw the attention of that court to one decision of a superior court of record. The general points to note about judicial notice of customs may be summarised as follows:

a. **Judicial notice of a custom is discretionary**. It has been argued in some quarters that when judicial notice has been taken of a custom, it constitutes a binding precedent on lower courts. This argument is difficult

[13] (2018) LPELR-44876 (CA); see also *Isu* v. *Abasa & Ors.* (2017) LPELR-42014 (CA).

> to absorb. The erudite Justice C.C. Nweze now a justice of the Supreme Court, seems to be of this school of thought. His Lordship writes that, "...a single decision of the apex court upholding the existence of a custom has all the attributes of every other decision of that court with regard to the principle of *stare decisis*. Such a decision, therefore, has its binding effect on the courts of inferior or coordinate jurisdiction."[14] It is submitted with undiluted respect that the above assertion is too sweeping and far-reaching and thus, should be absorbed with caution. It pushes the frontiers of the principle of judicial precedent beyond the limits permissible under the Evidence Act. The operative word in section 14(2) of the Old Act and section 17 of the 2011 Act is "May" which connotes an exercise of discretion. Furthermore, it appears that the learned *judex* did not advert his mind to the fact that customs are by their very nature, akin to a chameleon, changing its colours in accordance with changing situations and ought not to be made subject to the rigid governance of the doctrine of judicial precedents as that would be tantamount to an impediment to the development of customary law administration in Nigeria and its relegation to moribundity.

Just as we have earlier stated, judicial notice is not conclusive. A fact that enjoys judicial notice may be removed from its comfort zone by credible evidence in disproof of it. So, in the same wise, a custom that has been judicially noticed may still be displaced by contrary evidence. In *Danmole* v. *Dawodu*[15] the then Federal Supreme Court admitted evidence for the purpose of showing that in Lagos, the judicially noticed custom on succession, *Idi igi* (distribution of estates *per stripes*),has been displaced by the *Ori Ojori* custom (distribution of estate per capita): albeit, the court concluded that *Idi igi* was still in existence.

Finally, where a custom has been codified into a statute it enjoys judicial notice and evidence need not be given. It can be recalled that under section 122(2) which we have earlier discussed, statutes passed by the legislature enjoy mandatory judicial notice. Therefore, it is submitted that where a custom has taken the form of statutory provision, the word "may" in section 17 cannot operate to give the court a blank cheque when called upon to take judicial notice of it. The court "shall" notice such custom. The fortification for this logical view is the fact that the death of such custom cannot even be

---

[14] See C.C Nweze, *Contentious Issues and Responses in Contemporary Evidence Law in Nigeria,* Vol. 1 (Enugu: Institute for Development Studies, University of Nigeria, Enugu Campus, 2003) p. 112; See also *Abiodun.* v. *Erimilokun* (1961) All N.L.R 294; *Oyenwumi* v. *Ogunnesan* (1990) NWLR (pt. 137) 182

[15] (1958) F.S.C 46.

achieved by judicial activism: such custom must terminate only by way of legislative amendment of the statute codifying it. However, such codified customs do not automatically transform into rules of English Law and the codification cannot cause such custom to be treated as English Law. Belgore J (as he then was) had made this point in *Ehioghe* v. *Ehioghe.*[16] His Lordship remarked: "if certain ways of life are regulated by statutes for convenience owing to an advance in civilization, it will not in my view, be proper to say that such native ways of life henceforth ceased to be native."[17]

4. Judicial Notice of Facts Which Are Notorious

The courts are constituted by humans who also live in the same society as litigants. Therefore, the law is aware that those humans who perform judicial functions have the common knowledge which the ordinary citizens and inhabitants of society have. It is undesirable, for example, for a litigant to prove before a judge that 'hens lay eggs' This is so because the law assumes that the fact is too common that the judge is reasonably expected to know it. In such a case, it will amount to wastage of time and stretching the law and practice of evidence beyond reasonable limits to subject such facts to the crucible of proof. It is for the sake of this situation that section 124(1) of the Evidence Act has provided that the court shall take judicial notice of any fact which is of common knowledge in the locality where the court is situate or fact which is capable of verification by reference to a document, the authority of which, cannot be reasonably questioned.

In *Bauchi State House of Assembly & Ors* v. *Guyaba,*[18] His Lordship Mshelia, JCA posited that by virtue of section 124 of the Evidence Act, 2011, this Court (Court of Appeal) is empowered to take judicial notice of facts which is common knowledge in the locality in which the proceeding is being held. This suffices to say for instance that an assertion before an Enugu High Court sitting at Agbani Judicial Division that there is a campus of the Nigerian Law School at Agbani does not require proof because it is a fact that is common knowledge in Agbani locality. Also, a fact contained in a document of authority (like National Dailies) can be judicially noticed.

The list of facts which the court can judicially notice under section 124 is not closed. We agree with *Obiaraeri*[19] who opines that the discretionary powers given to the courts under section 124 are too wide as section 124(2)

[16] (1964) NMLR 30.
[17] Ibid., at pg. 35.
[18] (2017) LPELR-43295 (CA) P. 33, para. B.
[19] N.O. Obiaraeri, *op. cit.*, at pg 174.

provides that "the courts may acquire in any manner it deems fit, knowledge of a fact to which subsection (1) of this section refers and shall take such knowledge into account." It is however, submitted that no matter how powerful the courts may seem to be under the strength of this section, the court cannot invoke its powers under the section unless and until it has given ample opportunity and fair hearing to the parties involved so as to avoid any unfair prejudice against any of the parties.[20] Examples of facts that may be noticed under section 124 include: a fortnight is too short a period for human gestation; the advancement of learning is among the purpose for which the University of Oxford exists; that cats are kept for domestic purposes, etc.[21]

In *Beaumont Resources Ltd & Anor* v. *DWC Drilling Ltd,*[22] it was held that it is trite that the court before whom a proceeding is pending or has been completed takes judicial notice of all processes filed in the proceedings as well as the proceeding itself including the judgment as the case may be and so following from this proposition of law all the processes to be relied upon in any application made before that court in the proceeding are judicially noticed. In the same vein, in *Olusegun Debayo Doherty & Anor* v. *Tayibatu Ayoola Sunmonu & Ors,*[23] the court while ruling on the learned counsel to the appellants' contention regarding the learned trial judge's order to the effect that both the arrears of rents and mesne profits in the matter be paid by the appellants, at the current rate of exchange as stipulated by the Central Bank of Nigeria had this to say:

> It is indisputable, that the court in the quest to do substantial justice in any matter placed before it, has the power to take judicial notice of some glaring notorious facts. The reason is not farfetched. Judges are human beings who live in the society and not in the air. It is a notorious fact that the Nigerian currency, the naira, and its value fluctuates every now and then. Therefore, to my mind, it will sound very unrealistic and indeed unconscionable to suggest and insist that the value of the Naira in 1990 when the rents vide Exhibit 3 was paid is still the same today or when the trial judge delivered his judgment on 6th February, 2013.

[20] See section 124(3) of Evidence Act 2011.
[21] Examples are coined from Atsegbua, *op. cit.,* pg 242.
[22](2017) LPELR-42814 (CA).
[23](2018) LPELR-46725 (CA) Pp.39-40, paras. D-A.

In *Omorogbe & Ors* v. *Enehizena & Ors,*[24] the courts took judicial notice of public holidays in Nigeria. Furthermore, in *Kopek Construction Ltd.* v. *Ekisole,*[25] the Supreme Court took judicial notice that Nigeria is blessed with so many tribes, customs, languages and cultures. Also in *Ebe* v. *C.O.P.,*[26] the Supreme Court took judicial notice of the notorious fact that a Commissioner of Police is involved in so many cases at the same time and it would therefore be impossible for him to be physically present in all those cases.

5. Other Facts for Which Proof Is Not Required

There are facts that do not require judicial notice *stricto sensu* but proof of them is not required. Section 123 provides that any fact that has been admitted in writing by a party to a proceeding or his agent thereto, does not required proof. It is also provided in that section that any fact which is deemed by any rule of pleading to be admitted does not require proof.[27] This reminds us of the rule of pleading to the effect that any fact that is not unequivocally denied or which is evasively denied shall be deemed to be admitted and proof of it is not required.[28] However, by the *proviso* to section 123, the court has jurisdiction to require such facts referred to in that section to be proved.

---

[24](2018) LPELR-44833 (CA) P. 3, paras. B-C. The Court in the earlier case of *Essien* v. *Essien & Ors* (2008) LPELR-4049 (CA) P. 32, paras. B-C took judicial notice that Saturdays are work free days in the State.

[25] (2010) 3 NWLR (Pt. 1182) 618 655, Muhammad JSC.

[26] (2008) 1 SCNJ 462.

[27] See *Barau & Ors* v. *Consolidated Tin Mines Ltd & Ors* (2019) LPELR-46806(CA) P. 31-32, paras. F-A.

[28] Ibid.

Chapter 12

ESTOPPEL

1. Meaning and Types of Estoppel in Nigerian Terms

The definition of estoppel *strictu sensu* does not find expression in the Evidence Act. However, the Evidence Act did not leave it to conjecture. Copious provisions have been made with respect to the application of "estoppel" in the determination of the criminal and civil rights and obligation of the parties in judicial proceedings. In the course of our discussion, we shall diligently bring out these evidential provisions with heavy reliance on judicial interpretations of the subject matter.

In *Uwandu* v. *Chinagorom & Ors,*[1] the court defined estoppel in the following words:

> The doctrine of Estoppel connotes that where a man by word or conduct wilfully makes a representation of a state of facts to another, and thereby induced that other to believe that the state of things were as reputed by that person and that other took him by his words, and acted upon that representation, that person who made the representation either by himself or his representative in interest, cannot now turn around to say, or behave as if the state of things were not as he represented them.[2]

By operation of the rule of estoppel, a man is not allowed to blow hot and cold, to affirm at one time and deny at the other, or, as it is said, to approbate and reprobate. He cannot be allowed to mislead another person into believing in a state of affairs and then turning round to say to that person's disadvantage that the state of affairs which he had represented does not exist at all or as represented by him.[3] The plea of estoppel is generally employed as a shield for the protection of a defendant, but it can also be employed as a sword by a plaintiff in appropriate cases.[4] It then suffice to say

---

[1](2019) LPELR-46909(CA) P.16, paras. C-D.

[2] See *Achu & Ors* v. *Etta & Ors.* (2017) LPELR-43338(CA) Pp. 15-16, paras. E-C.

[3]*CMB Building Maintenance & Investment Co. Ltd* v. *Abolade* (2019) LPELR-47302 (CA) P. 24, paras. D-F.

[4]*Adams & Anor* v. *Fasasi & Ors.* (2018) LPELR-44379 (CA) Pp. 19-20, paras. F-A.

that this principle is founded on the ground that the law should not permit an unjust departure from an assumption of fact which one has caused another party to adopt for the purpose of their legal relations. However, this doctrine should not be stretched beyond its limit to be used to perpetuate injustice. Thus, the court in *Ntung & Ors* v. *Longkwang & Ors*[5] held that the doctrine of estoppel cannot be extended to cover up or condone an illegal, unconstitutional or criminal conduct and it will be against public policy to attempt to apply estoppel to shut up a complaint against such conduct. This suffices to mean that the doctrine of estoppel cannot work in favour of parties who mutually give their consent or agree to an illegality. Thus, estoppel will not be allowed to preclude the party against whom it is sought, from asserting and bringing to the notice of the court the illegality of such actions and/or instruments which are sought to be validated by acceptance of the estoppel pleaded.

Estoppel can also be seen as a bar to re-litigation of a suit especially once the suit has been settled with finality by a court of competent jurisdiction. The above judicial explanation of estoppel gained a statutory imprimatur in the provisions of section 169 of the Evidence Act which states thus:

> When one person has either by notice of an existing court judgment, deed or agreement or by his declaration, act or omission intentionally caused or permitted another to believe a thing to be true and to act upon such believe, neither he nor his representative in interest shall be allowed in any proceedings between himself and such person or such person's representative in interest to deny the truth of that thing.

From the foregoing provision, it is deducible that estoppel can arise in either two circumstances namely:

(a) by virtue of an existing court judgment, deed or agreement; or
(b) by virtue of a person's declaration, act or omission wherein the person intentionally caused or permitted another person to believe a thing to be true and to act upon same.

Where it arises by court judgment, it is to ensure that a litigation which has been prosecuted to conclusion cannot be resuscitated at the instance of a plaintiff. The rationale behind this is to make sure that litigation comes to an end and not necessarily repeated to the annoyance of the defendant and the entire administration of justice or the judicial system. But for the principle

---

[5](2018) LPELR-45624(CA) PP.68-69, Paras. G-B.

of estoppel and the twin principle of *res judicata*, litigation could not have had an end. Estoppel operates because of the twin reasons expounded in *Falaki & Ors* v. *Fagbuyiro & Ors.*[6] these are:

(a) that in the interest of the public, there should be an end to litigation as expressed in the Latin maxim *"interest reipublicae ut suit finis litium."*;

(b) that nobody should be sued twice on the same ground. If this is allowed, there will be no end to litigation except where the legal dexterity and ingenuity is exhausted.

In the same wavelength, in *Aja* v. *Aja & Ors,*[7] Estoppel is a rule that prevents a person from asserting the contrary of a fact, or state of things which he formerly asserted by words or conduct. Put in another way, a person shall not be allowed to say one thing at one time and the opposite at another time. Estoppel is based on equity and good conscience, the object being to prevent fraud and ensure justice between the parties, by promoting transparency and good faith. In *Ntung & Ors* v. *Longkwang & Ors,*[8] Hon. Justice Abiru JCA described estoppel as an admission or something that the law views as equivalent to an admission. By its very nature, it is so important, so conclusive, that the party whom it affects is not allowed to plead against it, or adduce evidence to contradict it. Estoppel prohibits a party from providing anything that contradicts his previous acts or declarations to the prejudice of a party who, relying upon them, has altered his position. It shuts the mouth of a party.

The court in *Attorney General Rivers State* v. *A.G. Akwa Ibom & Anor*[9] *per* Katsina-Alu JSC described estoppel as an admission or something which the law views as equivalent to an admission. By its very nature, it is so important and conclusive that the party whom it affects will not be allowed to plead against it or adduce evidence to contradict it. In *Adimora & Anor* v. *Adimora & Anor,*[10] it was held that a party is estopped by his failure to appeal against an adverse finding of a fact relevant to the issue. The court sees such failure to appeal against a decision as an admission.

According to Aguda,[11] estoppel bear resemblance with irrebuttable presumptions of law from which it can however be distinguished as it can be

---

[6](2015) LPELR-25848(CA).

[7](2019) LPELR-46840(CA).

[8] *Supra.*

[9] (2011) LPELR-633(SC) Pp. 21-22, paras. F-A.

[10](2018) LPELR-43959.

[11] A. Aguda, *The Law of Evidence*, 4th edn. (Ibadan: Spectrum Series, Spectrum Books Ltd, 2007) pg. 267-270.

waived whilst an irrebuttable presumption of law cannot be waived by the parties. Estoppel can also be regarded as a matter of pleading.[12] It is the law that a party seeking to rely on estoppel must specifically plead it unless it is so apparently clear that the court has a duty to consider it.[13] May we invite the statutory provision of section 174 of the Evidence Act to this effect. It provides thus:

> If a judgment is not pleaded by way of estoppel, it is as between parties and privies deemed to be a relevant fact, whenever any matter, which was or might have been decided in the action in which it was given, is in issue, or is deemed to be relevant to the issue in any subsequent proceeding.
>
> (2) Such judgment is conclusive proof of the facts which it decides, or might have decided, if the party who gives evidence of it has no opportunity of pleading it as an estoppel.

It is very pertinent to note that some of the rules relating to estoppel are found in the Evidence Act. Aside section 174 earlier treated, other relevant sections are sections 65, 169, 179, 171, 172 and 173 of the Evidence Act 2011 and it will be correct to describe them as rules of evidence.

Types of Estoppel

Under the common law, estoppel, like the biblical mustard seed, evolved from every modest origin as a generic term to include various undertakings resulting from conduct of the parties or matters of writing or record. This explains why Coke, in his commentaries on Littleton, simply classified estoppel as *estoppel in pais* (equitable estoppel), estoppel in writing and estoppel by matter of record.(Refer in footnote) Overtime, it blossomed into so many facets such that attempts to delineate its exact ambits have generated both conceptual and terminological problems. Indeed, the Law Lord, Lord Denning M.R in his erudition expressed in an appetizing prose and admitted this much problem of categorization as late as 1980 in *Mchll Kenny* v. *Chief Constable of West Midlands Police Force and Anor,*[14] where he brilliantly summed up this development thus:

---

[12] N.O Obiaraeri, *op cit.*, pg 138.
[13] *Asamu* v. *Lawanson & Ors* (2014) LPELR-24416 (CA) P. 23, para. E.
[14] (1980) 2 All ER 229 at 235.

> From that simple origin, there has been built up over the centuries in one law, a big house with many rooms. It is the house Estoppel. In Coke's time, it was a small house with only three rooms namely, estoppels by matter of record, by matter of writing and by matter in partes. But by our time, we have so many rooms that we are apt to get confused between them.

Thus from this, aside from these three types identified above, other species, forms or "Kaleidoscopic varieties" of estoppel include estoppel by representation, estoppel by conduct, promissory estoppel, estoppel by election, making estoppel and estoppel by certificate to mention a few.[15] Some of these classifications may with respect, be said to belong to period of antiquity or relevant purely for academic reasons as the Evidence Act itself does not regale in the luxury of classifications of estoppel in this moulds.

Again, in settling pleadings, it is unnecessary to state the particular form of estoppel that reliance is being placed upon, provided always there is sufficient fact on the pleadings pointing with clarity, the particular form of estoppel relied upon.

However, to clear this cloud of confusion hovering around the categorization of estoppel, the Supreme Court in its judgment in *Soronnadi & Anor* v. *Durugo & Anor*[16] per Kekere-Ekun, J.S.C held thus:

> It has been held by this Court that there are two types of estoppel: "cause of action estoppel" and "issue estoppel". The difference between the two was explained *Fadiora* v. *Gbadebo* (1978) 3 SC 219 @ 228 & 229, per Idigbe, JSC thus: "Now, there are two kinds of estoppel by record inter partes or per *rem judicatam* as it is generally known. The first is usually referred to as 'cause of action estoppel' and it occurs when: the cause of action is merged in the judgment. That is, transit in *rem judicatam*. See *King* v. *Hoare* (1844) 13 M& W 495 @ 1504. Therefore, on this principle of law (or rule of evidence), once it appears that the same cause of action was held to lie (or not to lie) in a final judgment between the same parties, or their 'privies, who are litigating in the same capacity (and on the same subject matter), there is an end to the matter. There is however, a second kind of *estoppel inter partes* and this usually occurs where an issue has earlier on been adjudicated upon by a Court of competent jurisdiction and the same issue comes incidentally in question in any subsequent proceedings between the same parties (or their

[15] See Black's Law Dictionary, Seventh Edition *op. cit.*, pages 570 to 572.

[16] (2018) LPELR-46319 (SC), pp. 35-36, paras. D-F.

> privies): in these circumstances, 'issue estoppel' arises. This is based on the principle of law that a party is not allowed to (i.e. he is precluded from)be contending the opposite of any specific point which having been once distinctly put in issue, has with certainty and solemnity been determined against him...Issue estoppel applies whether the point involved in the earlier decision is one of fact or law or one of mixed fact and law.

Notwithstanding the above proliferation in nomenclature, one fact cannot be gain said, namely: that the above types are only but a species of one genre. Denning M.R. made this instructive classification in the West Midlands Police case when he said:

> These several rooms have this much in common: they are all under one roof. Someone is stopped from saying something or other, doing something or other, contesting something or other...

2. Estoppel *Simpliciter*

Estoppel *simpliciter* as had been earlier established, is an admission of facts. Estoppel by its very nature is so important, so conclusive that the party whom it affects is not allowed to plead against it, or lead evidence to contradict it. It is very germane to note that there is a big disparity between "estoppel *simpliciter*" and plea of "estoppel per *rem judicatam* or *res judicata*" as will be seen in the course of our discussion. By virtue of section 169 of the Evidence Act, "estoppel *simpliciter*" do arise by reason of a person's declaration, act or omission whether the person intentionally caused or permitted another person to believe a thing to be true and to act upon such supposition or belief. This operates against both parties. To drive home the point we are trying to substantiate, recognition will be given to a genre of estoppel *simpliciter* called "Estoppel by Conduct" we shall also place reliance on cases to buttress same.

The principle of estoppel by conduct is that once a party has, by his words or conduct, made to the other a promise or assurance which was intended to affect the legal relation between them and to be acted upon accordingly, then once the other party had taken him at his word and acted on it, then the one who gave the promise or assurance cannot afterwards be allowed to revert to the previous legal relations as if no such promise or assurance has been made by him. This type of estoppel limits the capacity of a person to, after making another person to shift his position to the latter's detriment, seek to recline from his position he took or to call evidence to its contrary.[17]

This type of estoppel was succinctly captured in details in the recent case of *Azuasonogo* v. *Benue State Government & Anor.*[18] The court while relying on *A.G. Bendel State* v. *A.G. Federation & Ors*[19] and *A.G. Rivers State* v. *A.G. Akwa Ibom State & Anor,*[20] expounded on the principle thus:

> In *A.G. Bendel State* v. *A.G. Federation & Ors.* (1981) LPELR-605 (SC), the Law Lord, Obaseki, JSC at page 149 of the E-Report expounded: The doctrine of estoppel forms part of the law of evidence, and an estoppel, except as a bar to testimony, has no operation or efficacy whatsoever. Its sole office is either to place an obstacle in the way of a case which might otherwise succeed or to remove an impediment out of the way of a case which might otherwise fail. It has no other function. See *Rogers* v. *Pitcher* (1815) 6 Taunt 202. *Thompson* v. *Palua* (1933) 49 CLR 507 at 509; High Court of Australia per Sir Owen Dixon CJ. Estoppel does not lie in mere imagination or assertion, there must be facts proved which will give rise to estoppel.

The Court of Appeal, still relying on *Greenwood* v. *Martins Bank Ltd. (*1933) AC 51 at 57, listed the essential elements of the doctrine as stated by Lord Tomlin in the following terms:

> (1) A representation or conduct amounting to a representation intended to induce a course of conduct on the part of the person to whom the representation is made;
>
> (2) An act or omission resulting from the representation whether actual or by conduct by the person to whom the representation is made;
>
> (3) Detriment to such person as a consequence of the act or omission.

His Lordship then continued at page 29 in Azuasonogo's case as follows:

> In *AG Rivers State* v. *AG Akwa Ibom State & Anor* (2011) LPELR-633 (SC) at page 20-21, the Supreme Court again elucidated: "The doctrine of estoppel by conduct, though a common law principle has been enacted

---

[17] S.T. Hon's, *Law of Evidence, op. cit.,* at page 1207.
[18] (2019) LPELR-47270 (CA), pp.28-30 Paras. A-A.
[19] (1981) LPELR-605 (SC) P. 149.
[20] (2011) LPELR-633 (SC) Pp. 20-21.

> into our body of laws as Section 151 of the Evidence Act (now section 169 of the Evidence Act, 2011)." It is in these terms: "When one person has, by his declaration, Act or omission, intentionally caused or permitted another person to believe a thing to be true and to act upon such belief (a thing to be true and to act upon such belief), neither he nor his representative in interest shall be allowed in any proceedings between himself and such person or such person's representative in interest, to deny the truth of that thing." Also called *estoppel in pais*, this common law principle, which as shown above, has gained statutory acceptance in Nigeria, forbids a person from leading his opponent from believing in and acting upon a state of affairs, only for the former to turn around and disclaim his act or omission. Both common and statutory law do not permit this conduct; that is why Section 151 of the Evidence Act (now section 169) has used the emphatic phrase neither he nor his representative in interest shall be allowed.[21]

The notorious case of *Attorney General River State* v. *Attorney General, Akwa Ibom & Anor* cited above is very illustrative of this principle. The fact of this case will be fully deployed here to underscore the importance of estoppel by conduct. In that case which the Supreme Court pursuant to its original jurisdiction under section 232 of the 1999 Constitution, surmised that having regard to the nature of the claim before the court, the only relevant issue for determination by the court was simple. It was whether the defendants can unilaterally jettison the political solution agreement agreed between the two states (Akwa Ibom and Cross River) and revert to the historical solution on demarcating the maritime map of the littoral states contrary to the decision laid down by the Supreme Court in *A.G. Federation* v. *A.G. Abia State & 35 Ors*[22] and Article 15 of UNCLOS (United Nations Convention on Laws of the Sea) 1982. The plaintiff averred that it accepted the "Political Solution Method Agreement" arising from a peace meeting between the feuding parties including the present plaintiff and defendant presided over by the president of the country. So did the defendant. The said agreement that was reduced into writing and dated 31st October 2006 was admitted at the trial as "Exhibit AMB1." Thereafter and following the amicable resolution of the matter as embodied in the said letter from 1st November, 2006. On account of the foregoing, both plaintiff and defendants received 86 oil wells respectively and the revenue accruing therefrom with

[21]See also *CMB Building Maintenance & Investment Co. Ltd* v. *Abolade* (2019) LPELR-47302 (CA) p. 25, paras. A-D.

[22] (2002) FWLR (Pt. 10)1.

effect from November 2006. The parties faithfully implemented the agreement for some time before Akwa Ibom opted out. In this judgment, the full panel of the Supreme Court held among other things that the agreement in "Exhibit AMBI" brought the dispute to an end and that the parties are bound by the agreement and the parties are estopped by their conduct from disclaiming their act.

In the old case of *Oyeyemi* v. *Commissioner for Local Government Kwara*[23] although Nnaemeka Agu JSC did not cite section 169 of the Evidence Act in this case, there can be no doubt that his Lordship was describing the effect of estoppel by conduct. In this case, the plaintiff, at the High Court, claimed, *inter alia*, a declaration that he was recognised as the *Baale* of Oro by the defendants and that their purported withdrawal of the recognition and subsequent recognition of the 5th defendant was null and void. The High Court granted his reliefs but the court of Appeal upturned the judgment of the High Court. On further appeal, the Supreme Court restored the original judgment. Listen to Nnaemeka Agu JSC:

> The 3rd Defendant paid salary for the whole period. So, the Governor or indeed any of the defendants cannot be heard to say otherwise. The Defendants will not be allowed to approbate and reprobate on the same issue as it suits their convenience. They cannot be allowed to expressly recognize the appellant, pay him salary due to his office as *Baale* for about two years, make a solemn assertion on oath that he was duly selected and appointed according to custom and then, now that they are sued for improperly withdrawing his recognition as the *Baale*, be permitted to set up a case that he was not duly appointed. As they, by words, and conduct, wilfully made the appellant to believe that he was duly appointed as the *Baale* of Oro town and he believed them and acted as such, they cannot now be heard to deny the representation of facts which they had wilfully made in the matter of words or conduct. The law will hold them to their own wilful representations.

In summary, it must be stressed that the reliance on the representation must have been in good faith. That is to say, where the person so misrepresented to, had notice or knowledge, actual or constructive, of the true course of events, reliance cannot be said to have been placed on the declaration or conduct or representation. This was the position of the

[23] (1992) 21 SCNJ (Pt. 11) 266.

Supreme Court in *Lawal* v. *Union Bank of Nigeria*.[24] It needs however to be reiterated on record that section 151 of the repealed Evidence Act 2004, relied upon in some of the above cited cases is *in pari materia* with section 169 of the Evidence Act 2011 except to the extent that the latter accords additional recognition to estoppel by virtue of an existing "court judgment, deed or agreement."

3. Estoppel *Per Rem Judicatam* Or *Res Judicata*

As has been noted earlier in our preceding discussions, estoppel can arise under section 169 of the Evidence Act by virtue of an existing court judgment, deed or agreement. Nevertheless, the major section that touches on this particular genre of estoppel is rooted in section 73 of the Act. This section of course, poignantly brings to limelight, the applicability of the doctrine of estoppel per *rem judicatam*. It provides thus:

> Every judgment is conclusive proof, as against parties and privies, of facts directly in issue in the case actually decided by the court, and appearing from the judgment itself to be the ground on which it was based; unless evidence was admitted in the action in which the judgment was delivered which was excluded in the action in which the judgment is intended to be proved.

The doctrine of estoppel per *rem judicatam*, a Latin maxim, connotes that where a court of competent jurisdiction has settled by a final decision, the matter in controversy between the parties in an action, the said parties or their privies cannot re-litigate that matter again by bringing a fresh action.[25] An issue of *res judicata* is like a question of jurisdiction, which ought to be considered first before proceeding, where need be, to determine the merit of the case.[26] Estoppel per *rem judicatam* or *res judicatam* must be specifically pleaded; lest, it will not avail the party relying on it. This is the fulcrum of the decision of the court in *Faluyi & Ors* v. *Ogunseye & Ors*.[27] Estoppel per *rem judicatam* operates not only against the party whom it affects. As earlier stated, it goes to the question of jurisdiction. The party affected is estopped per *rem judicatam* from re-litigating afresh, the issue or cause of action already decided by a court of competent jurisdiction. In the more recent

---

[24] (1995) 21 SCNJ 13

[25] *Mahmud* v. *Hausawa & Ors* (2018) LPELR-46073 (CA) P. 22 paras. A-B. See also the recent Supreme Court decision in *Ezike & Anor* v. *Egbuaba* (2019) LPELR-46526 (SC).

[26] Per Onnoghen, JSC, in *Madam Ausatu Agboguleri* v. *Mr. John Depo & 3 Ors* (2008) 1 SCNJ 522 at 548

[27] (2019) LPELR-48015 (CA) P. 66, para. C.

decision of the apex court in *Zubair* v. *Kolawole,*[28] the court posited in its erudition thus:

> Estoppel per *rem judicatam* or res judicata arises where an issue of fact has been judicially determined in a final manner between the parties or their privies by a court or tribunal having jurisdiction in the matter and the same issue comes directly in question in subsequent proceedings between the parties and their privies. The principle operates where the subject matter and the question raised in the second matter are the same as the subject matter and question raised and decided in the first matter.

In my word, it is a settled matter with finality predicated on the premise that there should be an end to litigation. Thus, it is in the interest of public that there should be an end to litigation as expressed in Latin "*interest reipublicae ut sit finis litium.*" In *Mahmud* v. *Hausawa & Ors*[29] earlier cited, the court went further at page 22 to state the rationale of this principle of law thus:

> The rationale behind the doctrine was long ago underscored by Aniagolu JSC (of blessed memory) in the case of *Aro* Vs. *Fabolude* (1983)1 SCNLR p.58 in the following words:
>
> "There must be an end to litigation. Parties are not permitted to bring fresh litigations because of new views they may entertain of the law of the case, or new versions which they present as to what should be a proper apprehension by the court of the legal result either of the construction of the documents or the weight of certain circumstances. If those were permitted, litigation would have no end except when legal ingenuity is exhausted."

Another phase of this principle is that it can only serve to protect a defendant from vexatious cases caught in the web of this principle. It only avails a defendant as a shield and can never at any point be made available to the Plaintiff to foist a state of helplessness on the court's jurisdiction in which he brought an action before, since a successful plea of this principle erodes jurisdiction from the court to entertain the matter. In another decision of the Supreme Court in *Yanaty Petrochemical Ltd* v. *EFCC,*[30]

---

[28](2019) LPELR-46928 (SC) P 39 Paras. C-E.
[29] *Supra.*
[30] (2017) LPELR-43473 (SC) Pp. 40-41, para F-A.

while buttressing this position of the law, the Supreme Court per Ariwoola JSC held thus:

> Generally, the principle of law is well settled, that the plea of estoppel per *rem judicatam* is a shield rather than a sword. The plea is therefore ordinarily not available to a plaintiff to be pleaded in its statement of claim, as he would by that, be impugning the jurisdiction of the court to which he has brought his present action, since its successful plea would in effect, oust the jurisdiction of the court before which it is raised.

In *Ashorobi* v. *Akinole & Ors*[31] the respondents had applied *ex parte* in a special procedure of summary proceedings for possession of landed property occupied by squatters. The trial Court granted the *ex parte* application. The appellant's grievance was that the order of possession made in favour of the respondents on 16/2/2000, by the trial court in Suit NO ID/923M/99, had adversely affected her interest in the land. The appellant, by a motion on notice, prayed for an order, amongst other reliefs, that the court should set aside the order it made on 18th May, 2011, which was sequel to the ex-parte application of the respondents dated 1st March, 2011. The appellant's motion on notice was anchored on the ground amongst others, that the ex-parte order obtained by the respondents was tainted with material misrepresentation, misstatements and concealment of facts by the respondents and also to set aside the warrant of possession dated 4th August, 2006 and the writ of possession issued on the 7th October, 2010 for noncompliance with the provisions of the Rules of court. The appellant in her motion on notice urged the trial court to exercise the power of review conferred on it pursuant to the provisions of Order 53 Rule 8(1) of the 2004 of the Lagos State High Court (Civil Procedure) Rules, to review the orders it earlier made in Suit NO: ID/923M/99, since the proceedings in the same suit were conducted under the aforementioned Order 53. The respondents filed a counter affidavit against the appellant's application. The respondents *vide* a motion on notice dated 18th October, 2011, objected to the hearing of the aforesaid appellant's motion on notice, for want of jurisdiction, on the ground that the motion was caught by issue estoppel per *rem judicatam*. In his ruling, the learned trial judge upheld the respondents' objection and consequently the appellants' motion on notice was dismissed for want of the court's jurisdiction to entertain it as caught in the web of estoppel per *rem*

---

[31] (2019) LPELR-47506 (CA) Pp. 43-50, para. D.

judicatam. Dissatisfied, appellant appealed to the court of Appeal. Part of the issues the respondent raised for determination was whether the principle of estoppel per *rem judicatam* was rightly applied by the lower court?

The court while dismissing the appeal held thus:

> Upon my perusal of the record of appeal, it is clear to me as crystals, that appellant's motion on notice filed on 17th August, 2011, is with respect to part of the 398 acres of land in Agindingbi, Ikeja area, covered by the Survey Plan No. CK/LS/272 dated 22/12/1977, drawn by Abolade Coker, the Licensed Surveyor and the same land had been adjudged as belonging to the respondents vide the Suit NO:ID/216/77L, on 19/08/1983. The Lagos State Government, who was a party to the suit aforesaid, had wanted to re-litigate in respect of the said parcel of land and the Court of Appeal in her ruling on the Motion on Notice NO: CA/L/649M/2006, at the instance of the Lagos State Government, refused the application on 26/4/2007. On a further appeal to the Supreme Court vide the Appeal NO: SC.173/2009, by the Lagos State Government, the Apex Court on 24th May, 2010, ruled in favour of the respondents against the Lagos State Government...
>
> It should be remembered that the respondents vide the Suit NO: ID/216/77/L, had obtained judgment in their favour in respect of the 398 acres of land at Agindingbi on 19/08/1983 and the Lagos State Government was a party to the suit aforementioned. My Lords, I must say that I have no difficulty at all in agreeing with the submissions of the respondents' learned counsel to the effect that the foundation of the appellant's title to the plots of land at Agindingbi, Ikeja area, given to her by the Agindingbi community and regularized for her by the Lagos State Government who issued her with a Certificate of Occupancy in respect of the said plots of land. And if the attempt by the latter, described as Party Interested/Applicant, was adjudged by this Court in its decision rendered vide the Appeal No: CA/L/649M/2006 on 26/4/2007 and that by the Supreme Court on 24/5/2010 in re - Appeal NO: SC.173/2009, to be a re litigation of the action in Suit No: ID/216/77L, decided in favour of the respondents in 1983 at the court below, it follows that the appellant's motion on notice filed on 17th August, 2011 suffers the same fate, that is, it is tantamount to a re-litigation of the same subject matter which had been decided by the Court below in 1983...
>
> Therefore, it is not farfetched, to conclude that the appellant's motion on notice in question was caught in the web of estoppel per *rem judicatam*. The principle was well explained by the Supreme Court in *Yusuf* v.

> *Adegoke & Anor.* (2007) 11 NWLR (pt.1045) 332 @ 361-362, per Aderemi, JSC., thus: "It has become well entrenched in our civil jurisprudence that once a matter has been finally and judicially pronounced upon or determined by a Court of competent jurisdiction, neither the parties thereto nor their privies can subsequently be allowed to relitigate such matter in court. A judicial decision properly handed down is conclusive until reversed by a Superior Court and its veracity is not open to a challenge nor can it be contradicted. The term derives its force from good public policy which says there must be an end to litigation. The maxim is interest *republicae ut sit finis litium*...A successful plea of estoppel per *rem judicatam* ousts the jurisdiction of the Court before which it is raised...In the instant case, it is glaringly clear on the facts and circumstances already analysed earlier in this judgment, that the appellant is a privy in estate, of the Lagos State Government, from whom she derived her title to the plots of land given to her by the Agindingbi Community and later regularized by the Lagos State Government who issued her with a Certificate of Occupancy over her plots of land. Hence, the appellant is bound by the decision of this Court in CA/L/649M/2006 rendered on 26/4/2007, which was against her predecessor-in-title, the LagosState Government. Afortiori, the appellant is prevented by the operation of the doctrine of estoppel per *rem judicatam*, from reopening any issue with respect to the 398 acres of land at Agindingbi, Ikeja area, adjudged in favour of the respondents by the Court below, vide the Suit No: ID/216/77L in 1983; which is extant and binding on her.

The judgment of the court above was quoted *in extenso* to buttress the importance of *res judicata* and its applicability.

4. Pre-Conditions for Application of *Res Judicata*

As enunciated earlier, for the doctrine of estoppel per *rem judicatam* to apply, some condition sine qua non must be met. From the corpus of decided cases, one of which is the recent decision of the Court of Appeal in *Ezeala & Ors* v. *Ugah & Ors*[32] the court, while relying on the decision of the apex court in *Ogboloshingha* v. *BSIEC*,[33] finely distilled that for the doctrine of estoppel per *rem judicatam* to apply, it must be cumulatively shown that:

(i) the parties or their privies are the same in both the previous and present proceedings;

(ii) the claim or issue in dispute in both actions is the same;

---

[32](2019) LPELR-46904 (CA) Pp. 23, paras. A-C.

[33](2015) LPELR 24353 (SC).

(iii) the issues and subject matter of litigation must be the same in the two cases;
(iv) that the decision relied upon to support the plea of estoppel is valid, subsisting and final; and
(v) that the court that gave the previous decision relied upon to sustain the plea is a court of competent jurisdiction.

Unless all the above constitutional elements or requirements of the doctrine are fully established, the plea of estoppel per *rem judicatam* cannot be sustained. The Court of Appeal in *Ezeala's* case went further at page 23 to posit that it has also been held severally by the court that, unless all the above constitutional elements or requirements of the doctrine are fully established, the plea of estoppel per *rem judicatam* cannot be sustained.

This was also the infallible decision of the Court of Appeal in the earlier case of *Haruna* v. *Galadima & Ors.*[34] It is trite law that once these ingredients of res juidcata are established, the previous judgment estops the plaintiff from making any claim contrary to the decision in the previous case.[35]

Consequently, where an issue has been vigorously canvassed and duly adjudicated upon by a court of competent jurisdiction between two parties, it is binding in a subsequent suit between the same parties or their privies. *Res judicata* is not a technical doctrine; it applies to an order interlocutory in form which was meant to be a declaration of the rights of the parties. It equally applies in all courts; it is immaterial in what court the former proceedings was taken, provided only that it was a court of competent jurisdiction; provided it was for the same cause.[36]

The facts and decision of the apex court in the recent case of *Zubair* v. *Kolawole*[37] on the plea of *res judicata* is very germane to reproduce here. In this case, the contention of parties which formed the crux of the matter was: which of the two families, the appellant's Sunmonu Okunoye family or the respondent's Kolawole family, is entitled to produce the Baale of Ganmo through its male line by virtue of being the founder of Ganmo? On the appellant's side, there was an allegation that the respondent's predecessor in title had put himself out as *Baale* of Ganmo for which he was issued a warning in writing. On the respondent's side, it was also contended that

[34](2018) LPELR-44368 (CA) P. 10, para. A.
[35]*Kehinde* v. *Eneh* (2017) LPELR-43155(CA) P. 15, paras. B.
[36] See *Liasu & 5 Ors* v. *Salau & 3 Ors* (2012) 2 NWRL (Pt. 1283) 162 at 182.
[37](2019) LPELR-46928 (SC).

there was a decision rendered by the Traditional Council in 1978, after a thorough hearing, recognizing the respondent's family as the family entitled to the Baaleship. The defendant/respondent joined issues with the plaintiff/appellant and contended, inter alia, that in fact, it was his own great grandfather, named Ganna-Nganku, who founded Ganmo and that it is the male line of his own family that produces the *Baale*. The matter proceeded to trial. At the conclusion of the trial, judgment was entered in favour of the plaintiff/appellant. Dissatisfied with the judgment of the trial court, the respondent appealed to the Court of Appeal, which, by majority decision, allowed the appeal. Appellant therefore appealed to the Supreme Court. While dismissing the appeal at the Supreme Court and a consequent finding that the case of the appellant was caught in the web of estoppel per *rem judicatam*, the apex court held *inter alia*:

> I am unable to fault the sound reasoning above. It was the proceedings in Exhibits D1 and D2 that gave rise to the suit and the judgment of Oyeyipo, CJ in Exhibit D25. The parties, their privies and the cause of action in all three were the same as in the suit before the learned trial Judge. In the absence of any appeal against the decision in Exhibit D25, the trial Court was estopped from entertaining the suit. The decision of Oyeyipo, CJ that the court lacked jurisdiction to entertain the suit because the cause of action was not justiciable is valid and subsisting. The learned trial Judge ought to have struck out the suit. The first issue is accordingly resolved against the appellant. Having resolved the first issue against the appellant, there is no useful purpose to be served by delving into the remaining issues, which are now otiose. In conclusion, I hold that the appeal lacks merit. It is hereby dismissed.[38]

What needs to be re-emphasized is that a plea of *res judicata* will fail where all or any of these five conditions are not met by the party relying on it. In some instances, the two conditions that "issue" or "subject matter" must be the same are merged and treated as one condition thereby reducing the number of conditions to four.[39] However, there seem to be little variegated discrepancies in the decisions of the court as regards the number of conditions to be fulfilled for the doctrine of estoppel *per rem judicata* to apply. Though, we may not be so much concerned with numerical exactitude, but for the sake of clarity and precision of the law with its

[38] Pp. 42-43, Paras E-D.

[39] For instance, see Aguda, *op. cit.,* at pg. 272 to 282 and S.T. Hon, *op. cit.*, at pp. 1152.

predictability, we may point out some decisions that fell into this confusion. In *Madam Abusatu Agbogunleri* v. *John Depo & 3 Ors,*[40] three conditions were identified. The case of *Yakubu* v. *Ajaokuta Steel Co. Ltd*[41] also enumerated three conditions. Consequently, in *Dr. Oloruntoba – Oju &4 Ors* v. *Professor Abdul – Raheem & 3 Ors,*[42] five pre-conditions that must be present for estoppel to succeed were stated.

There may not be certainty of the number of conditions to be fulfilled for the doctrine to apply. However, there is solace in the more recent decision of the Supreme Court in *Yanaty Petrochemical Ltd* v. *EFCC*[43] *and* the recent decision of the Court of Appeal in *Haruna* v. *Galadima & Ors*[44] and *Ezeala's case supra* that identified five conditions that must exist for *res judicata* to operate. It is on this pedestal or consideration that the conditions identified in the latter decision of the apex court are spotlighted for discussion hereunder. This is because all conditions must exist before estoppel can operate and where one or more of the conditions are not met, plea of estoppel *per rem judicata* will not succeed.[45] The burden is on the party who sets up the plea of estoppel to conclusively establish that all the pre-conditions for its application exist. He has to marshal facts that would convince the court that the new action instituted by the Plaintiff is not merely a waste of time of the court but equally an abuse of the process of court. The court must steer clear of giving judgment in a case where a defence of *res judicata* is raised and there are no strong cogent and convincing evidence glaringly clear as to persuade the court to act in the manner the proponent of the defence pleads.[46] The conditions shall be discussed as follows:

i. The Parties or their privies must be the same

Before a judgment can operate as an estoppel per *rem judicatam*, the parties or the privies to the two proceedings must be the same.[47] This presupposes that there must be in existence, two suits; the earlier decided suit between the parties and the present one, wherein a party seeks to move the court to

---

40 (2008) 1 SCNJ 522 per Muhammad JSC.
41 (2010) 2 NWLR (pt. 1177) 167 at 178 per Bada JCA. Coram: M.U Peter-Odili, JCA, (as he then was), J.O. Bada, JCA, (read the lead judgment) A. Aboki, JCA Court of Appeal, Abuja Division, 2nd July 2009.
42 (2009) 6 SCNJ 1 at Per Adekeye JSC.
43 (2017) LPELR-43473(SC) P. 41 Paras. C-F.
44 *Supra* at page 10, paras. D-F.
45 *Naba'u & Ors* v. *Kashim & Ors* (2017) LPELR-43319 (CA) P. 23, para. G.
46 Ibid.
47 See the recent case of *Faluyi & Ors* v. *Ogunseye & Ors.* (2019) LPELR-48015(CA).

re-litigate on a matter that had been settled with finality between the same parties or their privies. It should be noted that this does not mean that all the parties in the previous suit must be made parties in the latter suit. It suffices where there were several parties in the previous suit, that those of the parties who are necessary parties to the issue in the previous suit are the same as in the latter suit.[48]

It is the law that every judgment is conclusive proof as against parties and privies.[49] "Parties" mean the actual parties named on record in the proceedings and this includes their privies as recorded under section 173 of the Evidence Act. The court also recognizes the categories of persons who litigate in undisclosed capacities.

In *Re: Agboyi-Ketu Local Development Area & Anor*[50] a "privy" was defined thus:

> The word "Privy" has been defined so succinctly as a person who is in privity with another. One who is a partaker or has any part or interest in any action or matter or thing.

In connection with the doctrine of *res judicata*, privy is one who after the commencement of the action has acquired interest in the subject matter affected by the judgment through or under one of the parties as by inheritance, succession, purchase or assignment.[51]The court in this case went further at page 20 to hold that a judgment of the court binds not only the parties but also all those who come within the legal ambit of privies to the parties on the record. In law, privies are of three classes, namely:

a. privies in blood such as an heir and ancestors;[52]
b. privies in law such as testators and executors or in the case of intestate succession, a successor and administrator;[53] and
c. privies in estate such as vendor and purchaser of land,[54] grantor and grantee or lessor and lessee.[55]

---

[48]Ayoola JSC in *Ikeni* v. *Efamo* (2001) 10 NWLR (Pt. 720) 1 See also *Ekennia* v. *Nka Kpara* (1997) 5 SCNJ 70.
[49]*Iseru* v. *Catholic Bishop of Warri Diocese* (1997) LPELR-1543(SC).
[50](2017) LPELR -41955 (CA) P. 21 paras. D-F.
[51] Ibid.
[52] See also *Gbadomosi* v. *Dairo* (2001) 6 NWLR (Pt. 708) 137, 167.
[53] See also *Tsokwa Oil & Marketing Co* v. *U.T.C Nig. Plc* (2002) 12 NWLR.
[54] See also *Lawal* v. *Salami* (2002) 2 NWLR (Pt. 752) 687, 717 – 718.
[55]*Nwosu* v. *Udeaja* (1990) 1 NWLR (Pt. 125) 188.

The general principle of law relating to privy in title is that in transactions relating to land, any person who derives title from or takes an assignment from, or is let into possession by or otherwise claims or "comes in" under the actual representor is bound by the same representation and consequent estoppel as that which binds the actual representor.[56]

ii. The issues and subject matter must be the same

The plea can only be relied on where the subject matter in the previous suit and the subject matter in the subsequent suit are the same.[57]In determining whether the issues and the subject matter of the two actions and the parties are the same, the court is permitted to study the pleadings, the proceedings and the judgment in the previous action. The court is entitled to look at the Judges reason for his decision and his notes of the evidence and is not restricted to the record. It may also examine other relevant facts to discover what was in issue in the previous case. It is entirely a question of fact.[58] Thus, a party will not be allowed to split a cause of action into two or more and litigate it in parts.[59]

In failure to satisfy this condition in *Ikoku* v. *Ekenkwu,*[60] the Supreme Court held that since the land in dispute in the present suit was different from the issue in the previous suit, it was futile to raise the plea of *res judicata.* The Court of Appeal while puncturing the case of the appellant in *Mbeda & Anor* v. *Fulani,*[61] held, *inter alia,*

> The second requirement that, the issue or subject-matter in dispute must be the same both in the earlier and second actions, postulates that once the issue in dispute has been raised and distinctly determined between the parties, the general rule, is that, neither party is allowed to fight that issue, irrespective of the facts or law involved or mixture of the two, all over-again. Hence, a party is precluded from re-litigating all over again a cause of action that has been previously determined. It will appear that the Appellants have no contention regarding this limb. I must again agree with the learned counsel for the Respondent that, the cause of action, in the two suits, that is, the suit filed by the 1st Appellant at the Upper Area Court, Gombe, which culminated in the appeal, Suit No. ADSM/4A/2013

[56] See *Coker* v. *Sanyaolu* (1976) 9-10 SC 203 at 233.
[57] *Izedonmwen* v. *Lawal* (2019) LPELR -47212 (CA).
[58] *Naba'u & Ors* v. *Kashim & Ors* (*supra*) at P. 25, paras. C-D.
[59] See *Gafai* v. *UAC Ltd* (1961) All NLR 785.
[60] (1996) 7 SCNJ 180.
[61] (2018) LPELR-46083 (CA) Pp. 21-23, Paras. F-C.

> and Suit No. ADSY/132/2016, the subject of this appeal, filed by the two Appellants at the trial Court, is the same...There is no question in my mind and I hold that, the subject-matter in dispute between the two sets of parties in the earlier and instant actions is the same and it is immaterial that the reliefs sought under each action are varied.

Thus, where the subject matter in the earlier or previous case is different from that in the subsequent or latter case, *res judicata* will not apply. It has also been held that the judgment relied on must not be imprecise, ambiguous, unclear, equivocal, implicit or nebulous, for a party is generally precluded from contending the contrary of any precise point which, having been once distinctly put in issue and has solemnly been pronounced upon or decided against him.[62] In *Adeshoye* v. *Olowolagba*,[63] it was held that where the previous matter is vague on the issue of subject matter and the parties, *res judicata* will not apply. In *Oya* v. *Ikalide*,[64] the court held that where the previous suit was a chieftaincy dispute while the present one was a land dispute, the rule of *res judicata* will not apply. It is needlessly superfluous to restate at this juncture that the doctrine will not apply where the subject matter is not the same even where there is a discrepancy in the measurement of the subject matter.

iii. The decision relied upon must be valid, subsisting and final

Another fundamental condition for the operation and applicability of estoppel per *rem judicatam* is that the judgment or decision relied upon must be valid, final and subsisting. Estoppel per *rem judicatam* can arise only out of an action in a court of competent jurisdiction which proceeded to final judgment. The question that should put dagger point in one's level of thinking is or agitate one's mind is: when can it be said that a decision or judgment is final? While giving a judicial insight on the test of finality of judgment, the Court of Appeal in *Vinet Estate Ltd* v. *Hon. Minister, FCT & Anor*,[65] answered this question thus:

> A decision of a court can only be regarded as finally disposing of the rights of the parties before it if the decision of the court is such that the

[62] See *Coker* v. *Sanyaolu (supra)*.
[63] (1996) 12 SCN 95.
[64] (1995) 7 SCNJ 122
[65](2018) LPELR-44797 (CA) P. 14, Paras. C-D.

matters in controversy between the parties would not be brought back to the court for adjudication.

This is predicated on the premise that issues before a court must be settled to finality and not left hanging on loose ends. The earlier decision relied upon must not only be subsisting and final, but must be valid. In *Ogunlana & Ors* v. *Fasanya & Ors,*[66] the originating processes in the action at the trial court (the previous suit upon which the plea of *res judicata* was premised in the case) having been signed by a law firm, not by an identifiable legal practitioner was held to be incompetent and the proceedings of the court leading to judgment in the case built on the incompetent processes was equally rendered incompetent and a nullity and thus liable to be set aside. Thus, the court pronounced that the principle of estoppel is inapplicable where the judgment is declared a nullity and hence, not a valid judgment. It therefore follows that a judgment that is a nullity has no legal validity and can confer no right nor impose any obligation on anybody and such judgment cannot operate as estoppel per *rem judicatam.* A null proceeding or judgment is deemed not to have even existed at all; it cannot therefore be the basis for the assertion of rights or to command obligation; it has no legal relevance. Such judgment cannot be employed as pedestal upon which to concrete a valid and sustainable decision. In *Kehinde* v. *Eneh,*[67] a judicial insight and illumination was thrown on the question of when is a judgment of the court said to be final? The court held that the test for deciding whether any order, decision or judgment of a court is final or interlocutory is, does the order or decision made dispose of the rights of the parties? If it does, then it is a final one, if it does not, it is an interlocutory one. Thus, where a decision of a court clearly and wholly disposes of all the rights of the parties in the case, that decision is final. But where the decision only disposes of an issue or issues in the case leaving the parties to go back to claim other right in the court, then, the decision is interlocutory. The court went further to hold that the judgment in suit No.KDC/7cv/2013 is final which has finally determined the claims of the parties. It is glaringly clear that the finality of a judgment for the purpose of *res judicata* is therefore viewed in contra distinction with an interlocutory judgment. A final judgment of that purpose is known as appealable judgment, definite judgment or final decree.[68]

---

[66](2019) LPELR-47875 (CA).

[67](2017) LPELR-43155(CA) P. 17, paras. A-C.

[68]See also *Palyvalent (Nig) Ltd* v. *Akinbote* (2010) 8 NWLR (Pt. 1197) 506.

It must be stressed at this juncture that a final judgment is one that confers rights that are enforceable. A judicial decision is said to be final judgment when it leaves nothing to be judicially determined or ascertained thereafter, in order to render it effective and capable of execution; and that it is one that is absolute, complete and certain and one that is not lawfully subject to subsequent recession or modification by the tribunal that pronounced it.[69] In the same wavelength, it was reiterated in *Chief Usung* v. *Chief Nyong*,[70] that there is need for a judgment or decision of a court to be final in its conclusion. No judgment or other proceeding can be final which does not once and for all, affect the status of the parties for whichever side the decision may be given. Put in another language, a final judgment is one which puts an end to an action by declaring that the plaintiff is or is not entitled to the remedy he sued for so that nothing remains to be done but execute the judgment.

iv. The court that gave the previous decision must be a court of competent Jurisdiction

Very fundamental and cardinal to the principle that guides the operation of *res judicata*, is that the court that gave the previous decision must be a court of competent jurisdiction; That is to say; a court with jurisdiction to hear and try the case. Question of jurisdiction is of a threshold issue in accusatorial system of criminal justice system. Jurisdiction is the fulcrum and the basis upon which the court stands. It is the 'linchpin', the 'life line' and the 'spinal cord' of adjudication. It is to adjudication, what oxygen is to mammals. Where there is a deficiency in jurisdiction, no matter how infinitesimal or minute, and the quantum of dexterity invested in such case notwithstanding, the case is, inescapably marooned in the web of nullity.[71] The question of jurisdiction is very paramount and crucial as it can be raised at any stage of the proceedings and even on appeal before the Supreme Court.[72]

The law is rock solid that the issue of jurisdiction of a court to adjudicate over matters is very pivotal. The word jurisdiction simply means, the authority which a court has to decide matters brought before it or take

---

[69] See *Honda Place Ltd* v. *Globe Motors Ltd* (2005) 14 NWLR (Pt. 945) 273.

[70] (2010) 2 NWLR (pt 1177) 88 at 115 per Omokri, JCA.

[71] *Magaji* v. *Ogele* (2012) LPELR-9476 (CA) per Obande Ogbuinya JSCA, *Shelim* v. *Gabang* (2009) 6 SCNJ 202 at 212 citing with approval *Mustapha* v. *Governor of Lagos State* (1987) 2 NWLR (Pt 58) *Utih* v. *Onoyivwe* (1991) 1 NWLR (pt 166) 206, *Madukolu* v. *Nkemdilem*. (1962) All NLR (Pt. 2) 581.

[72] *Onyekwuluje & Anor* v. *Animashaun & Anor* (2019) LPELR-46528(SC).

cognizance of matters presented to it in a formal way for its decision. Issue of jurisdiction can be raised in any form by any of the parties or *suo motu* by the court.[73] It is an elementary principle of law that any judgment or decision given without jurisdiction is a nullity and ought to be set aside.[74]

Courts are set up under the Constitution, Decrees, Acts, Laws, and Edicts. They vest the courts with powers and jurisdiction. If the statutes do not vest a court or tribunal with the jurisdiction to entertain a matter, the courts and the parties cannot by consent, endow itself (the court) with jurisdiction.[75] The jurisdiction of a court is confined, limited and circumscribed by the statue creating it.

It has for long been settled that a court is competent when-

(1) it is properly constituted with respect to the number and qualification of its members and none of the members is disqualified for any reason;
(2) the subject matter of the dispute is within its competence and jurisdiction;
(3) the action is initiated by due process of law and not in the abuse of the court's processes; and
(4) any condition precedent to the exercise of its jurisdiction has been fulfilled.[76]

Furthermore, the court while ruling on the fourth condition that for a successful plea of the defence of estoppel per *rem judicatam*, the court which adjudicated upon the earlier suit must be a court clothed with requisite jurisdiction held in *Mbeda & Anor* v. *Fulani*[77] that since the court that gave the previous decision (Upper Area Court) has been declared on appeal in Suit No. ADSM/4A/2013 as being devoid of jurisdiction, the judgment delivered by it cannot stand.

The court went further to posit thus:

> I must once again disagree with the Appellants learned counsel and hold that his answer to his own poser above is a total legal fallacy. As I already stated above, the judgment of the Upper Area Court, Gombe having been set aside on appeal had ceased to be in existence and was replaced by the decision in the appeal, Suit No. ADSM/4A/2013.

---

[73] Ibid.
[74] *Ovh Energy Marketing Ltd* v. *Virgin Fields (Nig) Ltd & Anor.* (2019) LPELR-47610 (CA).
[75] *FCMB* v. *Action Alliance* (2018) LPELR-44445 (CA).
[76] See *Oni* v. *Igbinedion University, Okada & Ors* (2018) LPELR-46161(CA); *Ashorobi* v. *Akinole & Ors.* (2019) LPELR-47506 (CA); *Madukolu* v. *Nkemdilim* (*supra*).
[77] (2018) LPELR-46083 (CA) P. 29.

In the final analysis, it must be noted that it is the claim that determines jurisdiction[78] and that no judge can set aside or vary the order or orders of any brother judge of the same High Court, except where the earlier one is a nullity. In the recent case of *Ogungwa & Ors* v. *Williams & Anor,*[79] the court of Appeal on the issue of the judge's inability to vary the ruling of a judge of coordinate jurisdiction held thus:

> It is settled that all courts established under the constitution derives their powers and authority from the constitution. And that once an issue has been distinctly raised and determined between the parties in a court, neither party is allowed to re-open such issue all over again. The issue of joinder of appellants having been determined by the order of Ilok J. on 22/10/2002 shall not be reopened again. By the rule of equality of courts, no court has the power to overrule the decision of another court of co-ordinate jurisdiction.

The doctrine or principle of *res judicata* cannot be considered in a vacuum and without the surrounding background facts of the case

In summary, a judgment or ruling handed down by a court that lacks jurisdiction to entertain the matter in which the ruling has been given, cannot operate as estoppel to debar the plaintiff from setting the law in motion against the defendant.

5. Cause of Action and Issue Estoppel

Oftentimes, cause of action estoppel and issue estoppel are conflated with each other. The reason could be as a result of its enclave under one 'umbrella' called *res judicata.* In a bid to streamline these off-springs of *res judicata,* we shall dissect their meanings with the aim of bringing out the dichotomy and applicability in them. In *Registered Trustees of Nigerian Association of Patent & Proprietary Medicine Dealers* v. *PCN & Anor,*[80] the court of Appeal held that the law is that if a party brings an action against another for a particular cause and judgment is given on it, he cannot institute another suit against the same party for the same cause (Cause of action estoppel). However, within one cause of action, there may be several

---

[78] *Esabunor & Anor* v. *Faweya & Ors* (2019) LPELR-46961 (SC).

[79] (2019) LPELR-47536 (CA) P. 18, Paras. C-E. See also *Onaopemipo* v. *UBN PLC* (2018) LPELR-46369 (CA) P. 16, paras. E-F.

[80] (2019) LPELR-47540 (CA) Pp.29-30, paras. G-C.

issues. Once an issue has been raised in a case and is determined between the parties, the same issue cannot be raised again by either of the parties in the same or subsequent proceedings. This is issue estoppel. What constitutes cause of action estoppel and issue estoppel in the realm of *res judicata* was clearly explained in the recent decision of the Supreme Court in *Zubair* v. *Kolawole*.[81] His Lordship, Kekere Ekun JSC posited thus:

> There are two types of estoppel: cause of action estoppel and issue estoppel. Cause of action estoppel arises where the same cause of action has been held to lie (or not to lie) in a final judgment between the same parties, or their privies, who are litigating in the same capacity (and on the same subject matter). Issue estoppel, on the other hand, arises where an issue has earlier on been adjudicated upon by a court of competent jurisdiction and the same issue comes incidentally in question in any subsequent proceedings between the same parties or their privies.

This is because, it is against the rule of public policy for anyone to be twice vexed on the same ground and for one and the same cause of action or the same issue. In appropriate cases, the parties affected are estopped per *rem judicatam* from bringing a fresh action before any court on the same cause and on the same issue already decided or pronounced upon by a court of competent jurisdiction in a previous action.[82]

Where *res judicata* is pleaded by way of estoppel to an entire cause of action, it amounts to an allegation that the whole legal rights and obligations of the parties were concluded by the earlier judgment, which may have involved the determination of question of law as well as finding of facts.[83]

On the second sphere of estoppel, it is known as "issue estoppel." In the recent case of *Faluyi & Ors* v. *Ogunseye & Ors*,[84] the court of Appeal while elucidating on the conditions to be fulfilled for issue estoppel to apply held thus:

> Now, issue estoppel is recognized by Section 174 of the Evidence Act, 2011. The application of issue estoppel is based on the principles of law that, a party is not allowed to contend the contrary of any specific point which had been distinctly put in issue and determined with certainty

[81] (2019) LPELR-46928 (SC) P.40, Paras. A-C.
[82] See *Oyelakin Balogun* v. *Adadosu Adejobi* (1995) 2 NWLR (pt. 376) 131.
[83] See *Liasu & 5 Ors* v. *Salau & 4 Ors* (2012) 2 NWLR (pt 1238) 162 at 181.
[84] (2019) LPELR-48015 (CA) P. 65 paras. A-G.

against him. For issue estoppel to apply, the following conditions must be satisfied:

(a) the parties in the previous and the current proceedings are the same;

(b) the issues are the same;

(c) the issues are material to the cause of action in the previous and in the latter suit; and

(d) the issue must have been resolved in the previous case...[85]

Obviously, it would be the duty of the party who relies on issue estoppel to plead and lead evidence of that fact. In other words, the specie of estoppel relied on must be pleaded and proved. However, it should be noted that all parties need not necessarily be parties to both cases before issue estoppel can apply; it is sufficient, where there are several parties in the previous suit, that those of the parties who were necessary parties to the issue in the previous suit are the same as in the latter suit. The rule being that once one or more issues have been raised in a cause of action and distinctly determined or resolved between the same parties by a court of competent jurisdiction, then as a general rule, no party or his agent or privy is allowed to re-litigate that or those decided issues all over again in another action between the same parties or their privies on the same issue. Generally speaking, within one cause of action, there may arise several issues raised which are necessary for the determination of the whole case. Once an issue has been raised and distinctly determined between the parties, neither party can be allowed to raise that issue all over again.

In the recent decision of the court in *Oseni* v. *Adesanya & Anor,*[86] it was held that a party is precluded from contending the contrary of any precise point which having once been distinctly put in issue, has been solemnly and with certainty determined against him. Even if the objects of the first and second actions are different, the finding on a matter which came directly (not collaterally incidentally) in issue in the first action, provided it is embodied in a judicial decision that is final, is conclusive in a second action between the same parties and their privies.

In another recent case of *Orioye & Ors* v. *Abina & Anor*[87] on determination of issue estoppel, one of the three issues formulated for

---

[85]See also *Falaki & Ors* v. *Fagbuyiro & Ors* (2015) LPELR-25848 (CA) P. 118 Paras. C-E.
[86](2019) LPELR-48051 (CA) Pp.22-23, Paras. E-A.
[87] (2019) LPELR-47864 (CA).

determination by the Court of Appeal was whether the lower court was not wrong in holding that issue estoppel barred the suit and that the suit disclosed no reasonable cause of action? In the case, the predecessor of the Appellants in the appeal was one Williams Sanyaolu. While the matter was pending, he died and was substituted by Mrs. Grace Abiade Majekodunmi, the Appellant in the Supreme Court's decision. The predecessor of the 1st Respondent in this appeal was Babatunde Badaru Abina. He equally died in the course of the proceedings and he was substituted with Mutiu Abina, the 1st Respondent in the Supreme Court decision and he is also the 1st Respondent in the appeal before the Court of Appeal. It all started with the application made by the 1st Respondent's predecessor to the Registrar of Titles, Lagos State, to be registered as the titleholder for No. 66 Karimu Street, Surulere, Lagos. The Appellants' predecessor opposed the application and the matter went to the Registrar of Titles' court, which upheld the right of the 1st Respondents' predecessor to be registered as the title holder for the property. The Appellants' predecessor was dissatisfied with the decision. He appealed to the appellate division of the High Court of Lagos State and his appeal was dismissed. He further appealed against the decision of the High Court to the Court of Appeal but his appeal further failed. Finally, he appealed to the Supreme Court. His appeal was dismissed in *Majekodunmi* v. *Abina* which the appellate court have already referred to. But for the Appellants, the decision of the Supreme Court did not bring a closure to the dispute. On 26th April 2002, which was three months after the decision of the Supreme Court on 18th January 2002, they commenced another action before the High Court of Lagos State in Suit No. LD/848/2002/MRS. *Elizabeth Abiola Orioye & Ors* v. *Mutiu Abina & Anor.* Pleadings were filed and exchanged between the Appellants and the 1st Respondent. The 2nd Respondent did not file any pleadings at the lower court. The Appellants called one witness in proof of their case and the witness, among other documents, tendered the certified copy of the Supreme Court decision in *Majekodunmi* v. *Abina,* and it was admitted in evidence as Exhibit C2. The 1st Respondent elected not to call any witness and rested his case on that of the Appellants. The Court of Appeal while dismissing the Appellants' case for being marooned in the web of issue estoppel held thus:

> There is, however, a second kind of estoppel *inter partes* and this usually occurs where an issue has earlier on been adjudicated upon by a Court of competent jurisdiction and the same issue comes incidentally in question in any subsequent proceedings between the same parties (or their

privies); in these circumstances, 'issue estoppel' arises. This is based on the principle of law that a party is not allowed to (i.e. he is precluded from) contending[sic] the contrary or opposite of any specific point which having been once distinctly put in issue, has with certainty and solemnity been determined against him. [See *Outram* Vs. *Morewood* (1803) 3 East 346]. Issue estoppel applies whether the point involved in the earlier decision is one of fact or law or one of mixed fact and law...The submission of the Claimants' Counsel that the Supreme Court did not decide the issue and that the Court left the issue hanging was very incorrect. And the Supreme Court having decided the issue against the Claimants, the issue cannot form the basis of another action by the Claimants. This is the essence of the doctrine of issue estoppel.

6. Estoppel By Deed

For the first time in our evidential rule, the Evidence Act under section 169 of the Act made provision for the creation of estoppel by deed. Perusing through the whole of the repealed Evidence Act 2004, no provision was made for estoppel by deed. For precision and better understanding, a deed is any written instrument that is signed sealed and delivered which conveys some interest in land or other property.[88] This paradigm shift, undoubtedly represent a radical departure from the repealed position of the law which did not recognize estoppel by deed either in section 151 dealing with estoppel by conduct or any other part of the entire repealed Evidence Act 2004.

Expressing an intellectual concern and the great lacuna that has clutched the old Evidence Act, Aguda had bemoaned that although writers on the English Law of Evidence usually have a heading for "estoppel by deed," there is nowhere in the Evidence Act where provision is made for this. There is no doubt that it is equally true here as in England that a party who has executed a deed will be estopped by a court from saying that the facts stated in the deed are not true. But its scope must be strictly limited.[89]

It is a welcomed development to note that estoppel by deed is now explicitly and precisely covered in section 169 of the Evidence Act 2011, although such inclusion was long overdue. Estoppel by deed prevents a party to a deed from denying anything in that deed if the party has induced another to accept or act under the deed.

---

[88] See Black's Law Dictionary, *op. cit.*, page 423. See also *Obuladike* v. *Nganwuchu* (2013) LPELR-21265 (CA) P. 44, paras. B-D.

[89] Aguda, *op. cit.*, page 238.

The case of *Orumwense* v. *Amu & Anor*[90] stated the general rule to the effect that a man is estopped by his deed, and that a party of full age and understanding is bound by his signature to a document, whether he reads or understands it or not. If, however, a party has been misled into executing a deed or signing a document essentially different from that which he intended to execute or sign, he can plead *non est factum* as a defence in an action against him.

But in most of the cases in which *non est factum* has been successfully pleaded, the mistake has been induced by fraud, even though it is not an invariable rule.[91] Furthermore, estoppel by deed is a rule of evidence founded on the principle that a solemn and unambiguous statement or engagement in a deed must be taken as binding between parties and privies and therefore as not admitting any contradictory proof.[92]

Estoppel by deed applies only to litigation arising on the deed and does not apply to actions on collateral matters. A deed that can be vitiated and declared void on ground of illegality, fraud or any other vitiating element cannot operate as estoppel.[93]

7. Estoppel By Agreement

Section 169 of the Act made provision of for Estoppel generally and in particular, estoppel by agreement can operate in the underlisted three circumstances namely:

(a) estoppel for tenant and of licensee of person in possession;
(b) estoppel of bailee, agent and licensee;
(c) estoppel of person signing bill of lading.

We shall traverse them seriatim.

i. Estoppel of tenant and licensee of person in possession

Under section 170 of the Evidence Act, no tenant of immovable property or person claiming through such a tenant, shall during the continuance of the tenancy, be permitted to deny that the landlord of such tenant had at the beginning of the tenancy a title to such immovable property; and no person who came upon any immovable property by the license of the person in

---

[90](2008) LPELR-8573 (CA) 18 B-E.
[91] Ibid.
[92]*Agboola* v. *Abimbola* (1969) LPELR-25473 (SC) 14 D-E while citing *Greer* v. *Kettle* [1938] A.C. 156 at p. 171, per Lord Maugham.
[93] See *Orumwense* v. *Amu & Anor* (*supra*).

possession of it shall be permitted to deny that such person had a title to such possession at the time when such license was given. This is so because, the granting of the tenancy and acceptance of rent by the landlord is a representation of the title by him[94] and payment of rent is an acknowledgement of the title by the tenant.

This principle of law has received judicial blessing in *Jovinco Nigeria Ltd & Anor* v. *Ibeozimako*[95] where one Chief Michael Okechukwu lbeozimako, who was the late father of the Respondent and the owner of the land in dispute known as "W2 Ahmadu Bello Way Kaduna" which he bought from one Ajulu in the year 1952. The W2 Ahmadu Bello Way Kaduna is a commercial premises. One Unachukwu was the care-taker of the property until he died and Vincent I. Okezue (PW1) became the care-taker. The 1st and 2nd Appellants were two of the four tenants who occupy shops in W2 Ahmadu Bello Way, Kaduna and were paying rent first to Chief M. O. Ibeozimako before his death and after his death to the Respondent through the care-taker. Before Chief M.O. Ibeozimako died, he gave the land to the Respondent his first son, who upon his father's demise inherited the land and thereafter became the landlord of the premises. The Appellants were paying their rent in respect of the shops occupied by them until 1994 when they stopped payment and 2nd Appellant who is the Managing Director of the 1st appellant started claiming that the place belongs to him. Meanwhile in 1996, the 2nd Appellant who presented to the Respondent and the caretaker (PW1) that the Respondents father who had applied to Kaduna North Local Government for a new Certificate of Occupancy in place of the missing one, was asked to pay the sum of ₦100,000 for the new certificate of occupancy (C of O). The Respondent sent all the required documents in respect of the house to Elder Vincent I. Okezue (PW1) who was to go together to the lands office with the 2nd Appellant but could not make it as he had to travel. He gave all the documents to the 2nd Appellant and the sum of ₦50,000. Second Appellant was to add another ₦50,000 which would be defrayed from his rent. However, instead of applying for the Certificate of Occupancy in the Respondent's name, the 2nd Appellant, in connivance with staff of the Lands & Survey of the Local Government, secured the Certificate of Occupancy in his own name. At the conclusion on the trial, the trial court granted the claim of the plaintiff as prayed. Judgment was entered for the Respondent against the Appellant at the trial court and the

[94] Nwadialo, *op. cit.,* at P. 160.
[95](2014) LPELR-23599 (CA).

Appellant's counter-claim also dismissed. The Appellants being dissatisfied with the judgment of the trial court lodged an appeal at the Court of Appeal. In its judgment, the Court of Appeal in its wisdom held thus:

> Section 170 of the Evidence Act provides: "No tenant of immovable property or person claiming through such tenant, shall, during the continuance of the tenancy, be permitted to deny that the landlord of such tenant had at the beginning of the tenancy, a title to such immovable property; and no person who came upon any immovable property by the licence of the person in possession of it shall be permitted to deny that such person had a title to such possession at the time when such licence was given." Obviously, the Appellants having acknowledged the right of the Respondent's father and later that of the Respondent to the land in dispute by which right the Appellants became the tenants of the Respondents thereby creating a landlord-tenant relationship, the Appellants cannot be permitted to deny the title of the Respondent or that the Respondent did not possess the title or right in the property. By operation of Section 170 Evidence Act, the Appellants who have been tenants to Respondent, are estopped from denying the title or interest of the Respondent in the disputed land. To allow the Appellants to deny the title of the Respondent, would amount to what the Supreme Court said while explaining the rule of the of estoppel in the case of *Ude* vs. *Nwara* (*supra*) as "blowing hot and cold, to affirm at one time and deny at the other; or as it is said to approbate and reprobate...[96]

ii. Estoppel of bailee, agent and licensee

Section 171 of the Act created another genre of estoppel by conduct known as Estoppel of bailee, agent and Licensee. This section provides that no bailee, agent or licensee is permitted to deny that the bailor, principal or licensor by whom any goods were entrusted to any of them respectively, was entitled to those goods at the time when they were so entrusted. However, a bailee, an agent or a licensee may be permitted to show that he was compelled to deliver up such goods to some person who had a right to them as against his bailor, principal or licensor or that his bailor, principal or licensor wrongfully and without notice to the bailee, agent or licensee, obtained the goods from a third person who has claimed them from such bailee, agent or licensee.[97]

---

[96] See Pp. 27-28, C-B.

[97] See the proviso to section 171 of the Evidence Act.

iii. Estoppel of person signing bill of lading

Under section 172 of the Act, every bill of lading in the hands of a consignee or endorsee for valuable consideration, representing goods to have been shipped on board a vessel, is conclusive proof of that shipment as against the master or other person signing the same, notwithstanding that some goods or some part of them may not have been so shipped, unless such holder of the Bill of lading had actual notice at the time of receiving the same that the goods had not been in fact laden on board. Provided that the master or other person so signing may exonerate himself in respect of such misrepresentation by showing that it was caused without any default on his part, and wholly by the hand of the shipper or the holder or some person under whom the holder holds.[98]

The above provision of section 172 of the Evidence Act applies only to a shipper, carrier, consignee or endorsee. This is the interpretation and application of section 172 of the Evidence Act as enunciated in *Comet Shipping Agencies Ltd* v. *Babbit Ltd.*[99] The fact of this case disclosed that the respondent sued the appellant for failure to meet its obligation under a contract of bailment because following the appellant's negligence in keeping the goods, some quantity of the consignment shipped by the appellant got missing. Appellant contended vigorously among other things that he was only entrusted with the containers containing the shipped goods for safekeeping and that the missing goods were not in the container. Relying on the bill of lading, the learned trial judge found the appellant liable for the lost goods and finally gave judgment for the Respondent. The Appellant appealed against the judgment while the Respondent also cross-appealed. Relying on the provision of section 154 of the old Evidence Act now section 172, the court of Appeal held that every bill of lading in the hands of a consignee or endorsee for valuable consideration representing goods to have been shipped on board a vessel is conclusive proof of that shipment as against the master or other person signing the same. A bill of lading serves as a receipt that the goods named therein have been taken on board and that a statement appearing on a bill is presumed to be a correct statement of what was shipped. The provision of section 154 of the Evidence Act 2004 (now re-enacted as section 172 of Evidence Act 2011) applies only to a shipper, carrier, consignee or endorsee. Therefore, the trial court was held to have misapplied the law when it held the appellant accountable on the ground

---

[98] See also section 375 (3) of the Merchant Shipping Act 2007 for a similar provision.

[99] (2001) FWLR (pt. 40) 1630.

that he failed to provide any evidence oral or documentary to prove that there is an error in the bill of lading. In a later case of *Sterling Bank Plc* v. *Katagum Enterprises Ltd,*[100] citing section 375(3) of the Merchant Shipping Act 2007 which is on all fours with section 172 of the Evidence Act 2011, the court of Appeal posited thus:

> A careful perusal of the above provision that generally, a bill of lading 'shall be' conclusive evidence of the shipment it relates to even where 'such goods or some part thereof' may not have been delivered except where as provided under the provision, where the 'holder of the bill of lading shall have actual notice at the time of receiving the same that the goods had not been in fact laden on board.' However, a party seeking to rely on the provision must show he/she/it is not caught up by the proviso to Section 375(3) of the Act (which is in *pari materia* with section 172 of the Evidence Act 2011), to the effect that the misrepresentation arising from the discrepancies evident from what was *ipso facto* delivered or supplied and what was actually endorsed on the bill of lading as being the quantity or quality of the goods shipped, 'was caused without any default on his part, and wholly by the fraud of the shipper, or of the holder, or some person under whom the holder claims

In the instant case, the Appellant has failed to show, by credible evidence that it is not caught up by the proviso of that section. Apparently, Exhibit D1 does not constitute conclusive evidence of the goods shipped and supplied having regard to the facts of this case.

8. Estoppel in Criminal Cases

Two twin pillars of the cardinal and one of the most revered fundamental rights to fair hearing guaranteed under section 36 of the Constitution, constitute estoppel in criminal cases. These two subsections under these fundamental rights are subsections 9 and 10.

Under section 36(9) of the 1999 Constitution (as amended), it provides that no person who shows that he has been tried by a court of competent jurisdiction or tribunal for a criminal offence and either convicted or acquitted shall again be tried for that offence or for a criminal offence having the same ingredients as that offence save upon the order of a superior court. This is expressed in the Latin phrase, *nemo debet bis vexari pro una et eadem causa.* In the same vein, section 36(10) of the 1999 Constitution (as

[100] (2015) LPELR-25874 (CA).

amended) stipulates that no person who shows that he has been pardoned for a criminal offence shall be again be tried for that offence.

Two bars to vexatious suits which serve as estoppel in criminal cases can be deductible from the wordings of section 36(9) of the 1999 constitution. There are *autrefois acquit* and *autrefois convict*. In *Dasuki (Rtd)* v. *FRN*,[101] the Court of Appeal while throwing judicial illumination to the workability of estoppel in criminal matters held thus:

> There is no dispute to the fact that the principle of estoppel applies to both civil and criminal matters as contended by the appellants counsel, per Aniagolu JSC, in the case of *Aro* vs. *Fabolude* (1983) LPELR SC 106/1981 , while agreeing with Lord Diplock in Mills and Cooper (1967) 2 All ER 100 @ 105, re-emphasized the fact that the general rule of estoppel indeed applies to criminal proceedings, but in a form modified by the distinctive character of criminal as compared with civil litigation, for in criminal proceedings, it takes the form of the rule against double jeopardy of which the simplest application is to be found in the plea of *autrefois* convict and *autrefois* acquit.

It should be noted that this subsection has similarity or congruity with doctrine of cause of action estoppel. Another point worthy to note is that in order for the plea to succeed, the offence charged must have been committed or allegedly committed at the time of the first prosecution. Thus, where, after a conviction of assault, the victim dies from the injuries, there is no bar to a subsequent prosecution for murder or manslaughter.[102]

Generally speaking, the provision of section 173 of the Evidence Act providing the legal imprimatur for the application of the plea of *res judicata* or estoppel per *rem judicatam* did not provide a dichotomy between civil and criminal proceedings. Out of abundant caution *(ex abuntia cautela)* we reiterate that section 173 of the Evidence Act provides that:

> Every judgment is conclusive proof, as against parties and privies, of facts directly in issue in the case, actually decided by the court, and appearing from the judgment itself to be the ground on which it was based; unless evidence was admitted in the action in which the judgment was delivered

---

[101] (2018) LPELR-43969 (CA) Pp. 35-36, paras. F-B.

[102] Adrian Keane, *The Modern Law of Evidence* 2nd edn (England: Butterworths 1989) page 438 – 439. See also *R* v. *Morris* (1867) LRICCR 90. For a fuller treatment of the essential procedural law relating to special pleas in bar, see generally Lord Morris' nine Principles in *Connelly* v. *DPP* (1964) AC 1254 and J. F Archbold, *Criminal Pleading, Evidence & Practice* 42 edn. (London: Sweet & Maxwell, 1985) Para 4 – 67.

> which is excluded in the action in which that judgment is intended to be proved.

It is clear from the foregoing that the "judgment" alluded to in section 173 of the Evidence Act can emanate from either civil or criminal proceedings.[103]

Effects of Judgment Not Pleaded As Estoppel

It is provided under section 174(1) of the Evidence Act that if a judgment is not pleaded by way of estoppel, it is as between parties and privies deemed to be a relevant fact, whenever any matter, which was or might have been decided in the action in which it was given, is in issue, or is deemed to be relevant to the issue in any subsequent proceeding. Under section 174(2) of the Act, such judgment is conclusive proof of the facts which it decides, or might have decided, if the party who gives evidence of it had no opportunity of pleading it as an estoppel.

There is an array of recent cases decided by our courts in an attempt to iron out the creases on the effect of judgment not pleaded as estoppel. In *Adekunle* v. *Ibru*,[104] the court held thus:

> It is well established in a long line of cases that the plea of estoppel is not required to be pleaded in a particular form. In *Chinwendu* vs. *Mbamali & Anor* (1980) 3-4 SC 21, the Supreme Court held as follows: "Undoubtedly the old rule was that estoppel by record and deed must be pleaded where, as here, there was an opportunity to do so; under modern practice it is not, however, necessary to plead estoppel in any particular form so long as the matters constituting the estoppel are stated in such a manner (as has been done in the pleadings of the respondents in these proceedings) to show that the party pleading relies upon it as a defence or an answer.

In *Alli* v. *Gbadamosi & Anor,*[105] the Court of Appeal held that it is the law that, for estoppel to be relied on as a defence, it must be specifically pleaded. However, it is not the law that estoppel must be pleaded in a particular manner. All that is required is that facts must be pleaded which show clearly that the party pleading intends to rely on estoppel as a

---

[103] See the dictum of Akawu Barka JCA in *Dasuki (Rtd)* v. *FRN* (*supra*).
[104](2018) LPELR-44119 (CA) P. 53, Paras. B-E.
[105] (2017) LPELR-42379 (CA) P. 28, Paras. A-B.

defence.[106] Thus modern legal thinking is that the courts will not allow themselves to be hampered by the undue and unnecessary technicalities in their quest to do substantial justice.

The issue is not therefore whether estoppel was pleaded specifically or not in a particular form, but whether there are sufficient facts in the pleadings which show that the pleader relies on it. This is to avoid sacrificing justice on the altar of technicality.

In summary, in the earlier decision of the apex court in *Ohiaeri* v. *Akabueze*,[107] it was categorically held that it is not mandatory that a defendant who seeks to rely on a previous judgment to support his plea of *res judicata* must use the words "estoppel" or "*res judicata*". It is sufficient if he refers to a previous judgment between the parties in respect of the matter in dispute, without alluding to its legal effect.

Customary Arbitration As Estoppel

It is well accepted that one of the many African customary modes of settling dispute is to refer the dispute to the family head or an elder or elders of the community for a compromise solution based upon the subsequent acceptance by both parties of the suggested award, which becomes binding only after such signification of its acceptance. Customary arbitration is a homegrown and efficacious alternative to dispute resolution mechanism devised by natives or indigenous people using their custom or culture to stability, method of social control, social cohesion and equilibrium.

Statutorily, custom has been defined under section 258(1) of the Evidence Act as a rule which in a particular district has from long usage obtained the force of law.[108] The Evidence Act regulates which custom is admissible and how custom may be proved. Section 16(1) of the Act provides that a custom may be adopted as part of the law governing a particular set of circumstances if it can be judicially noticed or can be proved to exist by evidence. The Act under sub 2 of the said section provides that the burden of proving custom shall lie upon the person alleging its existence. From the wordings of section 16(1) of the Act, two methods of proving custom can be deduced. There are by judicial notice and by leading evidence in the particular case or proof by evidence. Customary law has to be proved by calling witnesses or assessors who have special knowledge of the

---

[106] See also *Oseni* v. *Adesanya & Anor* (2019) LPELR-48051 (CA) P. 19, para. A.
[107] (1992) 2 NWLR (Pt. 221) 1.
[108] See the next chapter for a detailed discussion on proof of custom.

particular custom and it is only when such custom becomes notorious as a result of being adjudicated upon once by a court of superior record that judicial notice of it is taken without further proof. Custom of people varies; it differs from place to place and from community to community.

Going into the kernel of our discussion, estoppel can arise from customary arbitration where two parties to a dispute voluntarily submit the issue in controversy between them to arbitration according to customary law and agree expressly or by implication that the decision of such arbitration would be binding and final. Thus customary arbitration if proved and pleaded is capable of constituting an estoppel.[109]

While answering the question of what must be proved by a party relying on customary arbitration, the court of appeal in *Raphael & Ors* v. *Ukachukwu & Ors*,[110] held thus:

> It is also settled that before applying the decision of a customary arbitration as an estoppel, the party alleging arbitration must show that parties had voluntarily submitted to the arbitration, consciously indicated their willingness after the pronouncement of the decision, and unequivocally accepted the award. While it may be sufficient to simply plead the fact of a previous judgment by a regular court as the basis of an estoppel, merely pleading such a decision in respect of a customary arbitration without pleading the ingredients that project it as creating estoppel will not be proper pleading because not every decision of a customary arbitration, unlike that of a regular Court, can create an estoppel. In other words, the party alleging customary arbitration will have to adduce credible evidence of the relevant ingredients necessary to sustain the material plea of estoppel by customary arbitration.

Once the arbitrators reach a decision, it would no longer be open to either party to subsequently bend over backwards or renege from the decision so pronounced.

In *Nwosu* v. *Ekeigwe*,[111] the Court in its wisdom earlier reiterated *in extenso* what must be established for a customary arbitration to serve as *res judicata*. There are:

(a) that there had been a voluntary submission of the matter in dispute to an arbitration of one or more persons;

---

[109] See *Ejimadu* v. *Nwoko & Anor* (2018) LPELR-45022 (CA) P. 23, para, B.
[110] (2018) LPELR-43964 (CA) Pp. 15-16, paras. D-B.
[111] (2015) 12 NWLR (P.t 212).

(b) that it was agreed by the parties either expressly or by implication that the decision of the arbitration would be accepted as final and binding;
(c) that the said arbitration was in accordance with the custom of the parties or of their trade or business;
(d) that the arbitrators reached a decision and published the award;
(e) that the decision or award was accepted at the time it was made.[112]

Thus, in the instant case, there was evidence on record that the parties complied with all the above conditions in submitting to the arbitration panel and the parties agreed to oath taking in line with the decision of the arbitration panel to resolve the land dispute between them. The oath was taken; the oath taking meant that if the person who swears it (in this case, Simeon Nwosu) dies within a year, the land would be deemed to belong to the respondent but if he survives, the land would be taken to belong to the appellant. The said Simeon Nwosu died within one year of the oath taking. There was nothing inconclusive in the arbitration panel's decision. The decision of the panel therefore effectively created estoppel as between the parties and their privies. The decision of the arbitrators would thus, become *res judicata* within the context of the relevant native law and custom as in the instant case. The respondent satisfied the conditions laid down by the Court of Appeal for the applicability of Customary Arbitration Tribunal's decision.

At page 51, His Lordship Peter Olabisi Ige J.C.A continued while citing Nnaemeka-Agu, JSC in *Michael Ifeanyi Ojibah* v. *Ubaka Ojibah,*[113]

> In my view, the law is pretty settled that where two parties to a dispute voluntarily submit their matter in controversy to arbitration according to customary law and agreed expressly or by implication that the decision of the arbitrators would be accepted as final and binding, then once the arbitrators reach a decision, it is no longer open to either party to subsequently back out of such a decision. The decision of the arbitrators would thus become *res judicata* within the context of the relevant native law and custom as in this case.

---

[112] However in a latter case of *Nnadi & Ors.* v. *Odika & Ors.* (2017) LPELR-43448 (CA), only three conditions for the applicability of customary arbitration as estoppel were enumerated to with; if it is shown firstly that both parties submitted to the arbitration. Secondly that the parties accepted the terms of the arbitration, and thirdly, that they agreed to be bound by the decision.

[113](1991) 6 SCNJ 156 at 169.

We shall place heavy reliance on judicial authorities for a better appreciation of this topic. With respect to customary arbitration and how it can constitute estoppel, the following must be noted: customary arbitration has been recognized as an effective way of dispute resolution though not as a regular court. Efficacy of customary arbitration has been judicially recognized in a plethora of decided cases including *Agubuchie* v. *Onwudinjo & Ors*[114]and *Agu* v. *Ikewuibe*[115] wherein the court gave a firm judicial stamp of approval to the efficacy of customary arbitration when it held that it is well accepted that one of the many African customary models of settling disputes is to refer the dispute to the family head, or an elder or elders of the community for a compromise solution based upon the subsequent acceptance by both parties of the suggested award which becomes binding only after signification of its acceptance form which either party is free to resile at any stage of the proceedings up to that point.

In another recent decision of the court in *Nnadi & Ors* v. *Odika & Ors,*[116] the facts of the case disclosed that the parties were all from Dimboko Village in Umuoji. The Respondents stated that they wanted to reclaim their land but the Appellants refused. Prior to the suit, the dispute had been looked into by three arbitration panels - all of which were at the instance of the Respondents. This was because each time the arbitration panel finished and decided, the Appellants would continue to occupy the land in dispute, having rejected the award by the arbitrations. The Respondents then sued at the Customary Court Mbanano holding at Umuoji. The three Arbitration Panels were: (a) The Peace Committee; (b) Ndichie of Dimboko; (c) Uka Oye Dimboko Village Meeting. After the last mentioned body delivered its decision, the Appellants continued to stay on the land, and the Respondents sued them in the trial Customary Court. After testimonies of witnesses, tendering of exhibits and visit to locus in quo, the Customary Court delivered its decision on 15/4/1992 and dismissed the Respondents' case and granted title over the land to the Appellants. The Respondents appealed to the Customary Court of Appeal and the Court set aside the judgment of the trial Customary Court and granted the reliefs sought by the Respondents at the trial Customary Court. Dissatisfied with the decision, the Appellants appealed to the Court of Appeal. The Respondents also filed a Respondent's notice to vary the decision of the Customary Court of Appeal. One of the

---

[114](2017) LPELR-42720 (CA).

[115] (1991) 3 NWLR (pt 180) 385 per Karibi-Whyte, JSC (as then was).

[116](2017) LPELR-43448 (CA), Pp.15-19, Paras. E-A.

issues raised for determination at the Court of Appeal was: Whether the Customary Court of Appeal rightly held that the verdict of the three customary arbitrations were valid and operated as estoppel *per rem judicata* against the Appellants?

In the judgment of the court, the court posited thus:

> While a customary arbitration neither qualifies as a court of law or even an inferior court within the definition of the constitution, the Nigerian legal system recognizes customary arbitration upon the satisfaction of certain conditions. The conditions which a customary arbitration must fulfil before it becomes binding on parties are stated in the case of *Nzomah* v. *Ugochi* (2002) FWLR (Pt. 135) Pg. 694 at 702...It therefore means that when all these aforementioned conditions have been fulfilled, a customary arbitration is binding on the parties. See *Igwego* v. *Ezeugo* (1992) 6 NWLR Pt. 249 Pg. 561. The Respondents intend that the proceedings and conclusion of the arbitration panel should be made to bind the Appellants who had resiled from it. The Appellants refused to abide by the result of the customary arbitrations even though they clearly submitted to the jurisdiction of the panels. The point made by the Appellants counsel is that the arbitration was not final and that the Customary Court was right to have discountenanced it as the court cannot just act as a rubber stamp. As I said earlier, the decision of the customary arbitration would bind both parties if all the conditions precedent to its legality and applicability existed. It is clear that both parties agreed to be bound by the result of the arbitration panels. Immediately the panel was constituted, they had the opportunity to object to its composition and to refuse to give evidence before it. This they did not, it would be repugnant to good sense and equity to allow the losing party to resile from the decision of the arbitrators to which he had previously agreed. The question here is whether the decision of the customary arbitration panels constituted estoppel in law. To the extent that the Appellants submitted themselves to the arbitrations and gave evidence before the panels, one is bound to hold that they cannot resile from the decision of the native arbitrations. I am of the firm and humble view that the lower court was right to have held that the Customary Court was wrong when it ignored the decision of the native arbitrations to which parties subjected themselves. This issue is resolved against the Appellants.

In the same vein, another element that must be noted is that the dispute founded on the voluntary submission of the parties to the decision of the arbitrator or arbitrators who are either the chiefs or elders or the community traditional rulers, or family members. This is the gravamen of the decision in *Agu* v. *Ikewuibe,* [117] and restated in *Nwosu* v. *Ekeigwe.*[118]

These cases also re-echoed that submission to such arbitration shall not be by intimidation, coercion, inducement or undue influence on any of the parties.[119] The arbitrators may be the traditional rulers and members of his cabinet. The arbitration may be by chiefs and elders of the town, village or community as in *Agu* v. *Ikewuibe*[120] or body of elders as in *Nnadi & Ors* v. *Odika & Ors*[121] or by oath taking before a Juju priest as in the most recent Supreme Court case of *Pius Umeadi & Ors* v. *Victor Chibunze & Anor*[122] and *Omega* v. *Ebere*[123] and the latter case of *Nwosu* v. *Ekeigwe.* When all these conditions as stated in the recent case of *Nnadi & Ors* v. *Odika & Ors supra* have been met, arbitration would be liberally treated as a judicial proceeding and could be taken to operate as estoppel per *rem judicatam.*

To surmise it, as a general rule, a party who desires to lead evidence in support of his case must plead all the material facts in support thereof as evidence on facts not pleaded goes to no issue as was held in the most recent case of *Mr. Grant kayode Yankey* v. *Florence Austin.*[124] In the earlier case of *Isensee K.G.* v. *UBA Plc,*[125] the Court of Appeal held that the contention of the Appellant that the Respondent in the case did not specifically plead estoppel in his Statement of Defence at the lower Court cannot be supported. The Court went further to state that estoppel can be inferred from facts as it is sufficient to plead facts on which the issue could be founded. In the latter case of *Petkev Nig. Ltd & Anor* v. *Ogbogu & Anor,*[126] the Court of Appeal while citing Niki Obi JSC in *Odi* v. *Iyala,*[127] held that the law is elementary that estoppel per rem judicata is a special defence available to a defendant which must be specifically pleaded in the statement of defence.

---

[117] *Supra.*
[118] *Supra.*
[119] See *Aguocha* v. *Ubiju* (1975) 5 SECR 221.
[120] *Supra.*
[121] *Supra.*
[122] (2020) LPELR-49566 (SC).
[123] (2004) 6-7 SC 52. See also *Odonigi* v. *Oyeleke* (2001) 6 NWLR (Pt. 708) 12.
[124] (2020) LPELR-49540 (CA).
[125] (2012) LPELR-8028 (CA).
[126] (2016) LPELR-40069 (CA).
[127] (2004) 8 NWLR (pt. 875) 293.

Furthermore, in the 2019 case of *Oseni* v. *Adesanya & Anor,*[128] the Court of Appeal posited that it is not necessary to plead the ingredients establishing estoppel but that it is enough to avert to the existence of estoppel and thereafter adduce credible evidence of the ingredients in trial.[129]

It is humbly submitted that these are two conflicting decisions reached by our court. To lay to rest the incongruity stemming from the two contradictory judgments of the Court of Appeal, it was held in the more recent case of *Oseni* v. *Adesanya & Anor*[130] thus:

> The law is that estoppel need not be pleaded in any special form so long as the matters constituting estoppel are stated in a manner to show that the party pleading it relied on it as a defence or answer.

Thus the recent decision in Oseni's *case* above can best be resorted to in settling the incongruity as the court seeks to do substantial justice and will not allow justice to be slaughtered on the altar.

---

[128] (2019) LPELR-48051 (CA).

[129] See also the corroborating case of *Isensee K.G.* v. *Uba Plc* (2012) 16 NWLR (Part 1326) P. 357. However in the earlier decision of the same Court of Appeal in *Asamu* v. *Lawanson & Ors.* (2014) LPELR-24416 (CA), it was held that it is the law that a party seeking to rely on estoppel must specifically plead it unless it is so apparently clear that the Court has a duty to consider it...Estoppel per *rem judicatam* having not been pleaded, it ought not to have been considered by the lower Court as it is trite law that evidence at variance with pleadings go to no issue.

[130] Supra @ P.19 para. A.

Chapter 13

PROOF OF CUSTOM

A. Definition of Custom

The Evidence Act under section 258(1) defined custom as a rule which, in a particular district, has from long usage obtained the force of law. The Court of Appeal in *Abidoye & Anor* v. *Dosunmu & Anor*[1] gave an instructive definition of custom when it held that, the term "custom" as a noun denotes a practice that by its common adoption and long, unvarying habit, has come to have the force of law. It thus suffices to say that custom is a set of rules of conduct applying to persons and things in a particular locality. Let me say that it is of the characteristics of a custom that it must be in existence at the relevant time and must be recognized and adhered to by the inhabitants of the community to make it binding.[2]

In *Abidoye & Anor* v. *Dosunmu*,[3] the court while citing the case of *Princess Bilewu Oyewunmi* v. *Ogunesan*[4] per Obaseki JSC went further to posit thus:

> Custom is the organic or living law of the indigenous people of Nigeria regulating their lives and transactions. It is organic in that it is not static. It is regulatory in that it controls the lives and transactions of the community subject to it. It is said that custom is a mirror of the culture of the people. I would say that customary law goes further and imports justice to the lives of all those subject to it.

Custom is a mirror of acceptable usage. Custom has spatiotemporal variation.[5] Thus, it varies from place to place and from community to

---

[1] (2019) LPELR-47719 (CA) P. 38, para. D.

[2] See *Lewis* v. *Bankole* (1908) 1 NLR 81. See also *Okegbe & Ors* v. *Akpome & Ors* (2013) LPELR-21969(CA). However, this is without prejudice to the validity tests of admissibility that such custom must pass through to enjoy admissibility.

[3] *Supra* at Pp. 38-39, paras. F-A.

[4] (1990) 5 SCNJ 34.

[5] See *Oparaji* v. *Ohanu* (1996) 6 SC (Pt. 1) 41 per Igu JSC.

community. In this light, Muhammad, JSC in his erudition, In *Kopek Construction Ltd* v. *Ekisola*,[6] opined thus:

> Admittedly, Nigeria is blessed with so many tribes, custom, languages and legal cultures. It is not that easy for one to dismiss by mere waive of hand, the proposition that under some native laws and customs, the minimum requirement for a transaction to be valid is that there must be at least two witnesses.

This definition categorically accommodates our ethnic and cultural diversities. It is not in doubt whether African native law and custom in fact exists, though African native laws and customs have ironically been misconceived as primitive, arbitrary, archaic, and savage. Contrariwise, it is a well settled truism, that native laws and customs are organically dynamic. As once aptly reiterated by our court that, ever since the emergence of the sociological ideas of Roscoe Pound, with particular regard to the modern concept of law in a developing society, the most unreasonable and highly misplaced criticism about African Law (customary and native) is that it is merely custom, and not law. However, most cherishingly, concerted efforts have so far been made to sweep away the cobwebs, the myths, prejudices, and philosophical doubts of those who have all along denied that there was any such thing as African Law, customary or native law. Professor Allot, formerly of the School of Oriental and African Studies, University of London, was most pertinent where he wrote, *inter alia*, thus:

> African Law (customary law) is, in short, reasoned. It is not arbitrary, savage or non-existent. The difference between African and Western (European) Law is one of degree, not of kind.[7]

The recognition and proof of custom as a law regulating the life of persons subject to it has been recognized by the Evidence Act under section 161(1) of the Act. It provides to the effect that a custom may be adopted as part of the law governing a particular set of circumstances if it can be

---

[6] (2010) 3 NWLR (Pt. 1182) 618 per Muhammad, JSC.

[7] *Law Quarterly Review*, 1957, Pages 106 - 110; *Fundamentals of Nigerian Law*, 1989 at Page 10, Edited by Professor M.A. Ajomo and cited with approval in *Ogiefo* v. *Isesele I & Ors* (2014) LPELR-22333 (CA).

judicially noticed or can be proved to exist by evidence. This will be treated in details under the next topic.

Suffice it to say that the burden of proving a custom rests squarely on the person alleging its existence[8] as he who asserts, must prove.[9] A custom is not admitted as a matter of course. For custom to enjoy admissibility, it must be proved through the streamlined channels prescribed by the Evidence Act. Thus, in line with section 161(1), a custom which has not been judicially noticed is a question of fact which must be pleaded and proved by independent witness (es) through proof of evidence.[10]

B. New Impetus for Judicial Notice of Custom

As a general rule, customary law has to be proved by proof of evidence through calling of witnesses who have such personal knowledge of the particular custom and, it is only when such custom becomes notorious as a result of being adjudicated upon once by a court of superior record that judicial notice of it is taken without further proof. This is the fulcrum of the innovative section 17 of the Act.

Section 17 of the Evidence Act provides thus:

> A custom may be judicially noticed when it has been adjudicated upon once by a superior court of record.[11]

This provision came as a 'messiah' to salvage the interpretational difficulties that have bedevilled the poof of custom by Judicial Notice. In time past, the position of the law had been that a custom may be judicially noticed by the court if it has been acted upon by a court of superior or co-ordinate jurisdiction in the same area to an extent which justifies the court asked to apply it, in assuming that the persons or class of persons concerned in that area look upon the same as binding in relation to circumstances similar to those under consideration.[12]

---

[8]See section 16(2) of the Act. See also *Ugobo* v. *Ugobo & Ors* (2017) LPELR-43533(CA) P. 16, paras. A-C.

[9] See the most recent decision of the apex court in *Sharing Cross Educational Services Limited* v. *Umaru Adamu Enterprises Limited & Ors* (2020) LPELR-49567(SC) Per EKO, J.S.C (Pp. 7-8, paras. F-A); See also the Court of Appeal case of *Akanji* v. *State* (2020) LPELR-49531 (CA).

[10] *Okusanya & ORS* v. *Adetona & Ors* (2018) LPELR-44876(CA) P. 44, para. B.

[11] *Okusanya & Ors* v. *Adetona & Ors* (*supra*). See also *Isu* v. *Abasa & Ors* (2017) LPELR-42014 (CA).

[12] See section 14(2) of the repealed Evidence Act, 2004. See also the following decisions premised on the old law: *Olagbemiro* v. *Ajagungbade III & Anor* (1990) LPELR-2554(SC); *Romaine* v. *Romaine* (1992) 5 SCNJ 25 at 44-45; *Dung Jatua* v. *Pam Dung* (1993) 3 NWLR (Pt. 283) 558 cited in *Motoh* v. *Motoh* (2011) 16 NWLR (Pt. 1274) 474 at 522.

The extant and current position of the law as enunciated by section 17 of the new Act is devoid of ambiguity and completely eliminated the 'albatross on the neck' of proving customs by way of judicial notice. As an addendum, once a custom has been acted or adjudicated upon once by a superior court of record, such custom automatically becomes one that the court must take judicial notice of and thus, dispenses the need for further proof by calling a community or village of witnesses. In *Ngwakwe & Ors* v. *Ngwakwe,*[13] the court while relying on *Lewis* v. *Bankole,*[14] held that it is only where such custom has gained such notoriety as to acquire a force of law that the court can treat it as a matter of law, thereby taking judicial notice of such custom.

One point worthy of note here is the hierarchy of courts and the bindingness of decisions of superior courts on lower courts when faced with question of law with same fact or issue. This is the doctrine of judicial precedent[15] which has maintained precision and predictability in the dynamics of decided cases, though a case is authority for what it decides given its peculiar facts and circumstances.[16] Thus where a Superior court of record has adjudicated upon a particular custom once, it becomes binding on lower courts to take judicial notice of the existence of such custom without further proof.

It is submitted that the fact that a particular custom applicable in one locality has been judicially acted once by a superior court does not make it automatically applicable to all localities. A court will permit a party to lead evidence to show that a custom which has been judicially noticed has ceased to be a custom in a particular area in view of the fact that flexibility is one of the attributes of custom.[17]

C. Proof of Custom by Evidence

Section 16 of the Act made provision for two distinct ways of proving customs -to wit: by judicial notice or proof by evidence. Much has been said about the former. Premised on this where a custom has not been judicially

---

[13] (2018) LPELR-46125 (CA) P.30, paras. D-E. See also *Okusanya & Ors* v. *Adetona & Ors* (2018) LPELR-44876 (CA) 43 E-F.

[14] (1908) 1 NLR 82, 798.

[15] *Nigerian Army* v. *Bello* (2019) LPELR-47080 (CA) P.23, paras. A-B. See also *Nwabueze* v. *The People of Lagos State* (2018) LPELR-44113 (SC) and *Ugo-Ngadi* v. *FRN* (2018) LPELR-43903 (SC).

[16] *Adeniyi* v. *Ifelodun Local Government & Ors.* (2018) LPELR-44050 (CA) P. 13, para. D. See also *Udo* v. *State* (2016) LPELR-40721 (SC); *Director, S.S.S.* v. *Ibrahim* (2016) LPELR-41618 (CA); *One Laptop Per Child Association Inc. and Ors.* v. *Oyegbola & Anor* (2016) LPELR 41499 (CA).

[17] See *Okusanya & Ors* v. *Adetona & Ors* (*supra*).

noticed as provided under section 17 of the Act, such custom must be proved as a fact by way of evidence.[18]

Evidence in proof of a custom is led by calling of witnesses acquainted with the native custom to testify on the existence or otherwise of such custom.[19] This established principle of law has gained statutory blessing and attention under section 18(2) of the Act. It states emphatically that where the existence or the nature of a custom applicable to a given case is in issue, there may be given in evidence, the opinion of persons who would likely know of its existence in accordance with section 73 of the Act.[20] For a better appreciation of this provision, may i call in aid, the express statutory provision of section 73 of the Act so as to marry the two sections together. Section 73(1) of the Evidence Act provides that when the court has to form an opinion as to the existence of any general custom or right, the opinions, as to the existence of such custom or right, of persons who would be likely to know of its existence if it existed are admissible. Subsection 2 illuminated on what is regarded as "general custom or right" It states that the expression "general custom or right" includes custom or rights common to any considerable class of persons. It has been established through plethora of cases that it is extremely important that native law and custom must be pleaded and strictly proved by credible evidence.

With regard to the quality of evidence necessary to establish proof of a custom, the case of *Alabi* v. *Audu*[21] *is very instructive here.* In the instant case, the respondent and his younger brother Salawu Audu, by the Ebira Native Law and Custom, inherited the properties in dispute from their late sister, Ebun Audu, who died intestate without having any child. The family resolved that Salawu Audu should move into the completed buildings and manage the properties on the premises, whereby he rented two flats to the appellant. In 2003, Salawu Audu died and the respondent was introduced to the appellant who continued to pay rent to the respondent. Sometime in 2008, the respondent sent his daughter, Rali, to collect rents from the appellant and she noticed some construction on the uncompleted buildings in the land. The appellant was challenged but continued building hence, a report was made to the traditional ruler, who constituted a meeting to resolve the matter. It was at this meeting that the appellant for the first time

---

[18] See section 18(1) of the Evidence Act.

[19] *Ameh & Anor* v. *Suleiman & Ors* (2018) LPELR-46543(CA) P. 17, paras. B-C.

[20] See *Okwusogu & Ors* v. *Okadigbo* (2017) LPELR-42751(CA).

[21] (2017) LPELR-42872 (CA). P.22, paras. A-E.

in 2008 disclosed that late Salawu Audu sold the uncompleted buildings to her. The appellant filed an action at the Area Customary Court, Ogaminna to restrain Rali and Baka Jimoh from harassing her on the premises but later abandoned the suit. Thereafter, the respondent filed this suit to nullify the purported sale to the appellant, made without his knowledge.

Among other things, the appellant as defendant contended that the alleged Ebira Native Law and Custom upon which the respondent predicated his claim was not proved. He also contended vigorously that custom must be strictly proved, and cited authorities to show that the Courts have held that it is not enough that the person that asserts the custom should be the only person to testify in support of the custom. While dismissing the appeal unanimously, the court of Appeal in full appreciation and consciousness of the fact that there are some authorities supporting the contention of the respondent,[22] with regard to the quality of evidence necessary to establish proof of customary law held thus:

> The rationale in all the decisions of the apex court is on the quality of evidence. Hence, on the evidence required to ground proof of custom, what is important is the quality of the evidence adduced and not on the quantity of witnesses that testified. There is no law that requires corroboration of proof of customary law. There is no such provision in the Evidence Act. A single witness may suffice. A community of witnesses is not required, but what is essential is the quality of evidence adduced before the court, either it is given by the single witness or more witnesses. The general opinion of the apex court is that it is desirable, that in proving custom, a person other than the party asserting it should testify in support thereof. However, as rightly submitted by the learned senior counsel, this legal principle is not immutable...The colour of the cases so decided by the apex court shows that it is not mandatory that the evidence of the party alleging the custom must be corroborated. I am in agreement with the learned senior counsel when he submitted that corroboration is unnecessary.

---

[22] See *Giwa Abiodun* v. *Erinmilokun* (1961) 1 All NLR 294**,** where the Court held that although no particular number of witnesses is required to prove the existence of a custom or rule of customary law, the Court may not hold as sufficient proof the mere *ipse dixit* of the person alleging it. It is based on this pronouncement of the Court that many cases have now been decided on the premise that apart from the evidence of the party relying on a particular custom, another witness versed in the alleged custom should also testify. This is a matter of prudence and administrative grease in the wheel of justice. It should be noted that this principle evolved when there were no registered declarations on custom being relied upon by parties in a case as there is no provision of the Act to the effect that evidence on custom must be corroborated. See also *Eyo* v. *Onuoha & Anor* (2011) LPELR-1873 (SC).

Extrapolating from the above judicial authorities, corroboration is alien and unknown to our law vis-à-vis proof of custom. However, caution should be applied as it may be unsafe to accept the statement of the only person asserting its existence as conclusive. it is therefore desirable that a person other than the person asserting the existence of such customary law and tradition should testify in support of its existence. Under section 19 of the Act, it is declared that every fact is deemed to be relevant which tends to show how in particular instance a matter alleged to be a custom is understood and acted upon by persons then interested.[23] It is also the law that where customary law has been codified, registered or deposited with the appropriate authority, oral evidence will not be admissible to prove it.[24]

It should be noted however that a custom does not enjoy automatic admissibility. The law has placed a caveat by way of validity tests for the admissibility of such custom. These tests serve as a blueprint or litmus test to ascertain the acceptability and its admissibility. Thus, the Evidence Act does not leave it unguarded, unrestricted and untrammelled. To this effect, section 18(3) of the Act provides thus:

> In any judicial proceedings where any custom is relied upon, it shall not be enforced as law if it is contrary to public policy, or is not in accordance with natural justice, equity and good conscience.

From the statutory provision, it can be gleaned that any custom that is repugnant to natural justice, equity and good conscience or one that is contrary to public policy or incompatible with any law for the time being in force cannot enjoy enforceability. In *Mark* v. *Ironu & Ors,*[25] the court while discouraging the desperation of parents seeking for male children in African culture through a refusal to enforce a custom that allows a lady to bear a son while in her father's house to sustain the lineage of the father held thus:

> There are many decided authorities of this court and the apex court banishing discrimination against female children and upholding their right to share in the estates of their parents...Thus, parent(s) without a male

[23] See *Osolu* v. *Osolu* (1998) 1 NWLR (Pt. 535) 532.

[24] See *Fasade* v. *Babalola* (2003) FWLR (Pt. 161) 1707.

[25] (2019) LPELR-47026 (CA) P. 27, Paras. A-F. The court while giving its verdict, relied on litany of cases like *Ukeje* v. *Ukeje* (2014) 58 NSCQR 531; (2014) LPELR 22724 (SC); *Igbozuruike* v. *Onuador* (2015) LPELR 25530 CA and *Duru* v. *Duru* (2016) LPELR 40444 CA; See also section 42 of the 1999 Constitution, as amended.

> child, need not resort to the ridiculous extreme to deny his daughter right to marry, to confine her to immorality and amorous relationship with strange men, under her father's roof, to satisfy her parent(s) desperation for a male child to carry on his name, or perpetuate his lineage and inherit him. Children are gifts from God, who creates them, males and females gives[sic] and same as he wills, and every child should be received with utmost thanks, appreciated and nurtured to one's aspiration and ability, whether male or female, knowing that the child is entitled to succeed him/her (Parent), whatever the child turns out to be. One who is so obsessed about perpetuating his name on the earth should, in my opinion, rather work hard to leave worthy imprints on the sands of time by leading a good life of service to God and humanity; go into discovery, patenting, authorship of book(s), etc., and establishing good will. He does not necessarily require harvest of children (who may turn out to be vagabonds).

Thus, under the fireworks of these validity tests, where any native law and custom is in conflict with any Nigerian legislation such as the Evidence Act, the latter will prevail and such native law and custom will be void to the extent of its inconsistency.

Chapter 14

BURDEN OF PROOF AND STANDARD OF PROOF

1. Facts Proved, Facts Disproved or Facts Not Proved

The Evidence Act has made copious statutory provisions as to when a fact is said to be "proved", "disproved" and "not proved" and this has been found necessary in the understanding of the underlying principles associated with the concepts of burden of proof and standard of proof. Section 121(a) of the Evidence Act provides that a fact is said to be "proved" when after considering the matters before it, the court either believes it to exist or consider its existence so probable that a prudent man ought, in the circumstances of the particular case, to act upon the supposition that it does exist. This evidential principle gained judicial stamp in the recent Supreme Court decision in *Salau* v. *State.*[1]

In the like manner, section 121(b) of the Evidence Act posits that a fact is said to be "disproved" when after considering the matter before it, the court either believes that it does not exist or considers its non-existence so probable that a prudent man ought, in the circumstance of the particular case, to act upon the supposition that it does not exist. Finally the Act was so succinct and precise to state under section 121(c) that a fact is said to be "not proved" what it is neither proved nor disproved.

2. Burden of Proof

In general terms, "burden of proof" also known as "onus of proof" or "onus *probandi*" connotes the obligation on one or more parties in a suit to adduce sufficient evidence either in proof of the whole case or a particular fact.

The Supreme Court in its wisdom in the most recent case of *Sharing Cross Educational Services Limited* v. *Umaru Adamu Enterprises Limited & Ors*[2] reiterated the immortal evidential principle that the person who makes an assertion has the burden of proving same as whosoever that desires any

---

[1] (2020) LPELR-48114(SC) P. 10, paras. A-C.

[2] (2020) LPELR-49567(SC) Per Eko, J.S.C (Pp. 7-8, paras. F-A); See also *Akanji* v. *State* (2020) LPELR-49531 (CA).

court to give judgment as to any legal right or liability dependent on the existence of facts which he asserts must prove that those empirical facts exist. As fondly expressed in the principle that he who asserts, must proof.[3] This is explained by the maxim "*affirmati non negat incumbit probatio.*" Thus, where the party on whom this obligation is cast, fails, refuses or neglects to adduce the relevant evidence, then either he losses the whole case or fails to prove the particular fact.

In *Malhotra* v. *Bank of Singapore Ltd,*[4] It was held that a party must make out his case by the best available evidence. Therefore, where averments are just made without proof , then they must be discountenanced for lack of proof as the court do not make an order in vain where weaker, extraneous or insufficient or feeble evidence is given, that it will amount to failure of proof. In the same vein, the Court of Appeal in its recent decision in *Aderounmu* v. *FRN*[5] stated categorically that the law is settled that when there is any doubt in the course of proving any ingredient of the offence; the doubt will be resolved in favour of the defendant, as that will mean that the respondent has not proved his case beyond reasonable doubt.

In a well-considered judgment of the apex Court per Mary Peter Odili JSC while speaking on the burden of proof in the most recent decision of the Court in *Pius Umeadi & Ors* v. *Victor Chibunze & Anor,*[6] held thus:

> ...the onus is on the Plaintiff to establish his claim upon the strength of his own case and not upon the weakness of the case of the Defendant. The plaintiff must therefore satisfy the court that upon the pleadings and evidence adduced by him, he is entitled to the declaration sought.

The only verdict in such a circumstance is that of discharge and acquittal of the accused person.[7] It is submitted that burden of proof may either be "general burden" or "evidential burden". Where the burden is to prove the whole case, the burden of proof is then referred to as "general burden." But where it is a burden to prove a particular fact, it is known as evidential burden. Evidential burden shifts or swings like a pendulum as one scale of evidence or other preponderates and the onus continues to shift until it can

---

[3] See *Morrison* v. *Diamond Bank* (2018) LPELR-46005 (CA).
[4](2014) LPELR-22442 (CA) p.31, para. A.
[5] (2019) LPELR-46923 (CA) p. 14 paras, B-C.
[6](2020) LPELR-49566 (SC) p.50, paras. A-B.
[7]See also *Posu* v. *State* (2013) 3 NWLR (pt. 1234) 395 and *A-G Anambra State* v. *A-G Federation & Ors* (2005) 9 NWLR (Pt. 931) 572.

no longer be rebutted. This dichotomy was aptly captured in the recent Court of Appeal decision in *M.V. Long Island* v. *FRN*.[8] His Lordship held thus:

> There is a distinction between burden of proof and evidential burden, firstly in law, a distinction is drawn between burden of proof of a case which as an inflexible rule rests on the plaintiff in civil matters and evidential burden which places the onus of proof on one making a specific assertion over a particular point essential to his stand on the matter regardless of whether the person making the assertion is the defendant. It is undisputable that the burden of proof rests on the prosecution from beginning of a criminal trial to end. As a doctrine of law of Evidence, evidential burden imports that where a given allegation, whether affirmative or negative, forms an essential part of a party's case the onus of proof of such allegation rests on him.

However, the general burden is static. It is an immortal principle of law as earlier stated that he who alleges or asserts must prove and not the person who denies.[9]

Section 131(1) of the Evidence Act provides ample legal fortress for this by enacting thus:

> Whoever desires any court to give judgment as to any legal right or liability dependent on the existence of fact which he asserts must prove that those facts exist.

It is worthy of note that if the party fails to do so, the case will fail. Conversely, if the party succeeds in adducing evidence to prove the pleaded fact, it is said to have discharged the burden of proof that rests on him. It is at this point that the burden shifts to the adverse party to prove that the fact established before the honourable court is not compelling and sufficient enough to result in the court giving judgment in favour of the party.[10] The Supreme Court in *Jimoh* v. *Hon. Minister Federal Capital Territory & Ors*[11] restated the long hallowed principle of law that he who alleges must prove. Furthermore, in the most recent case of *Engr. Zubairu Yakubu & Anor* v.

---

[8](2018) LPELR-43479 (CA) Pp. 38-39 paras C-A.

[9] *Morrison* v. *Diamond Bank* (*supra*); See also *Ibrahim* v. *State* (2015) 11 NWLR (Pt. 1469) P. 164.

[10]See *Buhari* v. *Obasanjo* (2015) 7 SCNJ 1 at 47. See also Section 136 of Evidence Act on shifting of burden of proof.

[11] (2018) LPELR-46329 (SC).

Ministry of Housing Environment, Bauchi State & Anor,[12] the Court of Appeal held that a court of law ought not to award to a plaintiff a substantive relief he has not specifically claimed in his statement of claim and may not in fact desire. It is predicated on this same principle that Niki Tobi JCA (as he then was OBM) in *Ajikawo* v. *Ansaldo*[13] captured this in his usual fecund style of fervid prose thus:

> It is not the judicial function of a trial judge to embark on an unguarded voyage of facts which are not placed before him; a trial judge is not Vasco da Gama; a trial judge is not Christopher Columbus. Coming nearer home, a trial judge is not Mungo Park. A trial judge is a person whose duty is to inquire only on the facts placed before him in court. He is forbidden by our laws to go on a voyage of his own with a view of gaining greener pasture.

In the same vein, the Court of Appeal in the recent case of *County & City Bricks Development Co. Ltd & Anor* v. *MKC (Nig) Ltd* & *Ors,*[14] posited in so much eloquence, *inter alia,*

> A Court is not Santa Claus or a charitable institution; it cannot award a party what he has not claimed. A Court cannot award a claimant what he has not asked for as that would be an unusual charity and goodwill which a Court of law, *qua judex*, has no jurisdiction and is incompetent to do.

It is not within the province, purview and competence of the court to evolve or manufacture a case for the party. Thus, where a party to a case fails or refuses to submit to issues he raised in his pleading in the trial by giving evidence in support of same, the trial court must resolve the case against the defaulting party except there are other legal reasons to the contrary. Departing from the pleadings or case placed before the court and considering the issues that were not matters of contest between the parties will amount to conferring on the court with the position of Father Christmas or a charitable organization as enunciated in the cases above.

Analysing Section 131(2) of the Evidence Act will be germane in our present discussion. It provides that when a person is bound to prove the existence of any fact, it is said that the burden of proof lies on that person.

---

[12](2020) LPELR-49482 (CA); See also *Ugoloshinga* v. *BSIEC* (2015) 6 NWLR (Pt. 205 - 424).
[13] (1991) 2 NWLR (Pt.173) 359 at 372.
[14](2019) LPELR-46889 (CA) P. 38, paras. E-A.

Parties are by this provision saddled with the herculean task of proving their case with credible and cogent evidence.

Section 132 of the Act, made provision for who bears the burden of proof when it provided expressly that the burden of proof in a suit or proceeding lies on that person who would fail if no evidence at all is given on either side.[15] Parties are bound by their pleadings and the court cannot award a party what he has not pleaded and established. Hence, the fulcrum of a case is derived from the pleading and its success depends largely thereon for pleading that is bereft of facts needed to prove a case cannot be proved by evidence no matter how cogent.[16]

From the body of decided cases like *Buhari* v. *Obasanjo*[17] and others, burden of proof can be divided into three categories, namely:

(i) the legal burden under section 131 of the Evidence Act;
(ii) the evidential burden under section 132 of the Evidence Act;
(iii) burden on the pleading under section 133 of the Evidence Act.

It is the law that where the burden of proof of the existence or non-existence of a fact is in issue, regard must be had to the presumptions arising from the pleadings.[18]

3. Burden of Proof in Civil Cases

Burden of proof in civil cases is provided under section 133(1) of the Evidence Act. The said section provides thus:

> In civil cases, the burden of first proving the existence or non-existence of a fact lies on the party against whom the judgment of the court would be given if no evidence were produced on either side, regard being had to any presumption that may arise on the pleadings.

As a matter of law, pleadings of parties determines the general burden of proof in civil cases as usually decided by the court because it is a matter of law. As a general rule, he who asserts must prove in order to succeed in his claim as held in *Jimoh* v. *Hon. Minister Federal Capital Territory & Ors.*[19] This burden generally is on the plaintiff to establish all facts contained in his statement of claim. However, the burden of proof will shift to the defendant

---

[15] See also *Union Bank* v. *Ravih Abdul & Co. Ltd* (2018) LPELR-46333(SC) P.15, Para. F.
[16] See *Nwokorogu* v. *Nwogu* (2009) 5 SCNJ 218 at 233.
[17] (2005) 7 SCNJ 1 at 47 cited in *Adighije* v. *Nwaogu* (2010) 12 NWLR (Pt. 1209) 419 at 459.
[18] See *Archibong* v. *Ita* (2004) 1 SCNJ 141.
[19] *Supra.*

to prove contrary facts as canvassed in his statement of defence to refute and rebut the assertion of the plaintiff. For instance in the case of declaration of title to land, a party who seeks title to land *via* any of the five ways of seeking such, must prove the identity of the land in respect of which he seeks the remedy. Thereafter, the burden will shift to the defendant to state facts to rebut it and once the opponent/defendant admitted the identity of the land in dispute as pleaded in the pleadings either through pleadings or oral evidence, then identity has been established. Deducing from the probative nature of evidence adduced by both parties, after a careful and a painstaking analysis and evaluation, the court will give a well-considered judgment on the issue. As earlier stated, a court of law or trial judge is not Christopher Columbus or Mungo Park and thus cannot manufacture evidence on a bid to help or assist any of the parties as it were.

The courts are impartial umpire to hold balance between the two contending parties and thus, do not have any vested interest in the matter placed before them.[20] In *Nbaonu* v. *State*,[21] the Court of Appeal while citing the dictum of TOBI JCA (of the Blessed memory) in *Joseph Ugwu* v. *The State*[22] held thus:

> I find edification in the case of *Joseph Ugwu* v. *The State* (1998) 7 NWLR pt PAGE 392 and 408 where this court per Tobi JCA (as he then was, OBM) held that the professional duties of a lawyer do not take him as far as manufacturing evidence for the client. The judge has only the role to listen to both sides and decide. It is dangerous for the judge to participate in a judicial process by the addition of a piece of evidence which was not legally received in evidence by due process.

In addition, while a judge avoids descending into the arena of conflict but with all willingness to meet the justice of a case, a claimant must succeed on the strength of his case and not on the weakness of the defence; except where the defendant's case supports his case.[23]

Section 136(1) of the Act, provides that the burden of proof of any particular fact lies on that person who wishes the court to believe in its existence unless it is provided by any law that the proof of that fact lies on any particular person, but the burden may be shifted from one side to the

---

[20] See *Kaydee Ventrues Ltd* v. *Hon. Minister of FCT & Ors* (2010) 2 SCNJ 276. See also *Aboyeji* v. *Momoh* (1994) 4 SCNJ 302.

[21] (2018) LPELR-46058 (CA).

[22] (1998) 7 NWLR Pg. 392 at 408.

[23] *Arije* v. *Arije & Ors* (2018) LPELR-44193(SC).

other. It is a notorious principle of law premised on a hidden but resourceful truth that you can only warrant the court to believe by the evidence adduced and not you believing as you cannot put something on nothing and expect it to stand [24]*(ex nihilo nihil fit)*. This is because the something which has nothing to stand will fall owing to Newton's Law of gravity. Going to the realm of physics, this can also be likened to Sir Newton's second Law of Motion also known as "Inertia" which states that an object will remain in a state of rest except it is compelled by some external force. Thus, in law of evidence, nothing can put the court into activation of judgment except the weight of evidence adduced to prove ones case. When this is lacking, the court remains passive and does nothing with respect to the claim not substantially proved.

Section 136(2) of the Evidence Act states clearly that in considering the amount of evidence necessary to shift the burden of proof, regard shall be had by the court to the opportunity of knowledge with respect to the fact to be proved which may be possessed by the parties respectively.

Extrapolating from the foregoing, it is crystal clear that in civil cases, the burden is on he who asserts. Nevertheless, the law envisages that the burden may sometimes shift such as where there are presumptions arising from the state of the pleading or where the law places the burden on the party who otherwise would not have had that obligation or burden thrust on him. Some of the circumstances where shifting of the burden of proof may arise are as follows:

(i) where plea of *res ipsa loquitor* is raised;[25]
(ii) where constitutionality is presumed;[26]
(iii) where presumption of legitimacy is raised;[27]
(iv) under Section 167 of the Evidence Act, the court may presume the existence of any fact which it thinks likely to have happened, regard being had to the common course of natural event, human conduct and public and private business in their relationship to the facts of the particular case, and in particular, the court may presume that:
 (a) A man who is in possession of a stolen good soon after the theft is either the thief or has received the goods knowing them to be stolen, unless he can account for his possession.

---

[24] Lord Denning in *Macfoy* v. *UAC* (1961) 3 All ER 1169.
[25] See the old but important case of *Igbokwe & Ors* v. *UCH Board of Management* (1961) WNLR 173.
[26] *Cheranchi* v. *Cheranchi* (1960) NRNLR 24.
[27] Section 84 of the Matrimonial Causes Act.

(b) A thing or state of things which has been shown to be in existence within a period shorter than that within such things or state of things usually cease to exist, is still in existence etc.

The Supreme Court aptly captured the workability of the shifting of burden of proof in *Onobruchere* v. *Esegine*[28] when it held, *inter alia,*

> Where for instance the plaintiff pleads possession of the land in dispute as his root of title and the defendant admits that possession but adds that the land was given to the plaintiff on pledge, then the onus shift on to the defendant to prove that the plaintiff is not the owner of the land in his possession of which has been admitted. Once the defendant admits the plaintiff's possession of the land in dispute in his statement of defence, there and then, the plaintiff has on the pleadings discharged the onus of proof cast on him and...the Evidence Act...will impose a burden on the defendant to prove the negative – namely that the plaintiff is not the owner.

The Supreme Court in *Union Bank* v. *Ravih Abdul & Co. Ltd*[29] reiterated this dynamics of burden of proof when it held that the burden of proof keeps oscillating among the parties. The Evidence Act regulates in a special manner, the burden of proof but in specific circumstances, for instance, under section 142 of the Evidence Act, it provides that when the question is whether persons are partners, landlord, tenant or principal and agent, and it has been shown that they have been acting as such, the burden of proving that they do not stand or have ceased to stand to each other in those relationships respectively, is on the person who affirms it. Section 143 in like manner also provides that when the question is whether any person is the owner of anything of which he is shown to be in possession, the burden of proving that he is not the owner is on the person who affirms that he is not the owner.

Section 144 of the Evidence Act went further to provide that where there is a question as to the good faith of a transaction between parties, one of whom stands to the other in a position of active confidence, the burden of proving good faith of transaction is on the party who is in a position of active confidence. When any fact is specially within the knowledge of any person, the burden of proving that fact is upon him.[30]

---

[28] (1986) 1 NWLR (pt. 19) 799 cited in the illuminating but dissenting judgment of Onoade, JCA, in *Adighije* v. *Nwaogu* (2010) 12 NWLR 419.

[29] (2018) LPELR-46333 (SC).

[30] See section 140 of Evidence Act 2011.

It should be noted that in all cases in which a court places the burden of proof wrongly and in such error, proceeds to determine the case to the detriment of the party on whom the burden of proof was wrongly placed, it would clearly amount to a grave misdirection capable of rendering the entire decision of such a court or tribunal erroneous and liable to be set aside. In law, therefore, the consequences of misdirection as to the onus of proof could be very devastating on the judgment of the court appealed against and an Appellate Court would readily intervene to set aside such a judgment.[31]

4. Burden of Proof in Criminal Cases

It is an elementary feature of adversarial criminal procedure that the prosecution bears the burden of proving the defendant's guilt beyond reasonable doubt. This position has been succinctly captured in the recent Supreme Court decision of *Akibu* v. *State*[32] per Dauda Bage JSC. His Lordship copiously illuminated this principle in these words:

> The duty of the prosecution in any criminal matter is to prove the charges against an accused person beyond reasonable doubt. This is a settled position of the law. The onus of proving the guilt of any person accused of the commission of a crime lies on the prosecution and that the burden never shifts but must be discharged by credible evidence to ensure that all necessary and vital ingredients of the charge or charges are satisfactorily proved...By virtue of S.135(1) of the Evidence Act 2011 , the offence must be strictly proved by cogent and convincing evidence that leaves no iota of doubt or scepticism in the minds of the parties and members of the public, and I dare say this Court...

Under section 135(2) of the Evidence Act, it is well captured that the burden of proving that any person has been guilty of a crime or wrongful act is, subject to section 139 of the Evidence Act, on the person who asserts it, whether the commission of such act is or is not directly in issue in the action. Where the accused person puts up a defence of negligence, accident, provocation or self-defence, in that instance, the onus becomes even heavier on the prosecution. Apart from proving the case, the prosecution must go further to disprove the defence such as accident, self-defence, provocation and other defences entered by the accused. This principle is supported by a

---

[31] *Ogunde* v. *Abdulsalam* (2017) LPELR-41875 (CA) p.34, Paras. B-E.

[32] (2019) LPELR-47630 (SC) Pp. 10-11, paras. C-A.

long line of decided cases such as *Senu* v. *State*[33] including the Supreme Court decision in *Osuagwu* v. *State*[34] and the recent Supreme Court decision in a more recent case of *John* v. *State.*[35]

It will amount to a departure and miscarriage of intellectual ingenuity and utter disregard of the terminus of some principle of law if I fail to invite the eloquence of Viscount Sankey LC in this issue as stated in the old common law case of *Woolmington* v. *DPP.*[36] The Law Lord posited thus:

> Throughout the web of English Criminal Law, one golden thread is always to be seen: that it is the duty of the prosecution to prove the prisoners guilt subject to what I have already said as the defence of insanity and subject also to any statutory exceptions.

The general rule that the prosecution bears the burden of proof has a slight prospect of change as it admits of some remarkable exceptions. According to Glanville Williams,[37]

> When it is said that a defendant to a criminal charge is presumed to be innocent, what is really meant is that the burden of proving his guilt is upon the prosecution...Unhappily, parliament regards the principle with indifference; one might almost say with contempt. The statute book contains many offences in which the burden of proving his innocence is cast on the accused...The sad thing is that there has never been any reason of expediency for these departure from the cherished principle; it has been done through carelessness and lack of subtlety.

His Lordship Dauda Bage JSC in *Akibu* v. *State*[38] took cognizance of this limitation at page 11 paragraph E-F when it went further to state thus:

> ...However, the burden of proving the commission of a crime by the prosecution has constitutional limitation. Thus, where the burden shifts or a written law assumes or imposes the duty of proof of a particular fact on the accused person, the burden is not displaced by presumption of innocence.

---

33 (2016) LPELR-41229 (CA).
34 (2016) LPELR-40836 (SC).
35 (2019) LPELR-46936 (SC).
36 (1942) AC 1.
37 Glanville Williams, *The Proof of Guilt*, 3rd edn (London: Stevens, 1963) at p. 184 - 185.
38 *Supra.*

Section 139 of the Evidence Act recognizes these exceptional circumstances where the burden of proof can shift in criminal cases. It provides thus:

(1) Where a person is accused of any offence, the burden of proving the existence of circumstances bringing the case within any exception or exemption from, or qualification to the operation of the law creating the offence with which he is charged is upon such person.

(2) The burden of proof placed by this part upon a defendant charged with a criminal offence shall be deemed to be discharged if the court is satisfied by the evidence given by the prosecution, whether on cross-examination or otherwise, that such circumstances in fact exist.

Other circumstances of exceptions are

(A) The defence of Insanity or Intoxication under section 27 of the Criminal Code and section 139(3) of the Evidence Act.

(B) Where a fact is especially within the knowledge of any person as provided under section 140 of the Evidence Act.[39]

(C) Where the statutes impose the burden of proof.[40]

5. Standard of Proof

One common thread runs through all adjudicative proceedings: It is the conception of truth as a matter of probability, a term, which in itself, is amenable to degrees. This provokes the question as to degree of probability appropriate for a particular proceeding.[41] While burden of proof places an obligation on a particular party to adduce evidence either to prove a case or prove a particular fact, the standard of proof refers to the degree or level of proof demanded in a specific case, such as beyond reasonable doubt or by a preponderance of evidence. Standard of proof refers to the quantum of evidence required to prove a case. The usual question is whether the standard is very high or of a reasonable quality. The standard of proof required in both civil and criminal cases differ substantially and both of them are seen differently and the courts have interpreted them in this light.

This substantially different standard of proof in both civil and criminal cases will be discussed *in extenso*.

[39] See *Akhidime* v. *State* (1984) NSCC see also *Igbinovia* v. *State* (2001) FWNIL (Pt. 50) 1754 CA.
[40] Section 141 of Evidence Act.
[41] I.H. Dennis, *The Law of Evidence*, 2nd edn. (London: Sweet and Maxwell Ltd - 2002) p. 370.

6. Standard of Proof in Civil Cases

In civil cases, the standard of proof required to be met by the party seeking to discharge the legal burden of proof is on the balance of probabilities or on the preponderance of evidence placed on the scale of justice.[42] Section 134 was so succinct and explicit when it provides that burden of proof shall be discharged on the balance of probabilities in all civil cases. The Law Lord Denning .J. posited in his erudition in describing the standard of proof in civil cases thus:

> The degree is well settled. It must carry a reasonable degree of probability not as high as is required in a criminal case. If the evidence is such that the tribunal can say 'we think it more probable than not;' the burden is discharged but if the probabilities are equal, it is not.

It is pertinent for us to travel on a voyage to the old but germane decision of the Supreme Court in *Mogaji & Ors* v. *Odofin & Ors.*[43] The Supreme Court posited categorically without mincing words and with a high degree of statistical certainty that:

> A judge should use an imaginary scale of justice, by putting the evidence of the parties in two scales and the scales that is heavier based on credible, cogent, convincing and admissible evidence gets the judgment.

It should be noted that it is immaterial whether the parties flooded the court with a 'trailer-load' of witnesses whose evidence is not cogent and convincing, as the court will always base its decision on the cogent, compelling and convincing evidence of a witness even if it is just one witness. The Supreme Court further reiterated this position in a more recent case of *Anya* v. *Anya*[44] that civil suits are determined on the preponderance of evidence or balance of probabilities.

It should also be noted that by virtue of section 135(1) of the Evidence Act, where allegation of the commission of a crime by a party to the proceedings is directly in issue in a civil proceeding, it must be proved beyond reasonable doubt. This is a strict legal stipulation and the courts have never been deterred in interpreting it. In *Trustees of New Jerusalem Church*

---

[42] *Anya* v. *Anya* (2020) LPELR-49386 (SC) P.5, para. F; See also *A.B.C (Transport Co.) Ltd* v. *Omotoye* (2019) LPELR-47829 (SC) and *Sule & Ors* v. *Orisajimi* (2019) LPELR-47039 (SC).

[43] (1978) 4 SC 91. See also *Kaydee* v. *Minister of FCT* (2010) 2 SCNJ at 300 – 301.

[44] *Supra.*

of God, Warri & Anor v. *Ereku,*[45] the court held that the law is settled that the standard of proof of allegation of crimes which is the foundation in a civil cause or matter is provided by the legislature in S.13 (1)-(3) of the Evidence Act 2011 to the effect that it must be proved beyond reasonable doubt. In the instant case, the Respondent's allegation that "Exhibit D" is a forged document in civil proceedings should be proved beyond reasonable doubt. In the same vein, in *Odon* v. *Barigha Amange (No. 2)*[46] the court among other things held that:

> Membership of a secret cult is an offence or activity or act in breach of the law and prohibited by law. Consequently, an allegation of membership of a secret cult is an allegation of the commission of a crime which by the provision of section 138 of the Evidence Act 2004 (now section 135 (1) of the E. A. 2011) requires proof beyond reasonable doubt. The standard of proof remains the same even in election matters or petition that are considered to be sui generis or of a special nature. In the instant case, the allegation of being a member of a secret society or cult member made by the appellant against the 1st respondent is one that constitutes an allegation of a crime that has to be proved beyond reasonable doubt and not just on preponderance of evidence.

7. Standard of Proof in Criminal Cases

It is settled principle of law that the standard of proof in criminal cases as required by section 135(1) of the Evidence Act 2011 is 'proof beyond reasonable doubt'. In the exact words of the above section, it reads thus:

> If the commission of a crime by a party to any proceeding is directly in issue in any proceeding civil or criminal, it must be proved beyond reasonable doubt

The Supreme Court in the recent decision of *Edun & Anor* v. *FRN*[47] held thus:

> ...this is a criminal proceeding. Proof beyond reasonable doubt is the standard of proof. Sections 131(1), 132 and 136(1) of the Evidence Act, 2011 place the burden squarely on the party who asserts the existence of

[45] (2019) LPELR-46949 (CA) P. 20, paras. C-D.
[46] (2010) 12 NWLR (Pt. 1207) 13 at 55.
[47] (2019) LPELR -46947 (SC) P. 12, Paras. C-D.

a particular fact to prove the existence of that fact in order to be entitled to judgment.

Generally, proof beyond reasonable doubt simply means the prosecution establishing the guilt of an accused person with compelling and conclusive evidence; it means a degree of compulsion which is consistent with a high degree of probability. This is the decision of the apex court in the most recent case of *State* v. *Ahmed*.[48] Absolute certainty is impossible in any human adventure including the administration of criminal justice. Proof beyond reasonable doubt means just what it says. It does not admit of plausible and fanciful possibilities but it does admit of a high degree of cogency, consistent with an equally high degree of probability.[49] The court also gave a judicial imprimatur and impetus to this position as held in *Fabian Nwaturuocha* v. *The State*[50] that the standard of proof in a criminal trial is proof beyond reasonable doubt. It went further to posit that it is not enough for the prosecution to suspect a person of having committed a criminal offence. In the same case, the court gave a judicial insight to the meaning of the phrase "Proof beyond reasonable doubt." It submitted thus:

> Proof beyond reasonable doubt is not proof to the hill. It is not proof beyond all iota or scintilla or modicum of doubt. One thing that is certain is that where all the essential ingredients of the offence charged have been proved or established by the persecution, as done in the instant matter, the charge is proved beyond reasonable doubt. However, proof beyond reasonable doubt should not be stretched beyond reasonable limit.

The Apex Court in the recent case of *Ayinde* v. *The State*[51] also re-echoed this position of the law while citing *Fabian Nwaturuocha* v. *State*[52] when it held that "Proof beyond reasonable doubt" does not mean proof beyond all doubt or all shadow of doubt. It simply means establishing the guilt of the accused person with compelling and conclusive evidence, a degree of compulsion which is consistent with a high degree of probability. However, failure, refusal or neglect to prove any or all of the ingredients of the offence charged will be fatal to the case of the prosecution as you can

---

[48] (2020) LPELR-49497 (SC) P.18, paras, E-F.
[49] *Michael Ori* v. *The State* (2020) LPELR-49554 (CA).
[50] (2011) 6 NWLR (Pt 1242) 170 at 174.
[51] (2019) LPELR-47835 (SC) p.16, Paras. D-E.
[52] *Supra.*

only warrant the court to believe and the court will believe predicated on the establishment of all the ingredient of the offence charged through convincing, compelling and cogent evidence.

For full understanding of the workability of the degree or standard of proof in criminal matters, the facts of the earlier Supreme Court case of *Ibrahim* v. *State*[53] will be reproduced here. The facts of the case disclosed that the appellant was arraigned before the High court on a two court charges of conspiracy to commit armed robbery and armed robbery contrary to sections 6(b) and 12(a) of the Robbery and Firearms (special provisions) Act, Cap R.11, Vol. 14 Laws of the Federation of Nigeria, 2004. He was alleged to have committed the said offence with others at large on 7th March 2005 at Iguoil Petrol Station, Boluwaji, Ibadan, He pleaded not guilty to the charge. At the trial, the prosecution called five witnesses in proof of the allegations against him. Eighteen exhibits were equally tendered through the said witnesses. On his- part, the appellant apart from testifying in his defence, did not call any other witness. It was only at the trial in PW3's testimony that the appellant was identified as the witness' family's former houseboy. In other words, the witness knows the appellant very well. However, it was only during this testimony at the trial court, that he, for the first time, raised the issue of the appellant's involvement in the robbery incident in their private resident. He never mentioned the appellants name to the police. Also evidence adduced at the trial court shows that the robbery incident took place at Nos. 1 and 3, Bode Adebimpe close, Boluwaji, Atagba Road, Boluwaji Area, Ibadan. The trial court convicted and sentenced the appellant to death by hanging. The appellant's appeal to the court of Appeal was dismissed. Still aggrieved, he appealed to the Supreme Court who unanimously allowed the appeal and held as follows per C.C. Nweze JSC at page 172.

> ...In the instant case, having failed to lead any scintilla of evidence in proof of the ingredients of the offences which the appellant, allegedly committed on March 7, 2005 at Iguoil Petrol Station, Boluwaji, Ibadan, the prosecution failed in its duty to discharge the burden of proof which the law vests upon it. The prosecution also failed to prove the separate and distinct offence of conspiracy.

---

[53](2015) 11 NWLR (Pt. 1469) P. 164.

In the same vein, the Court of Appeal in *Hassan* v. *State*[54] allowed the Appeal of the Appellant, thereby quashing a verdict of death by hanging as held by Borno State High Court of Justice. The Court of Appeal held that the Respondent did not lead sufficient evidence to sustain their case against the Appellant. The court went further to hold that the case was largely built on suspicion and the lower court allowed itself to be influenced by sentiments and its personal whims in convicting the Appellant. The facts of the case reveal that on the 16th day of June, 2014 at about 0800hrs, one Hassan Idris of Kilabaliya village in Marte Local Government Area of Borno State reported at Marte Division that on 14/06/2014 at about 0700hrs, when he came back from his farm, he met his daughter, one Maimuna Hassan, 2 years old vomiting. Upon enquiring of what was wrong with her, his son one Saleh Hassan told him that when he left for his farm, their stepmother Hauwa Hassan diluted a chemical known as herbicide with water in a glass cup and administered same to her and as a result she fell sick and started vomiting. She was rushed to the primary health care clinic Kirenuwa town for treatment, but later died on the same day while receiving treatment. Appellant was arraigned before the High Court of Justice Borno State and charged her for the offence of Culpable Homicide punishable with death. Trial commenced before the High Court, wherein appellant pleaded not guilty to the charge. Both counsel addressed the Court after which the learned trial Judge evaluated the evidence and ascribed probative value to the evidence of the witnesses who testified. At the end, learned trial Judge in his Judgment found the Appellant guilty as charged, convicted the accused and sentenced her to death by hanging.

The law is that if an appellant assert that the prosecution failed to prove his guilt beyond reasonable doubt before conviction, it is for him to establish that it is so and it is the duty of an Appellate Court to examine the assertion against the whole background of the case and in particular, against the evidence leading to the guilt of the appellant. In the circumstance, the judgment of the lower court was upturned and the Appeal was allowed.

Just as we earlier stated in *Fabian Nwaturocha's case* on the connotation of the phrase "proof beyond reasonable doubt," the recent decision of the Supreme Court in *Ayinde* v. *State*[55] is also very instructive for proper understanding of the legal aphorism. In that case, it was decided that proof beyond reasonable doubt is not "proof beyond all shadow of doubt" or

---

[54](2018) LPELR-46817 (CA).

[55](2019) LPELR-47835(SC); See also *Audu* v. *FRN* (2018) LPELR-45642(CA) P. 33, paras, B.

"proof to the hill." It simply means establishing the guilt of the accused person with compelling and conclusive evidence, a degree of compulsion which is consistent with a high degree of probability.

Earlier, in the old English *locus classicus* of *Miller* v. *Minister of Pension,*[56] Lord Denning J (as he then was) in his appetising eloquence and characteristic candour adumbrated thus:

> Proof beyond reasonable doubt does not mean proof beyond the shadow of a doubt...If the evidence is so strong as to leave a remote possibility in his -favour which can be dismissed with the sentence, of course, it is possible but not in the least probable, the case is proved beyond reasonable doubt, but nothing short of that will suffice.

Albeit, being a foreign case, its persuasive nature has been crystallized into a binding decision when our court adopted the decision with approval and held in *Abdul Aziz* v. *State*[57] thus:

> ...While it is true, very true, that proof beyond reasonable doubt does not mean proof beyond the shadow of doubt, it has to be emphasised that proof beyond reasonable doubt is the highest standard of proof in law and that standard must not be compromised or watered down for any reason, not even on the ground of expediency.

The Court in *Omotosho* v. *State*[58] while citing Niki Tobi JSC (*of the blessed memory*) in *Tobi Abeke* v. *The State*[59] gave an expository meaning to the phrase "Reasonable doubt" in the following words:

> Reasonable doubt is a doubt founded on reason which is rational devoid of sentiment, speculation or parochialism; the doubt should be real and not imaginative. The evidential burden is satisfied if a reasonable man is of the view that from the totality of the evidence before the Court, the accused person committed the offence. The proof is not beyond all shadow of doubt. There could be shadows of doubt here and there but when the pendulum tilts towards and in favour of the fact that the accused person committed the offence, a court of law is entitled to convict even though there are shadows of doubt here and there.

---

[56] (1947) 2 All ER 372 cited in JUA v. *The State* (2010) 2 SCNJ 224.
[57] (2019) LPELR-47650 (CA).
[58] (2018) LPELR-44169(CA) P. 17, Paras. C-F.
[59] (2007) All FWLR (Pt. 366) 644 at 659 E-F;

Where the prosecution successfully proves its case beyond reasonable doubt, it is left for the accused to raise a reasonable doubt in his defence as posited under section 135(3) of Evidence Act. This burden on the accused is not as heavy as that placed on the prosecution. Under section 137 of the Evidence Act, where in any criminal proceedings the burden of proving the existence of any fact or matter has been placed upon a defendant by virtue of the provision of any law, the burden shall be discharged on the balance of probabilities.

8. Evaluation of Evidence

It is well settled that the evaluation of evidence and ascription of probative value to same is primarily the function of the trial court. This is the position of the law in the apex court's decision in *Enukora* v. *FRN*.[60] Evaluation of evidence involves the assessment of evidence so as to give value or quality to it, and that the records must show how the trial court arrived at its conclusion based upon such evaluation. The evaluation of evidence must therefore be a demonstration of the relationship or connection between the decision of the court and the evidence adduced before it, premised on the pleadings of the parties.

S.T. Hon in his book[61] while citing the Law Lord Oputa J. (as he then was) in *Ali* v. *Kadi Pet*,[62] quoted the Law Lord when he stated that the fact is that no one case is exactly like another and any court or tribunal for that matter would fall short of its duty if it did not first of all find the facts, believe or disbelieve material witnesses, then draw from the facts as found, inferences. It is on the facts as found and on the logical and reasonable inferences that could be drawn from those facts (as found) that the law can be applied.

In the recent decision of the Court of Appeal in *Otigbah* & Ors v. *Uwanaka* & *Anor*,[63] the court while adumbrating on the duty of the trial court in evaluation of facts stated thus:

> The lower court as the trial court has the duty of evaluation of evidence and ascription of probative value thereto. There is a duty on the trial court to receive all available relevant evidence on an issue. This is perception of evidence. After that there is another duty to weigh that

---

[60] (2018) 6 NWLR (Pt. 1516) 355.
[61] S.T. Hon, *op. cit.*, at Pg. 200.
[62] No. BO/ET/GI/79 (1966-1979) Vol. 3 Oputa Law Reports (Oputa LR).
[63] (2020) LPELR -49539 (CA) Pp.19-20, paras. F-B.

> evidence in the context of the surrounding circumstances of the case. This is evaluation of evidence. A finding of fact will entail both perception and evaluation.

In the light of the foregoing decisions, there are some notable point with respect to evaluation of evidence in both civil and criminal proceedings which are germane to be highlighted and discussed. One of such is that the law is trite that evaluation of evidence is the primary responsibility of the court particularly a trial court which watched the demeanour of the witness in the witness box.[64] An appellate court which does not enjoy this singular privilege of seeing and hearing witnesses will not therefore ordinarily interfere with findings of fact of the trial court.[65] An appellate court will only interfere if it is established that the findings were not supported by the totality of evidence on record. In *FRN* v. *Umeh & Anor*,[66] the Supreme Court clearly captured this in the following words:

> It is beyond contention that the evaluation of evidence and ascription of probative value to such evidence is the primary duty of the trial Court that had the opportunity of observing the demeanour of the witnesses while testifying. The appellate Court that deals with only the cold evidence on record, being handicapped, will not ordinarily, interfere with the trial Court's findings on the evidence. Where the trial Court, in spite of the advantage it has, however draws erroneous inferences from the evidence and occasions miscarriage of justice, the court below and indeed this court being appellate Courts will be duty bound to properly evaluate the evidence and make the correct findings to right the injustice occasioned by the trial Court's wrong findings arising from its wrong evaluation of the evidence.

In *Levi* v. *Adikwu & Ors*,[67] the court posited that evaluation of evidence entails the assessment of evidence so as to give value and quality to it. It involves a reasoned belief of the other or a reasoned preference of one version to the other. There must be on record how the court arrived at its conclusion of preferring one piece of evidence to the other. In the same vein, the court cannot pick or choose which set of evidence to believe and which

---

[64] *Timothy & Anor* v. *Okpein & Ors* (2018) LPELR-44182(CA) P. 61, para. B.

[65] See *Okonkwo* v. *Okonkwo* (2010) 14 NWLR (pt. 1231) 228.

[66] (2019) LPELR-46801(SC) Pp. 6-7, paras. E-B.

[67] (2018) LPELR-44261(CA).

set to disbelieve where there are material contradictions in the evidence of witnesses called by the party.[68] However in *Mamuda* v. *The State,*[69] the Supreme Court while bringing out the divergence between a mere slant in evidence of a witness and a clear material contradiction stated that for a statement to be contradictory, it should be a direct opposite of what was earlier stated or spoken. The court went further to state that the law is very clear that only grave and material contradiction (if any) which goes to the root of the case that can cause the evidence to tumble. Outside this, mere slant in the evidence of witnesses cannot be termed as contradictions. Thus, the applicable principle is that only material or grave contradictions in the evidence of a party which goes to the root of the case weakens the case of the party who relies on the evidence so bedevilled.

It is the duty of the trial court to receive in its record, all relevant evidence. The judge proceeds thereafter to weigh the evidence in the context of the surrounding circumstances of the case. That is evaluation. A finding of fact involves both perception and evaluation. There is a clear difference between finding of facts based on the credibility of witnesses and findings of facts based on evaluation of evidence.

For the sake of emphasis, it is a notorious principle of law that parties are bound by their pleadings as held in the most recent decision of the Court of Appeal in *Mr. Grant Kayode Yankey* v. *Florence Austin,*[70] where the court restated the law that a plaintiff swims or sinks with his pleadings. A judge cannot assist a plaintiff to win his case, because cases are not decided on emotions, sentiment or some misguided consideration. Cases must be held to the case pleaded by parties and will not be allowed to depart from the case in their pleadings and set up a different case in court. This is so even at the appellate stage.[71] Parties cannot under any guise be allowed to meander outside the penumbra of what they have pleaded. The court itself is also severely limited and restricted by the issues raised and contained in the pleadings of the parties. No party in litigation will be allowed to lead evidence at the trial which is contrary to his pleadings.[72] Cases are won on pleaded facts supported by compelling evidence. For facts needed to

---

[68] *Orient Photo Nig. Ltd* v. *Eco Bank Plc.* (2018) LPELR-44764 (CA) p. 41, paras. B-C; See also *Kayili* v. *Yilbuk & Ors.* (2015) LPELR 24323 (SC) p.68, Paras A-C.

[69] (2019) LPELR-46343 (SC) p. 32, paras, C-D.

[70] (2020) LPELR-49540(CA); See also *Adekeye* v. *Adesina* (2010) 18 NWLR (Pt. 1225) 450 at 493-494.See also *Adeleke* v. *Adesina* (2010) 18 NWLR (Pt. 1225) 450 at 493 to 494.

[71] *Giwa* v. *Anzaku* (2019) LPELR-46880 (CA) P.15, paras. E-F.

[72] *Emesekwe & Ors* v. *Igwe & Anor* (2015) LPELR-24904 (CA) P. 24, paras. B-C.

establish a right to a relief to be relevant, it has to be pleaded by the party seeking to rely on same to seek his claim or relief. Thus, evidence of facts not pleaded, goes to no issue[73] as parties normally join issues on the facts pleaded only by evidence, either oral or documentary, to establish the fact so pleaded. No party is allowed to present at the hearing, a matter different from that pleaded. So also, the court hearing the matter cannot make out for the parties, a case which they have not presented before him nor give to the parties what they have not asked for.[74] Where however, a court relies on evidence led in facts not pleaded, an appellate court has the duty to set aside any finding resulting from that reliance.

Through pleadings, parties know exactly the issue in contention and it is the law and commonsensical to lead evidence to prove the facts relied on by the party or to sustain allegations raised in pleadings. The court of law does not engage in exercise in futility[75] as it is not the judicial function of a trial judge to embark on an unguarded voyage of facts which are not pleaded before him in search of greener pasture as posited by Niki Tobi JCA (as he then was, of the blessed memory) in *Ajikawo* v. *Ansaldo.*[76] It is settled law that matters presented before a judicial body are determined purely on facts or evidence presented by the parties involved. Therefore, no pleading or the most forensic eloquence or advocacy of counsel can take the place of evidence or substitute evidence.[77]

In *TEC Engineering Co. (Nig) Ltd & Anor* v. *Salisu,*[78] the court explained that cogency of evidence led depends on series of factors and the duty of the trial court before arriving at the conclusion as to who to believe or disbelieve is to place the evidence of both parties in the different sides of the imaginary scale and weigh them together to see which evidence is heavier not necessarily by number of witnesses but by the quality or probative value of the testimonies of those witnesses. In doing this, regard is to be had to the following factors: (i) whether the evidence is admissible; (ii) whether it is relevant; (iii) whether it is credible; (iv) whether it is conclusive and (v) whether it is more probable than that given by the other party.

---

[73] *Rikichi & Ors* v. *Gambo* (2019) LPELR-47676 (CA) P. 17, para. D.

[74] *Union Bank* v. *Salaudeen* (2017) LPELR-43415 (CA) P. 35, paras. F-A.

[75] See *Uniben* v. *Efionayi & Ors.* (2019) LPELR-46737 (CA) while citing the Supreme Court in the earlier decision of *Agbakoba* v. *INEC* (2008) 18 NWLR Pt. 1119. Pg. 489.

[76] (1991) 2 NWLR (Pt.173) 359 at 372.

[77] *Ezeani* v. *FRN* (2019) LPELR-46800 (SC) p.29, B.

[78] (2018) LPELR-46654 (CA) P. 26, Paras. D-F.

In the *locus classicus* case of *Sodipo* v. *Leminkaninen*,[79] The Supreme Court brought out the sacred role of a judge. Hence it held that a judge exists to determine dispute and to examine with microscopic lens, all matters before him in the pursuit of justice. Indeed, a judge is like the goddess of justice or the lady of good counsel who must put the blindfold of justice on and refrain from peeping out of the blindfold in order to take an undue interest in the case before him.

We cannot discuss the weight of evidence to be attached to admissible statements in isolation of section 34 of the Evidence Act. It provides thus:

> In estimating the weight, if any to be attached to a statement rendered admissible as evidence by this Act, regard shall be had to all the circumstances from which any inference can reasonably be drawn as to the accuracy or otherwise of the statement, and in particular-
>
> (a) to the question whether or not the statement was made contemporaneously with the occurrence or existence of the facts stated and to the question whether or not the maker of the statement had any incentive to conceal or misrepresent facts; and
>
> (b) In the case of a statement contained in a document produced by a computer;
>
> (i) The question whether or not the information which the statement contained, reproduces or is derived from, was supplied to it, contemporaneously with the occurrence or existence of the facts dealt with in that information; and
>
> (ii) The question whether or not any person concerned with the supply of information to that computer or with the operation of that computer or any equipment by means of which the document containing the statement was produced by it, had any incentive to conceal or misrepresent facts.

These stipulations in section 34 of the Evidence Act, are expected to assist the trial court in ascribing probative value or weight to be attached to admissible evidence and especially the genre of evidence contained in a document produced by a computer. In the process of evaluating evidence, a judge is at liberty to comment on or rule decisively on the credibility of a witness or witnesses. To be able to exercise this judicial discretion

[79] (1986) 1 NWLR (pt 15) 220 at 234.

judiciously, the court must consider the following factors highlighted in *Ikekwem* v. *C.O.P.*[80] They are:

a the witness' knowledge of the fact he has testified on;
b his disinterestedness;
c his integrity; and
d whether his evidence is contradictory or has been contradicted by the surrounding or collateral circumstances.

For the lone purpose of meeting the justice of the case, the court must advert its mind to these factors. In evaluating evidence, a trial court should bear in mind that in civil appeals, the general ground that the judgment is against the weight of evidence is permissible. The purpose of raising this omnibus ground of appeal is that there is no acceptable evidence to support the findings of the trial court or that the judgment in favour of a successful party is against the totality of evidence adduced before the trial court.[81]

[80](2004) All FWLR (Pt. 213) 1246.

[81] See *C.O.P. Taraba State & Anor* v. *Dabo & Anor.* (2019) LPELR-47215 (CA) p. 15, para. C.

Chapter 15

TAKING OF ORAL EVIDENCE AND EXAMINATION OF WITNESSES

A. Introduction

Taking of oral evidence and examination of witnesses is governed by the Evidence Act. Thus, it is without prejudice to other procedures that may be available under the extant civil and criminal procedure laws or the different rules of court in force in Nigeria.

In this chapter, we shall x-ray copiously, the provisions of the Act that deal with the taking of oral evidence and examination of witnesses. Specifically, this is contained under PART XII of the Evidence Act. This part runs through sections 205 to 247 of the Evidence Act, 2011. We shall devote time to dissect these provisions as they relate to the general prescriptions of the law on examination of witnesses.

B. Oath of Affirmation before Taking of Oral Evidence

The first stage of reception or taking of oral evidence is either for the witness to affirm or be sworn on oath. Section 205 of the Evidence Act makes provision to that effect. It states thus:

> Save as otherwise provided in sections 208 and 209 of this Act, all oral evidence given in any proceedings must be given upon oath or affirmation administered in accordance with the Oaths Act or Law, as the case may be.

The law is explicit that a witness who wishes to give oral evidence must either give a sworn evidence or be affirmed subject to some exceptions cognizable under the law. This preliminary stage of taking of oral evidence is very pertinent, though an oral evidence of a witness is not rendered fundamentally defective and inadmissible only that it failed to be on oath or affirmation. The court has regarded this as a mere misnomer and shall in no case be construed to affect the credibility of a witness to state the truth provided that the other party does not suffer any injustice by such omission. In *Iloka* v. *Edokwe & Ors,*[1] while citing *Anatogu* v. *Iweka,*[2] the Court of Appeal captured this in the following words:

> Although S.205 of the 2011 Evidence Act provides that oral evidence given in any proceedings must be given upon oath or affirmation administered in accordance with the Oaths Act or Law as the case may be. The Supreme Court in *Anatogu* v. *Iweka* (*supra*) has held that the failure to take oath or make an affirmation and any irregularity as to form of oath or affirmation shall not affect its admissibility and probative value, and that such testimony shall be deemed to have been given as if under oath unless, it can be shown that a party has suffered a miscarriage of justice as a result of the omission or failure to administer the oath or affirmation before the testimony.

It should be noted that from the wordings of the provision of section 205 of the Act, an oral evidence can either be on oath or affirmation. The conjunctive word "or" makes it mutually exclusive.[3] In other words, an oral evidence cannot be by oath and at the same time by affirmation. One point must not be omitted here: the term "oral evidence" in appropriate cases also includes sign or body language demonstrated by an incapacitated person while testifying as a witness. This is the provision of section 176 of the Act which provides that a witness who is unable to speak may give his evidence in any other manner in which he can make it intelligible, as by writing or by signs; but such writing must be written and the signs made in open court. Sub 2 of section 176 states that evidence so given shall be deemed to be oral evidence.

This rule encapsulated under section 205 of the Act is applicable in both civil and criminal proceedings with two notable exceptions found in the provisions of section 208 and 209(1) of the Evidence Act. These exceptions are as follows:

i. Cases in which evidence is not given upon oath

To appreciate this exception, the Act provides for cases in which evidence not given upon oath can be received. Section 208 of the Act provides that:

---

[1] *Iloka* v. *Edokwe & Ors* (2016) LPELR-41027(CA) P. 27, para. C-E.

[2] No. 2 (2004) 47 WRN.

[3] See *Ugwu & Ors* v. *Alaebo & Ors* (2016) LPELR-41510(CA) P. 21, para. D where the court held that the word "or" when used in a statute is usually construed as disjunctive and as separating two distinct situations and or denoting an alternative.

> (1) Any court may, on any occasion, if it deems it just and expedient, receive the evidence, though not given upon oath, of any person declaring that the taking of any oath whatsoever is, according to his religious belief, unlawful, or who, by reason of want of religious belief ought not, in the opinion of the court, to be admitted to give evidence upon oath.
>
> (2) The fact that in any case evidence not given upon oath had been received, and the reasons for the reception of such evidence, shall be recorded in the minutes of the proceeding.

As a precursor to this section, the preceding section 207 of the Act made it emphatic to the effect that where an oath has been duly administered and taken, the fact that the person to whom the same was administered had, at the time of taking such oath, no religious belief, does not affect the validity of such oath." A combined reading of sections 207 and 208 of the Act clearly bring to bear the intendment of the draftsmen. By way of adumbration, these sections seek to remove the clog in the wheel of receiving oral evidence of an adult who by reason of religious belief, cannot give evidence on oath or affirmation.

The law respects the fundamental right to freedom of thought, conscience and religion encapsulated under section 38 of the 1999 Constitution of the Federal Republic of Nigeria (as amended). As a corollary, an adult witness by virtue of his/her religious affiliation, can elect to give an unsworn evidence or without an affirmation that all the evidence he shall give in the case will be the truth, the whole truth and nothing but the truth.

Where a witness elects to give an unsworn evidence, the court will proceed to receive the evidence and by virtue of section 208(2) make a precise record in the minutes of proceedings, the reasons for the reception of such evidence.

ii. Unsworn evidence of a child

In the spirit of encouraging an unimpeded and untrammelled reception of oral testimony, the law has another exception to the general principle that all oral evidence must be on oath or affirmation. This is contained under section 209 of the Act to the effect that in any proceedings in which a child who has not attained the age of 14 years is tendered as a witness, such child shall not be sworn and shall give evidence otherwise than on oath or affirmation, if in the opinion or the court, he is possessed of sufficient intelligence to justify the reception of his evidence and understands the duty of speaking the truth. Sub 2 went further to provide that "a child who has attained the age of 14 years shall, subject to section 175 and 208 of this Act give sworn evidence in all cases."

It is no doubt the settled position of the law that a child is a competent witness unless the court considers the child in question to be prevented from understanding the questions put to him by reason of tender years.[4] However, the law under section 209(1) and (2) has streamlined the reception of the evidence of a child by stating two cardinal tests. The first is when the child has not attained the age of fourteen years; and second is when the child has attained the age of fourteen years. If the child is below fourteen years, the court shall receive the evidence unsworn. If the child is determined to have attained the age of fourteen years and above, the court shall receive the evidence sworn. In both cases outlined above, the court shall on record be seen to have firstly determined the biological age of the child and the twin questions whether, in the opinion of the court, (a) the child is possessed of sufficient intelligence to justify the reception of his evidence and (b) understands the duty of speaking the truth.

Under section 209(3) of the Act, a strict legal safeguard is provided to the effect that a person shall not be liable to be convicted for an offence unless the unsworn testimony of a child (admitted by virtue of section 209(1) of the Act) and given on behalf of the prosecution is corroborated by some other material evidence in support of such testimony implicating the defendant. In *Ali* v. *Kano State*[5] the court held that the evidence of a child below the age of 14 years, requires corroboration both as a matter of law as stipulated in section 209 (1) and (3) of the Evidence Act and by established practice as a matter of prudence.[6]

Section 209(4) of the Act is a caveat to the evidence of a child to be a witness of truth at all times. It is provided that if a child, whose evidence is received under section 209 of the Act, wilfully gives false evidence in such circumstances that he would, if the evidence had been given on oath have been guilty of perjury, he shall be guilty of an offence under section 191 of the Criminal Code and on conviction shall be dealt with accordingly.

C. Witness to Be Cautioned Before Giving Oral Evidence

Section 206 of the Act provides that any witness summoned to give oral evidence in any proceedings shall before giving such evidence be cautioned

[4] See section 175 of the Evidence Act, 2011.
[5](2018) LPELR-44201 (CA).
[6]See also *Okwuka* v. *State* (2018) LPELR-45155(CA) and *Idi* v. *State* (2017) LPELR-42587(SC).

by the court or the registrar upon the court's direction, in the following words:

> You (full name) are hereby cautioned that if you tell a lie in your testimony in this proceeding or wilfully mislead this court, you are liable to be prosecuted and if found guilty, will be seriously dealt with according to law.

This innovative section has its basis on the offence of perjury under the Criminal Code. It is primarily formulated to make potential witnesses to realize, early enough in the proceedings, the solemn duty to tell the truth in court and that they may be exposed to criminal prosecution in the event of a failure, refusal or neglect to do so after the cautionary words had been administered. The court also sees an irregularity in the administration of the cautionary words as not fundamentally fatal to the probative value of such evidence provided it does not occasion a miscarriage of justice.

This is in line with what the justice of the case demands. It is already a clichй that gone are the days when justice is allowed to be slaughtered on the altar of technicality. It is an antiquated principle of law and admonition that when this host of the past stands in the path of justice clanging its medieval chains, the best form for a judge to take is to pass through them undeterred. In the recent case of *Apostle Peter Ekweozor & Ors* v. *The Registered Trustees of the Saviour's Apostolic Church of Nigeria,*[7] the apex court posited that attainment of justice is generally no longer allowed or tolerated to be controlled by adherence to technicalities or smart dexterity in court but rather to adherence to substance.

In the immortal case of *Coombe* v. *Edwards*[8] cited with approval in *Peter Ekweozor's case,*[9] Lord Penzance in an appetising prose captured it thus:

> The spirit of justice does not reside in formalities, or words, not in the triumph of its administration to be found in successfully picking way between the pitfalls of technicality. After all, the law is, or ought to be, the handmaid of justice, an inflexibility, which is the most becoming robe of law, often serves to render justice grotesque....if the choice is between legal technicality and justice, one ought to cast one's lot with justice. But it is not all that simple for justice in our Courts is, or ought to be, justice

[7](2020) LPELR-49568 (SC) P. 57, Para. D.
[8](1873) L.R. 3 P.D. 142.
[9] *Supra*.

> according to law.... I will at anytime, anywhere cast my lot for truth and justice...

In summary, the bench are at all point, duty bound by their oath of office and the dictates of the law to foster the interest of justice as it is said that let justice be done though the heaven falls "*Fiat justitia ruat caelum.*"

D. Examination of Witnesses

The order in which witnesses are produced and examined shall be regulated by the law and practice for the time being relating to civil and criminal procedure respectively, and, in the absence of any such law, at the discretion of the court.[10] However, the law went further to erect various procedural rules and regulations for production and examination of witnesses. We shall examine them in line with the provisions of the Evidence Act for proper appreciation of the subject matter.

i. Witnesses to be out of court and out of hearing

In view of the possibility of a witness to be influenced by the testimony of another witness who may be present while the latter witness is giving evidence, the Evidence Act has made provision to forestall such from happening.

Section 212 of the Act provides thus:

> On the application of either party, or of its own motion, the court may order witnesses on both sides to be kept out of court; but this provision does not extend to the parties themselves or to their respective legal advisers, although intended to be called as witnesses.

The essence of this glaring evidential rule above is to ensure that a witness remains a witness of truth whose testimony is not influenced by the oral evidence of a co-witness. To achieve this, witnesses who would testify in a matter may be ordered to be kept out of court. This application can either be made by either parties to the suit through their counsel or by the court *suo motu.* One exception to this principle is that it does not apply to parties to the suit although such party may be called as a witness in the matter. This principle does not also apply to counsel to the parties as the law guarantees them an untrammelled and uncircumscribed right to be present at all times during the trial. This principle has a constitutional bearing under section

---

[10]Section 210 of the Evidence Act.

36(4) (a) of 1999 Constitution of the Federal Republic of Nigeria (as amended). It states thus:

> Whenever any person is charged with a criminal offence, he shall, unless the charge is withdrawn, be entitled to a fair hearing in public within a reasonable time by a court or tribunal:
>
> Provided that-
>
> (a) a court or such a tribunal may exclude from its proceedings persons *other than the parties thereto or their legal practitioners* in the interest of defence, public safety, public order, public morality, the welfare of persons who have not attained the age of eighteen years, the protection of the private lives of the parties or to such extent as it may consider necessary by reason of special circumstances in which publicity would be contrary to the interests of justice.

The import of this provision is that parties to a proceedings have a constitutionally guaranteed right to be in court in the determination of his/her civil rights and obligations. Counsel on the other hand is under legal duty to be present to represent his client and assist the court to meet the justice of the case. However, the failure, refusal or neglect of a prospective witness to be out of court and out of hearing during examination of other witnesses does not lead to disqualification of such other witness; rather, it goes to the weight to be attached to his evidence. The Court of Appeal in *Adie* v. *Ochui & Ors*[11] while pronouncing on the evidence of such witness held thus:

> It is the duty of a Court to take such steps as it considers necessary to prevent communication between those who are in court and awaiting examination. That informs the call usually made to witnesses who are not parties to get out of court and out of hearing. In the event of a breach of any such steps, the proper approach is not to disqualify the witness but for the court to determine the weight to ascribe to such evidence after evaluation instead of dismissing him outrightly.

The order in which witnesses should be called at a trial is clearly a matter for counsel and in respect of which counsel must and does accept responsibility. If it turns out that the order chosen by counsel although not illegal yet offers an unjustified opportunity for one witness to have heard or

[11](2018) LPELR-46160 (CA) P. 39, paras. C-E.

overheard the testimony of another witness, clearly that is a circumstance which must go towards the assessment of the weight to be attached by the court to the probative value of the evidence concerned.

ii. Court to take reasonable steps to prevent communication with witnesses

Sequel to section 212 of the Act, a complementary section on the procedural safeguard on taking of oral evidence is provided for under section 213 of the Act.

Section 213 of the Act states that the court may during any trial take such means as it considers necessary and proper for preventing communication with witnesses who are within the court house or its precincts awaiting examination. This provision has become so imperative especially with the advent of so many sophisticated gadgets in the modern trend of technological innovations. Hence, to prevent any undue interference with the witnesses or any transmission of the proceedings of court by any means to a potential witness, the court is expressly authorized to take any step or step it considers necessary and proper for preventing communication with witnesses.

iii. Examination-in-chief, cross-examination and re-examination

In *Okuleye* v. *Adesanya & anor,*[12] it was clarified by the apex court that proceedings in civil proceedings commences with evidence in chief. The plaintiff states his case on oath as he understands it; thereafter he is subjected to cross-examination by counsel for the defendant. Cross-examination is to test the credibility of testimony given in evidence in chief. Re-examination is an opportunity for the witnesses to restore credibility to his testimony. Cases are hardly won on testimony from evidence in chief. Evidence is reliable and compelling and must be acted on when it goes through cross-examination and remains reliable. It must state that examination in chief is an opportunity to state the facts of his case by the plaintiff and his witness. Cross-examination is to test the correctness of the testimony of the plaintiff and his witnesses while re-examination is another chance to clarify facts but not an opportunity to restate the testimony given in evidence in chief all over again.

---

[12](2014) LPELR-23021(SC) Pp. 18-19, paras G-B.

These three uniform but separate and distinct steps for examination of any witness produced in court by any of the parties for oral testimony has gained judicial blessings in the Supreme Court decision of *Okuleye* v. *Adesanya & Anor.*[13] These step by step guidelines are recognized under section 214 of the Act. There are examination-in-chief, cross-examination and re-examination. May I reproduce the provision *in extenso.* Section 214 states thus:

> (1) The examination of a witness by the party who calls him shall be called "examination-in-chief."
>
> (2) The examination of a witness by a party other than the party who calls him shall be called "cross-examination."[14]
>
> (3) Where a witness had been cross-examined and is then examined by the party who called him, such examination shall be called "re-examination."

The order of examination of witnesses shall be first examined-in-chief then, if any other party so desires, cross-examined, then if the party calling him so desires, re-examined.[15] This is the order and direction of examination of witnesses as stipulated under the Evidence Act. Evidence in chief is an opportunity for the plaintiff and his witnesses to state their case on oath.[16] During examination-in-chief, the plaintiff proffers evidence to substantiate his case either in prove or rebuttal of a fact which the plaintiff has alleged.

It is a general rule pursuant to section 215(2) of the Act that examination and cross-examination must relate to relevant facts, but the cross-examination need not be confined to the facts to which the witness testified in his examination-in-chief.[17]

Where more than one defendant is charged at the same time, each defendant shall be allowed to be cross-examined.[18] Consequently, the Evidence Act also made provision for the sequence of examination of witnesses called by a co- defendant by another defendant. Section 217 of the

---

[13] *Supra.*
[14] *Nwabunike* v. *State* (2019) LPELR-47748 (CA).
[15] See section 215 of the Evidence Act.
[16] *Ayorinde & Ors* v. *Sogunro & Ors.* (2012) LPELR-7808 (SC) P. 17, paras. D. See also *Okoye & Ors* v. *Nwankwo* (2014) LPELR-23172 (SC) P. 18 para. F.
[17] *Oni* v. *Olajiga & Ors* (2018) LPELR-44929(CA) P.29, para. A.
[18] See section 216 of the Evidence Act.

Evidence Act provides that where more than one defendant is charged at the same time, a witness called by one defendant may be cross-examined by the other defendant and if cross-examined by the other defendant, such cross-examination shall take place before cross-examination by the prosecution.

It has become imperative since the introduction of written statement of oath as evidence in chief in civil proceedings that cross-examination is now the real test of the veracity of witnesses. The reason being that most written statement of oath nowadays are mere replica of the pleadings of the parties. It is thus by the cross-examination that the true worth of the evidence of a witness is ascertained.[19] In *Impact Solutions LTD & Anor* v. *International Breweries PLC,*[20] the Court of Appeal while citing the Supreme Court decision of *Oforlete* v. *The State,*[21] expounded on the law in this regard when he said among other things that cross-examination occupies an Olympian position in our adversarial system of adjudication. Cross-examination has been described as the noble art which constitutes a lethal weapon in the hands of the adversary to enable him effect the demolition of the case of the opposing party. Cross-examination if rightly employed, is a potent tool for perforating falsehood.[22]As a matter of fact, the law views evidence procured from the heat of cross examination as more reliable and compelling than the ones oozing out of examination-in-chief.[23]

It is always advisable for cross-examiners to avoid one-question-too-many that gives the witness an opportunity to come out with incriminating or damaging answers. This is in view of the fact that evidence before a court of law can be procured "from a witness under examination-in-chief, cross-examination and re-examination. Thus, where an opposing counsel cross examines a witness and relying on the misconceived clichй that the sky is his limit during cross examination and thus consequently opens the vista for the witness to state incriminating evidence against the party cross examining, the law is that such evidence is not rendered inadmissible only on the ground that it does not favour the party trying to puncture the evidence of the prosecution. In the Supreme Court of *State* v. *Yahaya*[24] the apex court held thus:

---

[19] See *African Songs LTD & Anor* v. *King Sunny Ade* (2018) LPELR-46184 (CA) P. 75, para. B-D.

[20](2018) LPELR-45441(CA) Pp.28-29, paras. F-A. See also *Kpandegh & Anor* v. *Kyenge & Ors* (2015) LPELR-41785(CA) Pp. 17-18, Paras. F-E per OGBUINYA JCA.

[21] (2000) 3 NSCQR 243 at 268, per Achike, JSC.

[22]*Ayan* v. *State* (2013) 15 NWLR (Pt. 1376) 34 at 36, per Fabiyi, JSC.

[23]*Okuleye* v. *Adesanya* (2014) 12 NWLR (Pt. 1422) 321.

[24](2019) LPELR-47611 (SC).

> There is no principle of the law of Evidence to support this implicit outrageous suggestion that evidence extracted, under cross-examination, from a prosecution witness, which evidence incriminates the accused person or defendant, is irrelevant and inadmissible in evidence. On the contrary, as Tobi JCA (as he then was) puts it poignantly in: *Okpokpo* v. *Uko* (1997) 11 NWLR (pt. 527) 94 at 113...once the Court is satisfied with the veracity of the evidence and the truthfulness of the witness, it will attach probative and evidential value (to the evidence). I know of no law, which attaches more probative or evidential value to evidence procured from examination-in-chief than to the evidence procured from cross-examination. An accused person or his counsel who had procured an inculpatory evidence from cross-examination of a witness is estopped from insisting that such inculpatory evidence does not bind him.

Thus, evidence elicited under cross-examination is just as potent as evidence given during evidence in chief, if believed by the court. This is premised on the principle enunciated by the apex court that cross-examination of a witness may also enhance the case of the party cross-examining by affirming or supporting his position.[25] Such evidence is good evidence on which a trial court can legitimately act to make appropriate findings of facts.[26]

The gravamen or the plank of cross-examination has been re-emphasized in a litany of cases. It has been established that cross-examination of an opponent and/or his witness is a very important process of determining the veracity of the evidence of a witness.[27] In *Registered Trustees of Peoples Club of Nigeria* v. *Registered Trustees of Ansar-Ud-Deen Society of Nigeria & Ors,*[28] the Court of Appeal while establishing the purport of cross examination stated, *inter alia,* that with the requirement of filing of Written Statements on Oath of witnesses of the new rules of the court, it is no longer anything strange seeing the Written Statement on Oath of a witness being almost word for word with the pleadings of the parties on whose behalf he is testifying. Thus, cross-examination has become invariably the crucible test by which separation between the truth and lies are attained in litigation process before the honourable court.

---

[25] See *MTN* v. *Corporate Communication Investment Ltd* (2019) LPELR-47042(SC) P. 20, para. C. See also *UNICAL & Ors* v. *Effiong & Ors* (2019) LPELR-47976(CA) P.35, para. E.

[26] *African Songs LTD & Anor* v. *King Sunny Ade* (*supra*) P. 76, paras. B. See also *Mothercat (Nig) Ltd & Anor* v. *Akpan* (2019) LPELR-47158 (CA) and *Aerobell (Nig) Ltd & Ors* v. *Fidelity Bank* (2018) LPELR-45338(CA).

[27] *Ayinde* v. *State* (2017) LPELR-42176 (CA); see also *Nwabunike* v. *State* (*supra*).

[28] (2019) LPELR-47523(CA) P. 45, paras. B-C.

Furthermore, the purpose of cross-examination cannot be over-emphasized. Once a party has concluded his examination-in-chief, the imaginary scale of justice weighs in his favour. Therefore, in order that the other party evens the balance, he has to take measures to place before the court enough facts in support of his own case. Some of these facts may be within the exclusive knowledge of his adversary who has just been led in examination-in-chief. He would therefore cross-examine his opponent and his witnesses with a view to eliciting facts within the knowledge of the adversary in his defence and/or in proof of his own case. In addition to which, the object of cross-examination is to weaken or destroy the case put forward by his opponent in his examination-in-chief.[29] Cross-examination is therefore a veritable and potent tool in the hand of a lawyer who knows his onions. Thus, it is therefore a good practice for a counsel to avail himself of this "noble art" in the demolition of the opponent's case and by- extension, build his case by puncturing the case of his adversary.

The court has bemoaned the disastrous implication of failure to cross-examine a witness on vital points in *Oforlete* v. *State*[30] where the court in its wisdom stated thus:

> Plainly, it is unsatisfactory if not suicidal bad practice for counsel to neglect to cross examine a witness after his evidence-in-chief in order to contradict him or impeach his credit while being cross examined but attempt at doing so only by calling other witnesses thereafter.

This could be associated with unprofessionalism and dearth of expertise in this great art of wits and mastery of forensic analysis of evidence. The mastery of art of cross-examination in the hands of a lawyer who has honed his skills in this field is very useful and important but same art in the hands of an inexperienced lawyer, will cause a serious dent to the case of even the lawyer cross examining. The supreme Court has held in avalanche of cases that the evidence of a witness which is not challenged or shaken by cross-examination, which evidence is not inadmissible by law, must be accepted as correct and uncontroverted.[31] In a later Supreme Court decision of *Ifedayo* v. *State,*[32] the apex court posited in its erudition thus:

---

[29] *Unum* v. *Asagh* (2018) LPELR-44254(CA); see also *Oforlete* v. *State* (*supra*).

[30] *Supra.*

[31] *Yusuf* v. *State* (2019) LPELR-46945(SC) P. 17, paras. A-B. See also *Elegushi & Ors* v. *Oseni & Ors* (2005) LPELR 1111 (SC) and *Ighalo* v. *The State* (2016) LPELR 40840 (SC).

[32] (2018) LPELR-44374(SC) P. 28, paras. D-E.

> It is settled that when a witness testifies on a material fact in controversy in a case, the other party, if he does not accept that it is true, should cross-examine him or at least show that he does not accept the evidence as true, and where he fails to do either, the court can, and will take his silence as acceptance that he does not dispute same.[33]

The Court of Appeal has always lent its voice to this settled position of the law. In *Mothercat (Nig) Ltd & Anor* v. *Akpan*[34] where Ogbuinya JCA in an appetising eloquence posited thus:

> I have, in due fidelity to the dictates of the law, visited the record, the spinal cord of the appeal, at the residence of the statement of oath of Mrs. Helen Victor Okuku, PW2, which colonises page 11 of it. The sworn deposition, on its adoption in the bowel of the court Metamorphosed into her evidence in-chief...At page 220 of the record, the PW2 passed through the crucible of cross-examination by the appellants counsel. It is startling that, the appellants, through counsel, in their infinite wisdom, failed/neglected to cross-examine the witness on the critical and decisive point. Indisputably, cross-examination occupies a kingly position in our adversarial system of adjudication. It has been described as a noble art which constitutes a lethal weapon in the hands of the adversary to enable him effect the demolition of the case of the opposing party. It is settled law, that where a party fails to cross-examine a party on a point, he is deemed to have admitted it. Thus, the dire consequence of the appellants neglect to cross-examine PW2 on the crucial piece of evidence is an undiluted admission of it. It follows, that the appellant's failure to cross-examine the witness on the pungent evidence, which snowballed into admission, punctures their learned counsel's seemingly alluring submission on the point.[35]

In an earlier decision of *Zakariya* v. *FRN*,[36] the Court of Appeal per Abiriya JCA further held that it is the law that where a witness is not cross examined on a crucial and material point, the only conclusion is that the adverse party who ought to have cross examined the witness accepts the evidence of the witness as true.

---

[33] *Simon* v. *State* (2017) LPELR-41988 (SC).

[34] (2019) LPELR-47158 (CA) P. 18-19, paras. F-D.

[35] See *Adeyemi* v. *State* (2018) LPELR-44737 (CA); *Al-Akim Investment (Nig) LTD* v. *FRN & Anor* (2018) LPELR-44083 (CA); *Ali* v. *State* (2018) LPELR-45995 (CA); *Andrawus & Anor* v. *Maksha* (2018) LPELR-46011 (CA) and *Nwokocha* v. *A.-G, Imo State* (2016) 8 NWLR (Pt. 1513) 141.

[36] (2018) LPELR-43999 (CA) P. 21, para. B.

From the armada of cases above, it can be gleaned that a failure, refusal or neglect to cross-examine a witness is deemed a complete admission of the evidence of such witness. However, it should be noted that where a witness refuses to yield himself to be cross examined, it is not deemed as an admission by the opposing counsel; rather , the law see such refusal as a flagrant breach of the right to fair hearing of the party who ought to cross examine the witness. In *Umukoro* v. *State,*[37] PW3 the IPO gave evidence in chief and tendered some exhibits including "exhibit D" which is the supposed confessional statement of the Appellant. The PW3 after his examination in chief, failed to yield himself to be cross-examined by the Appellant's counsel. It was therefore held that a denial of the right to cross-examine a witness to test the veracity of his evidence is a breach of fair hearing.[38]

It should be noted at this point that for cross-examination to stand its worth, it needed not be extensive before it could be relevant and sufficient, provided the crucial facts raised in the evidence in chief are examined and addressed thereon. It is only when a party completely refuses or fails to cross examine a witness that such a party will be deemed to have accepted the testimony of the said witness.[39]

It is not in question that re-examination of a witness after cross-examination by the adversary is a right that inures in the party that called the witness but it is a right which is not compulsory for a party to exercise, and where a party elects to exercise the right to clear some material ambiguity that arose after cross examination, he cannot be denied by a trial Court. Unlike examination-in-chief and cross-examination, re-examination is pertinent but basically optional. The Evidence Act under section 215(3), provides that re-examination shall be directed to the explanation of matters referred to in cross-examination and if a new matter is, by permission of the court, introduced in re-examination, the adverse party may further cross-examine upon that matter. The purpose of re-examination is to clear up any ambiguity that may have arisen as a result of cross-examination.[40] In a latter case of *Mohammed* v. *Gbugbu & Ors,*[41] re-examination is the witness' opportunity of explaining any seeming inconsistency in his answers, and of

---

[37](2018) LPELR-46159 (CA).

[38] See the following that were cited in *Umukoro* v. *State, Okereke* v. *Ibe* (2008) LPELR 4714, *Ogolo* v. *Fubara* (2003) 11 NWLR (PT. 831) Pg. 231, *Fulani* v. *Rafawa* (2013) LPELR 20384.

[39]*Ali* v. *State* (2015) LPELR-24711 (SC) Pp. 30-31, paras. E-A.

[40]See *Natsaha* v. *State* (2017) LPELR-42359 (SC) Pp.31 32 F-A.

[41](2018) LPELR-44494 (CA).

stating the whole truth of any matter which was touched on, but not fully dealt with, in cross-examination of clarifying facts and to restore credibility to his testimony. Re-examination is the time for the witness to explain or elaborate a particular fact which the counsel feels should be better explained without having to overreach the other party.

iv. Leading questions may not be allowed

Section 221(1) of the Evidence Act provides that any question suggesting the answer which the person putting it wishes or expects to receive is called a leading question. This definition in all aspect, is watertight because for a question to be "leading", it must not only suggest an answer, but the answer, must be one the person eliciting the evidence wishes or expects to receive. As a general rule, leading questions shall not be asked in examination-in-chief or in re-examination except with the permission of the court,[42] but leading questions may be asked in cross-examination.[43] However, the court shall permit leading questions under certain circumstances. These are:

1. matters which are introductory;
2. matters which are undisputed, or which have, in its opinion, been already sufficiently proved.[44]

A judge should always be in charge of his court to direct what happens therein in line with the dictates of the rules of court and our procedural laws. The court has the discretionary power to moderate questions put to witnesses during oral testimony. A party can also be allowed with the leave of the court to impeach the credit of his witness by general evidence of bad character especially when such witness has been declared a "hostile witness' by the court.[45] In such circumstance, leading questions will be allowed.

v. Evidence as to matters in writing or contents of a document

Section 222(1) of the Act provides that any witness may be asked, whilst under examination, whether any contract, grant or other disposition of property, as to which he is giving evidence was not contained in a document, and if he says that it was, or if he is about to make any statement as to the contents of any document, which, in the opinion of the court, ought to be produced, the adverse party may object to such evidence being given until such document is produced, or until facts have been proved which entitles

[42] See section 221(1) of the Act.
[43] Section 221(4) of the Act.
[44] Section 221(3) of the Act.
[45] See section 230 of the Act.

the party who called the witness to give secondary evidence of it. Furthermore, a witness may give oral evidence of statements made by other persons about the content of a document if such statements are in themselves relevant facts.[46]

vi. Questions lawful in cross-examination

The trite phrase that the sky is the limit of cross-examination is only but a myth. The Law itself is smacked of limitations and the law of cross-examination is definitely not an exception in our law of procedure. Certainly, relevancy is a limitation in all the three types of examination, including cross-examination.[47] This clichй of sky being the limit of cross-examination has often times been stretched beyond its bounds. There are permissible questions under cross-examination and the law has made copious provisions to that effect. It has been established that the gravamen of cross-examination is to demolish the case of the opponent and by extension, fortify the case of the party cross-examining and in doing so, leading questions can be asked. Consequent upon that, questions can be asked during cross-examination which tend to:

(a) test his accuracy veracity or credibility;[48] or
(b) discover who he is and what his position in life is;[49] or
(c) shake his credit by injuring his character.[50]

Furthermore, a person charged with a criminal offence and being a witness may be cross-examined to the effect, and under the circumstances, described in paragraph (c) of the proviso to section 180 of this Act,[51] meaning that, when the only witness to the facts of the case called by the defence is the person charged, he shall be called as a witness immediately after the close of the evidence for the prosecution.[52]

A successful cross-examination should be able to cast doubt upon the accuracy or veracity of the evidence already given by a witness if the cross-examiner optimally deploys, albeit in the permissible legal manner, the combative latitude or superior firepower of cross-examination.[53] Section 224(1) of the Act made provision to the effect that in relation to questions

---

[46] See section 222(1) of the Act.
[47] See the recent case of *Nwabunike* v. *State* (*supra*) at Pp. 10-11, paras. F-A.
[48] Section 223(a) of the Evidence Act.
[49] Section 223(b) of the Evidence Act.
[50] Section 223(c) of the Evidence Act.
[51] See the proviso to section 223 of the Act.
[52] Section 180(c) of the Evidence Act.
[53] N. O Obiaraeri, *op cit.,* at page 234.

permitted to be asked under section 223 of the Act, the court shall decide whether a question shall be asked and when a witness may be compelled to answer and may, if it thinks fit, warn the witness that he is not obliged to answer it especially when it relates to matters not relevant to the proceedings, except where it is to impeach the credit of the witness by injuring his -character. Thus, the following steps are provided under section 224(2) of the Act to guide the court in the proper exercise of this discretion.

In exercising its discretion, the court shall have regard to the following considerations:

(a) such questions are proper if they are of such a nature that the truth of the imputation conveyed by them would seriously affect the opinion of the court as to the credibility of the witness on the matter to which he testifies;

(b) such questions are improper if the imputation which they convey relates to matters so remote in time, or of such a character, that the truth of the imputation would not affect, or would affect in a slight degree, the opinion of the court as to the credibility of the witness on the matter to which he testifies; and

(c) such questions are improper if there is a great disproportion between the importance of the imputation made against the witness's character and the importance of his evidence.

The court may, if it deems fit, draw, from the refusal of the witness to answer, the inference that the answer if given would be unfavourable.

The avalanche of questions permissible under section 224 of the Act that has been copiously quoted above, may not be asked unless the person asking it or counsel on his behalf has reasonable grounds for thinking that the imputation which it conveys is well founded.[54] Section 226 of the Act is like a watch-dog to counsel's act of putting questions referred to in section 224 without reasonable grounds. It provides that if the court is of the opinion that any question referred to in section 224 of the Act was asked without reasonable grounds by any legal practitioner, it may report the circumstances of the case to the Attorney-General of the Federation or other authority to which such Legal Practitioner is subject in the exercise of his profession.

A very topical and controversial issue that has permeated the admissibility of evidence elicited from cross-examination is the effect of

---

[54] Section 225 of the Evidence Act.

answers obtained during such cross-examination on facts not pleaded. It is settled law that evidence elicited under cross-examination but not on facts pleaded does not enjoy a higher status than evidence in chief given on facts not pleaded merely because it was obtained under cross-examination as they both go to no issue.[55] Thus, it is only where the evidence elicited under cross examination is on facts pleaded either by the party being cross examined or by the party cross examining, that such evidence is good evidence for the cross examining party if it is in support of his case.

It suffices to say that evidence elicited from a party or his witness(es) under cross examination which goes to support the case of the party cross examining, constitute evidence in support of the case or defence of that party cross examining. The only snag to this principle is that the evidence so elicited under cross-examination must be on facts pleaded by the party concerned for it to be relevant to the determination of the issue in controversy between the parties.[56] It should be noted however that only facts are pleaded, not evidence. It is not every aspect of a fact that must be pleaded. Once an aspect of a fact has been pleaded, and learned counsel while cross-examining the witness, puts questions to the witness that helps the witness explain further, the facts pleaded or to supply elements of the facts left out, counsel cannot turn round to ask for the evidence to be expunged because that particular aspect was not pleaded.[57]

In *Oni* v. *Olajiga & Ors,*[58] the court while throwing its weight behind this principle of law posited that evidence elicited during cross-examination, if it relates to the fact in issue, has the same probative value, and is as valid and authentic, as evidence elicited during examination-in-chief. The court went further to hold that evidence elicited from a party or his witness under cross-examination, which goes to support the case of the party cross- examining, constitutes evidence in support of the case or defence of the party. If at the end of the day, the party c-ross-examining decides not to call any witness, he can rely on the evidence elicited from the cross-examination in establishing his case or defence. In such a case, it cannot be said that the party called no

[55] *Stanbic IBTC Bank* v. *Longterm Global Capital Ltd & Ors* (2018) LPELR-44053 (CA) Pp. 49-50, paras. F-B.

[56] *Ogbaji* v. *Utahile & Ors* (2019) LPELR-47186(CA) Pp. 34-35, Paras. E-A.

[57] See the case of *Ecobank (Nig) Ltd* v. *Aghazu* (2019) LPELR-46966(CA) P. 32, paras. C-E. Note the conflicting case of *Chioma* v. *Dimkpa* (2010) 9 NWLR (Pt. 1200) 482 at 503 to 504. However, this controversy has been laid to rest by the Supreme Court in the recent case of *MTN* v. *Corporate Communication Investment Ltd* (*supra*).

[58] (2018) LPELR-44929 (CA) PP. 29-30, Paras. A-B.

evidence in support of his case or defence. However, it can be said that the party called no witness in support of his case or defence, not evidence.

In the recent case of *MTN* v. *Corporate Communication Investment Ltd*,[59] the Appellant vehemently opposed the relevance of questions elicited from his witness under cross-examination as they were not pleaded. The apex court per Mary Ukaego Peter-Odili JSC while refusing such argument and stamping what is today referred to as the true position of the law on the subject matter, made this illuminating dictum:

> The appellant had urged the Court to expunge the facts admitted by the witness of the appellant under cross-examination as they were not pleaded. On this point, I agree with learned counsel for the respondent that that argument just cannot fly as cross-examination answers are not usually pleaded, since a party cannot be in the know or anticipate the mind of the other as to predicting what would be asked in cross-examination. Therefore if as happened in this case, the amount claimed by the respondent and admitted by the appellant's witness under cross-examination tallied with each other, there is no need for further pleading and it is to the advantage of --the respondent and nothing stops the court from utilising it as it is as valid as examination in chief.

Thus, in summary, the position of the law remains that relevance is and still remains the touchstone or the precursor of admissibility of evidence. Hence, answers to questions elicited during cross-examination are admissible. The facts that it was not pleaded notwithstanding, provided it is relevant to the fact in issue.

Vii. Questions which may not be allowed under cross-examination

Having established questions permissible under cross-examination, another side of the coin are questions which may not be allowed under cross examination. Section 227 of the Act specifically provides thus:

> the court in its discretion may forbid questions or inquiries which it regards as indecent or scandalous although such questions or inquiries may have some bearing on the questions before the court, unless they relate to facts in issue or to matters necessary to be known in order to determine whether or not the facts in issue existed.

[59](2019) LPELR-47042 (SC) P. 64, paras. A-E.

Furthermore, section 228 of the Act provides that the court shall forbid any question which appears to it to be intended to insult or annoy, or which, though proper in itself, appears to the court needlessly offensive in form.

In summary, questions that are not allowed under cross-examination are:

1. indecent and scandalous questions;
2. questions intended to annoy or insult; and
3. questions which appears to the court to be needlessly offensive.

These non-permissible questions justify some intermittent interception from the bench during cross-examination considering the line of questions of the counsel especially when they become destructive to the ends of the permissible questions under cross-examination. The court steps in to ask the cross examining counsel the purpose for which he intends to achieve through such questions.-

As much as a cross examiner is not permitted to bully or intimidate a witness under cross-examination, he is not in any way obliged to "romance", "caress" or treat him with "kid gloves" either. This is why cross-examination is regarded as the fire, the litmus test or the crucible and yardstick of measuring the probity of a witness oral testimony. A cross-examiner's question must not be anchored on unreasonable grounds as it can lead to unpleasant consequences.[60]

The Act also made provision for the exclusion of evidence to contradict answers to questions testing veracity. Under section 229 of the Act, it is provided that when a witness had been asked and has answered any question which is relevant to the inquiry only in so far as it tends to shake his credit by injuring his character, no evidence shall be given to contradict him, but if he answers falsely, he may afterwards be charged with the offence of perjury provided that if a witness is asked:

(a) whether he has been previously convicted or any crime and denies it, evidence may been given of his previous conviction; or

(b) any question tending to impeach his impartiality and answers it by denying the facts suggested, he may be contradicted.

In addition, under section 236 of the Act, the court may authorize questions tending to render evidence of relevant fact more probable or admissible. This section provides that when a witness gives evidence of any relevant fact, he may be questioned as to any other circumstances which he

[60] See sections 225 and 226 of the Evidence Act.

observed at or near to the time or place at which such relevant fact occurred, if the court is of the opinion that such circumstances if proved, would render more probable the testimony of the witness as to the relevant fact which he testifies. For instance, if "Mr. A", an eye witness to a crime of murder of "Mr. C" by "Mr. B" is called to testify,. Mr. A can be asked questions to the circumstance of threat to life of Mr. C (the deceased) by Mr. B (the accused) the previous day during an altercation in the neighbourhood where Mr. A was present. This story of threat to life if proved would render more probable the case of murder under determination.

viii. Special restrictions in respect of permissible evidence in trial for sexual offences

Section 234 of the Act made a novel provision for special restrictions placed on the defendant or his counsel with respect to permissible evidence in trial for sexual offences. This novel provision of the Act provides that:

> Where a person is prosecuted for rape or attempt to commit rape or for indecent assault, except with the leave of the court, no evidence shall be adduced, and except with the like leave, no question in cross-examination shall be asked by or on behalf of the defendant, about any sexual experience of the complainant with any person other than the - defendant.[61]

This provision seeks to protect the right to privacy and personal life of a victim of rape or indecent assault. In most cases, in attempt to discredit the testimony of a star witness in sexual offences, defence counsel seeks to ask questions during cross-examination which tend to show that a victim of rape or indecent assault was contributory to the offence which invariably would crystallize into a mitigating factor. The past sexual life of a victim or any evidence to show same should not be a point to cross-examine on except with the permission of the court.

ix. Production of documents without giving evidence

The law is crystal clear that any person, whether a party or not, in a cause may be summoned to produce a document without being summoned to give evidence, and if he causes such document to be produced in court, the court may dispense with his personal attendance.[62] A party can be issued with

---

[61] This new provision is a direct departure from the provision of section 211 of the repealed Evidence Act, 2004 which hitherto allowed for unfettered questioning of the prosecutrix in trial for sexual offences.

[62] Section 218 of the Evidence Act.

subpoena *duces tecum* by the court which primarily compels such party under subpoena to come and tender document and nothing more. Little wonder why he is usually neither sworn nor affirmed. The court can even excuse or dispense with the attendance of the party subpoenaed to tender a document if the latter can produce such document by any other means through his authorized representative as he has no other business to do with the court than to produce a document referred to in the subpoena *duces tecum.* This best explains the provision of section 219 of the Act which to the effect, provides that a person summoned to produce a document does not become a witness by the mere fact that he produces it and cannot be cross-examined unless and until he is called as a witness.

In *Michael & Anor* v. *Aduloju,*[63] the issue here touches on DW6, Chief Obayemi Aladetoyinbo, a witness subpoenaed to come and tender documents simply called subpoena *duces tecum.* The court posited in its wisdom that such a witness is summoned or ordered to appear to produce specified documents, and not to testify as in the case of subpoena *ad testificandum* which is to testify. The court in citing *Akintayo* v. *Jolaoye,*[64] highlighted different types of subpoena and posited that subpoena is an order of Court used for securing a witness' attendance in court of trial for the purpose of testifying and to produce some documents on behalf of the party who applied for the issue of such subpoena. Where the order is to secure the attendance of a witness for the purpose of testifying in Court, it is simply called subpoena *ad testificadum*; where the order commands the witness to produce certain documents at the trial of an action, it is called subpoena *duces tecum.* If it is expected that apart from producing the documents, the person is also to give evidence, the subpoena would be subpoena *ad testicandum et duces tecum.* The court summarized this position of the law when it held at page 20 paragraph D that the subpoena issued in this case was subpoena *tecum simpliciter* and therefore it was a command to produce documents and not to testify.

Where a party fails to produce the exact document he was subpoenaed to produce, the effect of it varies depending on whether it is breach of the rules of court which is to be treated as a misnomer and could be waived in the interest of justice,[65] or a breach of the procedural guideline by the Act, in which case, the law deems the document not produced and can either re-

---

[63](2018) LPELR-46312 (CA) P.19, para. E.

[64] (2010) LPELR-3688 (CA). See also *Olubeko* v. *Awolaja & Anor* (2017) LPELR-41854 (CA).

[65] See *Akpaji* v. *Udemba* (2009) 2 MJSC (Pt. 11) 152.

issue another subpoena *tuces tecum* or visit the defaulting party with the penalty for failure to produce the exact document.

In *Nata Ala* v. *Gabappa & Anor*,[66] the document produced by the Registrar of the Chief Magistrate Court who was subpoenaed to produce a document only was sought to be tendered by the Appellant at the trial Court. The said document fell short of the requirements of section 104 of the Evidence Act as it did not qualify as a Certified True Copy of the proceedings of the referred Magistrate Court. The appellate court while reacting to the issue as to whether the fault was that of the Registrar and as such could not be visited on the Appellant held thus:

> In my understanding, this was the objection of the learned counsel for the Respondent. His contention was that the document produced by the Registrar should not be admitted in evidence as the same was not the document he was subpoenaed to produce. As there was no controversy that the Registrar had failed to produce the exact document the Court subpoenaed him to produce, the Court ought to have noted that the document produced by the Registrar fell short of the document he was commanded to produce. Thereafter the Court would have had two options, which are to further command him to abide by the terms of its subpoena or to deem his act; failure to abide by its earlier command which carries a penalty.

The penalty could be a contempt proceeding against such person as subpoena is derived from two Latin words: "sub" meaning "under" and "poena" meaning "penalty." Therefore, when a person is either summoned to come and testify or to produce a document as in this case, he is a compellable witness under a solemn duty to so appear or produce the document, lest he stands the risk of being penalized by the court. In summary, it should be noted at this juncture that where the party goes to the witness box and tenders the document after being sworn or affirmed, he becomes a regular witness and he is liable to be cross-examined.[67]

x. Cross-examination as to previous statements in writing

Section 232 of the Evidence Act made provision for cross examination of a witness as to his previous statements in writing. It provides that a witness may be cross-examined as to previous statement made by him in writing or

---

[66](2018) LPELR-45379 (CA) Pp. 13-14, paras. E-C.

[67] *Akano* v. *Nigerian Army*. (2000) FWLR (Pt. 83) 2212.

reduced into writing and relative to matters in questions in the suit or proceedings to which he is cross examined without such writing being shown to him or being proved, but if it is intended to contradict such witness by the writing, his attention must, before such writing can be proved, or such contradictory proof given, be called to those parts of the writing which are to be used for the purpose of contradicting him: provided always that it shall be competent for the court at any time during the trial to require the production of the writing for its inspection, and the court may thereupon make use of it for the purposes of the trial, as it shall think fit.

This section presents two situations to wit:

1. where a witness may be cross examined as to his previous statements made by him in writing and relative to matters in question in the present suit in which the witness is being cross examined without the need to show such writing containing the previous statement to the witness;[68]
2. where it is intended by the cross-examination to contradict such witness by previous statement made by him in writing or reduced into writing. In this case, his attention must, before such writing can be proved, or such contradictory proof is given, be called to those parts of the writing which are to be used for the purpose of contradicting him.

This procedural safeguard has gained judicial attention in *Gwandu* v. *FRN*[69] the Court of Appeal held that the procedure for establishing a contradiction, if any, between the previous statement of a witness and his oral evidence in court is provided in section 232 of the Evidence Act 2011 and the Section reads: "A witness may be cross-examined as to previous statements made by him in writing or reduced into writing, and relevant to matters in question in the suit or proceeding in which he is cross-examined without such writing being shown to him, or being proved; but if it is intended to contradict him by writing, his attention must, before the writing can be proved, be called to those parts of it which are to be used for the purpose of contradicting him." While citing the Supreme Court, the Appeal Court went further to throw more illumination on this provision. It posited that this section was interpreted by the Supreme Court in *Madumere* v. *Okafor,*[70] where the court stated that the essential requirements of the section is that where a party intends to impeach the credit of a witness by

---

[68] See *Balogun* v. *A-G of Ogun State* (2002) FWLR (Pt. 100) 1287.
[69] (2014) LPELR-23992 (CA).
[70] (1996) 4 NWLR (Pt.445) 637.

showing that what that witness has said in the present proceedings contradicts his previous written statement:

(a) his attention must specifically be drawn to those parts of his evidence which are to be used for the purpose of contradicting him;
(b) he must be reminded of what he said on that previous occasion; and
(c) he must also be given an opportunity of making an explanation.

Where this procedure is not followed, the previous written statement cannot be used to contradict the oral testimony of the party before the court.

xi. Impeaching the credit of a witness

The credit of a witness may be impeached by any party other than the party calling him or with the consent of the court by the party who calls him by:

(a) by the evidence of persons who testify that they, from their knowledge of the witness, believe him to be unworthy of credit;
(b) by proof that the witness has been bribed, or has accepted the offer of a bribe, or has received any other corrupt inducement to give his evidence; or
(c) by proof of former statements inconsistent with any part of his evidence which is liable to be contradicted.

This is the clear or vivid provision of section 233 of the Evidence Act and impeaching the credit of a witness

Section 235 of the Act provides for evidence of witness impeaching credit. It states that a witness declaring another witness to be unworthy of credit may not, upon his examination-in-chief, give reasons for his belief but he may be asked his reasons in cross-examination and the answers which he gives cannot be contradicted as he is liable to be prosecuted for the offence of perjury under section 191 of the Criminal Code and on conviction, be dealt with accordingly. This is a complementary provision to section 233(a) of the Act. Whenever any statement admissible under sections 40 to 50 of the Act, (some of the recognized exceptions to the hearsay rule), is proved, all matters may be proved either in order to contradict or confirm it or in order to impeach or confirm the credit of the person by whom it was made, which might have been proved if that person had been called as a witness and had denied upon cross-examination the truth of the matters suggested.

It should be noted that where the credit of a witness is being impeached, this may be dislodged by showing consistency in the testimony of the witness or proof that his testimony is not an afterthought by relying on any former statement he may have made with respect to the subject matter under trial.

Categorically, under section 237 of the Act, it is provided that "any former statement made by the witness relating to the same fact or about the time when the fact took place or before any authority legally competent to investigate the fact, may be proved in order to show consistency in the testimony of the witness or to show that his testimony is not an afterthought." By way of adumbration, section 237 of the Act authorizes that the former statement of the witness be used to do any of two things namely: (a) show consistency in the statement; or (b) that his testimony is not an afterthought.[71]

xii. Hostile witness

A witness is considered hostile when, in the opinion of the court, he bears a hostile animus to the party calling him and so does not give his evidence fairly and with a desire to tell the truth to the Court.[72] It is settled that an application to treat a witness as hostile should be made as soon as it is obvious that he is hostile or that his testimony will be adverse to the interest of the party.[73] It should be noted that a witness does not become hostile merely because he gave evidence against the interest of the party who brought him to testify as it must be shown that he has no desire of telling the truth at the instance of that party.

The Court of Appeal has held that where witnesses called by a defendant give evidence which support the plaintiff's case, and the defendant did not treat them as hostile witnesses, the evidence of such witnesses must be treated as an admission against interest upon which the plaintiff is entitled to rely as further reinforcement of his case.[74] Thus, the time honoured practice of deciding on hostile witness must be borne in mind. Once the prosecution discovers that a witness is giving contrary evidence to what he already said in his depositions to the police, the options are as follows: one, if the witness intimates before he goes into the witness box that he would change his story, the prosecution will apply to the court that he would be called only for cross-examination as his evidence is contrary to his previous deposition. The court will accede to this and the evidence of this witness will be of no value to either side.

---

[71] This is in contra distinction with section 214 of the repealed Evidence Act, 2004 which authorized that the former statement of a witness be used for corroboration only.

[72] *R.* v. *Manning* (1968) Crim. LR 675.

[73] *Al-Mustapha* v. *State* (2013) LPELR-20995 (CA) P. 101, paras. D. *Turaki & Anor* v. *Sankara & Ors* (2011) LPELR-9203 (CA) P. 28, paras. A-B.

[74] *Ibrahim* v. *Yahaya* (2016) LPELR-41810 (CA) P. 58, paras, A-B.

Secondly and most importantly, if the witness resiles on getting into the witness box on his previous deposition on the same case, the prosecution applies to treat him as a hostile witness. In such cases, the witness will be declared a hostile witness if the court rules so. But before ruling, the court must be satisfied as to the discrepancy in his previous deposition and evidence on oath. Once satisfied, the court will rule the witness a hostile witness.[75]

As a prelude and for a better appreciation of the subject matter, the applicable provisions of the Evidence Act are now examined. Sections 230 and 231 of the Act govern the procedure for dealing with a hostile witness. Thus, as a general rule, formulated under section 230 of the Evidence Act, the party producing a witness shall not be allowed to impeach his credit by general evidence of bad character, but he may, in case the witness shall, in the opinion of the court, prove hostile, contradict him by other evidence, or by leave of the court, prove that he has made at other times a statement inconsistent with his present testimony; but before such last mentioned proof can be given, the circumstances of the supposed statement, sufficient to designate the particular occasion, must be mentioned to the witness and he must be asked whether or not he has made such statement.

Furthermore, section 231 of the Evidence Act, made provision for proof of contradictory statement of a hostile witness. Thus, if a witness upon cross-examination as to a former statement made by him relative to the subject-matter of the trial and inconsistent with his present testimony, does not distinctly admit that he has made such statement, proof may be given that he did in fact make it, but before such proof can be given, the circumstances of the supposed statement sufficient to designate the particular occasion must be mentioned to the witness, and he must be asked whether or not he has made such statement.

It is the law that if a witness is treated as hostile by the party calling the witness, then the sworn evidence of that witness as well as the witness's previous unsworn statement become unreliable and both must be rejected.[76] To narrow down this principle on how some witnesses suddenly turn to a 'viper' against the party calling him, the Supreme Court held in *Hassan* v. *State*[77] that if a witness who had made a statement to the police enters the witness box and decides to be funny, by attempting to detract or actually

[75] *Ibeh* v. *State* (1997) LPELR-1389 (SC) P. 20, paras. A-E.
[76] *Adeleye* v. *State* (2014) LPELR-23063 (CA) P. 21, paras. B.
[77] (2001) 35 WRN 175.

detracting from his previous statement, thereby making himself a hostile witness, the contents of the statement may be used to cross-examine him as to credit and no more.

xiii. Production of documents

Section 242 of the Act provides that subject to section 234 of this Act, a witness summoned to produce a document shall, if it is in his possession or power, bring it to court, notwithstanding any objection which there may be to its production or to its admissibility and the validity of any such objection shall be decided by the court. The court, if it deems fit, may inspect the document or take other evidence to enable it to determine on its admissibility.[78] If for the purpose of determining its admissibility, it becomes necessary to cause any document to be translated, the court may, if it thinks fit, direct the translator to keep the contents secret unless the document is to be given in evidence and, if the translator disobeys such direction, he shall be held to have committed an offence under section 97(1) of the Criminal Code.[79]

It is pertinent to note that the provision of section 242 of the Evidence Act on production of documents outlined above is nonetheless subject to the extant provision on exclusion of evidence on grounds of public interest contained in section 243 of the Act. This is glaring from the opening tone of section 242 above.

Section 243 of the Act provides as follows:

> (1) A Minister, or in respect of matters to which the executive authority of a State extends, the Governor or any person nominated by him, may in any proceeding object to the production of documents or request the exclusion of oral evidence when after consideration he is satisfied that the production of such document or the giving of such oral evidence is against public interest.
>
> (2) Any objection mentioned in subsection (1) of this section shall, if taken –
>
> (a) before trial, be by affidavit: or
>
> (b) at the hearing, be by certificate produced by a public officer.
>
> (3) The court shall have discretion whether or not to uphold any such objection, and may in determining how to exercise its discretion, inspect

---

[78] Section 242(2) of the Evidence Act.

[79] Section 242(3) of the Evidence Act.

such documents or be informed as to the nature of the oral evidence to which the objection relates.

xiv. Procedure for giving as evidence of document called for and produced on notice or procedure for using as evidence a document production of which was refused on notice

The procedure for giving as evidence of document called for and produced on notice is covered by the provision of section 244 of the Act to the effect that when a party calls for a document which he has given the other party notice to produce, and such document is produced and inspected by the party calling for its production, he is bound to give it as evidence if the party producing it requires him to do so. The procedure for using as evidence a document production of which was refused on notice is covered by section 245 of the Act. Thus, when a party refuses to produce a document which he has had notice to produce, he cannot afterwards use the document as evidence without the consent of the other party or the order of the court.

xv. Refreshing memory

In an attempt by the court to remove difficulties in the way of honest witnesses who would wish to refresh their memory during examination so as to speak the truth with exactitude, section 239 of the Act came to fulfil this mandate. It should be noted however that as a general rule, a witness is not permitted to give his evidence by referring to a prepared statement or writing. Myriads of exceptions exist to this general rule as a witness may, with leave of court, be allowed to refresh his memory in any of the ways provided by the law.

A witness may while under examination,[80] refresh his memory by referring to any writing which he made at the time of the transaction concerning which he is questioned, or so soon afterwards that the court considers it likely that the transaction was at that time fresh in his memory.[81] The witness may also refer to any such writing made by any other person, and read by the witness at the time of the transaction concerning which he is questioned, or so soon afterwards, if when he read it he knew it to be correct.[82]

---

[80]In this context, "examination" includes examination-in-chief, cross-examination and re-examination.

[81] Section 239(1) of the Evidence Act.

[82] Section 239(2) of the Evidence Act.

Sub 3 made provision for the special mode through which an expert can refresh his memory. An expert may refresh his memory by reference to professional treatises.[83] A witness may also testify to facts mentioned in any such documents or writing made by himself, any other person or professional treatises although he has no specific recollection of the facts themselves, if he is sure that the facts were correctly recorded in the document.[84]

The bottom line here, however, is that the statement, to be reliable, would have been made so close to the event when the vices of human frailty, forgetfulness, falsehood or outright mischief, will be ruled out and suspended to a certain degree.

To provide a fair and reasonable balance in the adjudicatory process, it is settled law that any writing which has been used by a witness to refresh his memory must be produced and shown to the adverse party upon demand and the adverse party is at liberty to cross-examine the witness upon the writing.[85] In the same vein, when a party refuses to produce a document which he has had notice to produce, he cannot afterwards use the document as evidence without the consent of the other party or the order of the court.[86]

It should be borne in mind that the opportunity to refresh memory by recourse to writings or treatises must be understood along the new, wide and encompassing interpretation of "document" in section 258(1) of the Act. In view of this novel development, a witness may, with leave of court, not only refresh his memory with writings in his diary, receipt or notebook but also with those contained in pager, phone or computer or other electronic devices by means of which information is recorded, stored or retrievable.[87]

xvi. Judge's power to put questions or order production of documents

Section 246 of the Act made a very encompassing provision and vested on a judge with so much powers under the Act to put questions to any witness or order the production of any document or thing in the course of a judicial proceeding with the sole purpose of clarifying some grey areas that arose *ex improviso.* This of course, does not clothe the judge with an unbridled

[83] Section 239(3) of the Evidence Act.
[84] Section 240 of the Evidence Act.
[85] Section 244 of the Evidence Act.
[86] Section 245 of the Evidence Act.
[87] See section 84 of the Evidence Act.

licence to descend into the arena of conflict and play the role of the prosecutor by asking probing and destabilizing questions. This is where the exception lies.

For ease of reference, it is worthy to reproduce the provision of section 246(1) of the Act which provides that the court or any other person empowered by law to take evidence may, in order to clear up ambiguities or to clarify points which have been left obscure in the evidence given by any witness, ask any question he pleases, in any form, at any time of any witness, or of the parties about any fact relevant or irrelevant; and may order the production of any document or thing; and neither the parties nor their agents shall be entitled to make any objection to any such question or order or, without the leave of the court, to cross-examine any witness upon any answer given in reply to any such question. The questions shall be based upon facts declared to be relevant under the Evidence Act and duly proved;[88] and a judge shall not compel any witness to answer any question or to produce any document which such witness would be entitled to refuse to answer or produce under this Act, if the question were asked or the documents were called for by the adverse party; nor shall the judge ask any question which it would be improper for any person to ask under section 224 or 225 of this Act nor shall the judge dispense with primary evidence of any document, except in the cases exempted in preceding sections of this Act.[89]

The case of *Madu & Anor* v. *Anozia & Anor*[90] is very instructive for proper comprehension and appreciation of the powers of the court to put questions or order the production of documents. In the instant case, the appellants *inter alia,* claimed against the defendants/respondents, a declaration that the plaintiffs/appellants are entitled to statutory right of occupancy over the land in dispute. Parties filed and exchanged their pleadings and the case proceeded to definite hearing. However, during the course of leading the appellants' witness PW5, the learned trial judge asked the witness a question to which answer was given by the said PW5. The appellants' counsel was not happy with the question posed by the learned trial judge to the witness, and he made his displeasure known by protesting against an alleged interference by the learned trial judge with the conduct of his case. The protest or objection was ignored by the learned trial judge and

---

[88] Section 246(2) of the Evidence Act.

[89] Section 246(3) of the Evidence Act.

[90](2018) LPELR-45484(CA) Pp. 24 -25, paras. E-A.

the court went ahead to put the question he posed to the witness and answer was given on record. The appellants being dissatisfied, through their counsel, sought for an adjournment which was refused. He therefore applied to withdraw his appearance for the appellants, and the said application was duly granted. Subsequently, the appellants filed a motion on notice on the 5th day of January, 1995, wherein they sought for the leave of the learned trial judge to allow the appellants' counsel; Prince N. I. A. Ohanyere, to continue as their counsel. The motion was dismissed for being unmeritorious. On the 22nd day of March, 1995, when the case came up for hearing, neither the appellants nor their counsel were present in court. Consequently, the learned trial judge was of the opinion that the appellants had abandoned their case. He dismissed it. Not in the least pleased, appellant appealed to the Court of Appeal. Among the issues formulated for determination was whether the question posed by the court to the Plaintiffs' 5th witness (PW5) during his examination in chief was necessary and justifiable in law? The Appellate court while allowing the appeal in part held thus:

> Finally, on the issue bordering on power of a court to put question to a witness. By virtue of Section 246(1) of the Evidence Act, 2011 (hereinafter referred to as the Evidence Act). A judge is empowered or has the power to put question(s) across to a witness in some certain circumstances, in order to clear some ambiguities or clarify certain point(s) in the evidence given by the witness...From the provision of the Evidence Act, reproduced above, it is clear that the learned trial judge has the power to put any question across to the appellants fifth witness as he did. This power as granted to the learned trial judge can be exercised at any stage of the evidence being adduced by the said witness, provided the questions are not scandalous, insultive, or falls into other categories of questions which the witness is at liberty not to answer or prohibited from being put to a witness by the Evidence Act.
>
> In the instant case, the question put to the appellants witness was asked to clarify a point from the evidence being given by the witness and nothing more. The question is innocuous as the learned counsel for the respondents has contended. It has no seemingly damaging effect whatsoever on the case of the parties especially that of the appellants. Thus, I do not agree with the learned counsel for the appellants that the learned trial judge has compromised his position as an impartial arbiter in this case by merely asking a question, aimed at clarifying a point or

clearing a perceived ambiguity in the evidence adduced by the appellants' witness.

However, in an earlier case of *Akinfe* v. *The State,*[91] the Supreme Court held that although a trial judge under sections 223 of the Evidence Act, 2004[92] and 200 of the Criminal Procedure Act, has very wide powers to ask any questions he pleases from any witness including the accused person, the powers of the judge to ask questions under those sections are not unlimited. They are limited by the implications of the adversary system which we operate, the absolute need for impartiality in fact and in appearance on the part of the judge and generally the principle of fair hearing enshrined in our constitution as the *grundnorm.* The court held that through the questions posed by the judge in *Akinfe's* case, the image of even handed justice was destroyed and the likelihood of bias against the appellant was established.

Finally, in certain circumstances, a judge is allowed by law, to put questions to a witness in order to clear some ambiguities or clarify certain point(s) in the evidence given by the witness.

---

[91] (1988) 3 NSCC 313.

[92] Comparable to section 246 of the Evidence Act, 2011.

Chapter 16

ADMISSIBILITY OF STATEMENT MADE IN SPECIAL CIRCUMSTANCE

1. Introduction

In our rules of evidence, it has long been recognized that under certain circumstance, statements made or contained in certain documents termed "special" will be relevant and admissible. This is of very significant implication in the understanding of the intricate principles of law on admissibility of statements made in special circumstance. Further, under section 258 of the Act, a wider approval was adopted in the definition of statement to include "any representation of fact whether made in words or otherwise." It is in the light of the foregoing that their relevance and admissibility under our current adjectival or evidentiary rules are discussed hereunder for what constitute, statements made in special circumstance.

2. Entries in books of account

Under section 51 of the Evidence Act, it provides thus:

> Entries in books of account or electronic records regularly kept in the course of business are admissible whenever they refer to a matter into which court has to inquire, but such statements shall not alone be sufficient evidence to charge any person with liability.

It is very important to note that before now, section 38 of the repealed Evidence Act had similar provision except that it only stated that such entries are merely "relevant" whereas the new law recognizes that such entries are admissible. It is submitted that this is a key shift and an upgrade of the probative value attached to entries in books of accounts. This is premised on the fact that any admissible piece of evidence is relevant but not all relevant evidence is admissible on the authority of *Ifaramoye* v. *State.*[1]

---

[1](2017) LPELR-42031(SC) p. 34, para. A.

It is beyond conjecture that entries in books of account are statutorily admissible as relevant facts and shall be treated as such in our adjectival law. Secondly, and very importantly too, section 51 of the Evidence Act expressly recognizes that "electronic records" regularly kept in the course of business are admissible thereby removing the old debate whether computer or electronic records are primary or secondary documents. The genre of admissible entries under the penumbra of section 51 of the Act is therefore very elastic and expansive in view of the meaning attached to "document" in section 258(1) of the Evidence Act and the expression "the species of admissible evidence" under section 51 of the Act will not be limited only to books which are usually bound and whose page are not easily replaced but they will include loose-leaf ledger[2] and electronic records. Under this interpretation in section 258 of Evidence Act, a book is a document and a document" includes any device by means of which information is recorded, stored or retrievable including computer output.

Furthermore, under the same section, the expression "banker's books and related expression" include ledger, daybooks, cashbooks, account books and all other books used in banking business.[3] The words or expression "such statements shall not alone be sufficient evidence to charge any person with liability" contained as a proviso to section 51 of Evidence Act means that no criminal charge or civil suit can be proved by mere statements in such books of accounts or electronic records. Therefore, some other corroborative evidence tending to establish the liability of the accused or the defendant will be required in addition to the solitary entries in such a book and electronic record.[4]

3. Entry in public record made in performance of duty

It is provided under section 52 of the Evidence Act 2011 that an entry in any public or other official books, register or record, including electronic record stating a fact in issue or relevant fact and made by a public servant in the discharge of his official duty, or by any other person in the performance of a duty specially enjoined by the law of the country in which such book, register or record are kept, is itself admissible. It is ostensibly clear that the above stipulation recognizes register or record that aside from entry in

---

[2] See *Esso West Africa Inc* v. *T. Oyegbola* (1969) 194 decided by the Supreme Court and cited with approval in Aguda, *op. cit.,* page 87.

[3] *Lufthansa German Airlines* v. *Ballanyne* (2013) 1 NWLR (part 1336) p. 52.

[4] N.O. Obiaraeri, *op.cit.,* at pg. 117.

public or other official books, registers or record, that entry in "electronic record" is also admissible.

Extrapolating from the language or wordings of the law above, for the entry in the electronic record to be admissible, it must be one kept for public or official purpose and not for private or unofficial reasons. It is also significant that section 52 of the Act declares such entry as "admissible" unlike the old law where they merely declared it as "relevant." It should be underscored that the expression "public or other official books, register or record" means no more than a public documents within the purview of section 102 of the Act as there is nothing in section 52 of the Act to suggest that a different meaning is intended by the draftsman. For the purpose of this section, public book, public register or public record including public electronic record are unarguably public documents since entry must have been made by "a public servant in the discharge of his official duty, or by any other person in the performance of a duty specially enjoined by the law of the country in which such book, register or record is kept."[5]

4. Statement in Maps, Chart and Plans

Under section 53 of the Act, it provides thus:

> Statements of facts in issue or relevant facts made in published map or charts generally offered for public sale, or in maps or plans made under the authority represented or stated in such maps, charts or plans, are themselves admissible.

Deducing from the above, the statement contained in the map, chart, or plan may relate to a fact in issue or relevant facts and they are admissible in either case. This provides broad accommodation under the law for the statements in the said map, chart or plan can be deployed in any of the various ways recognized by the law on relevancy. The map, chart or plan containing the statement may be one generally offered for sale in the market over to members of the public or official copies produced on the authority of Government. It is imperative that the relevant map, chart or plan must be

[5] For more understanding of the topic, section 102 provides for public document. It states that the following documents are public documents: (a) documents forming the official acts, records of the official acts; (i) the sovereign authority; (ii) officials bodies, legislative, judicial and executive, whether of Nigeria or elsewhere; and (b) public records kept in Nigeria of private documents like birth certificate, etc.

tendered in evidence in the required form in order to attract the presumption of genuineness under section 151 of the Evidence Act.

5. Statements as to facts of a public nature contained in certain Act or Notifications

Section 54 of the Act provides that when the court has to form an opinion as to the existence of any fact of a public nature, any statement of it made in a recital contained in any enactment or in any proclamation or speech of the President in opening the National Assembly or in any proclamation or speech, or in any statement made in a Government or public notice appearing in a state Gazette or the State Gazette of any other country is admissible.

The extant law declares such statement to be admissible and not merely relevant and further makes infinite allowance for the admissibility of any public notice appearing in "the Government Gazette of any other country" unlike under the defunct law which was limited or restricted only to "London Gazette or the Government Gazette of any part of the commonwealth.[6]

6. Certificate of specified government officers to be sufficient evidence in all criminal cases

Section 55(1) of the Evidence Act provide thus:

> Either party to the proceedings in any criminal case may produce a certificate signed by the Government Pharmacist, the Deputy Government pharmacist, an Assistant Government pharmacist, a Government Pathologist or Entomologist or the Accountant- General, or any other pharmacist so specified by the Government Pharmacist of the federation or of a state, any pathologist or entomologist specified by the Director of Medical Laboratories of the Federation or of a state, or any accountant specified by the Accountant-General of the federation or of a state (whether any such officer is by that or any other title in the service of the state or of the Federal Government) and the production of any such certificate may be taken as sufficient evidence of the facts stated in it.

Deducing from the foregoing, it is glaringly clear on the face of this provision that the certificate is authorized for use only in criminal

[6] Under section 41 of the repealed Evidence Act, 2004, this was limited to London Gazette or the Government Gazette of any part of the Commonwealth.

proceedings. It is open to the defence or the prosecution alike to produce and rely on such certificate signed by any of the designated government officers. In this connection, it must be observed that it is curious that nothing is mentioned of the Auditor-General for the federation and or Auditor- General for a state notwithstanding the fact that their offices are expressly created by the Constitution under sections 85 to 87 and 125 to 127 respectively and clothed with enormous powers to audit public accounts. There is also no provision for the Auditor General and Accountant General of the Local Government respectively. This is submitted as yet another lacuna graving to be filled in view of the fact that Local Government is a tier of government created in section 7 of the 1999 Constitution as amended. It is settled beyond conjecture that a certificate issued by a government officer not expressly mentioned in section 55(1) of the Act is therefore not admissible under the section as it is the law that the express mention of a word is to the exclusion of all others not stated as expressed in the Latin phrase "*expressio unius est exclusio alterius*". In *Afdin Ventures & Ors* v. *Chairman Abuja Municipal Area Council*,[7] it was held that it is well settled principle of construction of statute that where a section names specific things among many other possible alternatives, the intention is that those not named are not intended to be included. In *State* v. *Samson*,[8] a certificate issued by a government ballistician was held inadmissible under this section. However, in *Barewa Pharm. Ltd* v. *FRN*,[9] the court while considering section 55(1) and (2) of the Act and in deciding the question "whether certificate issued by government health officers is sufficient evidence in all criminal cases" held thus while answering the question in the affirmative:

> The process was clear and smooth and culminated in the certificates issued by PW6 and PW7 Exhibits T and U. I agree with learned senior counsel for the Respondent that based on these certificates emanating from NAFDAC laboratories in Yaba and Oshodi, the sample was contaminated with the contaminant Diethylene Glycol. I join the Respondent in asking "what other scientific evidence or proof could be more sufficient and convincing given the provision of Section 55(1) and (2) of the Evidence Act. The sections provide:

---

[7] (2014) LPELR-23509 (CA).
[8] (1971) UILR 26.
[9] (2016) LPELR-40536 (CA).

> 55 (1). Either party to the proceedings in any criminal case may produce a certificate signed by the Government Pharmacist, the Deputy Government Pharmacist; an Assistant Government Pathologist or Entomologist, or the Accountant-General, or any other Pharmacist so specified by the Government Pharmacist of the Federation or of a State, any pathologist or entomologist specified by the Director of Medical Laboratories of the Federation or of a State or any accountant specified by the Accountant-General of the Federation or of a State (whether any such officer is by that or any other title in the service of the State or of the Federal Government), and the production of any such certificate may be taken as sufficient evidence of the facts stated therein."
>
> (2). Notwithstanding Subsection one of this Section, any certificate issued and produced by any officer in charge of any laboratory established by the appropriate authority may be taken as sufficient evidence of fact stated in it.
>
> ...In the circumstances, the certificates presented by PW6 and PW7 Exhibits T and U have to be taken as sufficient evidence of the facts stated therein.[10]

The law stipulates that such certificate may be taken as sufficient evidence of the facts stated therein and not that it shall be taken as conclusive proof of the facts stated therein. Therefore the production of such certificate raises a rebuttable and not irrebuttable presumption of genuineness. This view is further reinforced by the provision of section 58 of the Act that the court shall, in the absence of evidence to the contrary, presume that the signature to any such certificate as is mentioned in sections 55 and 56 is genuine and that the person signing it held the office or authority which he professed at the time when he signed it.[11] A party tendering a certificate under this heading does not therefore have a stringent obligations to prove the signature on it unless and until there is evidence to the contrary but the court is entitled to allow evidence in rebuttal (to the contrary) to be laid. That is why the presumption is rebuttable.

In *Ufomadu* v. *Nigeria Army,*[12] one Dr. Innocent Onwumere (PW6), a trained doctor with degree in medicine and surgery who had practiced medicine for about twenty-one years after graduating from the University of

---

[10] Pp. 41-42, paras E-A; P.44, paras. C-D. See also *Abiodun* v. *FRN* (2016) LPELR-40535(CA) Pp. 40-42, paras. G-A.
[11] *Eromosele* v. *FRN* (2016) LPELR-40539 (CA).
[12](2017) LPELR-43046 (CA)

Nigeria, Nsukka in 1990 and under the employment of the Government of Enugu State at all-time material to this case, presented an Autopsy Report prepared by him though not being a pathologist. The court while rejecting his autopsy report (Exhibit 4) and applying *expressio unius exclusio alterius,* held that he lacked the requisite expertise and competence to have examined the corpse in order to issue an autopsy report. The court went further to state that the production of such autopsy report is not sufficient evidence of the facts stated in it. Not being a pathologist or a ballistician, the evidence of PW6 was held not to qualify to be admissible under section 55(1)-(5) of the Evidence Act, 2011 as he does not come within the persons named in the section under review.

The Supreme Court gave legal imprimatur to the provision of section 58 of the Evidence Act in *Posu and Anor* v. *The State.*[13] In that case, the appellants were charged with the offences of conspiracy to rape and rape, during the trial, PW1gave a graphic account of how he saw the appellants rape the victim PW2 and how PW2 was later taken to the hospital for medical examination. The prosecution among other things, tendered the medical report of PW2 which was admitted in evidence as "Exhibit C." The trial court found the appellants guilty and convicted them accordingly. The appellants appealed to the court of Appeal and the Court of Appeal dismissed their appeal and affirmed the trial court's verdict. The appellant's final appeal to the Supreme Court was dismissed as lacking in merit. On Exhibit C, the medical report, the Supreme Court held, *inter alia,*

> PW1 told the court that on the same night the incident took place, the matter was reported to the police who immediately took the PW2 soaked with blood to the hospital for examination in the early hours of 13/12/2008. The Doctors findings as noticed and indicated in Exhibit C were bruises on the thighs of PW2; semen in her vulva and tiny bruises at the entrance of her vagina. It is no deal and in no way a contested fact that Exhibit C is the report of Doctor's observation and treatment issued by one Dr. Itokem Michael of Ipokia General Hospital to PW 2. PW4 testified that he was on National Youth service at the Hospital at all times material to the case when he examined PW2 and issued Exhibit C. He had since completed his service and left the hospital to an unknown place. By section 44 of the Evidence Act, court shall, in the absence of evidence to the contrary presume that the signature of EN. C is genuine and that Dr. Itokem Michael who signed it held the office which he professed at the

---

[13] (2011) 2 SN3 at 45 to 46 per Galadima JSC. See also *Musa* v. *FRN* (2013) LPELR-22844 (CA).

> time when he signed it. I must therefore give Exhibit C the consideration it deserves having regard to the other evidence on record and the circumstances of this case. There was evidence from PW 2 to the effect that she was raped by the appellants.

Considering section 55(2) of the Act, it provides that "Notwithstanding subsection (1) of this section, any certificate issued and produced by any officer in charge of any laboratory established by the appropriate authority, may be taken as sufficient evidence of facts stated in it. The purport of this subsection will be well appreciated if read together with the explanations offered in section 55(5) of the Act which can be referred to as an 'interpretation subsection' to the effect that under the section.

(i) "Appropriate Authority" means the inspector General of police, the comptroller-General of customs or the minister of Health.
(ii) "Officer" means any officers-in charge of any laboratory established pursuant to this Act;
(iii) "Specified" means specified by notice as may be published in the federal or state Gazette.

This is to say that any certificate issued and produced by an officer in charge of any laboratory established by the inspector General of Police, the Comptroller-General of Customs or the Minister of Health pursuant to this Act may be taken as sufficient evidence of facts stated therein.

The "officer in charge" of the laboratory under section 55(2) of the Act does not need to be of the rank, status or designation of any of the government officers already listed in section 55(1) of the Act. This is also true of the class of officers whom the president may by notice in the *Federal Gazette* authorize to sign a certificate relating to any subject in the notice under section 55(4) of the Act. The said section 55(4) of the Act provides that:

> The president may, by notice in the *Federal Gazette*, declare that any person named in such notice, being an officer in the public service of the federation employed in a forensic science laboratory in a rank not below that of medical laboratory Technologist, shall for the purposes of subsection (1) of this section be empowered to sign a certificate relating to any subject specified in the notice, and while such section apply in relation to such person as they apply in relation to an officer mentioned in that subsection, provided that a certificate signed by such person shall not be admissible in evidence if in the opinion of the court it does not

relate wholly or mainly to a subject so specified as in such notice in relation to this subsection.

It was noted earlier that unless the content otherwise requires, "specified" means specified by notice as may be published in the federal or state Gazette" as explained in section 55(5) of the Act. It is clear that the President may by notice in the *Federal Gazette*, declare a specific person (the Act here speaks of any person named" and not an office or status) named in such notice entitled to sign a certificate relating to a specified subject matter. The named person must however be an officer in the public service of the federation employed in a forensic science laboratory in a rank not below that of medical laboratory technologist.

The production of certificate issued by any of the officers mentioned in section 55(1) and (2) above may be taken "as sufficient evidence of the facts stated in it. Unlike the production of a certificate issued under section 55(4) which is not admissible in evidence "if in the opinion of the court it does not relate wholly or mainly to a subject so specified as in such notice. It follows therefore that a certificate issued by any officer mentioned in section 55(5) and (2) is weightier in law than that issued by an officer mentioned under section 55(4) of the Act.

The certificate issued by a designated public officer under this section is a public document as stated under section 102 of Evidence Act. When a certificate signed by any of the specified officers is produced, it is unnecessary to call the officer to give evidence. This notwithstanding, under section 55(3) of the Act, it is recognized that the Court shall have the power, on the application of either party or of its own motion, to direct that such officer as is referred to in the subsections shall be summoned to give evidence before the court if it is of the opinion that, either for the purpose of cross examination or for any other reason the interest of justice so requires.

Section 57 of the Act contains a number of salient and mandatory stipulations on the other party before hearing. It provides that "where any such certificate as is mentioned in section 55 or 56 is intended to be produced by either party to the proceedings, a copy of it shall be served on the other party at least ten days before the day appointed for the hearing and if it is not so sent, the court may, if it thinks fit, adjourn the hearing on such terms as may seem proper." For purposes of computation of time, it can be gleaned that the law stipulates that the certificate shall be served at least ten clear days before the day appointed for the hearing. It is submitted that the use of the word "shall" to qualify the condition to be satisfied makes it mandatory[14] and as such, there must be evidence of proper service on the adverse party, preferably personal service or in lieu of same, substituted service duly ordered by a competent court. There must also be evidence of service at least ten clear days before the day appointed for the hearing. Where the service is not personal or through duly approved substituted means, it is submitted that this may prove fatal to the proceedings. Where the statutory time of service is abridged, the court is empowered to consider circumstances surrounding the matter and if it thinks fit, adjourn the hearing on such terms as may seem proper. The whole purport of the provision relating to time is to give reasonable and ample notice of the contents of the certificate to the adverse party in order to enable him prepare adequately for his defence. This is in tandem with the constitutionally guaranteed right to fair hearing[15] under section 36 of the 1999 Constitution (as amended). A party is not to be embarrassed or taken by surprise with the case of his adversary during trial. It is reasonable to think that the copy of the certificate served in the adverse party should be the same in character, content and effect with what is intended to be relied upon during trial. Therefore, if there is a material discrepancy or disparity between what has been served on the adverse party and what is sought to be relied upon in court during the trial, the court will not hesitate to hold that there is a violation of the provision of this section.[16] In summary, the court is under obligation to determine two key issues here namely:

(i) whether there was proper service; and

(ii) whether the service was effected within a minimum often clear days before the date fixed for the hearing. These two conditions are so sacrosanct for such hearing.

7. Certificate of central bank officers as evidence in criminal cases

Section 56 of the Evidence Act expressly provides that where in criminal proceedings, a certificate purports to be signed by an officer of the Central Bank of Nigeria who himself adds after his signature the words "duly authorized by the Governor of the Central Bank of Nigeria" it shall be accepted by all courts and persons as sufficient evidence of the facts stated in

---

[14] *Babatope* v. *Sadiku & Anor.* (2017) LPELR-41966 (CA) p. 16, para. A.

[15] *Ahmed & Ors* v. *Registered Trustees of Archdiocese of Kaduna of the Roman Catholic Church* (2019) LPELR-46414 (SC) p.14, para. B.

[16] N. O. Obiaraeri, *op. cit.,* at pg. 125.

the certificate, and no certificate shall be questioned on the ground only of the authorization; but subject to this, section 55(3) shall have effect with regard to any such certificate.

This provision no doubt, relates to criminal proceedings only. The court shall presume that the signature to any certificate of the Central Bank officer issued in the manner prescribed under this section is, in the absence of evidence to the contrary, genuine and that the person signing it held the office or authority which he professed at the time when he signed it. As already noted, the certificate issued by an officer of the Central Bank of Nigeria under this section is a public document under the interpretation of section 102 of the Evidence Act.

When a certificate signed by the officer of Central Bank of Nigeria is produced, it is unnecessary to call the officer to give evidence. However, under section 55(3) of the Act, the court is vested with the power, on the application of either party or of its own motion, to direct that any such officer of the Central Bank of Nigeria who issued the said certificate be summoned either to give evidence before the court or for the purpose of cross examination or for any other reason provided that the court makes a determination that it is in the interest of justice to do so as justice is the primary purpose of adjudication.

Where a certificate issued by an officer of the Central Bank of Nigeria is intended to be produced by either party to the proceedings, a copy of it shall be served on the party at least ten clear days before the day appointed for the hearing and if it is not sent, the court may, if it thinks fit, adjourn the hearing on such terms as may seem proper. The clarification already offered and views expressed in respect of necessity for proper service and need not to abridge time in respect of section 57 of the Act are applicable here and require no further adumbration.

Chapter 17

CORROBORATION

1. Introduction

The law is settled in a long line of cases that a party need not overwhelm the court with a trailer- load of witnesses to prove his case. Single testimony of one adult witness with a cogent, compelling, convincing and credible testimony can suffice to even send a man to the gallows.[1] It thus suffices to reiterate the undisputed position of the law that no particular number of witnesses shall be required for proof of any fact in issue. As the judge using the imaginary scale sees not the quantity or the number of witnesses called by each party but the quality and probative value of the evidence of those witnesses. Albeit, there are circumstances where the law will require that the evidence of a sole witness be supported by another independent witness for a court to decide such case in one way or the other. This is primarily what corroboration is all about.

2. General Principles

The general principle is that the law does not require a village or community of witnesses to prove a case. As it is an already established principle that the rational for the decision of the court is a collateral effect of the quality and the probative value of the testimony of the witnesses rather than quantity. Generally, corroboration is not needed to ground a conviction or prove liability; thus, the Evidence Act states that:

> Except as provided in sections 201 to 204 of this Act, no particular number of witnesses shall, in any case, be required for the proof of any fact.[2]

---

[1]The old case of *Sunday Akpan* v. *The State* (1967) NMLR 185 was predicated on this long-aged principle of law. See also *Okonofua* v. *The State* (1979) 5-9 SC 18; *Alabi* v. *The State* (1993) 7 NWLR (PT. 307) 511; *Olayinka* v. *The State* (2007) 9 NWLR (PT. 1040) 561 at 576D-E & 584 A-B and the recent case of *Ofordike* v. *State* (2019) LPELR-46411(SC) 27, paras. E-F.

[2] Section 200 of the Act.

Corroboration thus, refers to the act of supporting or strengthening a piece of evidence in a law court. It literally means "to support" or "make stronger". The Supreme Court in *State* v. *Yahaya*[3] defined Corroboration thus:

> On what corroboration means, one can posit with humility that it entails the act of supporting or strengthening a statement of a witness by fresh evidence of another witness.

In the same vein, the Court of Appeal in *Joshua* v. *State*[4] defined corroboration as an independent testimony, direct or circumstantial which confirms in some material particular not only that an offence has been committed but that the accused person has committed it. In the earlier case, the apex court per His Lordship Mary Ukaego Peter Odili JSC also defined corroboration as that evidence which tends to confirm, support and strengthen other evidence sought to be corroborated.[5] It does not mean that the witness corroborating must use the exact or very words, unless the maker involves some arithmetic.[6] The test to be applied to determine the nature and extent of corroboration is to establish that the evidence is an independent testimony which affects the accused by connecting or tending to connect him with the crime. The apex court in *Ikumonihan* v. *State*[7] has this to say on corroboration:

> The meaning of the legal term "corroboration" as stated by Lord Reading, CJ, in *Rex* v. *Baskerville* (1916) 2 KB 658, which was approved and adopted by this Court in *Okabichi* v. *State* (1975) 3 SC 96, is aptly captured as follows:
>
> Evidence in corroboration must be independent testimony, which affects the accused by connecting or tending to connect him with the crime- - It must be evidence, which implicate him, that is, which confirms in some material particular not only the evidence that the crime has been committed, but also that the prisoner committed it. Corroborative evidence is evidence, which shows or tends to show that the story that the Accused committed the crime is true, not merely that the crime has been committed, but that it was committed by him.

---

[3] (2019) LPELR- 47611 (SC) p. 31, para. F.
[4] (2019) LPELR -47358 (CA) P.12, Paras. D-E.
[5] *Nguma* v. *A.G Imo State* (2014) 7 NWLR. (Pt. 1405) P. 119.
[6] *State* v. *Yahaya* (*supra*) at P. 31, para. G.
[7] (2018) LPELR-44362 (SC) P.20, paras. B-E.

Corroboration or corroborative evidence therefore is that evidence that tends to support or confirm in some material particular, some other piece of evidence on any given issue of fact in a trial.[8] For a piece of evidence to be taken as corroborative of another, it must be an independent testimony which shows not only that an act has been committed, but that the act was committed by the party to whom it is attributed to.[9] This also, was lucidly stated in the time-honoured case of *R* v. *Bakerville.*[10]

Corroboration need not consist of direct evidence or the evidence of another witness nor does it need to confirm the whole story, provided it supports the evidence substantially. In *Nguma* v. *A.G. Imo State,*[11] the issue arose as to whether the black berate pistol, two life cartridges and axe (exhibits 1, 2 & 5 respectively) found at the appellant's house corroborated the appellant's confessional statement. In that case, the complainant had returned to Nigeria from America for the Christmas holiday. One night, he was robbed of all his money and jewelleries at his house. On seeing the appellant days later, he called the police who arrested the appellant and some other members of the gang. The pistol, axe, etc., were subsequently found at the appellant's house. The Supreme Court held that Exhibits 1, 2, & 5 being the black berate pistol, two life cartridges, the axe respectively were recovered from the appellant and when situated alongside the confessional statement, Exhibits 7, it would be seen that the items Exhibits 1, 2 and 5 are corroborative of the contents of Exhibit 7, the extra-judicial confessional statement. The statement itself gives graphic details of the planning, execution and the after-math of the robbery with some exhibits in tow.

Given that corroboration must be independent evidence, two different pieces of evidence from the same witness such as his extra judicial statement and oral evidence cannot amount to corroboration. Thus, the court held in *Shofolahan* v. *the State*[12] that a witness cannot corroborate himself and evidence of a witness which requires corroboration cannot be used to corroborate the evidence of another witness. In *Ali* v. *State,*[13] the Court of Appeal while citing the Apex Court with approval in the earlier case of *The*

---

[8] See the following: *Ifaramoye* v. *State* (2017) LPELR -42031 (CA); *Kolade* v. *State* (2017) LPELR-42362 (SC) and *Yusuf* v. *State* (2018) LPELR -46718 (CA).

[9] *Musa* v. *State* (2013) 9 NWLR (Pt.1359) 214 particular at pg. 243.

[10] (1916- 1917) All ER (Reprint) 38 at 43.

[11] *Supra.*

[12] (2013) LPELR-20998 (CA) P. 30, paras. D-E.

[13] (2019) LPELR-45995 (CA) P. 23, paras. A-B.

State v. *Gwangwan,*[14] stated that evidence that is regarded as corroboration is clearly not a repetition of the evidence sought to be corroborated, otherwise there will be no need for the original evidence. Hence, the evidence of PW5 in the case which was itself a repetition of the evidence of a co-accused was held to be far from being corroborative evidence.

A point to note Under the old Evidence Act[15] is the provision on self-corroboration when it provided that in order to corroborate the testimony of a witness, any former statement made by such witness relating to the same fact at or about the time when the fact took place, or before any authority legally competent to investigate the fact, may be proved. This obviously went against the provision on self-corroboration.[16] However, the 2011 Act modified section 214 of the previous Act by providing in section 237 thus:

> any former statement made by a witness relating to the same fact at or about the time when the fact took place, or before any authority legally competent to investigate the fact may be proved in order to show consistency in the testimony of the witness or to show that his testimony is not an afterthought.

This has, happily, resolved the conflict in the previous Act and protected the rule against self-corroboration.

3. Rational For the Corroboration Rule

In the earlier but a germane case of *Popoola* v. *State,*[17] the court while giving an exposition into the purpose or rational for the corroboration rule posited thus:

> What is the purpose of corroborative evidence? The answer to this was answered in the case of *Iko* v. *State supra* at page 241 para D - F where the learned jurist Kalgo J.S.C. referred to the case of D.P.P. vs. Hester (1973) A.C. page 296 at 315 Lord Morris said: "The purpose of corroboration is not to give validity or credence to evidence which is deficient or suspect or incredible but only to confirm and support that - which as evidence is sufficient, satisfactory and credible. Corroborative evidence will only fill its role if it is itself completely a credible evidence."

---

[14](2015) LPELR-24837 (SC) P.30, Paras, F-G.

[15] Section 214 of Evidence Act 2004.

[16] This was also noted by Nwadialo in F. Nwadialo, *op. cit.,* pg. 434.

[17] (2011) LPELR-4860 (CA) Pp. 15-16, paras. D-A; see also *Olasore & Anor* v. *Ajibolade & Anor* (2011) LPELR-8953 (CA); *Auta* v. *State* (2014) LPELR-23292 (CA) p. 37 para. B. and *Mbang* v. *State* (2010) 7 NWLR (Pt. 1194) P. 431

> While corroborative evidence must be independent and capable of implicating the accused in relation to the offence charged, it must be credible and must go to confirm and support that evidence which is sufficiently satisfactory and credible.

Lord Morris in the immortal case of *DPP* v. *Hester*[18] cited above, had a more expansive insight on corroboration generally when his Lordship posited thus:

> The reason for this are diverse...There may in some cases be motives of self-interest; or of self-exculpation, or of vindictiveness. In some situations, the straight line of truth is diverted by the influences of emotion or of hysteria or of alarm or of remorse. Sometimes, it may be that, owing to immaturity or perhaps to lively imaginative gifts, there is no true appreciation of the gulf that separates truth from falsehood. It must, therefore, be sound policy to have rules of law or of practice which are designed to avert the peril that findings of guilt may be insecurely based...All the rules which evolve are in accord with the central principle of our criminal law that a person should only be convicted of a crime if those in whose hands decision rests are sure that guilt has been established.

It should be noted also that evidence required to be corroborated by statute cannot corroborate another piece of evidence that is required to be corroborated by either law or practice. Finally in considering whether a piece of evidence is corroborative, one must take it as a whole; one must take all the little items together and consider whether they all add up to corroborate as a whole[19]

In summary, the rationale behind corroboration is that it helps to prevent an unjust sentence in cases where it would be risky to convict the accused based on the sole evidence of a witness or on a single piece of evidence for instance, offence of rape. Thus the essence of corroboration is to give support or strength to the assertion of the prosecution. That is why as a matter of practice, a trial court should be slow to convict on the uncorroborated evidence of the prosecution witness. It should be noted at this juncture that if an alleged corroborative piece of evidence is questionable, it will amount to insufficient corroboration.

---

[18] (1973) AC 296 at 315.
[19] *Omisade & Ors* v. *Queen* (1964) LPELR-25119(SC)

4. Cases in Which Corroboration Is Required

Corroboration is statutorily required in the following cases.

A. Treason and Treasonable Offences

The law recognizes certain exceptions where an accused person cannot be convicted by the evidence of a sole witness. One of such exceptions is the offence of treason and treasonable felony as provided under section 201 of the Evidence Act. A person charged with treason or with any of the felonies mentioned in sections 40, 41 and 42 of the Criminal Code Act cannot be convicted, except on his own plea of guilty, or on the evidence in open court of two witnesses at least to one overt act or the kind of treason or felony alleged, or the evidence of one witness to one overt act and one other witness to another overt of the same kind of treason or felony.[20]

The brief fact of the old but the immortal case of *Omisade & Ors* v. *Queen*[21] is very germane to be reproduced herein for a better appreciation of this subject matter. In this case, the accused persons were alleged to have solicited, incited and endeavoured to persuade and procure certain persons to take part in the levelling of war against the Sovereign Lady the Queen. Obafemi Awolowo between December, 1960, and February, 1962, procured Oladipo Akinwunmi Maja to arrange for the training of Nigerians outside Nigeria in the unlawful use of explosives, weapons, arms and ammunition in preparation for the said levelling of war within Nigeria against the Sovereign Lady the Queen. They were thus charged with treasonable felony. The first and fifth accused turned Crown witnesses. Four of them were not present in Court and the charges against them were withdrawn but not on the merits. Seven of them were discharged in the High Court. The remaining eighteen accused persons were convicted of various offences in the Information and sentenced to various terms of imprisonment. The sixth accused person died in prison whilst serving his term. Aggrieved by their convictions, they appealed against same to the Federal Supreme Court. The Supreme Court held that the only interpretation which, in their view, can be ascribed to subsection (2)(a) (now section 201(1) of the Evidence Act, 2011) is that if a defendant does not plead guilty to a charge of treason or treasonable felony, there must be two witnesses testifying in open court to the overt act alleged, or one witness to one overt act and one other witness to another overt act of the same kind of treason or felony. In effect, two different witnesses at least

[20] Section 201(1) of the Evidence Act.

[21] (1964) NMLR, 67.

are needed to prove a count of treasonable felony. This however must not be taken to mean that a witness must be able to testify to an overt act in its entirety: as Counsel for the 27th accused (Mr. Durand) put it, a number of witnesses may give evidence of "snippets" which add up to proof of an overt act.[22]

It will be imperative to state in a nutshell the provisions of sections 40, 41 and 42 of the Criminal Code as alluded to in the section under discourse. Section 40(1) creates the offence of accessory after the fact of treason and while subsection (2) makes the concealment of information of an intention to commit treason an offence. Section 41 of the Criminal Code provides for treasonable felonies – (a) plotting to overthrow the president (b) plotting to remove a state governor (c) to levy war against Nigeria (d) to instigate a foreigner to make any armed invasion of Nigeria or of any of the territories thereof. Section 42 makes promoting inter-communal war an offence.

However, it should be noted that these provisions will not apply where as a result of the overt act of treason or treasonable felony, the President is killed or there has been a direct attempt to endanger his life or injure his person.[23] Thus it is self-evident that corroboration will not be required in cases in which the overt act of treason alleged is the killing of the President or a direct attempt to endanger the life or injure his person. By express implication, the mandatory requirement of corroboration only ends with a charge for treason under section 201(1) of the Evidence Act and does not extend to sub (2) of the section.

B. Evidence in a charge of Perjury

Section 202 of the Evidence Act provides that a person shall not be convicted of committing perjury or for counselling or procuring the commission of perjury, upon the uncorroborated testimony of one witness contradicting the oath on which perjury is assigned, unless circumstances are proved which corroborated such witness.

C. Exceeding Speed Limit

A person charged under any road traffic legislation with driving at a speed higher than the allowed maximum shall not be convicted solely on the evidence of one witness that in his opinion the defendant was driving at such speed: provided that the evidence of a duly authorized officer of the relevant authority who was at the time of the commission of the offence operating

---

[22] Scc also *R.* v. *McCafferty,* 10 Cox C.C 603 at p. 611.

[23] Section 201(2) of the Evidence Act.

any mechanical, electronic or other device for the recording of the speed of a moving vehicle, the record of such device being additionally tendered in evidence against the defendant , shall not require further corroboration.[24] According to Murphy[25] on Evidence, the purpose of such provision is to provide a safeguard against the possible unreliability of such evidence of opinion, because of the likelihood of error in relating an impression of the speed of a vehicle to a precise speed limit. What this section portends are in two prongs and also conjunctive in nature: the oral evidence of the officer and the evidence from mechanical or other device for the recording of the speed of a moving vehicle. The nature of the corroborative evidence required in this circumstance is the mechanical or electronic device used for the purpose of recording such speed. This when tendered will corroborate the evidence of the authorized officer. At this point, it should be emphasized that the proviso in no stretch of imagination envisages a question of admissibility of the two genres of evidence. Rather, it goes to the issue of corroboration. It thus suffices to say that in the absence of such electronic corroboration mentioned in the subsection, there must be independent corroboration of the evidence to prove the traffic offence. In the germane case of *Agbonavibare* v. *Ogbebor,*[26] It was held that a person charged under the Road Traffic law of a State with driving at a speed greater than the allowed maximum shall not be convicted solely on the evidence of one witness that in the opinion he was driving at such speed.

It is submitted that it follows to say that such mechanical device will necessarily comply with the requirements for the admissibility of an electronically generated evidence as provided under section 84 of the Evidence Act.

D. Sedition

This is another offence that cannot be sustained successfully in the court of law solely on the evidence of a lone witness. This is to say that evidence of two or more witnesses are required for the proof of the offence of uttering seditious words under section 51(1) and (b) of the Criminal Code.

Section 204 of the Evidence Act provides that a person shall not be convicted of the offence of uttering seditions words under section 51(1) (b) of the Criminal Code Act upon the uncorroborated testimony of one

---

[24] Section 203(1) of the Evidence Act 2011.

[25] R. Glover and P. Murphy, *Murphy on Evidence,* 13th edn. (UK: Oxford University Press 2013) 666-667.

[26] (2007) All FWLR (Pt. 351)

witness. According to an erudite scholar, Fidelis Nwadialo,[27] he posited that the need for corroboration before conviction in a charge for sedition "derives from the effortless ease with which a charge for it would otherwise be proved." This position cannot be faulted in the light of the present society and how public office holders extremely guard 'reputation' thereby finding it extremely difficult to extricate their person from the office they occupy. Extrapolating from the wordings of section 204 cited above, it suffices to say that any conviction of sedition on the uncorroborated evidence of a sole witness is an effort in futility and of no moment as such cannot stand.

E. The Evidence of an Accomplice

The Court in *Alozie* v. *State*[28] while citing the Supreme Court per A. I. Iguh, JSC, in *Ogunlana & Ors.* v. *The State,*[29] at pages 20 -21 defined who an accomplice is in the following terms:

> One becomes an accomplice to a crime if he is *participes criminis* whether as principal or accessory before or after the fact with regard to the offence charged. The mere presence of a person at the commission of a crime does not *ipso facto* make one an accomplice to such a crime.

However, section 198(2) of the Evidence Act states that an accomplice as used in section 198 and 199 of the Evidence Act is "any person who pursuant to section 7 of the Criminal Code may be deemed to have taken part in committing the offence as the defendant or is an accessory after the fact to the offence of a receiver of stolen goods. Anyone who falls into any of these two categories is regarded as an accomplice. Thus, a person must be purposely facilitating or aiding the commission of a crime by his presence before he can be regarded as an accomplice. So too, the mere failure of a witness to report the commission of a crime will not *ipso facto* make the witness to the commission an accomplice.[30] The fact that one did not report a crime to the police until they interviewed him does not indicate complicity as it is common knowledge that in this country, witnesses often refrain from coming forward in case they might get into some sort of trouble. In *Ahmed* v. *State,*[31] the court held that merely participating in a

[27] Nwadialo, *op. cit.*, page 453.
[28] (2018) LPELR-45230 (CA) p. 17, para. C-D.
[29] (1995) 5 NWLR (Pt. 395) 266 at 285.
[30] *Alozie* v. *State* (Supra); See also *Nwachukwu* v. *State* (2014) LPELR- 22531(CA) p.32, para. E; *Imoke Onyikoro* v. *R.* (1959) NRNLR 103 and *Yaw Azuma* v. *R.* (1950) 13 WACA 87.
[31] (2018) LPELR-46606 (CA).

fight started by an aggressor does not make the one attacked an accomplice or a tainted witness.

The law regarding the evidence of an accomplice is by no means ambiguous. Section 198(1) of the Evidence Act states that:

> An accomplice shall be a competent witness against a Defendant, and a conviction is not illegal merely because it proceeds upon the uncorroborated testimony of an accomplice -Provided that in cases when the only proof against a person charged with a criminal offence is the evidence of an accomplice, uncorroborated in any material particular Implicating the defendant, the court shall direct itself that it is unsafe to convict any person upon such evidence.

The implication of the above provision is simply that an accused can be convicted on the uncorroborated evidence of an accomplice by a trial court, but such a court must be very cautious and must only do so when, on considerations of all the circumstances of the case, it is satisfied that it is safe to convict the accused.

This provision is an attempt by the Act to direct a court when faced with the evidence of an accomplice to first look out for corroboration. However, if this is absent, he must take all circumstances of the case into consideration, bearing in mind the danger of convicting the accused solely on the uncorroborated evidence of an accomplice. The courts have, sadly, taken this provision as the premise upon which the non-existent rule that the evidence of an accomplice required corroboration is based. It should be stressed again at this juncture that the intention of section 198(1) of the Act is expressly clear and leaves no room for conjecture and academic gymnastics. The purport of the said section is that evidence of an accomplice does not by law require corroboration; albeit, there is a duty inherently imposed on the Court by the Act to warn itself before convicting an accused on the uncorroborated evidence of such accomplice.

In *Shofolahan* v. *The State,*[32] the Court of Appeal with due respect fell into the error of stretching the limit of section 198(1) of the Evidence Act when it held that there was no proof that the appellant was guilty of murder because the two witnesses whose evidence implicated the accused were accomplices. It stated as follows:[33]

---

[32] (2013) 17 NWLR (pt. 1383) 281 C.A.

[33] At pg. 314.

> It is apparent that the learned trial judge convicted the appellant on the uncorroborated evidence of PW2 are PW3, indeed he indicated that the PW2 and PW3 are accomplices and that their evidence corroborate to a large extent the evidence of PW1 (Dr. Ore Falomo)...It is my view, in the circumstances of this Appeal that the learned trial Judge failed to properly direct himself to the unsafety of convicting on the un-corroborated evidence of an accomplice. PW2 and PW3's evidence remain uncorroborated as required by law and therefore lack probative value. And such a conviction based on such uncorroborated evidence must be quashed without much ado.

The court further stated that a witness cannot corroborate himself and evidence of a witness which requires corroboration cannot be used to corroborate the evidence of another witness. Corroboration decidedly must be external and independent evidence, outside what obtains from contested, confessional statements. The approach of the court in the above case is, to say the least, contrary to the provision of section 198(1) of the Evidence Act for it is not the position of the law that the evidence of an accomplice requires corroboration rather the law states that a judge must be cautious when the only evidence against an accused is the uncorroborated evidence of an accomplice. Evidence of such caution is evidence from the record of proceedings that the judge warned himself as to the danger of convicting the accused based on such evidence. In the above cases, the court merely concluded that since the evidence of the accomplices were not corroborated, they must be quashed. The correct position of the law was stated in a more recent case of *Ahmed* v. *State*[34] per Amina Audi Wambai J.C.A. His Lordship posited thus:

> I am of the candid view that merely participating in a fight started by an aggressor does not make the one attacked an accomplice or a tainted witness. Even if he were to wear such a toga and I am not saying so, the law remains that an accomplice is a competent witness for both the prosecution and the defence and *a conviction based on the evidence of such accomplice is not illegal even where such evidence is uncorroborated, though the judge should warn himself of the danger of doing so.*

---

[34] *Supra* at pp.15-16, paras. F-B.

F. Unsworn Evidence of a Child under the Age of 14

The unsworn evidence of a child constitutes another genre of evidence that requires corroboration. Section 209(1) of the Evidence Act 2011 state that "in any proceeding in which a child who has not attained the age of 14 years is tendered as a witness, such child shall not be sworn and shall give evidence otherwise than on oath or affirmation if in the opinion of the court, he is possessed of sufficient intelligence to justify the reception of his evidence and understands the duty of speaking the truth."

Section 209(3) further states that a person shall not be liable to be convicted for an offence unless the testimony admitted by virtue of subsection (1) of this section and given on behalf of the prosecution is corroborated by some other material evidence in support of such testimony implicating the defendant.

From the above, it can be gleaned that so long as a child is under the age of 14, if he gives evidence, which shall not be given on oath, his evidence must be corroborated to ground conviction for an offence. This does not apply to children above the age of 14 who must give sworn evidence which does not require corroboration.[35]

In *Ali* v. *State*,[36] the appellant was arraigned before the lower Court for the offence of rape contrary to the provision of Section 282 of the Penal Code and punishable under Section 283 of the Penal Code. The Appellant was alleged to have, on or about the 12th of March, 2012 at Jauro Abare Quarters of Gombe State, had unlawful carnal knowledge of one Hadiza Shaibu who was five years old at the time of the commission of the offence. The Appellant pleaded Not Guilty to the charge and the matter proceeded to trial and in the course of which the Respondent called six witnesses and tendered three exhibits as Exhibits A, B and C in proof of its case and the Appellant testified and called two other witnesses in proof of his defence. At the conclusion of the trial, Counsel to the parties filed and adopted the arguments in their written addresses. The lower Court found the Appellant guilty of the charge and sentenced him to ten years imprisonment without an option of fine. The Court of Appeal while dismissing the Appeal and quoting *in extenso* section 201(1) and (3) of Evidence Act held thus:

> It is clear that by the provision of Section 209(3) of the Evidence Act, the testimony of the victim, the fifth prosecution witness, required

[35] Section 209(2) of the Evidence Act.
[36] (2018) LPELR-45995 (CA).

> corroboration before the lower Court could act on it to convict the Appellant...

The medical report as one prepared by Dr. L. O. Akanbi was thereafter tendered and marked as Exhibit C. The lower Court relied on the medical report as a corroborating evidence of the victim and thus sustained the conviction of the Accused.

However in certain offences, though neither corroboration nor a warning is statutorily required, corroboration has by virtue of long practice, become the norm that the Court of law usually desire that some offences be corroborated to ground conviction. This is usually the case with Evidence of a tainted witness, voluntary confession, proof of custom and matrimonial cases. We shall devote some time to treat them one after the other as situations where corroboration can be required as a matter of practice. They are as follows:

Evidence of a tainted witness

In *Umar* v. *State,*[37] the Court of Appeal while citing Hon. Justice Nnamani, J.S.C. in *Mbenu* v. *State,*[38] had this to say about a tainted witness and how the court would treat such evidence:

> A tainted witness is a witness who, though not an accomplice, is a witness who may have a purpose of his or her own to serve. This Court has always held that the evidence of such a witness should be treated with considerable caution and should be examined with a tooth comb.[39]

The Court went further at page 21 to state the caution that indeed, trial courts have been advised to be wary in convicting on the evidence of such witnesses without some corroboration. The requirement that a trial Judge should in such circumstances, warn himself as one would in the case of accomplices, is one dictated by prudence not by law.

Voluntary Confession under section 28 and 29 of the Act

The law is trite on the point that, a man may be convicted on his own confession alone even without corroboration and there is no law against it. The position of the law is that if a suspect makes a free and voluntary confession in his extra judicial statement to the police, which confession is

---

[37](2019) LPELR-47617 (CA).

[38](1988) NWLR (Pt.84) 615, 626 267.

[39] Pp. 20-21, paras. F-A.

found to be direct and positive and the court is satisfied with its truth, such confessional statement alone is sufficient to ground conviction without corroboration.[40] This is the general rule. However, by virtue of practice, the court of law have been seen to lend a voice to the need to caution itself before convicting on the uncorroborated voluntary confession of the accused person and perhaps seek to find other supporting evidence to sustain such voluntary confession. The Supreme Court in *Olaoye* v. *State*[41] while alluding to the argument of the Appellant that the voluntary confession of the Accused person (Exhibit H) was not corroborated and thus the conviction of the accused should be set aside thus posited in its wisdom per Amiru Sanusi JSC:

> It is also part of the complaints of the appellant that the trial Court had convicted him on an uncorroborated and inadmissible evidence. According to him, the trial Court solely relied on the confessional statement (Exhibit H) to convict him of the offences charged. It needs be stressed here, that a confession of an accused person to the commission of an offence plays a vital role in the determination of his guilt. Therefore, a trial Court is free to convict him even on the confessional statement alone once that trial Court is convinced that the confession is voluntary as in this instant case. I said so because by his confession, the accused (now appellant) had confirmed the commission of criminal responsibility in terms of *mens rea* and *actus rea*. See *Okeke* vs. *State* (2003) 15 NWLR (Pt.842) 25...Now, coming to the issue of alleged want of corroborative evidence insinuated by the learned counsel for the appellant, I do not think that is true. As it could be fathomed, PW1 and PW2 were eye witnesses who had actually witnessed the entire criminal act perpetrated by the appellant and his partners in crime. Both of them gave uncontradicted and uncontroverted testimonies which had duly corroborated Exhibit 'H', the appellant's confessional statement. I must however state here, that a confessional statement which is made voluntarily and is direct, cogent credible and positive, is enough to ground conviction even without corroboration of any sort.[42]

It can be gleaned from the decision of the apex court in the instant case that the court considered the evidence of the eye witnesses (PW1 and PW2) as corroborative of "Exhibit H" which is the voluntary confession of the

---

[40] See the Supreme Court decision in *Ayedatiwor* v. *State* (2018) LPELR-43847(SC) Pp.23-24, Paras. F-A.
[41] (2018) LPELR-43601 (SC).
[42] Pp. 17-18, paras. G-C. Pp. 18-19, paras. E-B.

accused now the Appellant. It is submitted with respect that even though corroboration in this circumstance is not a requirement of the statute, the Court still adverted their mind to the testimony of the eye witnesses to hold that it strengthened the confessional statement even when the court could safely convict the accused on his confession, provided it is voluntary, cogent, credible, direct and positive.

Proof of Custom under Sections 16, 17 and 18 of the Act

Albeit it is not a requirement of the provisions of sections 16, 17, and 18 of the Evidence Act, our courts have always been insistent that any party alleging the existence of a custom must, apart from leading evidence in support thereof himself , should also call other witness(s) who would corroborate his evidence.

In *Alabi* v. *Audu,*[43] the Court of Appeal held thus:

> The appellant has contended vigorously that custom must be strictly proved, and cited authorities to show that the Courts have held that it is not enough that the person that asserts the custom should be the only person to testify in support of the custom. I am conscious of the fact that there are some authorities supporting the contention of the respondent, with regard to the quality of evidence necessary to establish proof of customary law. In case of *Giwa Abiodun* v. *Erinmilokun* (1961) 1 All NLR 294, the Court held that although no particular number of witnesses is required to prove the existence of a custom or rule of customary law, the Court may not hold as sufficient proof the mere ipse dixit of the person alleging it. It is based on this pronouncement of Court that many cases have now been decided on the premise that apart from the evidence of the party relying on a particular custom, another witness versed in the alleged custom should also testify.

In summary, from the gamut of judicial pronouncements, it has been described as unsafe to accept the testimony of the only person asserting the evidence of custom as conclusive. Hence, though not as a matter of requirement of the law on the subject matter, it is desirable and certainly good law that a person other than the party asserting the custom should also testify in proof thereof.

---

[43](2017) LPELR-42872 (CA).

Matrimonial cases

In matrimonial cases, it is highly desirable that the evidence adduced by the parties is corroborated by evidence of independent witnesses. This principle has gained judicial recognition and attention in *Ibrahim* v. *Ibrahim.*[44]

This is to say that in practice, the courts do require such corroboration, unless the absence of witnesses to provide such corroboration has been satisfactorily accounted for.

5. Corroboration in Civil Proceedings

As a general rule, corroboration is generally not required in civil cases. The only exception to this rule is the case of a breach of promise to marry. Section 197 of the Evidence Act provides that:

> No plaintiff in any action for breach of promise of marriage shall be entitled to succeed unless his or her testimony is corroborated by some other material evidence in support of such promise; and the fact that the defendant did not answer letters affirming that he had promised to marry the plaintiff is not such corroboration.

It is pertinent to note that the marriage envisaged here will mean "marriage validly contracted under the Marriage Act, or under Islamic Law or Customary law applicable in Nigeria."[45] In *Advanced Maritime Transport (Nig) Ltd* v. *Ojugboli & Ors,*[46] the Court of Appeal while restating the position of law on corroboration in civil cases held that it is to be noted that except in certain exception such as in action for breach of promise to marry, corroboration is not required in civil actions. Thus in *Olusanya* v. *Ibadiaro,*[47] it was held that in an action for breach of promise to marry, corroboration was a legal requirement which the trial court must examine with the greatest care. It is important to note that the fact that the defendant did not answer letters affirming that he had promised to marry the plaintiff is not such corroboration.[48] In summary, no plaintiff in an action for breach of promise to marry will succeed unless his or her testimony is corroborated by some independent material evidence in support of such promise.

---

[44] (2007) All FWLR (Pt. 346) 474 C.A.

[45] See the Interpretation section 258 (1) of the Evidence Act.

[46] (2018) LPELR- 46265 (CA) P. 48, para. E; See also *Eagle Transport Co. Ltd* v. *Anyia & Anor* (2017) LPELR-42020 (CA). See also *Onowhosa* v. *Odiuzou* (1999) 1 NWLR (Pt. 586) 173 SC.

[47] (1970) UILR 149.

[48] N.O. Obiaraeri, *op. cit.*, page 341.

6. Nature of Corroboration

As a general rule, the nature of corroboration is peculiar to the circumstance of each case as no case is entirely the same with the other. The test to be applied to determine the nature and extent of corroboration is to establish that the evidence is an independent testimony which affects the accused by connecting or tending to connect him with the crime. It does not mean that the witness corroborating must use the exact or very words, unless the maker involves some arithmetic. It is not expected that it would be tantamount to a confirmation of the whole evidence given by a witness, rather it must be such as corroborates some material aspects of the charge. It is enough even if it is only circumstantial and connects or tends to connect the accused with its commission.

It is settled law that even though evidence of corroboration must be an independent testimony, it needs not consist of direct evidence that the accused person committed the offence nor does it need to amount to a confirmation of the whole account given.[49] It has been held that the nature of corroboration depends on the peculiar circumstance of an individual case. In the offence of rape for instance, where an accused denies raping the victim, the evidence of corroboration the court should look out for, are thus: (a) medical evidence showing injury to the private part or to other part of the body of the victim which may have been brought about in a struggle. (b) Semen stains on her clothes or the clothes of the accused or to the place where the offence is alleged to have been committed, etc.[50]

In summary, the nature of corroboration needed in a particular circumstance varies from one case to another.

---

[49] *Olumuyiwa* v. *State* (2019) LPELR-46387 (CA) p. 28, paras. E-F.
[50] *Aliyu* v. *State* (2019) LPELR-47421 (SC) P. 21, paras, D-G.

Chapter 18

OFFICIAL AND PRIVILEGED COMMUNICATION

1. Introduction

There are circumstances where some sensitive information will not be disclosed and thus taken off from the public domain. It could be for some certain reasons like overriding public interest policy such as national security, public safety, public morality, public order or public defence that such information be concealed and withdrawn from the general public. Broadly speaking, a privilege could either be a private privilege or a state (public) privilege. For instance, section 36(4)(b) of the 1999 Constitution as amended expressly provides for privileged communication relating to affairs of the state. It provides that if in any proceedings before a court or such a tribunal, a Minister of the Government of the Federation, or a Commissioner of the Government of a State satisfies the court or tribunal that it would not be in the public interest for any matter to be publicly disclosed, the court or tribunal shall make arrangements for evidence relating to that matter to be heard in private and shall take such other action as may be necessary to prevent the disclosure of the matter According to Nwadialo,[1] the subject of privilege in the law of evidence is concerned with cases where a witness has a right or duty to refuse to disclose a relevant fact by not answering a question or refusing to produce a relevant document. The privilege may either be a privilege relating to a witness himself or that of other person whom he is representing. It then suffices to say that anything that a person is compelled to say after he has claimed his privilege will be treated as having been said involuntarily, they remain inadmissible in subsequent criminal trials brought against him.[2]

Privilege can be raised at any point during the oral hearing of the matter; and once raised, a judge has the duty to determine whether it avails or not;

---

[1] F. Nwadialo, *op. cit.*, page 100.
[2] Aguda, *op. cit.*, pages 317 and 325.

and in so determining, the judge is at liberty to call further oral or documentary evidence.[3]

Privileged communications thus deal with matters which a person is entitled not to disclose. They refer to those communications which by virtue of the injury that may be caused to the state or third party if disclosed are allowed to be withheld by a person.

2. For Privileged Communication

The rationale behind the law of privileged communication was aptly summarized by Imhanobe.[4] According to the learned writer,

> The justification for the law on privilege is to protect confidential relationship or the advancement of some other important public information which is considered more important than the concern to place all relevant evidence before a court.

Thus, privileged communications are regarded as one of the exceptions to the rule that all relevant facts are admissible.[5] Privilege may, at first glance, seem identical to non-compellability. But they are easily distinguishable. While a non-compellable witness cannot be mandated to give evidence or testify in court, a person who claims privilege enjoys no such immunity. He can be compelled to testify but not as to the specific matters which are privileged. In respect of those matters, he may merely refuse to answer such questions. Thus, his right to answer questions relates only to questions on the privileged matters. The obligation of the witness to testify on other matters remains unaffected despite the privilege.[6]

As S.T. Hon points out,[7] a witness should not refuse to be sworn merely because he is laying claim to a testimonial privilege; the proper procedure is for him to enter the witness box and be sworn and then refuse to testify or tender a document on the ground that he is entitled to a testimonial privilege.

Privilege extends to both oral and documentary evidence. Thus, a person may claim privilege in respect of a particular document, for instance a title deed. Usually, counsel raises privilege on behalf of a witness when asked to

---

[3] See *Birmingham, etc, Co.* v. *L. & N.W. Ry.* (1913) 3 KB 850 .

[4] S.O Imnhanobe, *Law of Evidence in Nigeria*, 1st Edn (Abuja: Imhanobe Law Books Limited 2013), pg 54.

[5] Section 1 of the Evidence Act.

[6] F. Nwadiola, *op. cit.* pg 465.

[7] S.T. Hon, *op. cit.*, Pg.1363.

disclose such matters in court, for the witness may be ignorant of his right not to disclose such matters. Though a judge is not under an obligation to do so, he may inform a witness of his right to claim privilege when appropriate.

3. Forms of Privileged Communications

The following are some of the official and unofficial privileged communications as recognized under our law. They are as follows.

1. Communications between Spouses

No husband or wife shall be compelled to disclose any communication made to him or her during marriage by any person to whom he or she is or has been married nor shall he or she be permitted to disclose any such communication, unless the person who made it or that person's representative in interest consents.[8] The exceptions to this rule are in suits between married persons or proceeding in which one married person is prosecuted for an offence specified in section 182(1) of the Evidence Act. Section 182(1) of the Evidence Act provides that when a person is charged with: (a) an offence under sections 217, 218, 219, 222, 224, 225, 226, 231, 300, 301, 340, 341, 357 to 362, 370 or 371 of the Criminal Code; (b) subject to section 36 of the Criminal Code with an offence against the property of his wife or her husband; or (c) with inflicting violence on his wife or her husband, the wife or husband of the person charged shall be a competent and compellable witness for the prosecution or defence without the consent of the person charged. In the same vein, by section 182(3) of the Act, neither a husband nor a wife shall be compelled to disclose any communication made to him or her, as the case may be, during their marriage. A combined reading of theses sections above points to one conclusion: the privilege nature of communications between a husband and wife christened from the sacrosanctity of marriage and the unity of spouse. It has been submitted that although the provisions of section 187 are wider than those of section 182(3) of the Act, the two are in agreement with each other as sections 182(3) is subsumed into section 187. The ingredient of both sections, therefore, includes:[9]

---

[8] Section 187 of the Evidence Act.

[9] S.T. Hon, *op. cit.* Page 1379.

(a) the fact that no husband or wife shall be compelled to disclose any communication made by either of them during their marriage.[10]

(b) the fact that this privilege against being compelled to disclose extends to even when the marriage is no more, because of the phrase *has married*.[11]

(c) the fact that apart from not being compelled, such husband or wife shall not even be *permitted* to disclose such communication.[12]

(d) the fact that such spouse may be *permitted* to disclose such communication if the other spouse that made it or his/her *representative in interest*, consents.[13]

(e) the fact that this privilege against disclosure and even the *permission* to disclose will not avail either spouse under two circumstances, namely: (a) in suits between the spouses; and (b) in proceedings in which either spouse is prosecuted for an offence specified under section 183(2) of the Evidence Act.[14]

To err on the side of surplusage, it has already been established that the definition of marriage envisaged by the Act is that as ascribed to the meaning of marriage under section 258 of the Act which is the interpretation section. It should be noted also that this privilege can be waived by either of the spouse where the husband or the wife does not object to such privilege communication to be offered in evidence.

2. Judicial Communications

Section 188 of the Evidence Act provides that no Justice, Judge, Grand Kadi or President of a Customary Court of Appeal and, except upon the special order of the High Court of the State or Federal Capital Territory, Abuja, or Federal High Court, no magistrate, or other persons before whom a proceeding is being held, shall be compelled to answer any questions as to his own conduct in court in any of the capacities specified in the section, or as to anything which came to his knowledge in court in such capacity but he may be examined as to other matters which occurred in his presence whilst he was so acting. As an explanation, magistrate, or other persons before whom a proceeding is being held, can be compellable to answer any question while discharging its official duty upon the special order of a High Court.

---

[10] Sections 182(3) and 187.

[11] Section 187 of the Act.

[12] Ibid.

[13] Ibid.

[14] Section 182(3) and 187 of the Act.

Section 189 of the Act also made provision for information as to the commission of an offence. It provides that no magistrate, police officer or any other public officer authorized to investigate or prosecute offences under any written law shall be compelled to disclose the source of any information as to the commission of an offence which he is so authorized to investigate or prosecute, and no public officer employed in or about the business or any branch of the public revenue, shall be compelled to disclose the source of any information as to the commission of any offence against the public revenue. In *Nwarata* v. *Egboka,*[15] the court of Appeal held that a police officer could not be compelled to disclose who his informer is as he was protected by sections 166 and 167 of the Act,[16] as a policeman giving evidence *qua* policeman, is under no compulsion to give evidence in Court.[17]

3. Professional communications between a legal practitioner and his client

Owing to the nature of the profession of a legal practitioner, communications between him and his client are bound to be sensitive and confidential. This is the rule of confidentiality under the Rules of Professional Conduct 2007. It is in view of this that the Evidence Act has made provisions governing such communications. For such privilege to subsist, the communication must be intended to be confidential; the legal practitioner must be acting in his or her professional capacity, and communication made is for the purpose of obtaining or giving legal advice. In *R* v. *Derby Magistrates, ex parte B.*[18] the House of Lords, emphasizing the rationale behind the rule, stated thus:

> A man must be able to consult his lawyer in confidence, since otherwise he might hold back half of the truth.

Two sections in the Evidence Act provide for privilege with respect to communications between a legal practitioner and his client. Section 192 (1) states thus:

> (1) No legal practitioner shall at any time be permitted, unless with his client's express consent, to disclose any communication made to him in

[15] (1964) A.C. 814.
[16] Equivalence of section 189 of the Evidence Act 2011.
[17] *Ita & Anor* v. *State* (2013) LPELR-21408 (CA) P. 18, para C.
[18] (1996) 1 A6 487 at 507, per Lord Taylor, C.J.

> the course and for the purpose of his employment as such legal practitioner by or on behalf of his client, or to state the contents or condition of any document with which he has become acquainted in the course and for the purpose of his professional employment or to disclose any advice given by him to his client in the course and for the purpose of such employment.[19]

It is immaterial whether the attention of such legal practitioner was or was not directed to such fact by or on behalf of his client.[20] This obligation continues even after the employment of the legal practitioner has ceased.[21] The very gravamen of this privilege was aptly captured by the court in *NSITFMB* v. *Adebayo*[22] per Aderemi JCA in the following words:

> Justice, the search for which is the pre-occupation of a lawyer is rooted in confidence. A client must at all times rely on and enjoy the confidentiality of his counsel. Indeed it is the cardinal duty of a lawyer or counsel to preserve his client's confidence. If justice is to be seen to be done, that duty of preserving confidence must out-last the employment of the counsel and even extend to those he (the lawyer) may later employ as his juniors or those who form partnership with him; if in the discharge of their professional duties to his later client, the disclosure or use of such confidence may ensue.

The exceptions to this rule are communications made in furtherance of any illegal purpose or any fact observed by any legal practitioner in the course of his employment as such, showing that any crime or fraud has been committed since the commencement of his employment.[23]

This obligation imposed on the legal practitioner, extends to interpreters and the clerks of the legal practitioners.[24] Also, if any party to a suit or proceeding gives evidence in such suit or proceeding, whether at his own instance or otherwise, he shall not be deemed to have by that reason consented to such disclosure as is mentioned in section 192 and, if any party to a suit or proceeding calls any such legal practitioner as a witness, he shall be deemed to have consented to such disclosure only if he questions such

[19] This evidential rule gained judicial blessing and recognition in *Iyeke* v. *Abu* (2015) LPELR-25735 (CA) Pp.19-20, paras. B-B.
[20] Section 192(2).
[21] Section 192(3) of the Evidence Act.
[22] (2003) FWLR (Pt.157) 1040.
[23] Section 192 (1) (a) & (b).
[24] Section 193 of the Act.

legal practitioner on matter which, but for such question, he would not be at liberty to disclose.[25] However, if the document or communication had already been made available to the public before the suit, section 194 will not be applicable. Thus in *Abubakar* v. *Chuks,*[26] the Supreme Court held that the document tendered in court by the appellant could not have been subject to section 170 of the Evidence Act (now section 192) because it had "upon the appellant's instructions, been published to third parties..."[27]

Another provision on privilege communications between a legal practitioner and his client is section 195 of the Evidence Act which states that:

> no one shall be compelled to disclose to the court any confidential communication which has taken place between him and a legal practitioner consulted by him, unless he offers himself as witness in which case he may be compelled to disclose any such communication as may appear to the court necessary to be known, in order to explain any evidence which he has given but no others.

Notwithstanding the above sections, a court may in exceptional cases compel a legal practitioner to disclose his client's privileged communication. As noted by Hon,[28] the question whether a court can compel a solicitor to disclose his client's privileged communication can only be answered based on the peculiar circumstance of each case. Thus, it is a question of fact. In *Oshunriode* v. *Akande,*[29] the Supreme Court held that a judge has power to order a solicitor to submit from the Bar to the Bench, the Solicitor's case file which will then be admitted in evidence to resolve an impasse on what had actually happened in court previously.

4. Privilege against Self-Incrimination

The rule against self-incrimination entitles a party to refuse to answer questions that may incriminate him or render him liable to a charge or penalty. It has long been recognized by the common law. In *Pyneboard Pty.*

---

[25] Section 194 of the Evidence Act 2011.
[26] (2008) All FWLR (Pt. 408) 207 S.C.
[27] Per Onnoghen J.S.C.
[28] S.T Hon, *op. cit.,* pg. 1376-1377.
[29] (1996) 6 NWLR (Pt. 455) 383.

Ltd v. *Trade Practices Commission,*[30] the English Court explained the rationale behind this rule thus:

> The privilege against compulsory self-incrimination is part of the common law or human rights. It is based on the desire to protect personal freedom and human dignity. These social values justify the impediment the privilege presents to judicial or other investigation. It protects the innocent as well as the guilty from the indignity and invasion of privacy which occurs in compulsory self-incrimination. It is society's acceptance of the inviolability of human personality.

Section 183 of the Evidence Act provides for this rule. It states as follows:

> No one is bound to answer any question if the answer to it would, in the opinion of the court, have a tendency to expose the witness or the wife or husband of the witness to any criminal charge or to any penalty or forfeiture which the judge regards as reasonably likely to be preferred or sued for.

From the above provision, an incriminating answer is based on "the opinion of the court." The court thus has a significant role to play in giving effect to this section. According to Nwadialo, where the question is patently objectionable on ground of this privilege, the court still normally warn the witness that he is not bound to answer it. In less obvious cases, the witness, or more usually his counsel, if he has one, raises the objection and supports it with reasons. If the objection is upheld, the question lapses and no answer will be required from the witness. If the objection is overruled, the witness is bound to answer the questions.[31]

The above section was examined in *Gallaher Ltd* v. *B.A.T (Nig) Ltd.*[32] In that case, the 1st and 2nd respondents commenced an action against 3rd respondent and another defendant. The 1st and 2nd respondents' claim against the 3rd respondent was for infringement of trademark and passing off. They contended that the package in which the Gold Band Brand of cigarettes was being manufactured and sold by the 3rd respondent was confusingly similar to the package in which their Benson and Hedges brand of cigarettes was being sold. The 1st and 2nd respondents alleged that they had registered as a trademark the design and colour of the package in which

---

[30] (1983) 152 CLR 328 at pg. 346.
[31] F.Nwadialo, *op. cit.*, pg. 112.
[32](2014) LPELR-24333 (CA).

their Benson and Hedges was being sold. The 1st and 2nd respondents also sought by an ex parte motion, leave to sue the 3rd respondent as representative of a defined class of persons; orders of interim injunction and an Anton-Pillar order against the 3rd respondent and all those persons on whose behalf, the 3rd respondent was sued. The trial court after hearing the motion, granted the orders sought. Subsequently, the appellants applied to be joined as defendants. After they were joined, they appealed for the discharge of the interim orders of injunction and the Anton-Pillar order, that they had registered Gold Bond and the package design of Gold Bond brand or cigarettes without colour limitation as trademarks. However, the trial court ruled against the appellant who, aggrieved, appealed to the Court of Appeal. On appeal, the appellant in defence of their failure to give information as to the manufacture, importation and sale of Gold Bond cigarettes in the alleged infringing packet, contended that such a disclosure would run contrary to section 183 of the Evidence Act which protects them from self-incrimination as it could expose them to a criminal charge or to a penalty or forfeiture likely to be sued under the provision of the Merchandise Marks Act (Cap M10) Laws of the Federation of Nigeria, 2004.

The Court of Appeal, rejecting the appellant's contention, stated thus:

> The Appellants' contention is that if they are allowed to comply with Order Nos. 5, 6 and 7 by giving information and making disclosure as to the manufacture, importation and sale of GOLD BOND Cigarettes in the packet the 1st and 2nd Respondents adjudged an infringement of their trademark, the information required may tend to expose them to a criminal charge or to a penalty or forfeiture likely to be sued under the provisions of Section 3(2) of the Merchandise Marks Act (Cap M10) Laws of the Federation of Nigeria, 2004.
>
> Starting with the provisions of Section 183 of the Evidence Act, 2011, I make no hesitation in agreeing with the learned trial Judge that the said section is inapplicable here. It only applies in the case of a witness in a proceeding before the court, Tribunal or any administration or adjudicatory body.[33]

Thus, as the appellant was not a witness in the case, he could not rely on section 183. The rule against self-incrimination is also inapplicable when the offence or penalty which the witness would have been charged with or liable

[33] At P. 52, paras. B-E.

to, ceases to exist. For instance, a pardon given to the witness by the Governor under section 212 of the 1999 Constitution of the Federal Republic of Nigeria, as amended. The rule of privilege against self-incrimination is not bereft of exceptions. According to section 183 (a)(b)(c) of Evidence Act 2011, the exceptions are:

1. A person charged with an offence, and being a witness in pursuance of section 180, may be asked and is bound to answer any question in cross-examination notwithstanding that it would tend to incriminate him as to the offence charged;
2. Anyone asked with a question which may establish or tends to establish that he owes a debt or is otherwise liable to any civil suit either at the instance of the Federal, State or Local Government or any other person;
3. A witness asked with a question required to be answered under section 458 of the Criminal Procedure Act at any inquiry by direction of the Attorney-General of the Federation, or of the Attorney-General of a State under Part 49 of the Criminal Procedure Act.

It is axiomatic to note that it is the duty of the witness or his counsel to raise this privilege, such duty does not extend to refusing to go into the witness box, but is limited to refusing to answer questions while in the witness box.[34] An objection can be raised by the counsel for the witness on the ground of this privilege. However, where such objection is overruled, the witness is bound to answer the question, otherwise the witness will be guilty of contempt of the court *in facie curia.*[35] It is important to note that where such objection was wrongly overruled and a witness is compelled to answer incriminating questions, the answers he has given will not be admitted against him in any subsequent criminal trial.[36] The witness also has the onus laid on him to prove to the honourable court that the risk of being prosecuted will be high if he answers the question.

A defendant standing trial is also a beneficiary to the exculpatory provision of section 36(11) of the 1999 Constitution as amended to the effect that "No person who is tried for a criminal offence shall be compelled to give evidence at the trial." A combined reading of section 36 (11) of the Constitution with section 183 of the Evidence Act will come to the aid of the defendant as provisions against self-incrimination.

---

[34] *Boyle* v. *Wiseman* (1885)10 EX 647.
[35] *Ex parte Fernandez* (1861) 30 LJCP 321.
[36] *R.* v. *Coote* (1873) LR 4PC 599.

5. Statements made without Prejudice

Two provisions of the Evidence Act govern such documents made "without prejudice." First, section 26 of the Evidence Act states that in civil cases, no admission is relevant, if it is made either upon an express condition that evidence of it is not to be given, or in circumstances from which the court infers that the parties agreed together that evidence of it should not be given. However, this provision does not by any means exempt any legal practitioner from giving evidence of any matter of which he may be compelled to give evidence under section 192 of the Act. Section 196 of the Act also provides that a statement in any document marked "without prejudice" made in the course of negotiation for a settlement of a dispute out of court, shall not be given in evidence in any civil proceeding in proof of the matters stated in it.

What these provisions seek to achieve is to encourage peaceful settlement of disputes, for the courts and the law as instruments of peace. Thus, when parties in dispute have resolved to settle such dispute and one of the parties has made admissions in the course of negotiation for settlement, the other party will not be allowed to tender such document or give evidence of such admission in court. The documents made available in the course of negations may therefore be marked "without prejudice." This signifies that such document is without prejudice to any suit or subsequent action. In *University of Abuja* v. *AMCON & Ors,*[37] the Court of Appeal while citing *La Roche* v. *Armstrong,*[38] stated the reason for this rule thus:

> It is the policy of the law that dispute should be amicably settled if possible and it would be unwise to enter into negotiations if statement made during such negotiations were admissible in evidence at the trial in the event of the attempt to settle not being successful.

In another recent case of the apex court in *Ashakacem Plc* v. *Asharatul Mubashshurun Investment Ltd,*[39] the case of the respondent from the pleadings was that, on the 24th of July, 2007, the parties entered into a contract for the supply and purchase of Low Pour Fuel Oil (LPFO) and it was agreed that the respondent would supply eleven million litres of Low Pour Fuel Oil (LPFO) to the appellant and which Low Pour Foul Oil (LPFO) was to be offloaded into the appellant's storage tanks at its offices in Ashaka

[37] (2019) LPELR -47306 (CA) p.34 para. D.
[38] (1922) 1 K.B 485.
[39] (2019) LPELR-46541(SC) pp. 23-24 para. E-C.

and Kano within six weeks. The unit price per litre for the supply to Ashaka would be ₦65.00, while that for Kano would be ₦59.50. Payment was to be made within two weeks of supply of the Low Pour Fuel Oil (LPFO) by the respondent and confirmation of its receipt by the appellant. Due to exigent circumstances, the respondent applied three times for extension of delivery period and the extension was granted and acceded to by the appellant. In the course of the supply, the price of the product rose and it became impossible for the respondent to continue the supply at the price agreed per litre. It wrote to the appellant requesting for a price review, which request was approved and a price of ₦75.00 per litre of Low Pour Fuel Oil (LPFO) was agreed. The review price of ₦75.00 per litre was a flat rate for all supplies to Kano and Ashaka storage facilities. The respondent supplied the product into the appellant's Kano storage facility and sent a delivery notification to the appellant where its Stores manager wrote via email that it supplied a total of 6,384,469 litres of LPFO into the Kano Storage tanks of the appellant. This was subsequently confirmed by a hard copy of a report on the quantity of LPFO reaffirming that 6,384,469 litres of Low Pour Fuel Oil (LPFO) was supplied into its Kano Storage tank and the appellant accepted the product, as the product supplied was found to be within the range of the appellant's quality parameters from the dip result conducted. The total price of the product supplied was ₦478, 835,175.00, out of which the appellant paid ₦352, 058,160.6, leaving a balance of ₦126, 777.014.37, which the appellant has failed to pay despite repeated demands. It was the appellant's case that he was no longer indebted to the respondent on the contract. That matter proceeded to trial. After the close of case of the parties, Appellant filed an application seeking to re-open its case to lead further evidence, which application was dismissed. At the conclusion of the trial, the trial Court entered judgment in favour of the respondent in the sum of ₦91, 662,435.44, together with interest at the rate of 10% from the date of judgment until full liquidation. Appellant and the respondent were dissatisfied with the judgment of the trial Court, against which they filed an appeal and a cross-appeal, respectively. The appellant's appeal was dismissed, while the respondent's cross-appeal was upheld. Dissatisfied, appellant appealed to the Supreme Court. The Supreme Court per Mary Ukaego Peter-Odili, (JSC) while ruling on whether a statement made without prejudice during negotiation can be admitted in court when such negotiation fails posited it its wisdom thus:

> ...it falls to reason that the letter dated 2nd March 2009 having been made in the process of reconciling the dispute between the parties and so the Court of Appeal was right to have upheld the decision of the trial Court on the document. The principle is anchored on the basis that at the point of mediation, parties should speak freely all in the quest for a peaceful resolution of the dispute. This principle of free discussion will be seriously prejudiced or impaired if any offer or admission made in the process of the negotiation could be given in evidence and used in support of a party's case in court afterwards where the negotiation breaks down. Therefore when those negotiations are reduced in writing they are usually marked "without prejudice" for the avoidance of doubt and so remain inadmissible against the parties or any of them in the ensuing suit in Court. However, if the words "without prejudice" is not stated in plain language, it does not detract from the fact that the words are implied in the negotiations conducted in documentary form or verbally.

However, if the document does not relate to negotiations between parties towards the settlement of an issue, section 196 will be inapplicable,[40] neither will it apply if a third party, not being a party to the dispute claims such privilege.[41]

6. Privilege attaching to title deeds and other documents

No witness who is not a party to a suit shall be compelled to produce his title deeds to any property or any document by virtue of which he holds any property as pledge or mortgage or any document the production of which might tend to incriminate him, unless he has agreed in writing to produce them with the person seeking the production of such deeds or some person through whom he claims.[42] Also, no one shall be compelled to produce documents in his possession which any other person would be entitled to produce if they were in his possession, unless such last mentioned person consents to their production.[43]

7. Doctor and Patient, Priest and Penitent

The Evidence Act contains no provision on communications made between a doctor and Patient or a priest and penitent. Hence, a doctor or priest can

---

[40] *Societies Commercials Del' Quest Africans* v. *Michael & Anor.* (1936) 13 NLR 104.

[41] *Nwadike & Ors* v. *Ibekwe & Ors.* (1987) 2 NSCC 12219.

[42] Section 184 of the Evidence Act.

[43] Section 185 of the Evidence Act.

give evidence in court as to what he has been told in the course of his employment. Thus, the fact that such priest may face sanctions from his church organization alone will not lawfully stop him from giving evidence in court concerning such confessions.[44] As bitter as it sounds, any priest who refuses to give evidence of his communication with his penitent may be guilty of contempt of court.[45]

8. State Privilege

State privilege is a common law evidentiary rule that allows the government to withhold information from discovery when disclosure would be inimical to national security. State privilege or official communication refers to those matters which are absolutely barred from disclosure subject to certain exceptions in the interest of the security of the state and good administration of public affairs. The essence of state privilege is that the information which cannot be disclosed without injury to the public interest are withheld and not merely because the information is confidential or official which alone is no reason for its non-production.

According to Murphy,[46] there is still a school of thought that certain documents of high importance should never be disclosed in litigation. An objection to disclosure of document relating to such matters should almost always be allowed, even on a class basis. Such documents relates to the workings of inner government, the formulation of national policy, and similar high matters. They were dealt with by Lord Reid in his exposition in *Conway* v. *Rimmer*[47] as follows:

> I do not doubt that there are certain classes of documents which ought not to be disclosed whatever their content may be. Virtually everyone agrees that cabinet minutes and the like ought not to be disclosed until such time as they are only of historical interest.

The most important reason for this was that:

> ..such disclosure would create or fan ill-informed or captious public or political criticism. The business of government is difficult enough as it is, and no government could contemplate with equanimity the inner workings of the government machine being exposed to the gaze of those

---

[44] *Normanshaw* v. *Normanshaw* (1894) 89 LT 468.
[45] *R.* v. *Hay* (1860) 2 F&F 4.
[46] Richard Glover & Peter Murphy, Murphy on Evidence, *op. cit.,* page 476.
[47] (1968) AC 910, 952.

ready to criticize without adequate knowledge of the background and perhaps with some axe to grind.

Coming home to our evidential jurisprudence, Section 190(1) of the Evidence Act 2011 provides as follows:

> Subject to any direction of the President in any particular case, or of the Governor of state where the records are in the custody of a state, no one shall be permitted to produce any unpublished official records relating to affairs of state, or to give any evidence derived from such record except with the permission of the officer at the head of the Ministry, Department or Agency concerned who shall give or withhold such permission as he thinks fit;
>
> Provided that the head of the Ministry, Department or Agency concerned shall, on the order of the court, produce to the judge, the official record in question or, as the case may be permit evidence derived from it to be given to the judge alone in chambers; and if the judge after careful consideration shall decide that the record or the oral evidence as the case may be, should be received as evidence in the proceeding, he shall order this to be done in private as provided in section 36(4) of the Constitution.

The proviso to the provision was included by the present Evidence Act, unlike the previous Evidence Act.[48] It gives the court the right to order the head of the ministry, department or agency to produce to the judge, the official record or to give evidence to the judge alone in his chambers. Depending on the judge's view after due examination of the evidence, he may order that it be received in evidence in private. This commendable amendment to the previous Act has brought the privilege of state affairs in accordance with section 36(1) of the 1999 Constitution as amended which enshrines the right to fair hearing.

Sections 191 and 243 of the Evidence Act further provide for official communications:

According to Section 191:

> No public officer shall be compelled to disclose communications made to him in official confidence when he considers that the public interest would suffer by the disclosure:

[48] Section 167 of the Evidence Act 2004.

> Provided that the public officer concerned shall, on the order of the court, disclose to the judge alone in chambers the substance of the communication in question; and if the judge is satisfied that the communication should be received in evidence, this shall be done in private in accordance with section 36 (4) of the Constitution.

Finally, section 243 provides that:

> A Minister or in respect of matters to which the executive authority of a state extends, the Governor or any person nominated by him, may in any proceeding object to the production of documents or request the exclusion of oral evidence when after consideration, he is satisfied that the production of such document or the giving of such oral evidence is against public interest.

Subsection 2 provides that any objection mentioned in subsection (1) of section 243 shall, if taken before trial, be by affidavit, or if taken at the hearing, be by certificate produced by a public officer. However, the court shall have discretion whether or not to uphold any such objection, and may in determining how to exercise its discretion, inspect such documents or be informed as to the nature of the oral evidence to which the objection relates.

The above provisions are welcome amendments which made the discretion of the Minister, whether by affidavit or certificate conclusive and barred a judge from examining the substance of the communication made to a public officer in official confidence.[49] Although the list of such privileged materials is not exhaustive, it includes:

A. Intelligence or security report [50]
B. Communication made to a public officer in confidence, for example, a report of an electoral officer to his superior.[51]
C. Source of information leading to the identity of an alleged terrorist,[52] or any other criminal.[53]
D. Facts or materials relating to military operations[54]or construction of military formations.[55]

---

[49] Section 220(2) of the previous Act...also see *Aregbesola* v. *Oyinlola* (2009) All FWLR (Pt. 472) 1147 C.A where the Court of Appeal held that it would amount to infringement of fair hearing of a party who wishes to rely on a state report classified "secret," if the report were withheld from being tendered.

[50] *Balfour* v. *Foreign and Commonwealth Office* (1994) 2 ALL ER 588.

[51] *Moruno* v. *Benson* (1996) NMLR 66.

[52] *Fox* v. *UK* (1991) 13 EHRR 157.

[53] *R.* v. *Smith* (2000) All ER (D) 2135 and *Morrow* v. *DPP* (91994) Crim LR 58.

[54] *Asiatic Petroleum Ltd* v. *Anglo-Persian Co. Ltd* (1961) 1 KB 822.

E. Correspondence between or among government departments, like Customs and Excise; Board of Internal Revenue,[56] reports of diplomats;[57] reports of the Internal Affairs Ministry on Prisons;[58]and communications between the military establishment and cabinet ministries[59]

In the light of the foregoing, a public officer claiming privilege to state affairs will have the responsibility or the *onus probandi* to satisfy the court that the information he is unwilling to disclose or the document he is withholding its production falls within the domain of exclusivity for which state privilege will attach.

---

[55] *Duncan* v. *Cammel Laird & Co. Ltd.* (1942) AC 624.
[56] *Re Joseph* (1990) 1 Ch 347 and *Hughes* v. *Vargas* (1893) 9 TLR 551.
[57] *M. Isaacs & Sons Ltd* v. *Cook* (1925) 2 KB 391.
[58] *Ellis* v. *Home Office* (1953) 2 All ER 149, (1953) 3 WLR 105.
[59] *Chatterton* v. *Secretary of State for India* (1895-9) All ER 1035.

Chapter 19

COMPETENCE AND COMPELLABILITY

Introduction

The term "competence" describes the legal qualification to testify in court. It means being legally fit to appear as witness in a court of law. A related but different concept is compellability. While competence deals with legal fitness to testify, compellability deals with the ability to enforce the appearance of such a witness in court. Also, a witness must first be competent to be compellable but all competent witnesses are compellable. Owing to the relationship between the two terms, they are usually treated together but as seen above, they are completely different legal terms.[1] Hence, they are examined separately in this book under this chapter.

Competence to testify must also be distinguished from another legal concept which is competence to give a particular type of evidence. As Nwadialo stated,[2] the basis of competence is mainly possession of unimpaired intellect while that of competence to give a particular type of evidence is dependent on special skill such as certain opinion evidence which may only be given by experts. Competence of a witness to testify is not about his educational standing or about the language or languages he can speak or about his inability to read and write in any particular language.[3]

Who may testify

The general rule in respect of competence to testify is that all persons are competent to testify in court.[4] This general rule is provided in section 175 of the Evidence Act as follows:

> All persons shall be competent to testify, unless the court considers that they are prevented from understanding the questions put to them, or from giving rational answers to those questions, by reason of tender

[1] C.C. Nweze, *Contentious Issues and Responses in Contemporary Evidence Law in Nigeria*, Volume Two, 1st edn. (Enugu: Institute for Development Studies 2006) pg. 43.
[2] F. Nwadialo, *op. cit.*, pg. 465.
[3] *Dame* v. *Usman J & Ors.* (2015) LPELR-40361 (CA) page. 35, Para. D.
[4] *Aboaba* v. *Ogundipe* (2017) LPELR-42922 (CA) p. 26, para C.

years, extreme old age, disease, whether of body or mind, or any other cause of the same kind.

A witness can be competent yet not compellable in the sense that he is not legally obligated or compelled to testify. Thus, everyone, subject to the exceptions mention above, is competent to testify. Also, blood relations and members of the same family or community are competent witnesses.[5] A person of unsound mind is not incompetent to testify, unless he is prevented by such mental infirmity from understanding the questions put to him and giving rational answers to them.[6] If a witness is unable to speak, he may give his evidence in any other manner in which he can make it intelligible, as by writing or by signs which must be written and the signs made in open court but such evidence is deemed to be oral evidence.[7] Evidence of an incompetent witness is inadmissible and any evidence given by such witness is expunged from the records if already taken.

i. Accomplice

An accomplice is a competent witness against the defendant; this is buttressed by section 198 of the Evidence Act. To further streamline the ambit of who an accomplice is, section 198(2) of the Act provides that an accomplice is any person who pursuant to section 7 of the Criminal Code may be deemed to have taken part in committing the offence as the defendant or is an accessory after the fact to the offence, or a receiver of stolen goods.[8]

An accomplice is very much accommodated by the provision of section 175 of the Evidence Act. In *Ahmed* v. *State*,[9] the Court of Appeal held that an accomplice is competent to testify and his evidence is not illegal even if it is not corroborated. It is also irrelevant that he is standing trial in a different court for an offence related to the one with which the accused is charged.[10]

ii. The President, Vice-President, Governor, Deputy Governor, Diplomatic and Consular Agents

As earlier established, "all persons" shall be competent to testify.[11] However, there are some notable exceptions to the compellability of some 'special

---

[5] *Ali* v. *The State* (2015) 10 NWLR (pt. 14666) pg. 36; *Popoola* v. *The State* (2015) 6 NWLR (Pt. 1456) pg. 487.

[6] Section 175 (2) of the Evidence Act.

[7] Section 176(1) & (2) of the Evidence Act.

[8] See also the decision of the court of Appeal in *Adoga* v. *FRN* (2019) LPELR-46931(CA) p. 13, paras, C-E while citing the apex court in *Agwuna* v. *AGF* (1995) 5 NWLR (Pt. 396) 418).

[9](2018) LPELR-46606 (CA) P.16, paras. A-B.

[10] The *Queen* v. *Omisade* (1964) NMLR 67.

[11] See Section 175 of the Act.

kind' of persons while occupying some certain offices that section 308 of the Constitution applies. It is a constitutional provision by virtue of section 308 of the 1999 Constitution of the Federal Republic of Nigeria (as amended) that no process of any court requiring or compelling the appearance of a person to whom section 308 applies shall be applied for or issued. Section 308 applies to a person holding the office of President, Vice-President, Governor or Deputy Governor.[12] This is the immunity enjoyed by this class of persons.

Under the Vienna Convention on Diplomatic Relations 1961,[13] envoys, consultant officers, members of their official and domestic staff and their families enjoy immunity from legal processes. Thus, they cannot be compelled to appear in court. This immunity may however be waived by them if they so desire.[14] This does not in any way suggest that they are not competent witnesses.[15] The case of *Zabusky* v. *Israeli Aircraft Industries*[16] is very instructive in this regard. In the instant case, the Court of Appeal held thus:

> I find it surprising that the court below founded its decision in avoiding the suit for want of jurisdiction on the provisions of the Diplomatic Immunities and Privileges Act, Cap. 99 Laws of the Federation of Nigeria, 1990. The ruling seemed to suggest that a foreign diplomat serving in Nigeria is neither a competent nor a compellable witness to testify in any proceedings in Nigerian Courts. Section 1(1) of the said Act clearly confers immunity to suits and legal processes against the Diplomats in Nigerian Courts. The effect is that such Diplomats are not compellable witnesses. But there is nothing in the Provisions of the Said Act to suggest that foreign diplomats are not competent witnesses. Sections 155 to 176 of the Evidence Act, Cap. 112 Laws of Federation of Nigeria, 1990[17] make provisions for competence and compellability of persons to testify in Nigerian Courts. Nothing in those provisions that a foreign Diplomat is not a competent witness in Nigerian courts. I hold that the Israeli Ambassador in Nigeria by virtue of Section 1(1) of the Diplomatic Immunities and Privileges Act is not a compellable witness in Nigerian Courts. He is however a competent witness and could have, if he so

[12] Section 308 (3) of the 1999 Constitution.
[13] This Convention is made applicable to Nigeria by virtue of the Diplomatic Immunities and Privileges Act, CAP. 99 LFN 1990.
[14] Section 2 of the Diplomatic Immunities and Privileges Act.
[15] Section 175 of the Evidence Act.
[16] (2007) All FWLR (Pt. 352) 1759 at 1794 CA.
[17] Now sections 175 to 186 of the Evidence Act 2011.

desired, testify for the appellants in the court below as to the publication of the libel complained of.

As a commentary on the ruling of the court, the judgment of the Court in the case represents the true and correct interpretation or position of the law of Evidence on the subject matter. It should be noted at this juncture that while the family members and the domestic staff and even the members of the family of the official staff of Diplomats and consular agent enjoy the immunity from court processes such immunity does not extend to the family members, official staff or family members of the official staff to the President, Vice-President, Governor or the Deputy Governor as that was never the intendment of the drafters of section 308 of the Constitution of the Federal Republic of Nigeria. The immunity under section 308 of the Constitution only applies to the sole holder of the office. The Immunity of these public office holders to which the section applies does not in any way inhibit the commencement of civil proceedings against them in their official capacity or estops the commencement of civil or criminal proceedings in which they are nominal parties.[18] There can also be criminal investigation of these officials while in office and this immunity automatically fizzles out upon the expiration of their tenure in office as it never inures in perpetuity.

iii. Children

The reception of the evidence of a child is aptly covered by section 209 of the Evidence Act. The provisions are too clear and unequivocal enough to invoke any confusion. It provides thus:

> (1) In any proceeding in which a child who has not attained the age of 14 years is tendered as a witness, such child shall not be sworn and shall give evidence otherwise than on oath or affirmation, if in the opinion of the court, he is possessed of sufficient intelligence to justify the reception of his evidence and understand the duty of speaking the truth.
>
> (2) A child who has attained the age of 14 years shall, subject to section 175 and 208 of this Act give sworn evidence in all cases.

The purport of the above section is that while a child who has attained the age of 14 years shall subject to sections 175 and 208 of the Act, give sworn evidence in all cases,[19] a child under the age of fourteen shall only give

---

[18] See section 308(2) of the 1999 Constitution (As amended).

[19] Section 209 (2) of the Evidence Act.

unsworn evidence if the tests of reception of such evidence as specified under sub 1 of section 209 have been met.

The effect of the above provision is that once a person has not attained the age of 14, he is to be regarded as a person to which the provision of section 209(1) of the Act applies and can only give unsworn evidence if in the opinion of the court, he is possessed of sufficient intelligence to be able to understand questions put to him and to give rational answers to them. This is the first hurdle to cross in reception of the evidence of a child who has not attained the age of fourteen years. To ascertain this condition, the court would normally put forward some preliminary harmless questions that is completely unconnected with the case in which he is expected to testify. According to the erudite author Lawrence Atsegbua,[20]The test of the child's ability to understand the questions put to him and give rational answer to them may be carried only by asking the child questions that do not necessarily have connection with the case before the court such as the name of his school, his teacher, his parents' name, etc. This is all in a bid to justify that the child possesses sufficient intelligence to understand the questions put to him. The second litmus test of reception of the evidence of a child to which section 209(1) applies, is to put questions to the child with the view of determining whether he understands the duty of speaking the truth. This may be done by asking the child questions such as the divine consequence of telling a lie or even telling a story whether it will be right to lie or tell the truth in that circumstances. Whenever the court having put forward these two tests as specified above for the reception of the evidence of a child who has not attained the age of fourteen, the court found out that such child does not possess sufficient intelligence to understand the questions put to him so as to give rational answers to them or lacks the capacity to understand the need to speak the truth, the child automatically becomes incompetent to testify at all by the operation of the proviso to section 175 of the Act that talks about competence to testify generally.

In *Abelegah* v. *State,*[21] the court of Appeal while citing Nnaemeka Agu JSC in the case of *Okon* v. *State, gave* a practical illustration for the reception of the evidence of a child under section 209 of the Evidence Act. In the case, the court held thus:

---

[20] L Atsegbua, *op. cit.,* pg. 198.

[21] (2015) LPELR-24793 (CA) Pp. 18-21, paras. A-A.

The legally, acceptable procedure in satisfaction of the provision was, graphically, captured by Nnaemaka-Agu, JSC, in *Okon* v. *State* (*supra*), at 182-183, thus:

It is my view that once a witness is a child...the first duty of the Court is to determine first of all whether the child is sufficiently intelligent to understand the questions he may be asked in the course of his testimony and to be able to answer rationally. This is tested by the Court putting to him preliminary questions which may have nothing to do with the matter before the Court. If the Court comes to the conclusion that the child is unable to understand the questions or to answer them intelligently, then that child is not a competent witness...If after passing the first test...then being a competent witness he will give evidence which is admissible...though not under oath. The procedure had been consolidated in a sea of later judicial authorities...At the time of the trial proceedings in the lower Court, PW5, Gift Abelegah, was about ten (10) years old. Obviously, he was a child as he had not attained the age of fourteen (14) years as ordained by Subsection (2) of Section 209 of the Evidence Act as to give evidence on oath or affirmation. In order to ascertain whether the lower Court respected the procedure outlined above, it is important to invite the printed record. In this perspective, let me pluck out, *verbatim et literatim*, what transpired in the lower Court before PW5 gave evidence, at page 72, lines 1-5, of the record, thus:

Mr. Wombo: our witness is in Court. He is ten years old.

Gift Abelega: I am ten years old. I am in Winners' Modern Academy and I am in primary 4 in the school. I go to Catholic Church; I do not know the name of the church (2015) LPELR-24793(CA)

Order: I will not put the witness on oath; with the Court room cleared...

Again, a calm look at the answers disclose that they have no nexus with the prosecution of the offence. They are, therefore, indications that the requirements of the provision were complied with, see *Dagayya* v. *State* (*supra*). The provision respects the opinion of the judex...In my humble view, the lower Court, based on the above juridical dissections, formed its opinion within the perimeter of our adjectival law and, de jure, free from appellate intervention. It implies that the lower Court's opinion that PW5 had the sufficient intelligence to give evidence and that he understood the duty of not fearing the truth is unimpeachable. In all, the conditions-precedent for the reception of the unsworn evidence of PW5, under Section 209 of the Evidence Act were fulfilled to the letter. I, therefore, hold that PW5 was a competent witness.

At the other flip side of the coin is section 209(2) of the Act. Under this subsection, where a child has attained the age of fourteen years, his evidence shall be received on oath as he is a competent witness under the law. Interpreting this subsection *stricto sensu* from its exact wordings, it can be said and correctly too that once a child has attained the age of fourteen, the test required for the reception of the evidence of a child under sub(1) becomes dispensed with but from long-aged judicial practice, it has been advised that the court still administer those test even to the evidence of child who has attained fourteen years.

Another sphere of this discussion that deserves an attention is whether the court is duty bound to record those preliminary questions put to the child? In *Idi* v. *State*[22] where the Court held thus:

> I agree with learned counsel for the respondent that there is no legal requirement that the Judge must record the questions put to the child and her responses thereto.

In *Abelegah* v. *State*,[23] the court, while ruling on the failure of the trial court to record the preliminary questions put to the child, held that it is apparent from the extracted proceedings that the questions put to PW5, which generated the answers, were not recorded by the lower court. That in itself is not fatal to the adjudicative inquisitive duty of the lower court as decreed by the provision.[24]

In *Idi* v. *The State*,[25] the Supreme Court held that what is required is that the record must show that the preliminary investigation was undertaken and that the court satisfied itself of the ability of the witness to testify. It thus suffices to say that failure of a court to carry out the preliminary tests renders the evidence of a child a nullity. In view of the present tests as explained above, this appears to be good law as it pertains to the effect of failure to carry out neither of the present preliminary tests.

However, if the child has not attained the age of 14 and his evidence sails through the first test provided by section 209(1) but the judge fails to ascertain if he understands the duty of telling of truth, the opinion has been expressed that the evidence of the child should not be expunged from the record but the court should see if it has been corroborated by other material

---

[22] (2017)LPELR-42587 (SC) P. 33, Para. D.

[23] Supra at page 19 paragraph F.

[24] See also *Solala* v. *State* (2005) All FWLR (Pt. 269) 1751. See also *Dagayya* v. *The State (2006) 7 NWLR* (Pt. 980) 637.

[25] *Supra* at page 33, para. E.

evidence implicating the accused. It is submitted that this approach is appropriate. Although a child who is to give evidence is generally compellable, courts of law are usually wary to compel his attendance by the use of contempt proceedings. However, a court will not allow a parent to ward off his child from attending court to give evidence.

In summary, the present tests required to determine if a child will give evidence are surmised thus:

(1) where the child has not attained the age of 14, the tests are:

(i) whether he has sufficient intelligence to justify reception of his evidence;

(ii) test as to whether he understand the duty of telling the truth;

(2) if the child has attained the age of 14, he will only be tested to ascertain if he has sufficient intelligence to justify reception of his evidence.

iv. Dumb, deaf and blind Witness

A dumb witness is a competent witness under the law and can regardless of this speech defect or impairment give direct oral evidence.[26] The evidence Act accommodated the evidence of these categories of witnesses under sections 175 and 176(1) and (2) of the Act. Section 175 applies to the deaf and blind witness or other persons with deformity. The court by virtue of the Act is mandated to receive their evidence in any manner that the court considers intelligible provided it is done in open court.

The provision of section 176(1) is pertinent to be reproduced herein:

> (1) A witness who is unable to speak may give evidence in any other manner in which he can make it intelligible as by his writing or by signs, but such writing must be written and the signs made in open court.
>
> (2) Evidence so given shall be deemed to be oral evidence.

This section underscores the aphorism that there is ability in disability. This section tends to accommodate the evidence of such witnesses with deformity in line with the letters, spirit and provisions of the constitutional safeguards and the right of every person to be heard in matters as to the determination of his right and liabilities, except where such deformity is such as to prevent the witness from understanding the questions put to him and thus fails to give rational answers to them.

---

[26] N. O. Obiaraeri, *op. cit*,, at 352.

v. Old Persons or Person

An old man or woman is competent to testify provided he or she is not prevented, by reason of senility, from understanding the questions put to him/her, or from giving rational answer to those questions.[27] Extreme old age often times lead to amnesia, or senility. These are mental incapacities which have all the capabilities of truncating the thought pattern of humans thereby causing the person to lose touch with reality and have obscurity in thought. Such impairments are fatal to the reception of the evidence of such witness as such persons cannot be seen as a competent witness under section 175 of the Act. The court is enjoined to administer the test of ability to recollect facts with accuracy without having to beat around the bush with all sort of distorted story lines.

If a witness is mentally infirm, his competence will be upheld during his compos mentis (lucid intervals); or if it a case of drunkenness, when he is sober.[28] Where, however such mental impairment will affect the witness in certain other aspects of his life without affecting his recollection of events concerning the subject matter of trial, the witness shall still be a competent witness.[29] It has been held that where possible, a Judge should adjourn proceedings to give an ailing witness, especially one suffering from a temporal illness or mental incapacitation, chance to improve on his health and, therefore, become a competent witness in the proceedings.[30] A point should be noted that, it is the exclusive prerogative of the trial court to make a determination that such person is prevented from understanding questions put to him or from giving rational answers to those questions by reason of the said disease. The Court in some cases might resort to the opinion of an expert to have an informed opinion of the state of the metal balance of the witness.

vi. Bankers

A banker or an officer of a bank or other financial institutions shall not in any legal proceedings to which the bank or financial institution is not a party, be compellable to produce any banker's book or financial book, the contents of which can be proved in the manner provided in sections 89 and 90 of the Act, or to appear as a witness to prove the matters, transactions and

---

[27]Section 175 of the Evidence Act.

[28] *R.* v. *Dunning* (1995) Crim. LR 372.

[29] *R.* v. *Barrat* (1996) Crim. LR 495.

[30] *R.* v. *Baines* (1987) crim. LR 508.

accounts in such book, unless by order of the court made for special cause.[31] Thus, bankers are also exempted from compellability by the Evidence Act from tendering some certain type of evidence.

Extrapolating from the wordings of the section above, it becomes crystal clear that for the bank to enjoy this limitation, it must not have been a party to the proceedings in question. Thus, where the bank or the financial institution is a party to the proceedings, the limitation becomes inapplicable and of no moment. Where in the circumstance, the bank or financial institution is not a party to the proceedings, a party may apply to court on "*special cause*" as used by the Act to dispense with the limitation. Here, the discretionary powers of the trial court comes to play as the court is not obligated to grant such request as a matter of right but the court is to look at the strength of the application vis-à-vis the fact of the case to decide whether or not to rule in favour of issuing an order of notice to produce on such banker or financial institution to produce the banker's book.

As a corollary, section 258(1) of the Act defines "banker's books and related expressions" to include ledger, daybooks, cashbooks, account books and other books used in banking business. This provision applies to both civil and criminal cases. It should be noted also that the Act under this section brings other financial institutions and officers of such financial institutions into contemplation which necessarily does not have to be a banker in the strict sense of it.

vii. Husband and wife of parties to suit (Civil and Criminal)

Section 178 of the Evidence Act states that subject to the exception applicable by virtue of section 165 of the Act, in all civil proceedings, the parties to the suit, and the husband or wife of any party to the suit, shall be competent witnesses.

With the above in mind, it remains to clarify that the competence and compellability of the husband or wife against the other depends on whether it is civil or criminal proceedings. This section suffices to say that the parties to the suit and the husband or wife are competent witnesses for each other in civil cases only and thus compellable. However, this provision is made subject to section 165 of the Act which provides for the legitimacy of the child.

[31] Section 177 of the Evidence Act.

The meaning of "wife and husband" has been expanded by the Evidence Act 2011 to mean "respectively the wife and husband of a marriage validly contracted under the Marriage Act, or under Islamic law or a Customary law applicable in Nigeria, and includes any marriage recognized as valid under the Marriage Act."[32] Though spouses of parties are competent witnesses, no husband or wife shall be compelled to disclose any communication made to him or her during marriage by any person to whom he or she is or has been married nor shall he or she be permitted to disclose any such communication, unless the person who made it, or that person's representative in interest, consents, except in suits between married persons, or proceeding in which one married person is prosecuted for an offence specified in section 182(1) of the Act.[33] This is known as spousal privilege or marital privilege as such husband and wife are seen as one, and for the purpose of unity of spouse as Murphy proffered in his book[34] that a wife cannot be produced either against or for her husband "*quia sunt duae animae in carne una*" and it might be a cause of implacable discord and dissention between the husband and the wife, and a means of great inconvenience. Also, where any proceeding is instituted in consequence of adultery, no witness in any such proceeding whether a party to them or not, shall be liable to be asked or bound to answer any question tending to show that he or she has been guilty of adultery unless he or she has already given evidence in the same proceeding in disproof of the alleged adultery.[35] Neither are parties to proceedings under the Matrimonial Causes Act 1970 compellable to give evidence proving or tending to prove that the parties to the marriage did not have sexual relation with each other at any particular time if it would show that a child born to the wife during the marriage was illegitimate.[36]

Conversely in criminal cases, save and except certain exceptions, the spouse of a defendant is not competent and thus not compellable. Two categories of competence and compellability exist here. One is the group of cases where because of the nature of the offence with which the defendant is charged his or her spouse is an automatic competent and compellable witness for the prosecution without the consent of the person charged. The second is the group of cases where a defendant's spouse is not competent

[32] Section 258 of the Evidence Act.
[33] Section 187 of the Evidence Act.
[34] Murphy on Evidence, *op. cit.*, at 566.
[35] Section 186 of the Evidence Act.
[36] Section 84 of the Matrimonial Causes Act 1970.

and compellable witness unless upon the application of the other spouse who is facing trial.[37] Section 179 of the Evidence Act, states that in criminal cases, the defendant, his wife or her husband, as the case may be, or any person jointly charged with such defendant and tried at the same time, and the wife or husband of the person so jointly charged, is competent to testify. As earlier mentioned, the "wife and husband" now includes polygamous marriage such as Islamic and Customary law marriages.[38]

These exceptions to the general rule above are encapsulated under section 182 of the Act where it provides that when a person is charged with an offence under section 217, 218, 219, 221, 222, 223, 224, 225, 231, 300, 301, 340, 341, 357 to 362, 369, 370 or 371 of the Criminal code; the wife or the husband of the person charged shall be a competent and compellable witness for the prosecution or defence without the consent of the person charged.[39]

The offences mentioned under the Criminal Code are indecent practices between male; defilement of girls under thirteen; householder permitting defilement of young girls on his premises; defilement of girls under sixteen and above thirteen, and of idiots; indecent treatment of girls under sixteen; procuration; procuring defilement of women by threats or fraud, or administering drugs; abduction of girls under eighteen with intent to have carnal knowledge; unlawful detention with intent to defile or in a brothel; indecent acts; duties relating to the preservation of human life (duty to provide necessaries), duty of the head of the family; endangering life or health of apprentice or servants; abandoning or exposing children; definition of rape; punishment of rape; attempt to commit rape; indecent assaults on females; abduction; abduction of girls under sixteen, slave dealing, bigamy and child-stealing respectively.

However, for an offence other than one of those mentioned in subsection (1) of section 182, the husband or wife of such persons is a competent and compellable witness but only upon the application of the person charged.[40]

In the same vein, under subsection (1)(b) of the same section, a person charged with an offence against the property of his wife or her husband or with inflicting violence on his wife or her husband, the wife or the husband of the person charged shall be a competent and compellable witness for the

[37] O.N. Obiaraeri, *op. cit.*, 355.
[38] Section 258 of the Evidence Act.
[39] Section 182 (1) (a) of the Act.
[40] Section 182 (2).

prosecution or defence without the consent of the person charged. However, this is made subject to section 36 of the Criminal Code.

Nothing shall make a husband compellable to disclose any communication made to him by his wife during the marriage or a wife compellable to disclose any communication made to her by her husband during the marriage.[41] This has been submitted to be a communication privilege and cannot be waived even after the marriage has been duly dissolved.

Furthermore, the failure of the wife or husband of any person charged with an offence to give evidence shall not be made the subject of any comment by the prosecution.[42] In other words, the prosecution is not allowed to react to the failure, refusal or neglect of the spouse of the defendant to testify whether for the prosecution or defence.

Viii Defendant as a witness for the prosecution or defence

Every person charged with an offence is a competent witness for the defence and prosecution at every stage of the proceeding whether the person so charged is charged solely or jointly with any other person. However, a person so charged shall not be called as a witness except upon his own application.[43] This provision is in tandem with an already established constitutional provision which has been settled beyond equivocation that no person who is tried for a criminal offence shall be compelled to give evidence at the trial.[44] Thus, though an accused is a competent witness even for the prosecution, he cannot be compelled by the prosecution to testify and it is highly unlikely, if not impossible, that an accused will testify for the prosecution against himself. However a co-accused could be a competent witness for the prosecution. For him to be a competent witness for the prosecution, it must not be in a trial which he is jointly charged with the accused unless he has pleaded guilty or has been convicted or has been acquitted or have the charges against him dropped.[45] This position of the law is an adoption of Lord Cockburn's dictum in *Windsor* v. *The Queen*[46] where he stated thus:

---

[41] Section 182(3).
[42] Section 182 (4).
[43] Section 180 (a) of the Evidence Act.
[44] Section 36 (11) of 1999 Constitution of the Federal Republic of Nigeria (As amended).
[45] *Umole* v. *Inspector-General of Police* (1957) N.R.N.L.R 8. Cited in Aguda, *op. cit.*, page 306.
[46] 10 Cox 276.

> Where two persons are in the same indictment, and it is thought desirable to separate them in their trail, in order that the evidence of the one may be taken against the other, I think, in order to ensure the greatest possible amount of truthfulness on the part of the person who is coming to give evidence under such remarkable circumstances, it would be far better that a verdict of not guilty should be taken first; or if the plea of not guilty is withdrawn, a plea of guilty taken. Sentence should be passed in order that the person coming forward to give evidence may do so with the mind free of all the corrupt influence which the fear of impending punishment and the desire to obtain immunity at the expense of the prisoner might otherwise be liable to produce in the mind of the witness.

Hon. Justice C.C Nweze has however strongly criticized the above practice as not being backed up by any statutory provision and impliedly contrary to section 175 of the Evidence Act.[47] His opinion is indeed not without merit, but it is submitted that the position taken by our courts is in complete accordance with common sense, especially as section 179 is drafted in general terms.

The competence and the legal limitations of a defendant as a witness for the defence is aptly captured *in extenso* under section 180 of the Evidence Act. It provides thus:

> Every person charged with an offence shall be a competent witness for the defence at every stage of the proceeding whether the person so charged is solely charged or jointly with any other person:
>
> Provided that-
>
> (a) a person so charged shall not be called as a witness in pursuance of this section except upon his application;
>
> (b) a person charged and being a witness in pursuance of this section may be asked any question in cross examination notwithstanding that it would tend to incriminate him as to the offence charged;
>
> (c) when the only witness to the fact of the case called by the defence is the person charged he shall be called as a witness immediately after the close of the evidence for the prosecution;
>
> (d) every defendant called as a witness in pursuance of this section shall, unless otherwise ordered by the court, give his evidence from the

[47] C.C. Nweze, *op. cit.*, pgs 70-71.

witness box or other place from which the other witnesses give their evidence;

(e) nothing in this section shall affect the right of the person charged to make a statement without being sworn;

(f) in cases where the right of reply depends upon the question, whether evidence has been called for the defence, the fact that the person charged has been called as a witness shall not of itself confer on the prosecution the right of reply; and

(g) a person charged and called as a witness in pursuance of this section shall not be asked, and if asked, shall not be required to answer, any question tending to show that he has committed or been convicted of or been charged with any offence other than that with which he is then charged, or is of bad character unless-

(i) proof that he has committed or been convicted of such other offence is admissible evidence to show that he is guilty of the offence with which he is then charged ; or

(ii) he has personally or by his legal practitioner asked questions of the witnesses for the prosecution with a view to establish his own good character or has given evidence of his good character, or the nature or conduct or the defence is such as to involve imputations on the prosecutor or the witnesses for the prosecution , or

(iii) he has given evidence against any other person charged with the same offence.

The provision of section 180 of the Act is so elaborate to cover in clear terms the competence of a person charged to give evidence. It covers the constitutional provision on the rule against self-incrimination as it provides that the defendant can only testify on his own volition and he is not duty bound to answer any question that tends to show his previous conviction. He has the right to remain silent even throughout his trial. If he testifies, he may be asked any question in cross-examination notwithstanding that it would tend to incriminate him as to the offence charged and he shall give evidence, unless otherwise ordered by the court, from the witness box or other place from which the other witnesses give their evidence. This is however without prejudice to his right to make a statement without being sworn.

ix. Compellability to produce a title deeds or other documents of witness

No witness who is not a party to a suit shall be compelled to produce his title-deeds to any property or any document by virtue of which he holds any property as pledge or Mortgage or any document the production of which might tend to incriminate him, unless he has agreed in writing to produce them with the person seeking the production of such deeds or some person through whom he claims.[48]

x. Counsel as witness for the client and opposing party

It is beyond dispute that a legal practitioner is competent to testify when appearing for himself but his competence to testify in a matter he represents another has been viewed with distaste. The Evidence Act does not in any way prohibit a legal practitioner from testifying in a matter in which he represents another and, hence, the Supreme Court in *Elebanjo* v. *Tijani*[49] held that a legal practitioner is competent to testify in a case which he appears as counsel. According to Oputa JSC:

> The position then is that counsel appearing should not ordinarily act as counsel and witness. But if it becomes necessary for such counsel to give evidence, his evidence is not rendered inadmissible by the mere fact that he has acted or is acting as counsel in the case. There can therefore be no doubt that counsel is not by the mere fact of being counsel for a party to a dispute, incompetent to give evidence in the case. He is competent.[50]

From the above, a legal practitioner is competent to give evidence even when he acts in his professional capacity. However, there have been both judicial[51] and academic dicta on the impropriety of counsel giving evidence. It has been criticized as against the professional ethics. Atsegbua[52] has expressed the view that counsel giving evidence should be the exception and not the rule as it is contrary to practice.

---

[48] Section 184 of the Evidence Act.

[49] (1986) 2 NSCC 1387 SC.

[50] This was followed in *Obi* v. *The State* (1997) 7 NWLR (Pt. 513) 352; *Abubakar* v. *Chuks* (2008) All FWLR (Pt. 408) 207 at 224 & 225 S.C.

[51] *Horn* v. *Rickard* (1963) 2ALL NLR 40; See also *Obadara* v. *President Ibadan West District Council Grade B Customary Court* (1965) NMLR 39.

[52] L. Atsegbua, *op. cit.*, pg. 203.

The Court of Appeal in *Federal Republic of Nigeria* v. *Martins*[53] expressed its distaste for a legal practitioner being a witness and a prosecutor in the same case in the following words:

> A legal practitioner cannot be a witness in a case that is not personal and then proceed to prosecute in the same matter. On the other hand, in a personal case, a legal practitioner can testify and represent himself. The reason is that counsel cannot prosecute and be put in the witness box to be cross-examined at the same time as it is not tardy and not in tandem with the rules of professional ethics and morals.

It has been advised that when a lawyer has a pre-information that he would be called upon to testify as a necessary witness in a case he is conducting except as to merely informal matters, such as identification of document, neither he nor his law firm should take up such matter. This is in a bid to also protect the rule of confidentiality between a legal practitioner and his client, more so when the legal practitioner becomes a witness for the defence in a case he is handling for his client.

---

[53] (2012) 14 NWLR (Pt. 1320) 287 at pg. 311.

Chapter 20

DOCUMENTARY EVIDENCE

Meaning and Types of Document or Copy of a Document

The Evidence Act contains copious provisions on the species of evidence known as documentary evidence. This is captured under sections 83 to 112 of the Evidence Act, 2011. It spreads across evidential subjects like admissibility of documentary evidence, admissibility of statements in documents produced by computers, primary and secondary evidence, proof of execution of documents, public and private documents, affidavit evidence etc. However, this chapter seeks to streamline the admissibility of documents in proof of facts in issue. But before delving into the discourse, it is of utmost importance to underscore and consider the scope of things that constitute "documents" under the Evidence Act, 2011.

Notwithstanding the narrow definition given to the word "document" under the old Evidence Act of 2004,[1] section 258(1) of the Evidence Act, 2011 expressly and exhaustively discussed the word "document" to include the following:

(a) books, maps, plans, graphs, drawings, photographs and also includes any matter expressed or described upon any substance by means of letters, figures or marks or by more than one of those means, intended to be used or which may be used for the purpose of recording that matter;

(b) any disc, tape, sound track or other device in which sounds or other data (not being visual images) are embodied so as to be capable (with or without the aid of some other equipment) of being reproduced from it;

(c) any film, negative tape, or other device in which more visual images are embodied so as to be capable (with or without) the aid of some other equipment) of being reproduced from it; and

(d) any device by means of which information is recorded, stored or retrievable including computer output.

---

[1] See Section 2 of the Repealed Evidence Act 2004.

In the interest of requisite emphasis, the only common ground between the old and the new law is the definition of document in paragraph (a) above while paragraph (b), (c) and (d) above are novel provisions under the Evidence Act, 2011. Sequel to this, another observation in the new Act is the statutory interpretation of the word or expression "Copy of a document." Section 258(1) of the Evidence Act Interprets Copy of a document to include:

> In the case of a document falling within paragraph (b) but not (c) of the definition of "document" in this subsection, a transcript of the sounds or other data embodied in it.

The use of the word "include" to introduce what constitutes a document under the Act goes without saying that the meaning of document is not exhaustively captured under section 258 of the Evidence Act. It suffices to say that the meaning of document under the Act can still accommodate other things of *ejusdem generis.* In the case of *Ports and Cargo Handling Services Company Ltd & Ors.* v. *Migfo Nig Ltd & Anor,*[2] the Supreme Court while expounding on the connotation of the word 'includes' when used in a statute held that when the word 'includes' is used in a statute or written document, it is capable of enlarging the scope of the subject matter it qualifies or tends to qualify.

Following from the broad definition of the word 'document' under section 258 of the Act, the Court of Appeal in *Holdent International Ltd* v. *Petersville Nigeria Ltd,*[3] held that plastic bottles bearing trademark inscriptions are documents. This is correct with all intents and purposes of the Act. It has been submitted that the meaning of 'document' should no longer be interpreted to have this narrow, restricted and compartmentalized meaning as this is not the contemplation of the Evidence Act 2011. In *Federal Polytechnic, Ede & Ors.* v. *Oyebanji,*[4] tape recordings tendered in evidence was accepted by the same court as documents. The Court subsequently adopted this position of the law in the latter case of *Obatuga & Anor* v. *Oyebokun & Ors.,*[5] where the court held that video tape qualifies as a document and thus, admissible under the Act. As earlier established, the meaning of document under the Act is not exhaustive. It is hoped that our

---

[2] (2012) LPELR-9725 (SC).
[3] (2013) LPELR 21474 (CA).
[4] (2012) LPELR -19696 (CA).
[5] (2014) LPELR -22344 (CA).

courts will continue to expand the horizon of the meaning of document to meet with the prevailing dynamics of the society as they arise

The court of appeal in *NBC Ltd* v. *Paully Joe & Co. (Nig.) Ltd* [6] while citing the Supreme Court per Achike JSC(as he then was) in *Okonyi* v. *Njokama*[7] laid down the three main basic condition precedent for the admissibility of documents as follows:

(a) The document must be pleaded (where the case is fought on pleadings).

(b) The document must be relevant to the enquiry undertaken by the court.

(c) The document must be admissible in law.[8]

Section 83(1) of the Evidence Act (2011), provides as follows:

In a proceedings where direct oral evidence of a fact would be admissible, any statement made by a person in a document which seems to establish that fact shall on production of the original document, be admissible as evidence of that fact if the following condition are satisfied:

(a) If the maker of the statement either;

(i) Had personal knowledge of the matter dealt with by the statement; or

(ii) Where the document in question is or forms part of a record purported to be a continuous record made (in so far as the matter dealt with by it are not within his personal knowledge) in the performance of a duty to record information supplied to him by a person who had, or might reasonably be supposed to have personal knowledge of those matters; and

(b) if the maker of the statement is called as a witness in the proceeding:

Provided that the condition that the maker of the statement shall be called as a witness need not be satisfied if he is dead, or unfit by reason of his bodily or mental condition to attend as a witness, or if he is outside Nigeria and it is not reasonably practicable to secure his attendance or if all reasonable efforts to find him have been made without success.

---

[6](2018) LPELR-46583 (CA) P. 7, para. B-D.

[7] (1999) 12 SCNJ 259 at 275.

[8] See also *Tar & Ors* v. *Ministry of Commerce & Industries & Ors.* (2018) LPELR-44216(CA).

The case of *FRN* v. *Samuel* [9] lends credence to this evidential rule of admissibility under section 83 of the Act. The above quoted section of the Evidence Act provides for the admissibility of documentary evidence, but for a document to be admitted in proof of fact in issue, there are conditions which must be satisfied before such document is rendered admissible in court. The court in *Lawan Wassah* v. *Kara*[10] elucidated thus:

> The procedure for admitting documents in evidence is for the trial judge to hear argument for and against the admissibility of the document and to ascertain whether the conditions for its admissibility has been duly satisfied, if not, the document in proof of a fact stands rejected and once it is rejected, the judge can never make recourse to such document so as to rely on it when preparing his judgment.

A. Types of Documents

There are basically two types of documents and these types of documents are accorded the recognition under the Evidence Act. They are:

A. private document;[11] and
B. public document.[12]

The classification of document as public or private is partly premised on the institutional terminus or origin of that particular document though it is not ironclad.[13] Two institutional origins exist: public and private institutions. A public institution encompasses certain acts or records of state officials and bodies while a private institution covers private individuals and bodies. Though there should be a distinction between the authorship or source of document and what it eventually becomes. The court held in *Onwuzuruike* v. *Edoziem &Ors*[14] that a petition addressed to the police, while in the hands of the appellant who wrote it, is a private document, but the moment it is received by the Police to whom it was addressed who are public officers within the meaning and intendment of section 109 of the Evidence Act, it becomes part of the record of public officers and thus a public document.

We shall examine the above listed categories of documents seriatim.

---

[9] (2017) LPELR -43417 CA pp. 38-39 paras. E-C.
[10] (2015) 4 NWLR (Pt. 1449) pg. 374 at 378- 780.
[11] Section 103 of the Act.
[12] Section 102 of the Act.
[13] *Gimser Commodities Ltd* v. *FCMB & Ors.* (2017) LPELR-43095 (CA). P. 18, para. D.
[14] (2016) LPELR-26056 (SC).

Section 102 of the Evidence Act states the following to be public documents:

(a) documents forming the official acts or records of the official act of

(i) the sovereignty authority;

(ii) official bodies and tribunals; or

(iii) public officers, legislative, judicial and executive, whether of Nigeria or elsewhere; and

(b) public records kept in Nigeria of private document.

The above categories of public document were recently recognised in *NAFDAC* v. *Reagan Remedies.*[15] In *Ogunleye* v. *Aina & 3 Ors.*[16] The Court defined a public document as:

> A document made by a public officer for the purpose of the public making use of it, being able to have access to it and refer to it.

Also, the Court in *House of Representatives and 5 Ors* v. *SPDCN & Anor*[17] posited and described a public document as a document made for the purpose of the public making use of it, especially in judicial or quasi-judicial duty and that the features of the public document are created over a public matter, preserved for the good of the public and always accessible for public inspection and use. Any document that is not meant for public inspection is not a public document. In *Onwuzuruike* v. *Edoziem & Ors,*[18] the supreme court while citing its earlier decision in *Tabik Investment Ltd & Anor* v. *GTB Plc,*[19] held that all documents emanating from the custody of a police officer being a public officer which is to be used in court are public document.[20]

In *PDP & Anor* v. *Kawuwa & Ors,*[21] a copy of a letter written by a private person sent to a public body or institution was held to be clearly a public document and it is immaterial that it was written in a private capacity as it falls squarely within the ambit of the clear provisions of Section 102(b) of the Evidence Act 2011.

---

[15] (2019) LPELR -47563 (CA) P. 38 paras. C-D; See also *Taiwo* v. *FRN* (2019) LPELR-47635 (CA); *Meka* v. *Chuba Ikpeazu & Ors.* (2017) LPELR-41920 (SC).

[16] (2011) 3 NWLR (Pt. 1235) pg. 479 at 537.

[17] (2010) 11 NWLR (Pt. 1205) pg. 479 at 253 per Aboki J.C.A.

[18] *Supra.*

[19] (2011) 17 NWLR (Pt. 1276) pg. 240.

[20] See also section 318(b) of the Constitution of the Federal Republic of Nigeria 1999 and Section 18(1) of the interpretation Act.

[21] (2015) LPELR-26044(CA).

On the other hand, section 103 of the Evidence Act emphatically declares that all documents other than public documents are private documents.[22] It must be emphasized that a private document may become or transmitted into a public document, such as when it is kept as a public record, but in no circumstances can a public document become transformed into a private document. As earlier noted, besides the origination of documents as partly a determinant for the classification of document into public and private, other factors are method of proving those documents and some consequential issues of admissibility of such documents under the Act. These other ancillary matters will be treated in subsequent sub-headings.

B. Proof of Public Documents

The position of the law remains that public documents are proved by the production of the original copies of such public documents which by themselves are admissible, and secondary copies are only considered where the original copies are unavailable.[23]

The Supreme Court in *Anagbado* v. *Faruk*[24] while restating this principle, held that original copies of public documents are surely admissible. It is only in the absence of such original public documents that only properly certified copies thereof are admissible as secondary copies of such public documents. It is sacrosanct to state here that a public document may be proved by the production of a certified true copy of it. In *Kassim* v. *State*[25] while citing *Ebu* v. *Obun,*[26] where the learned counsel for the Respondent erroneously submitted that originals of public documents ought to be certified to make them admissible. In response to this argument, the court per Opene, JCA bemoaned at the perversity of such argument thus:

> I do not know how the learned counsel come about this argument? When a document is certified, it is certified to be a true copy of the original. If then the original is to be certified, what will it be certified to be a true copy of itself (original)?

Clearly, in view of this decision, the court held that Exhibit B was wrongly rejected and ought to have been considered by the learned trial

---

[22] See *NAFDAC* v. *Reagan Remedies* (Supra); *Onochie* v. *Ikem* (1999) 4 NWLR (Pt. 116) Pg. 458. See also *Anatogu* v. *Igwe II* (1995) NWLR (Pt. 415) 542.

[23] See *Afolabi* v. *State* (2018) LPELR-44306 (CA) P.33, para. F.

[24](2018) LPELR-44909(SC).

[25](2017) LPELR-42586 (SC) P. 8, para. A-C.

[26](2004) 14 NWLR (pt. 892) 76 at 88.

judge in his judgment instead of treating it as if it had never been admitted. Thus, public documents must be certified in accordance with section 104 of the Act to be admissible in evidence. It is immaterial that they were pleaded and were relevant to the proceeding without having to fulfil the conditions as spelt out under the Act. At this point, section 104 of the Evidence Act provides that:

> (1) Every public officer having the custody of a public document which any person has a right to inspect shall give that person on demand a copy of it on payment of the legal fees prescribed in that respect, together with a certificate written at the foot of such copy that it is a true copy of such document or part of it as the case maybe.
>
> (2) The certificate mentioned in subsection (1) of this section shall be dated and subscribed by such officer with his name and official title and shall be sealed, whenever such officer is authorized by law to make use of a seal and such copies so certified shall be called certified copy.
>
> (3) An officer who, by the ordinary course of official duty, is authorized to deliver such copies, shall be deemed to have the custody of such document within the meaning of this section.[27]

However, the ultimate requirement of production from proper custody has no relevance to a duly certified public document under section 104 of the Evidence Act. In some cases, it can be tendered by a counsel from the bar to the court,[28] or by an officer authorized to do so by the other officer who has certified the document. A certified true copy of a document is by statute deemed original. Where there is no certification, the presumption of regularity will not be ascribed to it.

Where there is an issue in court and a party seeks to rely on a particular document which is kept in a public domain, the original cannot be gotten which is a requirement under the act; the public officer in charge of the document shall give the party relying on it a true copy (that is) a certified true copy which is equal to an original document. Therefore, for a public document to be certified as copy of the original, the court in a recent case of *Taiwo* v. *FRN*[29] while adopting with approval, the decision of the Supreme

---

[27] See *Ogbe* v. *Kogi State Government & Ors.* (2018) LPELR -44796 (CA) p.49 para. D.
[28] *Esezobor* v. *SAID* (2018) LPELR-46653(CA) P. 10, para. C.
[29] (2019) LPELR -47635 (CA) P. 14 paras. A-E.

Court in *Tabik Investment Ltd* v. *Guaranty Trust Bank* Plc,[30] emphatically postulated that before such public document can be tendered and accepted by the court as being certified, it must be shown that:

(a) it is paid for;
(b) there is an endorsement or certificate that it is a true copy of the document in question;
(c) the endorsement or certificate is dated and signed by the officer responsible for certification;
(d) it is sealed in cases in which the officer is entitled by law to use a seal.

The court went further at pages 14-15 to hold that Exhibit G which is a letter from the British Deputy High Commission, Lagos to the Acting Director NAPTIP Zonal Commander Lagos which shows an endorsement/certificate from NAPTIP on the face of the letter that it is a certified true copy, the name of the certifying officer, Salau Abiodun, and his rank, date and signature of the officer responsible for certification was done in compliance with the provision of Section 104 of the Evidence Act and therefore suffice.

It should also be noted that where a document was not rejected on the ground that it was inadmissible under the law, but on the ground that it was not tendered in accordance with the proper form required of a public document, though rejected, can still be re-tendered and admitted. Though the general position of the law is that a document tendered and marked rejected is no longer admissible in evidence. The court in the recent case of *Regency (Overseas) Co. Ltd* v. *Ariori & Ors*[31] was faced with this hard nut to crack. The court opined in the case that there is no dispute as to the fact that the proper foundation and certification necessary for the admissibility of the document in question was not complied with by the Respondents in the course of tendering of the document and the Appellant in the case rightly objected to its admissibility which the Court then marked as rejected. The Respondents then went back to put its house in order by getting the document certified and re-tendered same which was now admitted in evidence. It was held thus:

> The lower Court in admitting of the earlier rejected document made a distinction between when the general position of the law will apply and

[30] *Supra.*
[31] (2019) LPELR-47281 (CA).

what the exceptions are. The lower Court in its ruling at page 183 of the record held thus:

> At this stage, I must point out that basically a party cannot seek to tender a document which had been rejected earlier in the proceedings, but this position of the law has two broad classifications
>
> (1) Where the document sought to be tendered is the proper one but rendered inadmissible by a provision of the law in itself i.e. qua that document itself.
>
> (2) Where the document is one which even though proper, must be put in a particular condition before it can be admitted, like secondary evidence of public records, private documents of which public records were kept, bankers books, etc.
>
> The document in issue here falls into the second classification above. In respect of those in the first classification, once rejected, they are taken to have been dealt with on their merits. However in respect of those in the second classification, when the document which then was not put in conformity with what type or copy of it the law allows to be tendered, and were so rejected on that ground, it is permissible for an applicant to obtain the proper copy admissible in law and seek to tender it. If an applicant does so and so applies, that will not be taken as a second bite at the cherry and such permissions will be granted...The Respondents in the course of the trial was able to get the document certified and brought into conformity with the proper and acceptable mode of a public document, the lower Court then had no qualms in admitting the earlier rejected document. Having gone to regularise the document, I have no difficulty in aligning my view with that of the lower Court.

Relevancy and weight has been held to be a separate concept in the law of Evidence. It is also pertinent to state that admissibility of a document is one thing and the weight that the court will attach to the admitted document is another thing. In the recent case of *Odetola* v. *Togunde*,[32] the Court per Ojo JCA held *inter alia*:

> It is trite that admissibility of a document and the weight to be attached to such document are in two separate compartments. It is at the stage of writing its judgment that the Court takes a decision on the weight to be attached to the evidence presented by parties. The fact that a document

[32] (2019) LPELR -47505 (CA) pp.16-17 paras. G-H.

was tendered and admitted in evidence does not mean the Court must attach probative value to it.

There has been variegated decisions on whether only certified copies of public documents are admissible in legal proceeding.[33] However, the court has laid this controversy to rest in the recent Supreme Court case of *Sanmi* v. *State*[34] per Nweze JSC where the apex court held that the law remains that in the absence of the original document, only properly certified copies are admissible as secondary copies of public documents "but no other kind of secondary evidence." The Court of Appeal followed suit in *Mudashiru* v. *State*[35] to hold that public document that are admissible in evidence are either the original document themselves, or in the absence of such original copies, their certified true copies and no other.

The court at page 14 of *Mudashiru's case* went further to capture the rationale behind this well-considered decision that photocopies of a certified true copy of a document will not be admissible. It stated that by reason of the fact that we are in the age of sophisticated technology where photo tricks are the order of the day and secondary evidence produced in the context of Section 90(1)(a) could be tutored and therefore not authentic. Photo tricks could be applied in the process of copying the original document with the result that the copy, which is secondary evidence, does not completely and totally reflect the original and therefore not a carbon copy of the original as the Court has not the eyes of an eagle to detect such trick.[36]

Where the original copy of a public document cannot be produced, section 89 of the Act laid down conditions that must be satisfied for a secondary evidence of such document to be tendered and these conditions are:

(a) When the original is shown or appears to be in the possession or power-
   (i) of the person against whom the document is sought to be proved; or
   (ii) of any person legally bound to produce it and when after the notice mentioned in section 91 such person does not produce it;
(b) the existence, condition or contents of the original have been proved to be admitted in writing by the person against whom it is proved or by his representative in interest;

---

33 *Chevron Nigeria Ltd* v. *Aderibige* (2012) 4 NWLR (Pt. 1289) pg. 1 at 13 and *Okere Affia* v. *Agwu* (2012) 1 NWLR. (Pt. 1282) 425 CA answered this question in the affirmative.
34 (2019) LPELR-47418(SC) P. 31, para. D.
35 (2019) LPELR-47946 (CA) p. 9 para. G.
36 See *Araka* v. *Egbue* (2003) 7 SCNJ Page 114 At 126 Per Tobi (JSC) of blessed memory.

(c) the original has been destroyed or lost and in the latter case, all possible search has been made for it;
(d) the original is of such a nature as not to be easily movable;
(e) the original is a public document within the meaning of section 102; the original is a document of which certified copy is permitted by this Act or by any other law in force in Nigeria, to be given in evidence, the originals consist of numerous accounts or other document which cannot be conveniently be examined in court, and the fact to be proved is the general result of the whole collection or
(f) the document is an entry in a banker's book

The above section crystallizes the admissibility of certified true copy of a public document under the Act.

C. Proof of Execution of Documents

Under this sub-topic, we shall evaluate proof of execution of private and public documents. However, can a person relying on either a private or public document prove that such document has been duly and properly executed?

A private document is considered a document of private interest which may be issued by a private person whereas a public document is a document of public interest issued or published by a public body or authority connected with public business. It is very germane to closely take a look at the classical case of *Sturia* v. *Precia*[37] where Lord Blackburn defined a public document as one made by a public officer for the purpose of the public making use of it and being able to refer to it especially where there is a judicial or quasi-judicial duty to inquire into it. This definition was adopted with approval in *Agonsi* v. *Okwu.*[38]

A public document ordinarily should be easily accessed and also members of the public cannot lay hold or access a private document unless where the private document has become a public record as contemplated by section 102(b) of the Evidence Act.

Proving the existence and execution of private document does not raise an eyebrow. It has been surmised that in proof of public document, the court concerns itself with being satisfied that the document is duly certified, whether the certifying officer had been duly authorized and whether the public document is in substantial form and executed according to law.

---

[37](1880) A.C. 623.

[38]*Agonsi* v. *Okwu* (2016) LPELR-40614(CA) P. 27, para. C-A.

Also, in proving the existence and execution of private documents, the court is concerned with three questions to wit:

a. who is the author of the document?;
b. is the document authentic?;
c. is the document relevant and admissible?[39]

An issue of execution and authentication helps the court to determine whether the document is relevant to the fact in issue. It was held by the court in *Bright & Ors.* v. *Iwuoha*[40] that an unsigned document is a worthless document which cannot be countenanced by the law. Authorities abound to the effect that an unsigned document is not only worthless, it is inadmissible. Where it is admitted, it attracts no weight or probative value at all. Where a document which ought to be signed is not signed, its authenticity becomes in doubt.[41] In another case of *Ikeli & Anor* v. *Agber,*[42] the Court per Ogbuinya JCA held that in the province of the law, an unsigned document commands no judicial value of validity.

The court of Appeal in a more recent case of *FCDA Staff Multi-Purpose (COOP) Society & Ors* v. *Samchi & Anor*[43] while stating the effect of an unsigned document, succinctly puts it in the following words:

> Where a document which ought to be signed is not signed, for whatever reason, then the very essence of the document is now questionable, because its authenticity is in serious doubt; it is like a man without a face, only worse; and for that reason, the ambiguity created as a result will be construed against the maker or whoever sought to present it.

An unsigned document may not be admitted in evidence and where admitted, it does not attract any weight because it has no origin in terms of its maker. It has been established that the requirement of signature is to ascertain its origin and authenticity vis-à-vis its maker. However, there are instances where an unsigned document though prima facie inadmissible, becomes admissible by virtue of the peculiarity of such omission and clarification of authorship by *viva voce* evidence. In the recent Supreme

---

39 *Kuforji* v. *V.Y. B Nigeria Ltd* (1981) 6- 7 SC, 40.

40 (2018) LPELR-43758 (CA). P. 7, paras. D-E.

41 Per ALAGOA JCA (as he then was) in *Iki* v. *Idowu* (2006) 9 NWLR (pt. 984) 47 cited and relied upon *in Nwosu North and South Int. Ltd. & Anor.* v. *Nig. International Trd* and *Bright & Ors* v. *Iwuoha Industrial* (2014) LPELR 23425 (CA).

42 (2015) All FWLR part 785 p. 296.

43 (2018) LPELR-44380 (CA) Pp. 12-13, paras. G-A.

Court decision in *Ashakacem PLC* v. *Asharatul Mubashshurun Investment Ltd*[44] per Mary Ukaego Peter Odili JSC, the court in its erudition held thus:

> The point has to be made that the requirement of signature is made by the law to determine its origin and authenticity with regard to its maker and so where certain situations exist, an unsigned document could be admissible as in this instance where oral evidence clarifying the document and its authorship as in the case at hand thereby rendering such an unsigned document admissible.

Thus, a signed document though valuable as putting it beyond peradventure what terms the parties have agreed to is not essential to the existence of some contracts. Where the immediate parties to an agreement do not deny their agreement or the existence of the contract and there is no doubt about their intention that they should be bound, barring statutory provision to the contrary, the existence of the contract cannot be impugned on the ground that the document embodying the terms they have agreed to was unsigned, unless the parties have made such a condition of their being bound.[45]

Also, where the judgment or order of a court is not certified by the Registrar of court or where it does not carry the signature of the judge that delivered it, an order for it to be admissible in evidence attracts the presumption of genuineness and at times may be rendered inadmissible if its genuineness is rebutted.[46] The courts have held the question of certification of public document very seriously and have refused to treat same with kid gloves. The need for certification also extends to where such public document is attached to an affidavit except where it is not the gravamen of the case and ought not to be relied upon by the court for its judgment. The court in *Shagaya & Anor* v. *Useni & Ors*[47] had this to say:

> The copies of the rulings of 23rd June, 2015 and 8th July, 2015 attached to the affidavit in support of the application of the applicants having not been certified in accordance with Section 104(2) of the Evidence Act are therefore of no probative value in the consideration of the application of the applicants. As to the contention of Ngyou, Esq. that the documents

[44] (2019) LPELR-46541(SC) P. 27, paras. D-F.

[45] See also *Awolaja & Ors* v. *Seatrade G.B. V.* (2002) LPELR-651.

[46] *Global Soap & Detergent Ind. Ltd* v. *NAFDAC* (2010) 5 NWLR (Pt. 1294) pg. 511; see also *Ezeora* v. *FRN* (2016) LPELR-41144 (CA).

[47] (2015) LPELR-25822 (CA) Pp.15-16, paras. G-C.

attached to the affidavit require no certification, I am of the view that where such document is the pivot or the basis for a Court to take a decision in a matter, same must be certified. It is only where the document does not formed the basis of the decision of the Court, that it may not be certified when attached to an affidavit.

In order to underscore the proof of execution of documents, the following sundry provisions of the law must be noted and they are:

i. Proof of Signature and Handwriting and Electronic Signature

The word 'signature' is not a modern invention. Its meaning pre-dates the advent of computer age.[48] It is a recognized principle that signatures can be made in a person's handwriting or by electronic ways. It has been held in *Clarisdon Industries Ltd.* v. *A.I.B Ltd*[49] that the basic function of signature is to authenticate a document and assure that a person is bound by the document or process. A signature is a person's mark written by that person. Signature has always been understood as a person's distinctive name, or mark that he uses on a document.[50] The Signature to a memorandum may be any symbol made or adopted with an intention to authenticate the writing as that of the signer.[51] An electronic signature may be a digital signature which is secured, electronically transmitted or of unique identity. There appears to be no legislative attempt to defining electronic signature in Nigeria.[52] However, section 93(2) of the Evidence Act, 2011 merely acknowledged the existence of electronic signature. For proper appreciation of this section, we shall reproduce it *in extenso.*

Section 93 of the Evidence Act provides that:

1. If a document is alleged to be signed or to have been written wholly or in part by any person, the signature or the handwriting of the document of so much of the document as is alleged to be in that person's handwriting must be proved to be in his handwriting

---

[48] A.O Ajileye, *op. cit.,* p.90.
[49] (2002) FWLR (Pt. 128) 1355.
[50] Black's Law Dictionary, *op. cit.,* p. 1507; See also *Oko* v. *Ntaji & Ors* (2014) LPELR -24248 (CA) P.38, Para. D.
[51] *Michmerah Intl. Ltd* v. *Nigeria Intl. Bank. Ltd* (2015) LPELR- 25768 (CA) P. 15, para. B.
[52] There also appears to be no judicial interpretation to the definition of electronic signature in Nigeria.

> 2. where a rule of evidence requires a signature, or provides for certain consequences if a document is not signed; an electronic signature satisfies that rule of law or avoids those consequences.
>
> 3. An electronic signature may be proved in any manner, including by showing that a procedure existed by which it is necessary for a person, in order to proceed further with a transaction to have executed a symbol or security procedure for purpose of verifying that an electronic record is that of the person.

By this provision, though an electronic signature was not statutorily defined with exactitude, however, it naturally follows to mean that the legal effect of an electronic signature is on all fours with a hand-written signature.

The Cybercrimes (Prohibition, Prevention, etc.) Act, 2015 is also unhelpful in defining with exactitude, the meaning of electronic signature as it simply accepts the validity of electronic signature in commercial transactions. Essentially, it attempts to ensure that transactions conducted electronically are not denied legal effect.[53] Thus, the Cybercrimes Act stipulates that electronic signature in respect of purchase of goods, and other transactions shall be binding.[54]

At a basic level, therefore, any mark or method that captures a person's intent to approve or accept the contents of electronic document constitutes electronic signature of that individual. The nature of the mark or how it was created is immaterial. What is germane is proving who made the mark and the fact that the document was not changed subsequently. The burden of proving that the electronic signature does not belong to a purported originator of such signature is placed on the contender.[55] Section 17(2) states thus:

> whenever the genuineness or otherwise of such signature is in question, the burden of proof, that the signature does not belong to the purported originator of such electronic signature shall be on the contender.

It must be noted that when the court is to form an opinion upon identity of handwriting and finger impressions, the opinion of handwriting or signature experts as to the identity of handwriting or finger impressions are admissible. In the recent case of *Iyua* v. *Paul & Anor*,[56] the Court of Appeal,

---

[53] A. O. Ajileye, *op. cit.*, p.92.
[54] Section 17(1) of the Cybercrimes (Prohibition, prevention etc) Act, 2015.
[55] Ibid., at Section 17(2).
[56] (2019) LPELR-47266 (CA) pp. 28-32 para. F-B.

per Otisi JCA while quoting the Supreme Court with approval in the case of *Tomtec Nig Ltd* v. *Federal Housing Authority*,[57] posited thus:

> The law is well settled that a court of law faced with two disputed signatures has the power to compare the disputed signature with any signature agreed to be an undisputed or genuine signature.

It is trite law that when the objection is that the signature or handwriting is not that of the person by whom it purports to have been made, then the need arises to prove that the writing or signature was made by such person. The law provides how such proof should be made. In such circumstance, a person specially skilled in questions as to identity of handwriting or finger impression may be needed. The owner of the disputed signature need not swear to any affidavit or testify to deny the purported signature particularly as they exist before the court.

The identification and proof of handwriting or signatures including electronic signature can be done under the following:

(1) by the admission of the writer;
(2) by the evidence of a person who knows the writing and signature;
(3) by a person who witnessed or attested to the document;
(4) by an expert called to provide forensic analysis;
(5) by the court, comparing in open court such writings and signatures.[58]

With these ways of proving handwriting or signature in mind, the court has been able to resolve such disparity that associates with proving of signatures and handwriting including electronic signature.

ii. Identification of person signing a document

The Evidence Act under section 94 made provision for the identification of persons signing a signature. Section 94(1) and (2) of the Act provides that:

> (1) Evidence that a person exists having the same name, address, business or occupation as the maker of a document purports to have, is admissible to show that such document was written or signed by that person.
>
> (2) Evidence that a document exists to which the document, the making of which is in issue purports to be a reply, together with evidence of the making and delivery to a person of such earlier document, is admissible

[57] (2009) LPELR-3256 (SC).
[58] *C. G. G. (Nig) Ltd* v. *Ayovuare & Ors* (2015) LPELR-24437(CA).

> to show the identity of the maker of the disputed document with the person to whom the earlier document was delivered.

In order to illustrate and give a vivid explanation of the principle of law enunciated in section 94(1) of the Evidence Act, the Court of Appeal in *Arije* v. *Arije*[59] submitted that the question arising in the context of the appeal before it was whether the findings of the learned judge after comparing the signatures in line with section 108(1) of the Evidence Act, 2011 (similar to 94 of the Evidence Act 2011) is correct and whether having found that no fraud was established, the court below rightly proceeded to hold that the appellant did not established their claim. The court of Appeal subsequently held that if the names are not the same as is obvious having not been pleaded, the natural inference is that they are not the same person and the incidental presumption is that the different signatures found by the learned trial judge is in respect of two different names.

iii. Evidence of sealing and delivery of document[60]

By virtue of section 95 of the Act, it provides that evidence that a person signed a document containing a declaration that a seal was his seal is admissible to prove that he sealed it. Sub 2 provides that evidence that the grantor on executing any document requiring delivery expressed an intention that it should operate at once is admissible to prove delivery.

iv. Proof of Instrument to the validity of which attestation is necessary

Section 96 of the Act, provides that:

> (1) in any proceeding whether civil or criminal, an instrument to the validity of which attestation is required by law may, instead of being proved by an attesting witness, be proved in the matter in which it might be proved if no attesting witness were alive. Provided that nothing in this section shall apply to the proof of wills or other testamentary documents.
>
> (2) If no attesting witness is alive, an instrument to the validity of which attestation is required by law is proved by showing that the attestation of one attesting witness at least is in his handwriting, and the signature of the person executing the documents is in the handwriting of that person.

---

[59] (2011) 13 NWLR (Pt. 1264 at 265.

[60] Evidence Act 2011, Section 95.

v. Admission of execution by party to attested document

The admission of a party to an attested document of its execution by himself shall be sufficient proof as against him, though it is a document required by law to be attested.[61]

vi. Cases in which proof of execution or of handwriting is unnecessary[62]

In some circumstances, it may not be necessary to prove execution or handwriting. This is succinctly captured under section 98 of the Act which provides that:

> (1) A person seeking to prove the due execution of a document is not bound to call the party who executed the document or to prove the handwriting of such party or of an attesting witness in any case where the person against whom the document is sought to be proved-
>
> (a) Produces such document and claims an interest under it in reference to the subject matter of the suit: or
>
> (b) Is a public officer bound by law to produce its due execution, and he has dealt with it as a document duly executed.

Without prejudice to that contained in subsection 1 of section 98, subsection 2 provides that nothing contained in this section shall prejudice the right of a person to put in evidence any document in the manner mentioned in section 89 and 90 and under section 155 of this Act.

vii. Proof when attesting witness denies the execution

By virtue of section 99 of the Evidence Act, it states that if the attesting witness denies or does not recollect the execution of the document, its execution may be proved by other evidence. The Evidence Act did not define or interpret the word execution. However, "Execution" is a validation of a written instrument or document such as a contract or will by fulfilling the necessary legal requirements.

viii. Proof of document not required by law to be attested[63]

The above topic is unstintingly encapsulated under section 100 of the Act which provides that: "An attested document not required by law to be attested may be proved as if it was unattested."

---

[61] Section 97 of Evidence Act 2011.

[62] See the marginal note to Section 98 of the Evidence Act 2011.

[63] Evidence Act 2011, Section 100.

ix. Comparison of signature, seal or finger impression with others admitted or proved[64]

The Evidence Act under section 101 of the Act provides that:

> (1) In order to ascertain whether a signature, writing, seal or finger impression is that of the person by whom it purports to have been written or made, any signature, writing, seal or finger impression admitted or proved to the satisfaction of the court to have been written or made by that person may be compared with the one which is to be proved although that signature, writing seal or finger impression has not been produced or proved for any other purpose.[65]
>
> (2) The court may direct any person present in court to write any word or figure or to make finger impressions for the purpose of enabling the court to compare the words, figures or finger impressions so written with any words, figures or finger impressions alleged to have been written or made by such person: Provided that where a defendant does not give evidence, he may not be so directed to write such words or figures or to make finger impressions.
>
> (3) After the final termination of the proceeding in which the court required a person to make his finger impressions, such impression shall be destroyed.

A judge has the untrammelled right to compare and contrast a disputed signature with an allegedly admitted or genuine one especially in an open court. In that juridical exercise, the court rely on section 101 of the Evidence Act. Incontestably, the law grants the court the unbridled licence, under the provision of Section 101(1) and (2) of the Evidence Act to engage in such adjudicative exercise of comparison of signatures.[66] It has been held not to be an investigation forbidden in a judicial trial. However, it has been decided that as laudable as the provision of section 101 of the Evidence Act is, parties to a case must present a request to the court for comparison of signature, before a court can employ its discretion to grant or refuse such a request. To embark on the exercise of comparing signatures will have the effect of descending into the arena of contest, where none of the parties has requested for such an exercise. Courts are forbidden from descending into the arena of

---

64 Evidence Act of 2011, Section 101(1) (2) & (3).

65 See *Aliyu* v. *Okoye & Ors.* (2018) LPELR-45429(CA) p. 29 paras. E-G.

66 See *Akpan* v. *Obot & Anor.* (2019) LPELR-47150 (CA).

contest and conducting cases for any of the parties.[67]It is also pertinent to note that where the maker denies his signature, the court of law is presented with the option to compare the signature already admitted by the alleged signatory to be his own with the one that he was asked to sign or write in open court under the provision of section 101 of the Act.[68] In *Aliyu* v. *Okoye & Ors.,*[69] the Court held thus:

> The law permits the Courts to compare writings and or signatures in order to discover their authors only in cases where the writings and or signatures are in dispute and therefore in issue. Also in such cases, proven or acknowledged writings or signatures of the disputants must be before the Court.[70]

Before making a ruling on the signatures in one way or the other, a trial judge can significantly differentiate two signatures or handwritings of the same person and call for their reactions in line with the sacrosanctity of one of the twin pillars of natural justice: this is the doctrine of fair hearing.

x. Document signed or executed by illiterates

Where a class of document is signed by an illiterate, special attention is required. One clear instance is where the Evidence Act under section 119 (1)(d) of the Act provides that where the deponent is illiterate or blind, the affidavit shall state that fact and shall be accompanied with a jurat. The jurat shall be written without interlineations, alteration or erasure immediately at the foot of the affidavit and towards the left side of the paper, and shall be signed by the person before whom it is taken.

It was judicially decided in the immortal case of *PZ & Co Ltd* v. *Gusau*[71] that an illiterate person is a person who is unable to read and write in any language, that is, he is totally unread. In the more recent decision of the Supreme Court in *Sunday* v. *FRN,*[72] the apex court per Sanusi JSC has this to say about the question: who is an illiterate?

> My understanding of who can be regarded as an illiterate is that such person must be a person who cannot read, understand and express his

---

[67] *Sanmi* v. *State* (2019) LPELR-47418 (SC).

[68] *Ndoma-Egba* v. *ABC Plc.* (2005) 14 NWLR Pt. 944P. 79 see also *Dagaash* v. *Bulama* (2004) All NWLR (Pt. 212) P. 1666 and *Odutola* v. *Mabogunje* (2013) 7 NWLR (Pt. 1354) 52.

[69](2018) LPELR-45429 (CA).

[70] Ibid., at P. 30, paras, C-D.

[71] (1962) All NLW (Pt.1) 242.

[72] (2018) LPELR-46357 (SC) PP.17-18 paras. C-A.

> opinion by writing in the language which is used in writing it on his behalf. In other words, a person who is unable to read and write in some other language is not an illiterate within the meaning of the Illiterate Protection Act. Therefore, the issue or question on who is actually an illiterate cannot be presumed by Court, but it is an issue or question which must be proved by evidence and as I stated supra...the burden to prove such assertion of illiteracy lies squarely on the person who alleged such illiteracy.

Another protection offered to illiterates in reference to documents is under the Illiterate Protection Act which has also received statutory re-enactment in various states of the federation as State law. It should also be noted that where a document is executed without an illiterate jurat where needed, such document is voidable only at the instance of the illiterate himself.[73] Though it is a requirement that any person who shall write any letter or document at the request or on behalf of, or in the name of an illiterate person shall also write on such letter or other document, his own name as the writer and his address. The law is designed to protect illiterate from being exploited.[74]

In conclusion, any document which does not comply with the illiterate protection Act may nevertheless be admissible for example, in support of the case of an illiterate.[75] As earlier established, it is the law that the jurat is for the protection of the illiterate from possible fraud. It is therefore to be used as a shield and not as a sword. The failure to insert a jurat on a document only makes it unenforceable as between the illiterate, the maker and the writer/preparer of the document if the document fails to comply with the requirement of the law.[76] A party alleging illiteracy must specifically plead and prove it failing which any finding thereon will go to no issue.[77]

D. Admissibility of documentary evidence as to fact in issue

The Evidence Act recognizes the admissibility of documents as to facts in issue under section 83 of the Act. In other to appreciate the provision of section 83 of the Act, it is very germane to quote *in extenso,* the section. It provides thus:

---

[73] *Laarokun & Ors* v. *Kadir* (2019) LPELR-47715 (CA).

[74] Ibid. @ page 40 para. E; *Itauma* v. *Akpe-Ime* (2000) 80 LRCN 248.

[75] Aguda *op. cit.,* pages 180-181.

[76] *Tar & Ors* v. *Ministry of Commerce & Industries & Ors* (2018) LPELR-44216(CA); See also Section 3 of the Illiterates Protection Act.

[77] *Sunday* v. *FRN* (*supra*); see also *Kano* v. *Oyelakin* (1993) 3 SCNJ 65.

(1) In any proceeding where direct oral evidence of a fact would be admissible, any statement made by a person in a document which seems to establish that fact shall, on production of the original document, be admissible as evidence of that fact if the following conditions are satisfied.

(a) If the maker of the statement either-

(i) Had personal knowledge of the matters dealt with by the statement; or

(ii) Where the document in question is or forms part of a record purporting to be a continuous record, made by the statement (in so far as the matters dealt with by it are not within his personal knowledge) in the performance of a duty to record information supplied to him by a person who had, or might reasonably be supposed to have, personal knowledge of those matters; and

(b) if the maker of the statement is called as a witness in the proceeding: provided that the condition that the maker of the statement shall be called as witness need not be satisfied if he is dead, or unfit by reason of his bodily or mental condition to attend as a witness or he is outside Nigeria and it is not reasonably practicable to secure his attendance, or if all reasonable efforts to find him have been made without success.

It should be noted at this point that before a document is admitted under section 83(1) of the Act, there must be a witness in the witness box through whom such document can go in,[78] especially when it is a private document unlike a public document that can be tendered through a lawyer from the bar where the procedure is not contested. However, where a witness or the maker is shown to be dead or unfit by reason of his bodily or mental condition to attend as a witness, or if he is outside Nigeria and it is not reasonably practicable to secure his attendance, or where all efforts to secure his attendance prove abortive, in such circumstance, the presence of the maker can be dispensed with under the exculpatory provision of section 83(2) of the Act. In the absence of these exceptions, a maker of a document must be called and thus tender the document through him. In *Oloruntoki* v. *Johnson*[79] it was held that in the absence of such established exceptions, a survey plan sought to be tendered must be tendered through the surveyor

---

[78] *Abdulsalam* v. *State* (2018) LPELR-45371(CA).
[79] (1990) 6 NWLR (pt. 158) 600 CA.

who drew it. A statement as earlier noted, includes any representation of fact whether made in words or otherwise.[80]

It can be gleaned from the above provisions of section 83(2) that in any proceedings, if having regard to the circumstances of the case, it is satisfied that undue delay or expense would otherwise be caused, the court shall make an order that such a statement as is mentioned in subsection (1) of this section be admissible as evidence or may without any such order having been made, admit such a statement in evidence notwithstanding that:

(a) the maker of the statement is available but is not called as witness; and

(b) the original document is not produced if in lieu of it, there is produced a copy of the original document or of the material part of it certified to be a true copy in such manner as may be specified in the order or as the court may approve, as the case may be.

The Court can *suo motu* or upon an application by a party to a suit, authorize that the same document be admitted even where the maker is available, if securing his attendance, undue delay or expense would otherwise be caused. It is also observed that section 83(1) of the Act applies "in any proceedings" which can be criminal or civil proceedings. This is submitted to be a great expansion to the applicability of the section.[81] Section 83(2)(b) gives the court the discretion to allow the admission of a copy of an original document or a certified true copy of a document in lieu of the original document.

Section 83(3) of the Act, also provides thus:

> Nothing in this Section shall render admissible as evidence any statement made by a person interested at a time when proceedings were pending or anticipated involving a dispute as to any fact which the statement might tend to established.[82]

The above section covers the admissibility of documents made during the pendency of a law suit. The general rule is that a document made by a person interested during the pendency of a suit or when litigation is anticipated is inadmissible.[83] A person is held to be "interested" within the meaning of this subsection if he has pecuniary or other material interest in the result of the proceeding. He is a person whose interest is affected by the result of the

---

[80] Section 258 (1) Evidence Act, 2011.

[81] Section 91(1) of the repealed Evidence Act, 2004 applied only to civil proceedings.

[82] *Olorunzoki* v. *Johnson* (1990) 9 MWLR (Pt. 158) 600.

[83] See *Osuji* v. *Osuji* (2019) LPELR -46621 (CA) P. 29, para. E; see also section 83(3) Evidence Act 2011.

proceedings, and therefore would have a temptation to pervert the truth to serve his personal or private ends. It does not mean an interest in the sense of intellectual observation or an interest purely due to sympathy. It means "an interest in the legal sense, which imports something to be gained or lost.[84]

Here, the purpose the law seeks to achieve is to render inadmissible, a document prepared by an interested person with the primary intention of defeating the course of justice. It should be noted that a person who is not personally interested in the result of the litigation cannot be regarded as one who is "interested" in the proceedings. Thus, what this means is that documents tendered by such persons as independent contractors, or persons who are purely on official assignment, such as policemen, officials or servants without interest of a personal nature in the litigation or the result thereof , are admissible.[85] Thus, in *Disu Olomo* v. *Sunday Ape,*[86] the court elucidated that in considering section 83(3) of the Evidence Act, 2011, a person who is performing an act in his official capacity cannot be a person interested under the above provision. The court's view in *Disu Olomo* v. *Sunday Ape* above was reiterated in *Sterling Bank Plc* v. *Sola Ltd*[87] In a more recent case of *Oyebo & Anor* v. *Lasisi & Ors,*[88] the Court of Appeal while citing the *Olomo* v. *Ape*[89] with approval, stated the rationale behind section 83(3) of the Evidence Act in the following words:

> ...In *Olomo* Vs. *Ape* (2013) LPELR 22327 (CA), this Court stated the rationale behind the enactment of section 83(3) of the Evidence Act in the following words: "Coming to the first question of whether the trial Court was not wrong in rejecting the survey plan sought to be tendered by the surveyor same having been prepared during the pendency of this suit..."On the question of the second arm of when proceedings were pending or anticipated," there is no doubt that Section 83 (3) of the Evidence Act is anchored on the doctrine of *lis pendens* which prevents the admission of documents made *pende lite*.

The court further laid down criteria for admissibly of documents and these criteria are pleadings, relevance and admissibility in law. A document

---

[84] *U. T. C. (Nig) PLC* v. *Lawal* (2013) LPELR-23002(SC) P.26, paras. B-D.
[85] S.T Hon, *op. cit.,* page 921.
[86] (2013) LPELR -22327 (CA).
[87] (2015) 5 NWLR (Pt. 1453) pg. 405.
[88] (2019) LPELR-47882 (CA) pp. 40-41 paras. E-B.
[89] *Supra.*

is admissible in evidence if it is relevant to the fact in issue and admissible in law.

Also section 83(4) of the Act provides thus:

> for the purpose of this section, a statement in a document shall not be deemed to have been made by a person unless the document or the material part of it is written, made, or produced by him with his own hand, or was signed or initialled by him or otherwise recognized by him in writing as one for the accuracy of which he is responsible.

This section must be read and understood in the light of the fact that under our law, it is now recognized that signature can be made in a person's handwriting or by electronic means.[90]

Finally in section 83(5) of the Act, it provides that:

> for the purpose of deciding whether or not a statement is admissible as evidence by virtue of this section, the court may draw any reasonable inference from the form or contents of the document in which the statement is contained, or from any other circumstances, and may, in deciding whether or not a person is fit to attend as a witness, act on a certificate purporting to be certificate of a registered medical practitioner.

E. Relationship between oral and documentary evidence

This topic seeks to x-ray the connection, the legal nexus or relationship between oral evidence and documentary evidence since the distinction between both categories of evidence must be borne in mind at all times. It should be systematically noted that oral evidence and documentary evidence are types or species of evidence recognized under the Evidence Act.

It is trite law pursuant to section 125 of the Evidence Act that all facts, except the contents of documents may be proved by oral evidence. Thus, the law precludes a party from giving oral evidence of the contents of a document.[91] This principle recently received judicial blessing in the most recent decision of the court of Appeal per Ita George Mbaba JCA in *Akanu & Anor* v. *Osisioma Ngwa Local Government.*[92] In this case, the erudite justice of the Court of Appeal in an appetising prose held thus:

---

[90] See Section 17(2) of Cybercrimes (Prevention, Prohibition, etc.) Act, 2015.

[91] See *West African Utilities Metering & Services Ltd* v. *Akwa Ibom Property and Investments Co. Ltd* (2019) LPELR-47089(CA) P. 27 para. C.

[92] (2020) LPELR -49549 (CA) p. 17 para. D-E; See also *Edeh* v. *Mac-Tino* (Nig) Ltd (2018) LPELR-45859 (CA) p. 18 para. E

> Of course, in law, an oral evidence will always surrender to the dictates of a documentary evidence on a given issue, since the latter is superior and more reliable, and one cannot use oral deposition to vary what was agreed upon in a written agreement.

Section 128(1) of the Act provides the general rule thus:

> When any judgment of the court or any other judicial or official proceeding, contract or any grant or other disposition of property has been reduced to the form of a document or series of documents, no evidence may be given of such judgment or proceeding or of the terms of such contract, grant or disposition of property except the document itself, or secondary evidence of its content in cases in which secondary evidence is admissible under the Act; nor the contents of any such document be contradicted , altered, or added to or varied by oral evidence.[93]

The courts have been able to decide that where there is documentary evidence showing the sale of land, oral evidence to prove it is inadmissible.[94] The Supreme Court in the recent case of *Ashakacem Plc* v. *Asharatul Mubashurun Investment Ltd*[95] applied this rule to hold that the contracts of supply of Low Pour Fuel Oil (LPFO) having been reduced into writing no oral evidence can be led to add or vary it. It was held that it is now trite law that oral evidence is inadmissible either to add to or subtract from the contents of a document as a document speaks for itself with the result that parties cannot give evidence contrary to its contents. However, where the subject matter of a grant is inadequately described or identified, extrinsic evidence is allowed to be led to make it certain. It must appear possible that the subject matter can be made certain and in addition evidence must actually be led to make it certain. This is the decision of the court in *Agba & Ors* v. *Jubu*.[96]

Section 128(2) of the Evidence Act provides that oral evidence of a transaction is not excluded by the fact that a documentary memorandum of it was made, if such memorandum was not intended to have legal effect as a contract, grant or disposition of property.

---

[93] See also *Edeh* v. *Mac-Tino (Nig) Ltd* (Supra). See the following: *Ayemnwenre* v. *Evbuomwan* (2019) LPELR -47213(CA); *Mohammed & Ors.* v. *Umoru* (2019) LPELR-47499 (CA) and *Ambursa* v. *Ahmed & Ors.* (2018) LPELR-46419(CA).

[94] See *Akanu & Anor* v. *Osisioma Local Government* (Supra).

[95] (2019) LPELR-46541 (SC) P. 14, para. E.

[96] (2019) LPELR-47189 (CA) Pp. 100-101, Paras. G-A.

In the same vein, under section 128(3) of the Evidence Act, oral evidence of the existence of a legal relationship is not excluded by the fact that it has been created by a document when the fact to be proved is the existence of the relationship itself, and not the terms on which it was established or is carried on. Subsections 128(2) and (3) represent exceptions to the general rule that oral evidence will not be allowed to prove or vary the content of a document. This can best be described as the inter-connectivity of oral evidence and documentary evidence.

The court in *Eze* v. *State*[97] posited that where documentary evidence supports oral evidence, oral evidence becomes more credible. Thus, documentary evidence should be used as a hanger from which to assess oral evidence.

Another relationship between documentary evidence and oral evidence is found in cases where there is conflict in affidavit evidence. The court held in *APC & Anor* v. *Agoda & Anor*[98] that where there is a conflict in affidavit evidence, oral testimony will be called in aids to resolve it. It is trite law that where a judge is faced with an affidavit that is irreconcilably in conflict, the judge can resolve same by calling for oral evidence or by resorting to authentic documentary evidence which supports one of the affidavits in conflict with another.[99] It is also notable that where there is documentary evidence before the court, the court can *suo motu* resolve such conflicting evidence by resorting to the document present.[100] Affidavit evidence is treated in detail in Chapter Twenty-Two.

---

[97](2018) LPELR-43715(SC) P. 13, para. A.

[98](2019) LPELR-47174(CA) P.39, para. G.

[99] *Collins Commermex Nigeria Ltd & Anor.* v. *Skye Bank PLc* (2019) LPELR-46892(CA).

[100] *Collins Commermex Nigeria Ltd & Anor.* v. *Skye Bank PLc* (ibid.).

Chapter 21

PRIMARY AND SECONDARY DOCUMENTARY EVIDENCE

A. Primary documentary evidence

The law is trite that documents shall be proved by primary evidence except in the cases where secondary evidence is permissible.[1] The court was very emphatic when it held in *Hassan* v. *Vixen Ent. (Nig) Ltd & Anor*[2] that the contents of documents must be proved either by primary or secondary evidence. This is in agreement with the provision of the Evidence Act which states in section 85 that the contents of documents may be proved either by primary or secondary evidence. It is also the position of the law in the Supreme Court case of *Udo* v. *State*,[3] that the best evidence of the contents of a document is the document itself produced for the inspection of the Court; this is the primary documentary evidence.

The Evidence Act listed the categories of what qualifies as primary evidence. By virtue of section 86 of the Evidence Act 2011, the term primary evidence means the document itself produced for the inspection of the court.[4] Where a document has been executed in several parts, such part shall be primary evidence of the document.[5] It is the law that where a document has been executed in counter parts, each counterpart being executed by one or some of the parties only, each counterpart shall be primary evidence as against the parties executing it.[6] Where a number of documents have all been made by one uniform process, as in the case of printing, lithography, photography, computer or electronic or mechanical process, such shall be primary evidence of the contents of the rest, but where they are all copies of

---

[1] Section 88 of the Evidence Act.

[2] (2015) LPELR-40357(CA).

[3] (2016) LPELR-40721(SC) P. 12, paras. B. See also *PDP & Anor* v. *Kawuwa & Ors* (2015) LPELR-26044 (CA)

[4] Section 86(1) of the Evidence Act.

[5] Section 86(2) of the Evidence Act; See also *Eneji* v. *State* (2013) LPELR-20393(CA).

[6] Section 86(3) of the Act. *Ngadiukwu* v. *Moghalu & Ors* (2014) LPELR-24366(CA).

a common original, they shall not be primary evidence of the contents of the original.[7]

Extrapolating from the foregoing provisions of the law, primary evidence means the document itself produced for the inspection of the court. By the language of section 86(1) of the Evidence Act, this is the original document tendered or produced as evidence. Any other genre of evidence other than the original in that natural state is not primary evidence and same is liable to be discountenanced except for reason coming under section 89 of the Evidence Act where secondary evidence is allowed.

The court in *Ikpeazu* v. *Ogah & Ors*[8] held that in the adversarial system of jurisprudence, proof of a content of a document must be by the document itself. In the same breath, the court in *Alarufe & Ors* v. *Olabayo & Ors* ,[9] while relying on *Aja* v. *Odin*[10] held that by virtue of the provision of section 86(4) of the Evidence Act 2011, a number of documents made by one uniform process, as in the case of printing' lithography, photography, computer or other electronic or mechanical process, each shall be primary evidence of the contents of the rest; but where they are all copies of a common original, they shall not be primary evidence of the contents of the original. Thus, carbon copies of receipts as in the case of Exhibits P1 to P10 made by the same mechanical process were held to be primary evidence of the contents of the rest.

In *Idi* v. *State,*[11] the apex court while rejecting the argument of the appellant's counsel on a misconceived assertion held thus:

> In this case, the learned appellant's counsel made copious reference to Sections 85 , 86(1) , 88 , 89 (1)(e) & (f) , 90(1)(c) and 102(a)(iii) of the Evidence Act to submit that Exhibit B, a medical report made by the Pw.4, was inadmissible in its original form. The court while rejecting such erroneous submission and misconception of the law held that there seems some erroneous impression, or misconception, that Evidence Act outlaws the production of the original of a public document. Section 88 of Act is permissive of secondary evidence of the contents of a document only when the primary evidence is not available. In any case, primary evidence is not outlawed by Section 88 of the Act. Section 89(e) of Act does not

[7] Section 86(4) of the Evidence Act.
[8] (2016) LPELR-40843 (CA) P.49, para. E.
[9] (2015) LPELR-25816 (CA) P.27, paras.B-D.
[10] (2011) 5 NWLR (1241) 531, 532.
[11] (2017) LPELR-42587 (SC) Pp. 40-41, paras. F-E.

categorically say that the only admissible public document is the secondary evidence of it.

In our adversarial system, a party must prove his case on the strength of primary documentary evidence (where he intends to prove contents of a document) if he wishes the court to give judgment in his favour. Where the production of the primary evidence is not practicable, he must fall back to the helping hands of section 89 of the Act where secondary evidence relating to such document can be tolerated.

B. Secondary Evidence

This is like a default provision on proving contents of document where primary evidence is not available. By reason of the provision of Section 88 of the Evidence Act, a litigant is required to prove the contents of his documents by primary evidence only except in circumstances provided for under section 89 of the same Act or where primary evidence is not available. This provision opened the vista for secondary evidence. Thus, resort cannot be had to secondary evidence at the first instance without necessary compliance with the procedure for the admissibility of such secondary evidence as a pre-condition. Secondary evidence comes in handy only where proper foundation has been laid as to why it is not possible for the litigant to prove his case by primary evidence.

The law gave a statutory imprimatur to this provision under section 89 of the Evidence Act. It provides that secondary evidence may be given of the existence, condition or contents of a document when:

(a) the original is shown or appear to be in the possession or power -

(i) of the person against whom the document is sought to be proved; or

(ii) of any person legally bound to produce it and when after the notice mentioned in section 91 such person does not produce it;

(b) the existence, condition or contents of the original have been proved to be admitted in writing by the person against whom it is proved or by his representative in interest;

(c) the original has been destroyed or lost and in the latter case all possible search has been made for it;

(d) the original is of such a nature as not to be easily movable;

(e) the original is a public document within the meaning of section 102;

(f) The original is a document of which a certified copy is permitted by this Act or by any other law in force in Nigeria, to be given in evidence;

It is crystal clear from the above provision that court does not admit secondary evidence of a document as a matter of course. A party who seeks to rely on such secondary evidence does not simply tell the court that "I have a secondary evidence on which I seek to rely on." A proper foundation must be laid as to the unavailability of the primary document which is the original. This is where section 89 of the Act comes to aid wherein among other things, the party relying on the secondary evidence either prove that the original is in the possession of the adverse party or the original has been destroyed or lost and all possible search has been made for it, etc.[12] If the original is in the custody of the adverse party, the person seeking to rely on secondary evidence, must first put that other party on notice to produce the original. It is only then can secondary evidence be resorted to in the event of failure by that other party to produce the original. Section 85 of the Evidence Act is not a licence for the admissibility of such secondary evidence in the face of Section 88 of the Evidence Act. This evidentiary rule gained judicial blessing, recognition and attention in *Tamkeyar* v. *Bussa & Ors.*[13]

The Act went further to list what constitutes secondary evidence under section 87 of the Act.[14] It includes: (a) Certified copies given under the provision hereafter contained in this Act; (b) Copies made from the original by mechanical or electronic process which in themselves ensure the accuracy of the copy, and copies compared with such copies; (c) Copies made from or compared with the original; (d) Counterparts of documents as against the parties who did not execute them and (e) Oral accounts of the contents of a document given by some person who has himself seen it.

Section 87 of the Evidence Act reveals types of secondary evidence that are admissible which is already stated above. It is pertinent to note that the only document of which certified copies are permitted by the Act are public documents as provided in section 104(1) of the Act.[15]

The Evidence Act does not accept all forms of secondary evidence in proof of a document. The law in clear terms provided for certain categories of secondary documentary evidence which may be received in evidence in lieu of the original documents listed under section 89 of the Act. Where the original document is not present, the law will not therefore allow for the

---

[12] See section 89 of the Evidence Act.
[13](2017) LPELR-42987 (CA).
[14]Evidence Act 2011, Section 87(1) (a) (b) (c) (d) and (e).
[15] See the recent Supreme Court decision of *Sanmi* v. *State* (2019) LPELR-47418(SC) P.31, para D.

admissibility of any other type of secondary evidence except as authorized by law.

This submission finds statutory flavour in section 90 of the Evidence Act, 2011, which provides that:

> (1) The secondary evidence admissible in respect of the original document referred to in the several paragraphs of section 89 is as follows:
>
> (a) In paragraphs (a), (c) and (d), any secondary evidence of the contents of the document is admissible;
>
> (b) In paragraph (b), the written admission is admissible;
>
> (c) In paragraph (c) and (f), a certified copy of the document, but no other secondary evidence is admissible;
>
> (d) in paragraph (g), evidence maybe given as to the general result of the document by any person who has examined them and who is skilled in the examination of such documents; and
>
> (e) in paragraph (h), the copies cannot be received as evidence unless it is first proved that –
>
> (i) the book in which the entries copied were made was at the time of making one of the ordinary books of the bank;
>
> (ii) the entry was made in the usual and ordinary course of business;
>
> (iii) the book is in the control and custody of the Bank, which proof may be given orally or by affidavit by an officer of the bank; and
>
> (iv) the copy has been examined with the original entry and is correct, which proof must be given by some person who has examined the copy with the original entry, and may be given orally or by affidavit.

In conclusion, some sections of the Evidence Act cannot be read in isolation without making reference to other sections. Section 89 of the Act should be read in conjunction with section 90 of the Act; failure to do so, the intendment of the Act may be defeated.

C Notice to produce

The very essence of notice to produce under section 91 of the Act is to create a leeway for a person proposing to give secondary evidence under section 89(a) of the Act as the person upon whom the notice is given may not necessarily produce it. It is primarily for the party seeking to rely on such primary document to give secondary evidence of it. One can safely say that it can be likened to laying of foundation for the admissibility of such secondary evidence. The law provides that secondary evidence of the contents of the documents referred to in section 89(a) shall not be given unless the party proposing to give such secondary evidence has previously given to the party in whose possession or power the document is, or to a legal practitioner employed by such party, such notice to produce it as is prescribed by law; and if no notice to produce is prescribed by law then such notice as the court considers reasonable in the circumstances of the case.[16]

The purpose and essence of notice to produce is not to give the party served the notice an opportunity to prepare a defence to it, but it is to clear the way for the person serving, so that, he can give secondary evidence of it.[17] The gravamen of service of Notice to Produce and the consequences of non-response to such service was aptly captured in the recent case of *Ibironke* v. *MTN*.[18] In this case, the Court of Appeal while citing Adeleke JCA in *Anoka* v. *Yunusa*[19] held thus:

> On the issue of notice to produce, I have to say that a party on whom notice to produce is served is not under any obligation to produce the document. The service of the notice to produce only entitles the party serving the notice to adduce secondary evidence of the document in question by virtue of Section 98 of the Evidence Act.
>
> In other words, the service of a notice to produce a document does not relieve the person serving the notice of the burden of producing the document if he can or of proving its contents. Consequently the non-response to a notice to produce will not cause the Court to invoke the presumption of withholding of evidence under Section 149(d) [sic][20] of the Evidence Act against the defaulting party.

It should be recalled that among other things that section 167(d) of the Act provided for, it states that the court may presume that evidence which could be and is not produced would, if produced, be unfavourable to the person who withholds it. This provision is not for the party issuing notice to produce to explore as he cannot establish his case on the failure, neglect or refusal of the adverse party to produce such document. It is an established

---

[16] Section 91 of the Evidence Act. See also *Onwuzuruike* v. *Edoziem & Ors.* (2016) LPELR-26056 (SC).
[17] Aguda *op. cit.*, page 205.
[18] (2019) LPELR-47483(CA) P. 37, paras. B-E.
[19] (2008) LPELR-3663 (CA).
[20] This should read section 167(d) of the Evidence Act 2011.

principle of law settled beyond conjecture that a party must win his case on the strength of his case and not on the weakness of the defence as the court has outlived the era of technicality. The Court of Appeal in another recent case of *Jurassic Communications (Nig) Ltd* v. *Adeyeye*[21] where the Respondent complained that he served notice to produce on the Appellant to produce ledger in its possession but the Appellant failed to produce same at the trial Court. The court, *inter alia,* held that it is trite law that where a party on whom a notice to produce is served fails to produce document, it is the duty of the party serving the notice to adduce secondary evidence of the document in question. Since the Respondent did not adduce secondary evidence of the alleged Ledgers, Section 167(d) of the Evidence Act 2011 cannot be invoked. After all it was the Respondent who asserts the existence of the ledger and the burden is on him to prove same.

Having established the intendment of the spirit and the provision of section 91 of the Act on notice to produce, it should be noted however that this provision is not bereft of exceptions. In other words, there are circumstances where secondary evidence of a document under section 89(a) can be admissible without service of notice to produce. There is a caveat or a proviso to the applicability of this section under review.[22] It went further to state that provided such notice shall not be required in order to render secondary evidence admissible in any of the following cases, or in any other case in which the court thinks fit to dispense with it-

a. when the document to be proved is itself a notice;
b. when, from the nature of the case, the adverse party must know that he will be required to produce it;
c. when it appears or is proved that the adverse party has obtained possession of the original by fraud or force;
d. when the adverse party or his agent has the original in court;
e. when the adverse party or his agent has admitted the loss of the document.

This exception gained judicial imprimatur in *The Registered Trustees of Abosso Apostolic Faith Church of Jesus Christ* v. *NNA & Ors*[23] where the court held thus:

---

[21](2019) LPELR-46498(CA) P. 31, paras. B-F; see also *Nweke* v. *State* (2017)15 NWLR (Pt. 1587) 120 at 140 paras B-C.
[22] See the proviso to section 91 of the Act.
[23] (2014) LPELR-22826 (CA) Pp.11-12, paras.C-C.

> Learned counsel for the Respondents had argued vigorously that for secondary evidence of a document to be admissible in evidence there must be proof that notice to produce the original was given to the adverse party. The learned trial judge also in her ruling towed this line of reasoning. However, I do not subscribe to that line of thought. I am fortified in this regard by the provision of Section 91 of the Evidence Act, 2011 where instances when notice can be dispensed with were aptly stated. Specifically, Subsection b of Section 91 clearly provides: "when from the nature of the case, the adverse party must know that he will be required to produce it." In the instant case, the existence or contents of the letter of suspension is not in dispute. From the pleadings the Respondents are only disputing the powers of the Appellant through the bishop to suspend them. In essence, the Respondents are merely disputing their suspension which came into effect via copies of the letters sent to them. The Respondents are well aware that they were never served with any original of the suspension letters, only copies. It is therefore obvious that where the original of the secondary document is not alleged or believed to be in custody of the adverse party as in this case, then notice to produce same cannot be given to them as it would serve no useful purpose since the Respondents obviously cannot produce what they do not have. Under the circumstance, notice to produce can safely be dispensed with since proper foundation had already been laid for its admissibility.

Thus, a party is only to be served a notice to produce a document only if the original document is in his possession or power as a man cannot give what he does not have as out of nothing, nothing flows. This is expressed in the Latin maxim *ex nihilo nihil fit.* As you cannot put something on nothing and expect it to stand.[24] This will amount to an effort in futility as the law only deals with serious live issue and does not have time for frivolities or hypothetical questions.[25]

A person who is not a party to the cause or matter cannot be served with a notice to produce because this procedure relates only to parties.[26] It is also the law that when a party calls for a document which he has given the other party notice to produce, and such document is produced and inspected by the party calling for its production, he is bound to give it as evidence if the party producing it requires him to do so.[27] Where the party calling for its

---

[24] See the immortal dictum of Lord Denning in *Macfoy* v. *UAC* (1961) 3 All ER 1169.
[25] *Uniben* v. *Efionayi & Ors* (2019) LPELR-46737(CA).
[26] *Kossen* v. *Savannah Bank Ltd* (1995) 12 SCNJ pg. 29.
[27] Section 244 of the Evidence Act.

production refuses to tender same in evidence upon inspection, it is submitted that such failure, refusal or neglect to produce it when called upon can raise the presumption of withholding evidence under section 167(d) of the Evidence Act. However, where a party refuses to produce a document which he has had notice to produce, the same party who refused to produce the document cannot afterwards use the document as evidence without the consent of the other party or the order of the court.[28]

D. Proof that bank has made returns or been duly licensed

The Act also made copious provisions on some special secondary evidence to be admitted in proof that a bank has made returns or that it has been duly licensed.

Section 92 of the Act provides thus:

> (1) The fact of any bank having duly made a return to the Central Bank, the Nigerian Deposit Insurance Corporation or Federal Inland Revenue Service may be proved in any legal proceeding by the production of a copy of its return verified by the affidavit of an officer of the bank, or by the production of a copy of a copy of a Newspaper purporting to contain a copy of such return published by the Central Bank, Nigerian Deposit Insurance Corporation or the Federal Inland Revenue Service, as the case may be.
>
> (2) The fact of any bank having been licensed under the Banks and other Financial Institutions Act may be proved by the production of a certificate by an officer of the bank that it has been duly licensed under the Act.

Basically, section 92(3) is the interpretation subsection. It defined major institutions used in the provision. For the purpose of this section, "Central bank" means the Central Bank of Nigeria established by the Central Bank of Nigeria Act, 2007. "Federal Inland Revenue Service" means the Federal Inland Revenue Services Act 2007 and "Nigerian Deposit Insurance Corporation" means the Nigerian Deposit Insurance Corporation established by the Nigerian Deposit Insurance Corporation Act.

---

[28] Section 245 of the Evidence Act.

Chapter 22

AFFIDAVIT EVIDENCE

A. Introduction

It is a matter of domestic knowledge that there is no explicit definition of affidavit in the Evidence Act, even in the repealed Evidence Act of 2004 which was in operation before Evidence Act 2011, which also followed the same trend of failure to provide a definition of affidavit even in the interpretation section.[1]

Nevertheless, etymologically speaking, the word "affidavit" is derived from the Latin word "*affidare*" which at common law means "to swear faith to" or "to pledge one's faith or do fealty by making an oath.[2] In the same view, affidavit can simply be defined as a court process in writing deposing to facts within the knowledge of the deponent usually made under oath or affirmation. In *Anyaeche & Anor* v. *Nduka,*[3] the Court of Appeal while quoting erudite Justice Tobi, JCA *(*as he then was OBM*) in Ojukwu* v. *Onyeabor*[4] defined affidavit as a documentary evidence which the court can admit in the absence of any unchallenged evidence. In the same vein, in a more recent decision of the Court of Appeal in *Princess* v. *Governor of Ogun State & Ors,*[5] the court defined affidavit thus:

> Generally, an Affidavit has been judicially defined as a statement of fact which the maker or deponent swears on oath to be true to the best of his knowledge, information or belief.

An affidavit is also a written or printed declaration or statement of facts made voluntarily and confirmed by the oaths or affirmation of the party making it, taken before a person having authority to administer such oath or

---

[1] Section 258 of the Act.

[2] *Maraya Plastics Ind. Ltd* v. *Inland Bank of Nigeria Plc.* (2002) FWLR (Pt. 120) 1732 at 1737 per Omage, JCA.

[3](2017) LPELR-42459(CA) P.27, Para. D-E.

[4] (1991) 7 NWLR (pt. 2013) 286.

[5] (2018) LPELR-44986 (CA) p. 37, para. F.

affirmation.[6] The meaning of affidavit gained judicial attention in the Supreme Court decision in *Josien Holdings Ltd* v. *Lornamead*[7] as thus:

> Statement of facts which the maker or deponent swears or affirms to be true to the best of his knowledge or which are based on information which he believes to be true.

Section 107 of the Evidence Act 2011 provides that a court may in any civil proceedings make an order at any stage of such proceeding directing that specified facts may be proved at the trial by affidavit with or without the attendance of the deponent for cross-examination, provided that where a party desires the attendance of such deponent for cross-examination, the court shall require his attendance for that purpose where this would not result in unjustifiable delay or expense.

From the provision above, it is deducible that the Act contemplates that an affidavit should be used only in civil proceedings. However, in practice, an affidavit can also be used in interim or interlocutory applications such as application for bail in criminal proceedings. The proviso has an obligatory tone as it used "the court shall" oblige attendance of a deponent if the attendance is so desired for the purposes of cross-examination. It thus suffices to mean that where a party desires the attendance of such a deponent, he may apply to the court and the court *shall* grant the application unless doing so may lead to unjustifiable delay or expenses.[8]

From the present position of the law, it is submitted that a party to a suit is at liberty to request to be given an opportunity to cross-examine a deponent and the trial court is under a mandatory duty to oblige the request. Any unreasonable refusal of the trial court to allow either an opportunity to cross-examine a deponent or to lead oral evidence to clear material conflicts in an affidavit amounts to denial of fair hearing on the part of the party that has made the application.[9] The Act further provides that before an affidavit is used in court for any purpose, the original shall be filed in court, and the original or an office copy shall alone be recognized and admissible in court.[10] This section is explicit that secondary documentary evidence of an affidavit is not admissible in court as only the original or an office copy is

---

[6] The Oath Act, Cap. 01 LFN 2004.

[7] (1995) 26 LRCN 1.

[8] See the recent Supreme Court decision in *FRN* v. *Maishanu & Ors* (2019) LPELR-46380 (SC) p.30 para. A.

[9] See *Ebon* v. *Ikpe* (2002) 17 NWLR (pt. 797) 504.

[10] Section 108 of the Act.

permissible. An affidavit may be sworn or affirmed before a commissioner for Oaths usually the Registrar of court, or a Notary Public. An affidavit may be admissible in court if it is sworn in Nigeria Embassy, High commission or consulate in a foreign country. An affidavit sworn before any judge, officer or other person duly authorized to take affidavits in Nigeria may be used in the court in all case where affidavits are admissible. This is the statutory provision of section 109 of the Act.

Under section 110 of the Act, it provides thus:

> Any affidavit sworn in any country other than Nigeria before-
>
> (a) a judge or magistrate being authenticated by the official seal of the court to which he is attached, or by a notary public; or
>
> (b) the duly authorized officer in the Nigerian Embassy, High Commission or Consulate in that country may be used in court in all cases where affidavits are admissible.

The fact that an affidavit purports to have been sworn in the manner prescribed under the law shall be a prima facie evidence of: (a) the seal or signature, as the case maybe, of any such court, judge, magistrate or other officer or person mentioned in, or appended or subscribed to, any such affidavit; and (b) the authority of such court, judge, magistrate or other officer or person to administer oaths although it is a rebuttable presumption.[11] This rebuttable presumption makes it unnecessary to prove the signature or seal of a person before whom an affidavit is sworn or that has authority to take oaths as it attracts presumption of regularity. Conversely, it is clearly spelt out in section 112 of the Evidence Act that an affidavit shall not be admitted which is proved to have been sworn before a person on whose behalf the same is offered, or before his legal practitioner. This is an important mandatory restriction on the calibre or type of persons who may legally receive an affidavit and the law frowns at its contravention to the detriment of the offending party.[12]

B. What an Affidavit Should or Should Not Contain

As defined earlier, an affidavit is a statement of facts which the maker or deponent swears or affirms to be true to the best of his knowledge or which are based on information which he believes to be true.[13] The question then

[11] Section 111 of the Act.
[12] See *Maraya Plastic Industries Ltd* v. *inland Bank of Nigeria Plc* (2002) FWLR (Pt 120) 1732.
[13] *Josien Holdings Ltd* v. *Lornamead* (*supra*).

is: what should or should not be contained in an affidavit? The question was answered with judicial insight in *Enwo-Igariwey & Anor* v. *Anozie & Ors*[14] where the court in its wisdom categorically stated without mincing words that by virtue of the provision of section 115(1) and (2) of Evidence Act 2011, an affidavit shall contain only statements of facts and circumstances derived from the personal knowledge of the deponent or from information which he (deponent) believes to be true. Such deposition shall therefore not contain extraneous matters such as objections, prayers, or legal arguments or conclusions.[15] In determining whether an affidavit contains an extraneous matter, objection, prayer or legal argument, the Court of appeal in the recent case of *Princess* v. *Governor of Ogun State & Ors*[16] while relying on the earlier decision of *Bamaiyi* v. *State*[17] posited in its wisdom thus:

> In the case *of Bamaiyi* v. *State & Ors.* (*supra*), the Supreme Court, per Uwaifo, JSC stipulated the test for determining whether an affidavit contains extraneous matter as follows: I think the legal position is clear, that in any affidavit used in the Court, the law requires, as provided in Sections 86 and 87 of the Evidence Act (now section 115 & 117 of Evidence Act 2011), that it shall contain only a Statement of facts and circumstances derived from the personal knowledge of the deponent, or from information which he believes to be true, and shall not contain extraneous matter by way of objection, or prayer, or legal argument or conclusion. The problem is sometimes how to discern any particular extraneous matter. The test for doing this, in my view, is to examine each of the paragraphs deposed to in the affidavit to ascertain whether it is fit only as a submission which counsel ought to urge upon the Court. If it is, then it is likely to be either an objection or legal argument which ought to be pressed in oral argument, or it may be a conclusion upon an issue which ought to be left to the discretion of the Court either to make a finding or to reach a decision upon through its process of reasoning. But if it is in the form of evidence which a witness may be entitled to place before the Court in his testimony on oath and is legally receivable to prove or disprove some fact in dispute, then it qualifies as a Statement of facts and circumstances which may be deposed to in an Affidavit.

When a person deposes to his belief in any matter of fact, and his belief is derived from any source other than his own personal knowledge, he shall set

---

[14](2018) LPELR-45766 (CA) P.7, paras. B-C.

[15] Relying on *Bamaiyi* v. *State* (2001) 8 NWLR (Pt. 715) p. 222, para G-H.

[16] *Supra* @ pp. 39-40 paras C-D.

[17] *Supra.*

forth explicitly the facts and circumstances forming the ground of his belief.[18]

Subsection 4 of section 115 further provides that when such belief is derived from information received from another person, the name of his informant shall be stated and reasonable particulars shall be given respecting the informant, the time, place and circumstance of the information. Any averment in an affidavit that is incongruous with this settled rules will suffer the danger of being struck out as it amounts to inadmissible hearsay. In *Jimoh* v. *Hon. Minister Federal Capital Territory & Ors,* the apex court per EKO JSC embarked on a judicial insight on this subject matter in the following words:

> A deponent of an affidavit in any proceeding before a Court of law is a witness in the matter. Section 115(1) of the Evidence Act, 2011 enjoins the deponent as a witness, to depose to facts in an affidavit that "either of his own personal knowledge or from information which he believes to be true". It is not enough to set out in the preamble paragraphs of an affidavit for the deponent to restate the facts that he has been authorized either by his principal or employer, and the client to make the affidavit; and that he derived the facts averred in the affidavit in the course of his employment and/or from his personal knowledge and/or information generally. For every assertion in a specific averment [sic) the deponent, consistent with Section 115 (1), (3) & (4) of the Evidence Act, must disclose with particulars his source of information and belief. The counter-affidavit of Charles Jibuaku, Esq., a Legal Practitioner, is replete with obvious hearsay and unverifiable facts...The source of this information on which the weighty allegation is predicated remains a matter for conjecture.[19]

As earlier stated, in as much as the court may permit an affidavit to be used notwithstanding that it is defective in form if the court is satisfied that it has been sworn before a person duly authorised, nevertheless, the court shall not admit an affidavit which has been sworn before a person on whose behalf the same has been offered, or before his legal practitioner or before a partner or clerk of his legal practitioner as this offends the letters, spirit and provisions of the Evidence Act.[20]

---

[18] Section 115 (3) of the Act. See also *Gumau* v. *Abdullahi* (2017) LPELR-43421(CA).

[19](2018) LPELR-46329 (SC) pp. 10-11, paras. A-C.

[20] Section 112 of the Act.

A deponent is not allowed to correct his defective affidavit in open court, because it is an oath that was not taken before the judge but before the commissioner for Oaths.[21] This is so because Section 118 of the Act provides explicitly that the person before whom an affidavit is taken shall not allow it, when sworn, to be altered in any manner without being re-sworn; and may refuse to allow an altered affidavit to be re-sworn and require instead of a fresh affidavit. An affidavit that offends the provision of the Evidence Act will be struck out and amounts to nothing. This was the decision in *Sami* v. *APC & Ors.*[22] The court in this case went further to posit thus:

> I am in total agreement with the submission of the appellants counsel that they are legal conclusion and argument and to that extent offensive to section 115(2) of the Evidence Act. These paragraphs of the counter-affidavit being so offensive and poisonous have also contaminated the other paragraphs which have also become as poisonous as the offensive paragraphs rendering the entire counter-affidavit liable to be struck out as the Court cannot and should not make any attempt to pick and choose the contaminant from the contaminated.

A defective or erroneous affidavit may be amended and re-sworn by leave of the court, on such terms to time, costs or otherwise as seem reasonable.[23]

C. Mandatory Provision in Taking Affidavit

It is settled like the rock of Gibraltar under the Evidence Act what may be considered an irreducible minimum and mandatory guideline on the forms an affidavit used in a case or matter must take. Section 117 of the Act is very clear and unequivocal on this point. It provides thus:

> (1) Every affidavit taken in a cause or matter shall-
>
> (a) Be headed in the court and in the cause or matter;
>
> (b) State the full name, trade or profession, residence and nationality of the deponent and
>
> (c) Be in the first person, and divided into convenient paragraphs numbered consecutively.
>
> (2) Any erasure, interlineations or alteration made before the affidavit is sworn, shall be attested by the person before whom it is taken who shall

---

[21] *Agbakoba* v. *DSSS* (1993) 7 NWLR (Pt. 305) 353.
[22] (2019) LPELR-48045 (CA) P. 24, paras. A-C.
[23] See section 114 of the Act.

> affix his signature or initial in the margin immediately opposite to the interlineations, alteration or erasure.
>
> (3) Where an affidavit proposed to be sworn is illegible or difficult to read, or is in the judgment of the person before whom it is taken so written as to facilitate fraudulent alteration, he may refuse to swear the deponent, and require the affidavit to be re-written in an unobjectionable manner.
>
> (4) An affidavit when sworn shall be signed by the deponent or if he cannot write or is blind, marked by him personally with his mark in the presence of the person before whom it is taken.[24]

Among other things, one observation of semantic display is visible in the various subsections. It is explicit that the use of the word "shall" in conspicuous positions in subsection (1), (2) and (4) are in contra opposition to the word "may" as used in subsection (3) of section 117 of the Act quoted above. It then goes to say that the provisions of section 117(1) and (2) are mandatory and leave the courts with no discretion in the matter.

The principle was judicially recognized in *Babatope &* v. *Sadiku & Anor*[25] where the Court of Appeal held that the word "shall" has received countless pronouncements of the Apex Court and this Court as to its interpretation when used in an enactment or rules of Court. It is almost in all cases, interpreted as denoting a command. It is never a word that gives room for deviation or option. It requires strict compliance since it is obligatory.

Another point worthy of note is section 118 of the Act which makes another obligatory provision for altered affidavit. It provides thus:

> The person before whom an affidavit is taken shall not allow it, when sworn, to be altered in any manner without being re-sworn; and may refuse to allow an altered affidavit to be re-sworn and require instead a fresh affidavit.

After an affidavit has been sworn, it offends the very thread and fabrics of section 118 of the Act to alter same in any way without been re-sworn. It is clear on the surface of the Act. Furthermore, section 114 of the Act provides for amendment and re-swearing of affidavit. It provides that a defective or erroneous affidavit may be amended and re-sworn by leave of the court, on such terms as to time, costs or otherwise as seen reasonable. Where a court directs that a defective affidavit be amended or re-sworn, it follows that the

---

[24] An unsigned affidavit is invalid. See *Chevron Nig Ltd* v. *Enioye* (2005) All FWLR (Pt. 265) 1168.

[25](2017) LPELR-41966 (CA) P. 15, paras. D-E.

deponent of the defective affidavit should amend or re-swear fresh affidavit before the person whom an affidavit is taken and not otherwise. In *Agbakoba* v. *Director State Security Service.*[26] The court of appeal held that a deponent cannot be allowed to correct his defective affidavit in open court because, it is an oath that was not taken before the judge but before a commissioner for oaths. The case of *Afrijet Airlines Ltd* v. *Elias & Anor*[27] is also in support of this principle though the court went further to add that the provision applies where the deponent makes the alteration and not when the alteration was made by the court. In the same vein, counsel cannot by the best of eloquence and advocacy, correct a defective affidavit. Rather, a further and better affidavit should be filed to highlight and correct the error.[28]

The illiterate or blind deponents were not also left out in the contemplation of the law vis-à-vis their ability to depose to an affidavit. Under section 119 of the Act, it stated in clear terms that:

> (1) Where the deponent is illiterate or blind, the affidavit shall state that facts and shall be accompanied with a jurat.
>
> (2) The jurat shall-
>
> (a) Be written without interlinations, alteration or erasure immediately at the foot of the affidavit and towards the left side of the paper, and shall be signed by the person before whom it is taken;
>
> (b) State the date of the swearing and the place where it is sworn,
>
> (c) State that the affidavit was sworn before the person taking the same; and
>
> (d) Where the deponent is illiterate or blind, state such fact and shall state that the affidavit was read over to such illiterate or blind deponent or translated into his own language (in the case of a deponent not having sufficient knowledge of English), and that he appeared to understand it.
>
> (3) Where the deponent mark instead of signing, the jurat shall state that fact, and that the mark was made in the presence of the person before whom it is taken.
>
> (4) Where two or more persons join in making an affidavit, their several names shall be written in the jurat and it shall appear by the jurat that

---

[26] (1993) 7 NWLR (Pt. 305) 353.
[27] (2019) LPELR-47304 (CA).
[28] *Daladi* v. *Ali & Ors* (2014) LPELR-23595 (CA) P.31 para. B.

> each of them has been sworn to the truth of the several matters stated by him in the affidavit.
>
> (5) If the jurat has been added and signed on an altered affidavit, the person before whom it is taken shall add a new jurat on the affidavit being re-sworn and in the new jurat, he shall mention the alteration.

D. Affidavit May Be By Declaration or Affirmation

It is expedient and pertinent to highlight that it is not the law that an affidavit must be taken only on oath. Thus, an affidavit may be by an affirmation or declaration without oath. Reason may be on religious grounds or want of religious belief which are constitutionally guaranteed or immature age which ought not, in the opinion of the person taking the declaration to be on oath subject however to some conditions precedent being satisfied.

This principle of law is graphically provided for in section 120 of the Evidence Act as follows:

> The person before whom an affidavit may be taken may take without oath the declaration of any person who-
>
> (a) affirms that the taking of any oath whatsoever is, according to his religious belief unlawful; or
>
> (b) by reason of immature age or want of religious belief, ought not, in the opinion of the person taking the declaration to be admitted to make a sworn affidavit.
>
> (2) The person taking the declaration shall record in the attestation, the reason of such declaration being taken without oath.

The reason for the provision of section 120 of the Evidence Act providing that a person may declare some facts in an affidavit without oath can be likened to the same reasons for the exceptions to the general principle of law embedded in section 205 of the Evidence Act that oral evidence is to be on oath or affirmation.[29] These exceptions are found in sections 208 and 209(1) of the Act. Specifically, 208 of the Act provides that any court may on any occasion, if it deems it just and expedient, receive the evidence, though not given upon oath, of any person declaring that the taking of any oath whatsoever is according to his religious belief unlawful, or who, by reason of want of religious belief ought not, in the opinion of the court, to be admitted

---

[29] N.O, Obiaraeri, *op. cit.*, page 317.

to give evidence upon oath. The fact that in any case evidence not given upon oath has been received and the reasons for the reception of such evidence shall be recorded in the minutes of the proceeding.[30] It should be stressed at this point that applying the golden rule of canon of statutory interpretation, the intention of the law here is that relevant and admissible evidence of an adult witness should flow in the court unimpeded or unhindered by reason of presence or absence of religious belief. In the same vein, section 209(1) of the Act provides that a child who has not attained the age of fourteen years shall not be sworn and shall give evidence otherwise than on oath or affirmation. This is another circumstance where an affidavit can be by affirmation or declaration other than on oath. An affidavit should be precise, elegantly worded and not vague, verbose or a complete distortion of facts. It is commendable that the concluding part of an affidavit should be clear as to the fact whether it is on oath or an affirmation. The concluding part of an affidavit should comply substantially with the format prescribed under the Oaths Act or Oaths law of a state as the case may be.[31] However, the Oath Clause of an affidavit may not necessarily comply with the exact wordings used in the Oath Act. It has been held that that it suffices once there is substantial compliance with the Oaths Act. The court in *Dasofunjo* v. *Ajiboye*[32] while discountenancing the argument of the respondent's counsel that failure of an affidavit to strictly conform with the format in the schedule to the Oaths Act, rendered the entire affidavit incompetent. The court held that where an affidavit having substantially conformed to the requirements of the Oaths Act, and having been duly sworn to before a recognized Commissioner of Oaths, it will be a misconception and misapplication of the law which can occasion grave injustice for court to disregard such affidavit. Courts must seriously be admonished, and must fall in line with the fact that the hay days of technicalities are indeed over, that fundamental justice means deciding a case on the merits.

In the recent decision of the Court in *Abolase M & Ors* v. *Messrs Chevron (Nig) Ltd & Anor,*[33] the Court of Appeal while relying on *Lonestar Drilling Ltd* v. *Triveni Engr & Ind. Ltd*[34] in determining the competence or otherwise of the Counter-Affidavit of the Respondent when it used the following words as the Oath Clause: "*I depose to this affidavit in good faith*

---

[30] Section 208(2) of the Act.
[31] See The Oaths Acts, Cap 01 LFN, 2004; *Ogwuegbu* v. *Agomuo* (1997) 7 NWLR (pt 609) 114.
[32](2017) LPELR-42354 (CA) Pp. 19-20, para. E-A.
[33](2019) LPELR-47516 (CA) Pp.11-12 paras. A-A.
[34](1999) 1 NWLR (PT 588) 622 at 629.

conscientiously believing same to be true and in accordance with the Oaths Act in force" held thus:

> In paragraph 6 of the Further Counter Affidavit of 6th December, 2018, it is deposed thus: *6. I depose to this affidavit in good faith conscientiously believing same to be true and in accordance with the Oaths Act in force.* I am unable to see the incompetence which the Applicants allude to. In truth, the exact words of the Oaths Act may not have been used in the counter affidavits, but the words used substantially comply with the letters, spirit and intent of the Oaths Act. In *Lonestar Drilling Ltd* vs. *Triveni Engr & Ind Ltd* (1999) 1 NWLR (PT 588) 622 at 629...this Court per Akintan, JCA (as he then was) held:
>
> In as much as I believe that there is need to comply with the provision of the Oaths Act, I believe that failure to use the exact words prescribed by the Act will not necessarily render an affidavit invalid. Rather, I believe that in deciding whether an affidavit should be declared invalid, it is necessary to examine the words used with a view to determine if there was in fact a substantial compliance with the requirement of the Act. The counter affidavits are therefore not incompetent.

The courts overtime have also lend voice to substance rather than form as justice should and ought not to be sacrificed or slaughtered on the altar of technicality.

E. Legal Effect of Unchallenged Facts in an Affidavit

It is trite that where a party in litigation is served with an affidavit containing some allegations against him or facts which are against his interest and he fails to contradict those facts through a counter affidavit, he is deemed to admit the contents of the plaintiff's affidavit as true more so when there is nothing suggesting that the facts stated in the affidavit are unreliable. This principle was diligently restated and emphatically applied in *Mato* v. *Hember & Ors.*[35]

In the recent decision of the apex court in *Obumseli & Anor* v. *Uwakwe,*[36] per Aigue JSC, it was held thus:

> Besides, it is trite law that depositions in an Affidavit, which are not challenged, are deemed admitted *Magnusson* v. *Koiki* (*supra*). The

[35](2017) LPELR-42765(SC) P. 38, paras. F-G; See also *Akiti* v. *Oyekunle* (2018) LPELR-43721 (SC) and *Ihua-Maduenyi* v. *Robinson & Ors.* (2019) LPELR-47252 (CA).

[36](2019) LPELR-46937 (SC) Pp. 19-20, paras. F-A.

> Appellants only have themselves to blame, faced with an Affidavit, they failed to file a Counter-Affidavit to controvert the facts therein, and therefore, the Court of Appeal was right to hold as it did against them.

Facts in an affidavit are contradicted by facts in a counter affidavit or affidavit in opposition and not by the most eloquent advocacy of counsel as argument of counsel cannot crystallize, metamorphose or take the place of admission of facts in the affidavit.[37] In effect, submission of counsel, no matter how brilliant does not constitute or take the place of evidence.[38]

At this point, it should be noted that for a counter affidavit to completely collapse or traverse averments in an affidavit, it must be such a nature as to controvert all material averments in the said affidavit sought to be punctured. Thus, the court in the recent case of *Apph & Ors* v. *Oturie,*[39] posited thus,

> ...where in a counter affidavit, a respondent makes some feeble and shallow averments in denial of specific facts in an affidavit such averments are mere general denials which are ineffective as a challenge to serious averments made against him.

Thus, the party filing the counter affidavit is expected to specifically, vigorously and roundly challenge and disprove any and every material deposition in his adversary's affidavit in view of the general rule than an unchallenged fact in an affidavit is deemed admitted. However, to controvert averments in an affidavit, it is not in all cases that a Counter-Affidavit must be filed especially when the affidavit sought to be controverted is unfounded in law and fact. Hence, counter affidavit does not act as a magic wand that it must be filed in all cases to demolish any form of averments in an affidavit. In the light of this, the court in the case of *NDIC* v. *Ette*[40] held thus:

> ...failure to file a counter-Affidavit by a party is not a fiat or a warrant to grant the reliefs which are totally unfounded. This is so because there is no law which provides that a party must file a Counter-Affidavit or else there is an automatic victory for the Applicant.

---

[37] *Maryland Comprehensive Secondary School, Olabode & Ors* v. *Awoh & Ors.* (2017) LPELR-44042 (CA).

[38] See *Ezeani* v. *FRN* (2019) LPELR-46800 (SC); *Oduwole* v. *David West* (2010) 10 NWLR (Pt. 1203) 598.

[39] (2019) LPELR-46301 (CA) p. 19 para. D.

[40] (2015) LPELR-40607 (CA) pp. 23-24 paras. G- A.

It should be noted also that an affidavit not served on an opponent cannot be used even if no counter affidavit has been filed by the opponent.

A counter affidavit is an affidavit and must as such, conform to all the rules already discussed under section 117 of the Act for making of an affidavit. Finally, a counter affidavit is expected to counteract or depose to the contrary or opposing facts vis-à-vis the affidavit in support like a statement of defence in relation to statement of claim. The main function of a counter affidavit is to be in opposition to the affidavit in support in so far as the main issues in dispute are concerned. It is good law that a denial in pleading or in an affidavit must not give room for any conjecture or speculation. A denying paragraph in an affidavit should therefore specifically deny the averments in the particular paragraph or paragraphs of the affidavit in support.[41]

F. Conflicts in Affidavit and How to Resolve Them

The courts and our statute book (Evidence Act) in clear terms have resolved this issue and made a copious provision for what should be the effect of such conflict and how to resolve them in an affidavit. Section 116 of the Evidence Act provides to the effect that when there are before a court affidavits that are irreconcilably in conflict on crucial facts, the court shall for the purpose of resolving the conflict arising from the affidavit evidence, ask the parties to proffer oral evidence as to such facts, and shall hear any such oral evidence of the deponents of the affidavits and such other witnesses as may be called by the parties.

The Court of Appeal in a recent decision gave a judicial credence to this question in *APC & Anor* v. *Agoda & Anor*[42] when it held thus:

> The general rule of the law is that where a Court is faced with affidavits which are irreconcilably in conflict, in respect of material facts, the Court should take oral evidence to resolve the conflict. See Section 116 of the Evidence Act, 2011 and the cases of *Uku* v. *Okumagba* (1974) 3 SC 35; *Falobi* v. *Falobi* (1976) 1 NMLR 169; *Faluyi* v. *Oderinde* (1987) 4 NWLR (pt. 64); *Pepple* v. *Green* (1990) 4 NWLR (Pt. 142) 108 and *Oyefeso* v. *Omogbehin* (1991) 4 NWLR (Pt. 187) 596. However, it is not in all cases that the Court will resort to oral evidence to resolve conflicting affidavits. Where the parties have tendered documentary evidence, which is sufficient to resolve the conflicting affidavits, the Court can rely on such

---

[41] *Ugwuanyi* v. *NICO PLC* (2005) All FWLR (Pt. 259) 202.

[42] (2019) LPELR-47174(CA) pp. 39-40 paras. G-C.

> documentary evidence and apply its God-given wisdom and learning to resolve the conflict.

The court in the same case further posited in its wisdom and pedantry that it is not every conflict that arises from different affidavit evidence that requires oral evidence. The court can *suo motu* resolve conflicting affidavit evidence by resorting to the documentary exhibits. Also, where conflicts in the affidavits do not touch the material substance of the matter before the court, decisions may be based on the evidence in those affidavits without resort to oral evidence to resolve such immaterial facts.

From the armada of the judicial decisions handed down with regards to this subject matter of how to resolve conflicting affidavits, it can be surmised that the court can resolve this conflict in two ways to wit:

a. by calling for oral evidence; or

b. by resorting to authentic documentary evidence which supports one of the affidavit in conflict with another.

Where a court fails to resolve the material conflict in affidavit evidence before him by calling oral evidence to resolve the conflict, it is treated as a serious error on the part of the court.[43]

G. How Exhibits Attached To an Affidavit Are Treated

It has been established beyond conjecture in a long line of cases[44] that a document attached to an affidavit is part of the affidavit and must be considered together. Thus, in the recent decision of the Court of Appeal in *Mbora* v. *Ekpenyong & Anor*, [45] the court in an expository prose, held thus:

> A document attached to an affidavit as an exhibit forms part of the affidavit and any person who is entitled to inspect the affidavit has a right to demand an inspection of the exhibit being an integral part of the affidavit.

The Supreme Court in *Ezechukwu & Anor* v. *I. O. C. Onwuka*[46] while reiterating the earlier position held that all documents attached to an affidavit form part of the affidavit in question and it is not possible to raise

---

[43]See *Akinsete* v. *Akindutire* (1966) ISCNLR 389 & *Ajani* v. *Taiwo* (2012) 5 NWLR (pt. 1295) 141.

[44]*Eyemi & Anor* v. *Onah & Anor* (2013) LPELR-20328(CA); *Abah* v. *UBN Plc & Ors.* (2015) LPELR-24758(CA); *Minaj Holdings Ltd* v. *AMCON* (2015) LPELR-24650 (CA); *Ezechukwu & Anor* v. *I.O.C. Onwuka* (2016) LPELR-26055 (SC) and *Mbora* v. *Ekpenyong & Anor* (2019) LPELR-48169 (CA).

[45](2019) LPELR-48169 (CA) P. 34 paras. E-F.

[46] *Supra* at page 37 para. C.

objection to its admissibility in the affidavit without running counter to the principle governing same.

All exhibits attached to an affidavit must be distinctly marked and serially identified in the body of the affidavit. The exhibit itself should bear the certification of the person before whom the affidavit is deposed disclosing that this is the document already referred to as exhibit in the relevant paragraph of the body of the affidavit. Although, there is no generally acceptable standard for making reference to exhibits attached to affidavits. A dichotomy should be created at this point as to how court treats an exhibit attached to an affidavit but marked with any distinct identification and an exhibit that is not so marked as an exhibit at all. In *NDCA & Gaspa Projects Management Engineering Ltd* v. *Gaspa Project Mgt. Group Ltd & Ors,*[47] the Court of Appeal while relying on its earlier decision in *Ogundehin* v. *Olubowale*[48] held that it is settled law that any document attached to an affidavit but which is not so marked as an exhibit, cannot be countenanced. It is very pertinent for a party to properly identify an exhibit for ease of reference and usage by the court. The court has expressed its distaste for such untidy practice of leaving exhibits unmarked. In *Ogumbambo* v. *FRN & Ors,*[49] the court held thus:

> It is curious to me that none of the parties endorsed their respective exhibits and this is highly deprecated. Counsel is expected, indeed it is expedient that counsel endorses on the documents exhibited thus "This is the document referred to as Exhibit XXX in the affidavit /counter affidavit..." It is not the function of the Court to fish out exhibits. It is the function of parties to identify exhibits by marking them.

A party seeking to rely on an exhibit attached to an affidavit must specifically identify each of the several exhibits attached to an affidavit. It has been held that documentary evidence which is before a court that is relevant and admissible in the determination of an issue before the court should not be excluded simply because it was not identified by an exhibit number or not attached to an affidavit. In summary however, it should be noted also that a court can only make use of exhibits properly admitted before it.[50]

---

[47](2019) LPELR-47607 (CA).

[48] (2016) LPELR-41125 (CA).

[49](2013) LPELR-20551 (CA).

[50] See *Obeya* v. *Okpoga Microfinance Bank Ltd* (2019) LPELR-47615(CA). P. 24, para. B.

Chapter 23

ADMISSIBILITY OF COMPUTER AND ELECTRONIC EVIDENCE

A. The Unsettled Old Order

Prior to the emergence of the Evidence Act, 2011, the repealed Evidence Act, 2004 had no provision expressly stating or providing for computer generated documents. The Evidence Act that was repealed after so many years of operation lagged behind the electronic revolution. This trend is not alien to our jurisprudence as it did not start today. Going down the memory lane of judicial appraisal, the Evidence Act 1943 which came into force on 1st June, 1945 became the first legislation governing matters of evidence in judicial proceedings before courts in Nigeria, thus providing the primary source of the law of evidence. The role of the courts has been largely interpretative and through numerous decisions, the courts have defined the intendment, applicability and ambit of specific provisions of the Act. Some of the decisions have also alluded to lacunae in the legislation, one of which is the need for a reform or an amendment to accommodate electronically generated evidence to suit the modern day realities. In a bid to remedy or fill these lacunae, our courts have always made resort to the common law rules of evidence which constituted subsidiary source of our law of evidence.[1] It is interesting to note that the Evidence Act 1943 remained in force for about sixty-six (66) years and did not, at least prior to 2011, undergo any major amendment besides its republication in the different editions of the Laws of the Federation of Nigeria.[2] Given that the Nigerian society is not static, it is

---

[1] *Rex* v. *Onitiri* [1946-1949] 12 WACA 58, where the court admitted in evidence the expert opinion of a Police officer on the authorship of a typescript by reference to the English common law because s. 56 of the Evidence Act Cap 62 did not deal specifically with the matter; similarly in *Queen* v. *Itule* [1961]1 ANLR 481 at 485, a confessional statement which had both inculpatory and exculpatory contents was admitted in evidence by reference to the common law since s. 27 of the Evidence Act did not deal explicitly with the subject-matter.

[2] The two amendments prior to 2011 were introduced by the Evidence (Amendment) Act 1977 and the Evidence (Amendment) Decree 1991; the Act was first published as Cap 62 in the 1958 Edition of the Laws of the Federation of Nigeria and Lagos and later as Cap 112 in the 1990 Edition of the Laws of the Federation of Nigeria and as Cap E14 in the 2004 Edition of the Laws of the Federation of Nigeria.

very arguable that a legislation that had remained in force for that long would invariably have had some disconnections with the realities of modern day judicial proceedings and the need to ensure even-handed dispensation of justice by our courts.

Chief of the major contentious issues prior to the passage of the Evidence Act, 2011, was on the issue of whether the definition of "document" contained in section 2 of the Evidence Act, 2004 includes electronic or computer generated evidence. Under section 2 of the now repealed Evidence Act, 2004, "document" was interpreted in a very narrow compartment to include only "books, maps, plans, drawings, photographs and also includes any matter expressed or described upon any substance by means of letters, figures or marks or by more than one of these means, intended to be used or which may be used for purpose of recording the matter. On the 3rd day of June 2011, the Evidence Act received a fresh breath and an injection of novel issues of great importance to our modern day practice which is believed to be long overdue. One fundamental and monumental innovation of the new Evidence Act 2011 is the express provision for evidentiary rule of admissibility of statements in document produced by computer.[3]

There were controversial opinions on whether a computer printout was admissible as a document in the context described under section 2 of the repeated Evidence Act, 2004. These opinions are contentious and largely unsettled to the extent that there were conflicting decisions of the Court of Appeal over the subject-matter.[4]

It was observed by the Supreme Court as far back as 1969 in *Esso West Africa Inc.* v. *Oyegbola*[5] that "the law cannot be and is not ignorant of modern business methods and must not shut its eyes to the mysteries of the Computer. Admissibility of computer-generated evidence remained a debatable or arguable point till the enactment of the Evidence Act of 2011. This controversy was provoked in the main by the absence of specific or direct evidentiary rules authorizing the admissibility of computer-generated evidence in Nigeria. It was premised on this unsettled order that the court in the case of *Udoro & Ors.* v. *The Governor, Awka Ibom State & Ors,*[6]

---

[3] Section 84 of the Evidence Act 2011.

[4] See *UBA Plc.* v. *Abacha Foundations* (2003) FWLR (Pt. 178) Pg. 997.

[5] (1969) NNLR 194 at 198.

[6] (2008) LPELR -4094 (CA) pp.7-9, para. D.

rejected the admissibility of a video cassette and as a document under section 2(1) of the old Evidence Act. The court bemoaned when it held thus:

> ...it is worthy to note that the Appellant are not really perturbed by the definition of the word "document" as were stated in the Evidence Act. They simply want the court to interpret or elongate the meaning of the word "photograph" to include videocassette. Needless belabouring this issue, it is clear and crystal that photograph and videocassette are two different forms of recording events. If the law makers had intended to include video tape as a kind of documentary evidence, they would have expressly done so without having to put the court under the strain of analysing whether photograph could be interpreted to include video cassette and tape...it is interesting to note that in countries such as the United Kingdom, where their Civil Evidence Act, 1988 etc., have been amended to make video recording admissible, it was clearly and expressly stated that video is a different aspect of documentary evidence. Their laws which right from time included photograph as a form of documentary evidence were specially amended to include video tape or videocassette as another form of admissible documentary evidence. If the views expressed by the learned counsel for the Appellant were correct in law, the English man, whose mother tongue is English, should not have bothered him about amending his country's procedural law to include video tape or video recording evidence as a form of admissible documentary evidence.
>
> It is also necessary to point out that since it was not the word "photograph" that S.2(1) of the Evidence Act defined, it would, therefore, be wrong to invoke the rules of construction to interpret that word. Attempts had been made in the past by the Law Reform Commission to amend our Evidence Act to officially include computer print outs, etc. and video tapes as documentary evidence, though they have not been passed into law. So, in the absence of any legislation in Nigeria amending our Evidence Act by incorporating the same therein, it would be wrong for any court to attempt to include video cassette in section 2(1) of the Evidence Act which was concise and precise as to what it intended to be regarded as document...it is also clear that if the legislature had intended to include video cassette in the class of photographs or document , it would have expressly done so and, it would not have resulted to one now trying to smuggle in through the back door what was never in the contemplation of our Evidence Act as Amended... it must be restated that the item attached as Exhibit B to the Appellants' affidavit is, for all intents

and purposes, not a document as envisaged by Section 2(1) of the Evidence Act.

This decision, though sound in the old order is no longer a good law under the dispensation of the new Evidence Act as video cassette and other range of novel means of transmission of information can now receive admissibility under the new Act.

In *UBA* v. *SAPFU*,[7] the Court of Appeal in the same vein held that a statement of account contained in a document produced by a computer could not be admitted in evidence under the old Evidence Act. Another gripping issue associated with the 'old order' was whether computer generated evidence could be classified as primary or secondary evidence.[8] In *Anyaebosi* v. *R.T. Briscoe*, the Supreme Court held that the computer printout tendered was admissible as secondary evidence. It is submitted that the apex court in Anyaebosi's case must have taken into account of electronic evidence and its place in Nigeria within the globalized world and its dynamics. The judgment stands as an ideal example of how courts can assist in expanding the bounds of the law by being proactive.[9] There was also another controversial issue as to whether or not a computer printout not found physically with an accused but printed out of his e-mail box after his arrest can be said to be in his possession.[10] There was also contentious nature of the conditions to be fulfilled for a computer printout of a statement of account to be admissible.[11]

Because of the stringent nature and controversial upheavals associated with the unsettled nature of the old law, there were clarion calls from the judicial arm to the legislative arm to intervene and proffer solutions to this controversy. This lingered until the outstanding statutory changes introduced under the Evidence Act, 2011 were exhaustively discussed.

---

[7] (2004) 3 NWLR (Pt. 861) 516.

[8] *Anyaebosi* v. *RT Briscoe* (1987) 3 NWLR (Pt.59)108.

[9] It will be seen that upon the emergence of the new order, so many things were tinkered with. For instance, in *Holdent International Ltd* v. *Petersville Nig Ltd* (2013) LPELR- 9725 (CA) it was held that plastic bottles bearing trademark inscriptions are documents. This must be correct in the light of the meaning ascribed to the word "document" under the new Act as it is no longer to be construed in a narrow compartment. Furthermore, Tape recordings tendered *in Federal Polytechnic Ede & Ors* v. *Oyebanji* (2012) LPPELR 19696 (CA) were accepted by the court as document within the meaning of section 258 and thus regarded as a document capable of proving a fact in issue. Also in *Obatuga & Anor* v. *Oyebokun & Ors*, (2014) LPELR 22344 (CA) the Court posited that a video tape was held to qualify as a document within the meaning of section 258 of the new Act which is to be read in conjunction with section 84 of the Evidence Act, 2011. Much of these will be treated in details as we proceed.

[10] *FRN* v. *Abdul* (2007) 5 EFCLR 204 at 228.

[11] *Oghoyone* v. *Oghoyone* (2010) LPELR 4679.

B. Admissibility of Computer-Generated Evidence

The National Assembly enacted the Evidence Act in 2011. This enactment represents the response of the legislature to ceaseless clamour for amendment of the old Evidence Act.[12] It took the legislature a long time to act when it eventually acted, it went beyond merely amending the Act, but it repealed it. Significantly, the legislation attempts to bring the law in line with the modern day reality of advancement in the area of electronic and computer technology as it clearly provides for admissibility of electronically generated documents.

Section 84 of the Act stands out noticeably as a towering provision. It provides for admissibility of a statement contained in a document produced by a computer. Furthermore, section 258 of the Act went further to define a '*statement*' as any representation of fact whether made in words or otherwise.

It further defined '*computer*' to mean any device for storing and processing information, and any reference to information being derived from other information is a reference to its being derived from it by calculation, comparison or any other process. This is a trail-blazing provision in the new Act as computer was not defined under section 2 of the old Act. This gave rise to so many bottlenecks as to whether a computer-generated evidence is admissible or not.

Section 84(2)(A)-(D) on its own part, elucidates four conditions that must be satisfied before such statement becomes admissible. Section 84 (4) requires a certificate to be signed to authenticate the document by a person occupying a responsible position in relation to any matter mentioned in subsection (2).

Without further ado, section 84 has been introduced to fill the wide gap that existed in the repealed Evidence Act which hitherto made no specific provision for admissibility of electronically generated evidence.

The provision of section 258 of the Act was also readjusted and additional words were included. As a corollary, section 258 of the Evidence Act, 2011 unequivocally provides that a 'document' includes the following:

(a) books, maps, plans, graphs, drawings, photographs and also includes any matter expressed or described upon any substance by means of letters, figures or marks or by more than one of those means, intended to be used or which may be used for the purpose of recording that matter;

---

[12] *Egbue* v. *Araka* (1996) 2 NWLR (Pt. 433) p. *688; Udoro & Ors.* v. *The Governor, Awka Ibom State & Ors.* (*supra*).

(b) any disc, tape, sound track or other device in which sounds or other data (not being visual images) are embodied so as to be capable (with or without the aid of some other equipment) of being reproduced from it;

(c) any film, negative tape, or other device in which more visual images are embodied so as to be capable (with or without) the aid of some other equipment) of being reproduced from it; and

(d) any device by means of which information is recorded, stored or retrievable including Computer output.

In *Ibrahim* v. *State,*[13] the Supreme Court held that when the word "includes" is used in a statute, the words or phrases mentioned are intended to be construed as comprehending not only such things as have been mentioned in the statute according to their ordinary and natural meaning but also other things not specifically mentioned but which may reasonably be held to come within the purview of what is mentioned. In *Ports and Cargo Handling Service Co Ltd* v. *Migfo Nig Ltd,*[14] the court held that when the word *"includes"* is used in a statute or written enactment, it is capable of enlarging the scope of the subject matter it qualifies or tends to qualify. This canon of construction of document opened the vistas for several decisions of the court upon the commencement of the new Act that widened the scope and meaning of document under section 258 of the Act.

The court having stated in Oyegbola's case while giving the early warning that the law cannot be and is not ignorant of modern time's reproduction in inscriptions on ledgers or other documents by mechanical process,[15] re-shaped our evidentiary rules just like statement of account. Of course, by Section 51 and 52 of the Evidence Act, 2011, electronic records and computer generated documents are now admissible in our Courts.

It is a breath of fresh air in our evidential *corpus juris* for the introduction of this novel and pragmatic provision in our evidence Act. This could best explain the dynamics of law as an instrument of social change and vice versa. A deep insight on the workability of this novel provisions will be treated in the subsequent subtopics.

C. Condition Precedent for Admissibility of Electronic Evidence

From the glaring provision of the law on the conditions for admissibility of electronic evidence, one common thread runs through them: the need to

---

[13](1991) LPELR-1404 (SC) P. 38, para. C-D.

[14](2012) LPELR-9725 (SC).

[15]The learned trial Court had considered the above warning and other cases including *Trade Bank* v. *Chami* (2004) All FWLR (Pt.235) 118 in the issue of computer-generated documents.

have security and reliability of the computer system that handles such records that is tendered for admissibility. Under the Evidence Act, it clearly specifies the rules governing the admissibility of computer output. The court in its usual duty of interpretation of the law carries out this task with an eagle's eyes to ensure compliance with the laid down conditions for the admissibility of such electronic generated evidence to ensure authenticity of documents emanating therefrom.

On the question of admissibility of statements in documents produced by computers, section 84(1) of the Evidence Act, 2011 provides thus:

> In any proceedings, a statement contained in a document produced by computer shall be admissible as evidence of any fact stated in it of which direct oral Evidence would be admissible.

The admissibility of such document is not automatic. The Evidence Act was very detailed when it made copious provision on the conditions that must be met before such document produced by computer can be admissible. Section 84(2) of the Act outline these conditions to wit:

A. the computer containing the statement was produced by the computer during a period over which the computer was used regularly to store or process information for the purposes of any activity regularly carried on over that period whether for profit or not, by anybody, whether corporate or not, or by any individual;
B. that over that period there was regularly supplied to the computer in the ordinary course of those activity information of the kind contained in the statement or of the kind from which information so contained is derived;
C. that throughout the material part of that period the computer was operating properly or, if not, that in any respect in which it was not operating properly or was out of operation during that period was not such as to affect the production of the document or the accuracy of its contents; and
D. that the information contained in the statement reproduces or is derived from information supplied to the computer in the ordinary course of those activities.

It is crystal clear that the admissibility of computer generated evidence has been settled beyond conjecture in the new Evidence Act. The intendment and the demands of Section 84 has been settled by the Supreme Court of Nigeria on how to determine admissibility of electronically generated evidence.[16] The main objective of these provisions is to authenticate and validate the reliability of the computer which generated the evidence sought to be tendered.[17]

From the prefatory statement of section 84, it is clear on the face of it that computer generated evidence is admissible "*in any proceedings*", which means that it applies to both civil and criminal Proceedings. The provision of Section 84(2) of the Evidence Act, 2011 is mandatory and allows for no discretion. It is mandatory for a party who seeks to tender a computer generated evidence to comply with the conditions stipulated in Section 84(2).[18] This is the decision of the court in *Loben Investment Co-Operative Multipurpose Society Ltd* v. *FRN*.[19] The courts do not treat any failure to fulfil the above conditions with levity. In *Kubor* v. *Dickson,*[20] the Supreme Court, per Onnoghen, JSC, affirmed that computer-generated evidence or documents which did not comply with the pre-conditions laid down in Section 84(2) were inadmissible. The court frowns at such fundamental defect from the party who seeks to tender such computer generated evidence without having to pass through the crucible of these conditions as he who assert must prove. In *Davou* v. *C.O.P Plateau State Command,*[21] the Court of appeal rejected pictures of the deceased marked "Exhibits P6A and P6B" as their admissibility offends Section 84 of the Evidence Act, 2011. The pictures were tendered without recourse to the requirements of Section 84 of the Evidence Act, 2011. The court went further to state that the pictures were just tendered without the negatives nor any explanation. Where if the photographs were taken with a digital camera or produced from a digital camera, that becomes a computer generated document by virtue of Section 84(5)(c) of the Evidence Act, 2011. The camera that was used in taking the photographs ought to have been tendered in evidence, but that was not

---

[16]See *Hon. Henry Seriake Dickson* v. *Chief Timipre Marlin Sylva & Ors.* (2017) 8 NWLR (PART 1567) 167 At 200 F - H TO 202 A - H per Nweze JSC.

[17]*Brila Energy Ltd* v. *FRN* (*supra*) P. 159, para A.

[18]See the following cases of *Collins Commermex Nigeria Ltd & Anor* v. *Skye Bank Plc.* (2019) LPELR-46892 (CA).

U.B.N. Plc v. *Agbontaen & Anor* (2018) LPELR-44160 (CA); *Brila Energy Ltd* v. *FRN* (2018) LPELR - 43926(CA); *Kubor* v. *Dickson* (2013) NWLR (Pt. 1345) 534, 577-578; *Omisore and Anor* v. *Aregbesola & Ors.* (2015) 15 NWLR (Pt. 1482) 205.

[19](2019) LPELR-47325 (CA) P. 37, para C.

[20](2012) LPELR-9817 (SC).

[21](2019) LPELR-47040 (CA).

done. Rather the printed photographs were tendered in evidence. Also, the certification which is a pre-requisite for its admissibility in evidence under Section 84 of the Evidence Act, 2011 was not made and as such, was expunged.

We shall x-ray the above conditions one after the other.

A. The Document containing the statement was produced by the computer during a period over which the computer was used regularly to store or process information for the purposes of any activity regularly carried on over that period

The plank of this condition is to ensure that the computer from which the document emanated is reliable. The test of reliability of the computer is proved by way of evidence to establish that such computer was used regularly to store or process information for the purposes of any activity regularly carried on over that period whether for profit or not or by anybody, whether corporate or not. A computer output or computer generated evidence that would sway the mind of the court to admit same must be one whose workability and reliability is not in doubt as the court is not oblivious of the intermittent malfunctions of computer systems which at times can be attributed to virus attack which is capable of altering an output of a computer.

B. That over that period there was regularly supplied to the computer in the ordinary course of those activities information of the kind contained in the statement or of the kind from which information so contained is derived

This section deals with the genuineness and correctness of the computer generated evidence which is the document itself. One could ponder why the drafters of the Act added this? One point should be noted: as the society evolves with new technology, so is the birth of some mischievous activities to distort the ordinary course of event. Here, it is concerned with the vulnerability of computer records to manipulation and tampering. The essence is to weed out or eliminate suspicious or spurious documents. The Court of Appeal in *Brila Energy Ltd* v. *FRN,*[22] while adopting the decision of the Apex Court in *Dickson* v. *Sylva & Ors,*[23] held as follows:

---

[22] *Supra.*
[23](2016) LPELR-41257(SC) P. 15.

> In this digital age when different creations can be achieved electronically, the reason for the requirement of authentication or certification of the gadget or computer used in producing and processing the electronically generated documents is not farfetched. The party seeking to rely on such evidence must be able to show that the data and information contained in the electronically generated document is truly what it claims to be. The pre-conditions for admissibility set down by Section 84 are to establish this fact. The relationship between the computer and the information is crucial. The electronic evidence must be produced from a computer or gadget that is inherently reliable and has been in operation over the relevant period.

This condition seeks to answer questions like did the computer produce what is programmed into it or was it tampered with either by mechanical or manual means? Evidence must be shown to prove that there is no material discrepancy between what is keyed into the system and the output as any incongruity will be resolved against the admissibility of such computer generated evidence.

C. That throughout the material part of that period the computer was operating properly or, if not, that in any respect in which it was not operating properly or was out of operation during that period was not such as to affect the production of the document or the accuracy of its contents

Just like the frailty of human nature, section 84(2)(c) of the Act accommodates the susceptibility of computer device through whom computer evidence is generated. A computer device as earlier established can malfunction. This of course, leads to the inaccuracy of the output from such computer. Just the same way it is not all errors in judgment that can invalidate same, any defect in the operation of a computer that is capable of affecting the admissibility adversely must be such as to affect the production of the document or the accuracy of its content. Thus, if a computer printout for example is blurred by virtue of low toner in the cartridge of the printer but still legible without any alteration of the content, the court will overlook any objection on its admissibility premised on this conditions. In *Director of Public Prosecution* v. *McKeown and Jones,*[24] a driver was arrested for driving with excess alcohol. At the police station, he was to be tested with the

[24] (1997) 1 All ER 737.

Lion Intoximeter. The officer tested the machine and it calibrated correctly. This was at about a quarter after midnight; the sergeant's watch read 23:00. Part of the discrepancy was explained by the fact that, as the print-out made plain, the machine was set to GMT. But there was no explanation for the balance of the difference. The court while relying on Police and Criminal Evidence Act 1984 and the Road Traffic Act of 1988 held that failure of an internal computer clock was not a sufficient indication of a computer malfunction to make a reading from the breath analysing machine inadmissible in evidence. Thus the conviction of the defendant was upheld.

E. That the information contained in the statement reproduced is derived from information supplied to the computer in the ordinary course of those activities

Another condition that must be fulfilled for a computer generated evidence to be admissible is that the information contained in the statement is one that was supplied to computer in the ordinary course of its normal use similar to the condition under section 84(2)(a). From the armada of cases handed down by our superior courts of record, the conditions stipulated under section 84(2) of the Evidence Act are not disjunctive in nature but rather cumulative as a party who establishes one condition to the exclusion of others is deemed to have failed in its entirety to discharge this burden placed on him; all the conditions must be proved.[25] It is worthy of note that he whose desires the court to give judgment in his favour must first establish that the fact exist as he who asserts must prove. Thus the *onus probandi* or the burden of proof of the conditions outlined in section 84(2) of the Act lies squarely on he who wants the court to give judgment in his favour while relying on the document produced by a computer.

Section 84(3) of the Evidence Act, 2011 provides that:

> Where over a period the function of storing or processing information for the purposes of any activities regularly carried on over that period as mentioned in subsection (2) of this Section was regularly performed by computers, whether –
>
> (a) by a combination of computers operating over that period;
>
> (b) by different computers operating in succession over that period ;

[25] See *Collins Commermex Nigeria Ltd & Anor* v. *Skye Bank PLC* (2019) LPELR-46892 (CA); See also *Kubor & Dickson* (*Supra*); *Brila Energy Ltd* v. *FRN* (*supra*); note the use of the word "and" at the end of paragraph 84(2)(c) that connects 84(2)(d), clearly indicates connectivity of all the conditions which means that all the conditions must be met.

(c) by different combination of computers operating in succession over that period; or

(d) In any other manner involving the successive operation over that period, in whatever order, of one or more computers and one or more combinations of computers, all the computer used for that purpose during that period shall be treated for the purposes of this section as constituting a single computer and references in this section to a computer shall be construed accordingly.

D. Supply of Information to Computer

Besides the conditions for the admissibility of a computer generated evidence already treated in the preceding sub topic, section 84(5) of the Act in clear terms, governs the mode of reception of information to a computer in order that the statements in document produced by such computers cross the hurdles or Rubicon of admissibility. Pursuant to this section under review information shall be taken to be supplied to a computer if it is supplied to it in any appropriate form and whether it is supplied directly or by means of any appropriate equipment.[26] Where, in the course of an activity carried on by any individual or body, information is supplied with a view of it being stored or processed, that information, if duly supplied to that computer, shall be taken to be supplied to it in the course of those activities.[27] Under the extant provision of the law, a document shall be taken to have been produced by a computer whether it was produced by it directly or (with or without human intervention) by means of any appropriate equipment.[28] Obiaraeri expressed his concern as to this far reaching provision in that the law did not state what amounts to "any appropriate form" and "appropriate equipment." The learned author now opines that it will therefore require exercise of judicial discretion to interpret the expression "any appropriate form" and "appropriate equipment" in any given case under judicial inquest.[29]

E. Endorsed Certificate Raises Presumption of Genuineness

In a bid to ensure reliability of a computer and also the authenticity of the information or statement contained in a document generated by such computer, the Act made provision for certificate under section 84(4) of the

---

[26] Section 84 (5) (a) of the Evidence Act 2011.
[27] Section 84 (5) (b) of the Evidence Act 2011.
[28] Section 84 (5) (c) of the Evidence Act 2011.
[29] N.O Obiaraeri, *op. cit.,* at page 330.

Act. The Act further states *in extenso* what the certificate must contain for its admissibility.

According to Section 84(4):

> In any proceedings where it is desired to give a statement in evidence by virtue of this section, a certificate-
>
> (a) identifying the document containing the statement and describing the manner in which it was produced;
>
> (b) giving such particulars of any device involved in the production of that document as may be appropriate for the purpose of showing that the document was produced by a computer;
>
> (ii) dealing with any of the matters to which the conditions mentioned in Subsection (2) above relate, and purporting to be signed by a person occupying a responsible position in relation to the operation of the relevant device or the management of the relevant activities, as the case may be, shall be evidence of the matter stated in the certificate, and for purpose of this subsection, it shall be sufficient for a matter to be stated to the best of the knowledge and belief of the person stating it.[30]

This provision raises presumption of genuineness under section 146 of the Evidence Act as it is crystal clear that upon fulfilment of the above provision, it shall be evidence of the matter stated in the certificate. It is also sacrosanct to note that a computer or electronic evidence sought to be tendered in court, must first of all have its foundation laid to show proper substantial compliance with the evidential rules on the subject matter. In *Weekly Insight and Communication Network Ltd & Anor* v. *Peter & Ors.*,[31] it was held that rebuttable presumption of genuineness is raised when a document is substantially in the proper form required by law. It is also the provision of the law that any person "occupying a responsible position" in relation to the operation of the relevant device or the management of the relevant activities, as the case may be, can sign such certificate. This simplifies the onerous demand that could supposedly be associated with who can sign the certificate. By the use of "any person occupying a responsible position in relation to the operation of the relevant device or the management," even a computer operator can sign such signature and not

---

[30] See also *Ayodeji* v. *FRN* (2018) LPELR-45839(CA); *Onwuzulike* v. *State* (2017) LPELR-41889 (CA).

[31] (2019) LPELR-46847 (CA).

necessarily an expert. In *Brila Energy Ltd* v. *FRN*,[32] the Court of Appeal while lending its voice to this innovative provision held thus:

> Another condition for the admissibility of electronic evidence under Section 84(4) of the Act is the production of an authentication/trustworthiness certificate of the computer used in producing the documents. From case law, this subsection permits even non-experts to issue such a certificate, especially persons who, though not possessing the required professional qualifications may have acquired some practical knowledge and being in the position described in the subsection to bring him within the definition of an expert by the expanded definition of an expert in *Oando Nig. Plc* v. *Adijere W/A Ltd* (2013) 5 NWLR (Pt. 1377) 374...

Thus, once it can be shown that a person occupying a responsible position has by virtue of his experience and long practice, acquired practical knowledge and can vividly describe the operation of the relevant device, his signature suffices under this provision. Pursuant to section 146(2) of the Act, the court shall presume that any officer by whom any document purports to be signed or certified, held, when he signed it, the official character which he claims in such document.

F. Weight To Be Attached To Admissible Statement

While the admissibility of computer-generated evidence is one thing, the weight or the probative value the court would attach to it is a different thing. The weight the court will attach to the document will depend on the circumstances of the case as contained or portrayed in the evidence. Consequent upon the innovative provision and the acknowledgment of electronically generated documents as admissible evidence, the Act went further to give a guide to courts on how to assess such evidence. Section 34 of the Act provides that in estimating the weight to be attached to statement rendered admissible as evidence by this Act, regard shall be had to all the circumstances from which any inference can be reasonably be drawn as to the accuracy or otherwise of the statement, and in particular-

(a) to the question whether or not the statement was made contemporaneously with the occurrence or existence of the facts stated, and to the question whether or not the maker of the statement had any incentive to conceal or misrepresent facts; and

---

[32] *Supra* at Pp.22-23, para. E-A.

(b) in the case of a statement contained in a document produced by a computer –

(i) the question whether or not the information which the statement contained, reproduces or is derived from, was supplied to it, contemporaneously with the occurrence or existence of the facts dealt with in that information; and

(ii) the question whether or not any person concerned with the supply of information to that computer or with the operation of that computer or any equipment, by means of which the document containing the statement was produced by it, had any incentive to conceal or misrepresent facts.

In *Viwanu-Ojo & Anor* v. *Towakennu & Ors*[33] the Court of Appeal while citing the cases of *Agballah* v. *Chime*[34] and *Adefarasin* v. *Dayekh*[35] held thus:

> However, the fact that a document has been admitted in evidence does not necessarily mean that it must be automatically, attached probative value or weight. In determining the weight, if any, to attach to an admitted document the Court will take into consideration the entire circumstances from which inferences can reasonably be drawn as to the accuracy or otherwise of the document especially regard being had to the question whether or not the document was made contemporaneously with the occurrence of existence of the facts stated, and whether or not the maker of the said statement in the document had any incentive to conceal or misrepresent facts. In essence, admissibility of a document and the evidential value ascribable to it are two different things.

As earlier noted, the question of weight to be attached to a document is quite a different kettle of fish from mere admissibility of the document. The court has held in *Odetola* v. *Togunde*[36] that it is trite that admissibility of a document and the weight to be attached to such document are in two separate compartments. It is at the stage of writing its judgment that the court takes a decision on the weight to be attached to the evidence presented by parties. The fact that a document was tendered and admitted in evidence does not mean the court must attach probative value to it. The fact that a document has been admitted in evidence with or without objection does not

---

[33](2015) LPELR-41989 (CA) pp. 42-43, paras. G-D.

[34] 1 NWLR (PT.1122) P.373 at 443 - 444.

[35] (2007) 11 NWLR (PT.1044) P.89 at 115.

[36](2019) LPELR-47505 (CA) Pp. 16-17, paras. G-A.

necessarily mean that the document has established or made out the evidence contained therein and must be accepted by the trial Court. This is not automatic. The above prescriptions assist the court in determining the ascribable probative value to be attached to such documents as this is the evidence that finds its place on the imaginary scale.

G. Need For Continuous Law Reform

Generally, the law has come to stay with the reality of the vast changing technological advancements in the area of computer generated evidence. Computers and other electronic information and communication devices represent a new millennium in the age of technology development. The advent of computers brought with it a new form of record keeping in software-microfilms, microchips, diskette, flash drives, etc., which was not contemplated under the old Evidence Act. But for the emergence of the new Act with its innovative provisions for admissibility of statements in documents produced by computers and the expansive meaning of document, such genre of evidence that were hitherto inadmissible has been made admissible by reason of this innovative provision. This of course, is highly commendable as document produced by computers are now admissible under section 84 of the Act same with entries in books of account or electronic records under section 51 of the Act.

However, it should be noted that we are not there yet. The promise land is yet to be attained even in the light of the present Act. Except we resolve to settle for a static evidentiary rules while the world advances and leaves the law at a distance to turn back to cry and yearn for continuous reform as the dynamics of the society demands; This is never the expectation of any proactive society. It is against this backdrop that our Law Reform Commission must be proactively conscious of the dynamics of the law to timeously and continually bring our law *in tandem* with the ever-evolving society. It is also humbly submitted that there ought to be a definition section in section 84 of the Evidence Act and not to take the definition of "computer" to section 258(1) of the Evidence Act. Furthermore, the word "document" should have also gone to Section 83 to specifically define what a document is. No wonder, section 258 has 258(1) a-d, and another a-d, and another a-b. The question is: How do you now cite the section properly in law that will look legalistic and perfect? Are we going to say; section 258(1) a-d of another a-d and of a further a-d? It is recommended that the appropriate changes be effected otherwise, there will certainly be confusion in citing the appropriate section of the law.

Consequently, there is need for the Evidence Act to incorporate the issue of electronic recorded video evidence of confessional statement of the Defendant (Accused Person) which is recognized in the Administration of Criminal Justice Act of most states of the federation. It is submitted that the provision of the Evidence Act dealing with confessional statement ought to be amended to incorporate the new video electronic record of confessional statement. There is therefore the need to incorporate this in Section 29 of the Evidence Act vis-à-vis Section 31 in order to make confessional statement more reliable.[37]

In summary, lawyers as worshippers in the temple of justice and judges as impartial umpire holding balance between contending parties should constantly improve themselves by engaging in continuous legal education, symposia, seminars, workshops and other avenue of intellectual expansion and stimulation. Through this mean, the players in the legal field can get abreast and acquainted with modern technology for the development of the law.

---

[37]See Amuda Kannike "Admissibility of Evidence as it relates to Electronic Devices" Being a paper delivered at the Conference organized by the Magistrate Association of Nigeria; Bayelsa State Chapter on Thursday the 12th day of April 2018 at the Multi Door Court Complex Ovom Yenagoa.

www.ingramcontent.com/pod-product-compliance
Lightning Source LLC
Chambersburg PA
CBHW050520240926
51846CB00003B/631